IMAGINING
BOUNDARIES

SUNY series in Chinese Philosophy and Culture
David L. Hall and Roger T. Ames, editors

IMAGINING BOUNDARIES

Changing Confucian Doctrines, Texts, and Hermeneutics

EDITED BY
Kai-wing Chow,
On-cho Ng,
and
John B. Henderson

STATE UNIVERSITY OF NEW YORK PRESS

Published by
State University of New York Press, Albany

Printed in the United States of America

For information, address State University of New York Press,
State University Plaza, Albany, N.Y., 12246

Production by Cathleen Collins
Marketing by Patrick Durocher

Library of Congress Cataloging in Publication Data

Imagining boundaries : changing Confucian doctrines, texts, and
    hermeneutics / edited by Kai-wing Chow, On-cho Ng, and John B.
    Henderson
        p.   cm. — (SUNY series in Chinese philosophy and culture)
    Includes bibliographical references and index.
    ISBN 0–7914–4197–0 (alk. paper). — ISBN 0–7914–4198–9 (pbk. :
alk. paper)
    1. Confucianism.   I. Chow, Kai-wing, 1951–   II. Ng, On-cho.
III. Henderson, John B., 1948–   . IV. Series.
BL1855.I43 1999
181′.112—dc21   98–38760
                                                                          CIP

10 9 8 7 6 5 4 3 2 1

Contents

1

Introduction

Fluidity of the Confucian Canon and Discursive Strategies

On-cho Ng
Kai-wing Chow

> To presuppose that every combination of elements is inferior to their original is to presuppose that draft 9 is obligatorily inferior to draft number H—since there can never be anything but drafts. The concept of the *definitive* text complies only with religion or weariness.
>
> —Jorge Luis Borges, "Versions of Homer"

In our historical conception of Confucianism, we are understandably apt to view it as a grand cultural *Weltanschauung*, a worldview with dominant motifs, telling themes, guiding logic, and governing problematics that may be encapsulated in a master narrative. Elegant and cogent narratives of this sort abound in contemporary studies of Confucianism, masterfully woven by a host of erudite scholars. David Hall and Roger Ames pinpoint what they call "analogical or correlative thinking" as the first-order strategy of coming to grips with reality and the human condition in classical Chinese culture.[1] Tu Wei-ming sees Confucianism as a moral universe in which the self, with its immanent qualities of fundamental goodness, is the locus of ultimate transformation, in the sense of soteriological transcendence.[2] In pondering the "trouble with Confucianism" in the context of modernity, Wm. Theodore de Bary posits the critical, prophetic role of the *chün-tzu* (the noble man) as the fulcrum of a politicosocial community in which this figure must play the ambiguous roles of a conscientious critic of the dynastic state, a loyal servant of the ruler and a caring representative of the people whose voice could only speak through him.[3] Thomas Metzger suggests looking at Neo-Confucianism as a shared cultural "grammar" that involves a "sense of predicament," the result of the nagging awareness that there is a chasm between

1

the idealized goal of life—transforming state and society by the heroic moral self—and the dismal realities of the given world—the source of the anxiety of moral failure.[4]

These systematic interpretations, in one way or another, afford supreme guidance for understanding Confucianism as an integrated system of thinking.[5] They are, however, essentially contemporary attempts to engage the "Confucian tradition" in a dialogue in order to re-invent the tradition. They are *moments* in the hermeneutics of Confucianism, moments when the heterogeneous nature of the tradition is suppressed and subordinated under a dominant motif. The trouble with this kind of macroscopic explanation is that it can be at times deterministic and reductive, excluding the contingent, the exceptional, the unexpected and the alternative. Needless to say, to point to such a problem is not to impugn the explanation itself. It is to remind us that a certain degree of determinism and reductionism is the besetting sin of all generalizations, no matter now tenable and valid they are. The point is that even if the general and somewhat stable intellectual boundaries of the Confucian tradition are correctly drawn, their inexorable constant shifts and alterations, here and there in time and space, must also be duly traced. The transmission of the Confucian canonical texts perforce means their undergoing changes as part of the process of being reinterpreted by various groups for different reasons. These changes in turn were indicative of the dynamic unfolding of Confucian doctrines. Both the texts and doctrines of any vital cultural tradition, such as Confucianism, are always in the midst of transformation, drift, and rupture, *in medias res*, relocated and remapped in ongoing interpretations and publications. Hence, the constant need to canonize and legitimize texts and ideas, that is, to fix a boundary to establish a sense of stable authority. This imposed finality is, of course, fictive, and all canonical traditions are ephemeral.[6] Ideas and texts will be reconfigured, their boundaries reimagined.[7]

This reconfiguration and reimagining is both conservative and radical in nature. It is conservative in that its oft-avowed intention is to save and preserve the original ideas by retrieving them. It is also radical because often, the substantiation of the value of a doctrine or a text does not depend on a certain condition, especially the original condition. Take the *Ta-hsueh* (The Great Learning) and *Chung-yung* (Doctrine of the Mean), for example. Both originally were chapters in the *Li-chi* (The Classic of Rites), but they were taken out of the classic, classified as independent treatises, and then grouped with the *Analects* and *Mencius* to form the *Ssu-shu* (Four Books). The forging of the Four Books was in essence the reterritorializing and resituating of Confucian texts and their corresponding Confucian teachings, an act that was not intended by the original authors. Nonetheless, such a radical move in no way undermined their value but instead elevated it, for such transience of the classics was sanctioned and demanded by the cultural and intellectual changes of the time.

It should also be noted that this unavoidable engagement with the shifting of boundaries of a tradition, be it in the form of texts or doctrines, is not only submission to the tyranny of temporality; it is also acknowledgment of the different temporalities in the dynamic development of a cultural tradition. For instance, how did the Confucian classics relate to histories? How did philosophy interact with exegesis? How did Confucian theory and practice interpenetrate? Foucault had a point when he said that "it is not enough to indicate change. . . . We must define precisely what these changes consist of: that is, substitute for an undifferentiated reference to *change*—which is both a general container for all events and the abstract principle of their succession—the analysis of *transformation*."⁸ Regardless of whether using the word "transformation" as opposed to "change" is merely semantic legerdemain, the plea is to provide more concrete and substantive illustrations of the vicissitudes of culture. Our inquiry begins with the assumption that the Confucian tradition was not a neatly packaged organic whole in which the constitutive parts fall naturally into their places, but that it displayed the ruptures of all cultural constructions. It was forged and reforged, configured and reconfigured.

This anthology of essays is about the mapping of the intellectual tradition of Confucianism in Chinese history. It is not devoted to delineating a body of texts, doctrines, discourse, and practices in order to define what Confucianism is in any given period, but rather to showing how Confucianism was mapped along the grids of text and discourse, sometimes in relation to *other* traditions such as Taoism and Buddhism, at other times with reference to internal sectarian interests. The authors are interested in understanding how the boundaries between Confucian and other traditions were imagined, negotiated and shifted. There are a common set of issues that all the chapters seek to address:

1. The fluidity of the Confucian canon;
2. The constant need to negotiate the boundaries of Confucianism in relation to other intellectual traditions;
3. The dialogical relations between text and discourse in establishing boundaries for the Confucian tradition;
4. Specific textual and discursive strategies employed in the imagining of boundaries;
5. The range of expansive and contractive strategies used to enlarge or restrict the Confucian tradition's intellectual space vis-à-vis other traditions.

Guided by these common concerns and issues, our volume argues that to understand Confucianism is to understand how imaginary boundaries were created in order to define a set of texts as Confucian canon and to identify ideas, and hence discourses, as uniquely Confucian. The boundaries were imagined and created to map out the discursive space of Confucianism. The demarcating lines are created through the use of textual and discursive strategies such as taxonomy of genres and knowledge, as well as textual criticism on authorship and authenticity, to include and exclude texts and ideas. With these strategies, texts and ideas were moved in and out of the imagined boundaries. Thus, in the Confucian tradition, the relationship between texts/ideas and readers/interpreters was open and constantly changing. The essays in this volume are devoted to re-presenting the specific temporal relationships between Confucianism and its interpreters with their textual and discursive strategies. These temporal engagements were the various hermeneutical moments in the history of Confucian thought, in which the Confucian tradition was re-invented. The authors, in one way or another, reveal one central phenomenon represented metaphorically—the constant crossing, negotiating, and imagining of the boundaries that strained to circumscribe Confucianism.[9]

By drawing attention to the heterogeneous nature of the earliest Confucian texts and ideas, Michael Nylan's essay questions that most cherished of historiographic assumptions regarding the Han, the assumption that there was a recognizable Confucian synthesis achieving orthodox status at the time but later dismissed as deficient. This apparent historiographic truism and platitude owed much to the later Ch'eng-Chu masters' strong distaste for Han Confucianism. They presumed that empire, a strong political order, and orthodoxy, an equally vigorous ideological order, must go hand-in-hand. They found Han Confucianism to be insufficiently "orthodox," being neither unitary nor faithful to Confucius's precepts. Ironically, their determined efforts to denigrate all of Han Confucianism might have lent it the essentialized air of a uniform entity, so much so that many eminent Sinologists once spoke confidently of the Han "victory of Confucianism."

Nylan helps us discern the blurry boundaries that defined the complex world of Confucian—she uses often the Chinese term of "Ju"—beliefs and practices. Adducing historical evidence from the Han, she challenges the five fundamental premises that underlie the contention that there was a "Han orthodox synthesis" resulting in the "victory of Confucianism":

1. That we can easily identify who the Confucians really were, as a distinct group with a clearly identifiable ideology;
2. That the empire, that is, its rulers and administrators, like the later Neo-Confucians, presumed an absolute need for a single ruling orthodoxy;
3. That state sponsorship of Confucian activities was consistent;
4. That state promotion of Confucian activities was also effective, leading to markedly greater uniformity in thought and practice;
5. That this accomplished greater uniformity represented something quite different from what had existed in the pre-Han period.

In the process of showing the flaws of these premises, Nylan also reveals the tremendous tensions inherent in the Han Confucian tradition. By dint of the "moral quandaries, paradoxes, and polarities, all of which resulted from inexplicable mysteries that lay at the very center of the Han Confucian way, no amount of painstaking explication by would-be rationalizers could excise these mysteries from the Confucian enterprise." Challenging the conventional view of a homogeneous Confucian orthodox synthesis, Nylan enjoins us to appreciate the lessons that the heterogeneous Han Confucianism may teach about the role of intellectual ferment, diversity, and inclusiveness in maintaining empires.

A basic reason why a text and discourse cannot be closed permanently is that they all share the same linguistic system despite attempts to develop their own vocabularies in order to exclude the multivocality inherent in all the languages in use.[10] The same term signifies differently in different discourses; multiple and often competing meanings may be inscribed on it. When the interpreter chooses to cross the semiotic boundaries in rendering the *other* text in the language of his/her own intellectual traditions, boundaries become blurred. To articulate such fuzziness or hybridity in intellectual cross-breeding, scholars resort to terms like syncretism or accommodation. Yuet Keung Lo's chapter on Huang K'an's (488–545) commentary on the *Analects* explores the dialogical relationship between the commentator and the canon, demonstrating the problem of the multivocality of the text. Writing commentary was Huang's discursive strategy to break down intellectual boundaries at the canonical level. Primarily by focusing on an emerging Confucian metaphysics as documented in Huang K'an's *Lun-yü chi-chieh i-shu* (Subcommentaries on the Collected Commentaries on the *Analects*), Yuet Keung Lo examines the survival and revival of Confucian doctrines after the fall of the Han in the early third century. Lo demonstrates how Confucian learning accommodated ideas from Neo-Taoism and Buddhism by realigning its doctrinal boundaries, yielding in the end a new metaphysics that would have been quite alien to Han Confucians.

The fundamental impact on the formation of early medieval Confucian metaphysics came from a dualistic ontology of Neo-Taoism. According to Wang Pi (226–249) and other Neo-Taoists, the origin of the universe is identified as Nonbeing from which the myriad things and beings originate. The dichotomy of Nonbeing and being creates a metaphysical dualism of the transcendental and the phenomenal. Confucians like Huang K'an accepted this bifurcation of reality, and wrote about the two realms and their possible relations. To Huang, Principle, which resides in the transcendental realm, finds expression in the human realm, whereas all things and affairs in the human realm are governed by Principle. Hence their mutual interdependence. Unlike the Neo-Taoists, however, Huang did not necessarily consider Nonbeing as the ultimate, accessible only to the sage. Rather, he established a metaphysical hierarchy of selfhood, with sagehood at the pinnacle. It is also noteworthy that this notion of hierarchy bore a striking resemblance to a line of early medieval Chinese Buddhist thought, which argued for sequenced and gradual cultivational progression toward nirvana.

For the early medieval Confucians, the goal of self-cultivation is sagehood, which is the embodiment of Nonbeing. In embodying Nonbeing, the sage's mind becomes always empty, without encumbrance and pruned of desires. He then can naturally and appropriately respond to all circumstances. Huang's theory of no mind is quite similar to the Chinese Buddhist theory of self-cultivation most notably expounded in the commentaries on the *Vimalakīrtinirdeśa* by Kumārajīva—the Buddha's mind is free of discrimination and distinction—and his student Seng Chao—the sage's mind is free of defilement so that everything is treated equally as emptiness. But as Lo also reminds us, medieval Confucianism did manage to claim its distinctiveness for its method of self-cultivation by displaying a much stronger interest in nurturing the immanent human nature, so that desires and feelings are not always condemned as intrinsically bad.

Thus, whether as metaphysics or as existential praxis, the principal philosophical issues that animated a third-century Confucian such as Huang K'an could not eschew and in fact invited the mediation by Neo-Taoism and Buddhism. The boundaries of medieval Confucianism shifted as Confucians came to terms with the concept and practice of sagehood and self-cultivation championed by Neo-Taoist and Buddhist metaphysics. Lo's study shows how the Confucian status of the *Analects* was subverted by Huang K'an's commentary, problematizing the practice of assigning intellectual identity to a text. The common language and discourse on metaphysics—the nature of the "sage" and "self-cultivation"—that Taoism and Confucianism shared rendered the boundaries between the two traditions blurred. The meaning of the *Analects* mediated by Huang's commentary could not be categorically either Confucian or Taoist.

As Sung Neo-Confucians developed discursive strategies to identify heresies, Confucian scholars like Ou-yang Hsiu sought to renarrate the history of the Five Dynasties from a Confucian perspective. Tze-ki Hon's essay explores the ways in which a historical narrative was imbued with Confucian messages. In the process, he shows how the past might be manipulated to endorse particular Confucian visions of state and society in the present. Hon compares and contrasts two major accounts of the Five Dynasties: the *Old History of the Five Dynasties* (Chiu Wu-tai shih) by Hsueh Chu-cheng (912–981) and the *New History of the Five Dynasties* (Hsin Wu-tai shih) by Ou-yang Hsiu (1007–1072). The former gives a positive reading of the Five Dynasties as a period with its own unique way of ordering the world; the latter, conventionally labeled as Confucian, condemns the period as a dark moment in Chinese history marred by political chaos and moral degeneration.

Hon argues that these two diametrically opposite views actually represented two different conceptions of the body politic embraced respectively by two generations of Northern Sung literati, separated by some seventy years. Hsueh, as a first-generation Northern Sung literatus, had served in the governments of various dynasties. He took for granted the military governance that had been in ascendancy since the last decades of the T'ang dynasty. Ou-yang, on the other hand, lived in a time when civil rule had been securely restored. He spoke for a new generation of literati intent on molding a civil culture founded on Confucian ethicomoral principles.

To bring out the differences between Confucian and un-Confucian views of the past in full relief, Hon thematically and systematically examines the way Hsueh and Ou-yang dealt with these issues: (1) the concept of the Mandate of Heaven; (2) Sino-Khitan relations; (3) kinship based on adoption; and (4) the moral mission of a Confucian scholar. Each of them involved discrimination and distinction, that is, a sense of boundary based on a set of unequivocally Confucian criteria. The concept of the Mandate of Heaven separated the ultimately profound from the merely human; the Sino-Khitan relations distinguished the barbaric from the cultured; kinship questioned the value of the patrilineal family system; the moral mission of a Confucian clarified right and wrong, good and evil. In their divergent historical renderings of the meaning and significance of these important issues, Hsueh and Ou-yang presented two different sets of criteria for delineating the boundaries of a Confucian polity. Thanks to Hon's careful analysis of the differences, we have here a revealing example of how boundaries were drawn in historical texts and discourse.

The need for discursive strategies in erecting boundaries between intellectual traditions is further explored in John Henderson's critical examination of Neo-Confucian efforts to identify heresies. Henderson synthetically presents the rhetorical strategies and arguments that the orthodox Ch'eng-Chu school devised to deal with heresies (*i-tuan*), including varieties of Buddhism and Taoism as well as renegade forms of Confucianism. The simplest of these was to reduce heresy to the terms of orthodoxy, to present heresy as a partial or one-sided apprehension of orthodox truth, thus depriving heresy of its autonomy and even its language. Second, orthodox heresiographers schematically related heresies to one another in various uncomplimentary ways. One of these ways was to pair two heresies as complementary opposites centered on an orthodox middle way. Another was to array several heresies in hierarchical orders, for example according to their relative degree of harmfulness to the orthodox way. Third, heresiographers often reduced diverse heresies to a common denominator of error, or to some primal ur-heresies such as that of Mencius's alleged archrival, Kao-tzu. Fourth, and conversely, Neo-Confucian heresiographers were also fond of depicting the most objectionable contemporary heresy, such as that of Ch'an Buddhism or Wang Yang-ming, as a monstrous composite or summa of several earlier heresies.

The last two of these strategies tended to blur the boundaries between various heresies instead of clarifying them. Neo-Confucian heresiographers also obscured the boundaries between orthodoxy and heresy in arguing that the latter had grown to be increasingly subtle through the ages, and thus increasingly difficult to distinguish from orthodoxy. The subtlety of latter-day heresies was matched by the precariousness of latter-day orthodoxy. In view of the straitness of the orthodox gate, Neo-Confucians had good reason to be watchful over themselves even while they were alone.

What is particularly interesting in Henderson's dissection of the heresiographic strategies is the revelation of the *aporia* that inhered in Neo-Confucian heresiography—at the same time that it erects clear-cut boundaries demarcating the straight from the crooked, its professed putative orthodoxy depends entirely on the supposed constant presence of the heterodox. Moreover, by failing to understand heresies on their own terms and by insisting that these pernicious ideas were deviant variations of genuine truths, these protectors of the true way were forever placing the undesirable elements at the core of orthodoxy.

The strategies of identifying heresies were of no use to those Confucians who sought an expansive approach to Confucianism. Wang Yang-ming, the purveyor of the harmful stock of heresy in the eyes the Ch'eng-Chu partisans, is the subject of Kandice Hauf's inquiry. Wang's emphasis on the subjective experience of moral truths threatened to break down all intellectual and social boundaries. Hauf illustrates Wang's expansion of the boundaries of Confucianism by addressing three issues. First, Wang, in his earnest attempt to open up the quest for sagehood through "goodness unbound," that is, the recovery of the innate moral knowledge (*liang-chih*), purposefully and ecumenically engaged Taoism and Buddhism so that some of their teachings figured prominently in his intellectual universe. The innate moral knowledge gave him, and ultimately everyone, the autonomy to judge what was of value in alternate spiritual traditions, and therefore, the ability to transcend the boundaries between sage and commoner, and between Confucianism, Buddhism, and Taoism.

Second, Hauf describes Wang's Confucianism in action by providing an account of his experience with the non-Han peoples in Kweichow between the years of 1508 and 1510. In accordance with his optimistic belief in the innate knowledge of the good, Wang was convinced of their transformability. Their rough and improper behavior on the outside did not harm their innate goodness. Such outward vulgarity would dissipate and be transformed if Confucian superior persons (*chün-tzu*) were in their midst exercising their moral and scholarly influences. Instead of repudiating outright the characters and practices of the peoples he encountered, Wang took pains to transform them. Hauf proffers an interesting example wherein Wang appropriated a popular cult of the Miao people by re-inscribing Confucian meanings on this local religious practice. Rather than treating the Miao worship of Hsiang, the evil stepbrother of the sage-king Shun, as a "profane cult" (*yin-tz'u*), Wang reinterpreted the legend of Hsiang, making him a paragon of a morally transformed figure, and in the process, Wang used this occasion to sing a paean on filial piety, converting a popular religious cult into a sort of Confucian worship.

Third, Hauf considers the question of intellectual boundaries in terms of the use of physical space by evaluating the use Wang and his followers made of Buddhist, and to a lesser extent, Taoist establishments, such as shrines, temples, and monasteries. Wang Yang-ming often visited, stayed, and taught in Buddhist temples. The point is that Confucians encroached on and shared space with Buddhists and Taoists, often peacefully and matter-of-factly. In all, both in practice and in doctrine, Wang's life and teachings exemplified the elasticity of Confucianism in action. In Wang's thought, goodness, experienced subjectively, became unbounded and flowed freely across intellectual, social, and even ethnic boundaries.

While the idea of goodness cannot be frozen and claimed exclusively by any intellectual tradition, a text can similarly pass through different discursive moments. In Kai-wing Chow's essay, we find a brief history of the hermeneutic contestations that surrounded the classical text of the *Great Learning* (Ta-hsueh), beginning with the Ch'eng-Chu elevation of the text to a separate canon and ending with its branding as heterodox writing by Ch'en Ch'ueh (1604–77). Chow, using the *Great Learning* as a particular instance, addresses the theoretical issue of the fluidity of canonicity in Chinese exegesis. What were the criteria for placing a text within the boundary of an intellectual school? How were the boundaries imagined and of what were they constituted? Chow refers to the change in the status of a text in discourse as the "moment" of the text, signifying the fluidity of its discursive status, rather than the true, objective identification of it as canonical. To use the term "moment" is to avoid organizing the different variations of a text into a rigid schema of development.

As Chow reveals, Chu Hsi created two paradigms for reading the *Great Learning*. The first was structural, whereby Chu divided the text into two parts: *ching* (the classic proper) and *chuan* (the commentary proper). Propelled by his own philosophic emphasis, he himself further added a commentary on the classical passage of "*ko-wu chih-chih*" (investigation of things and extension of knowledge to the utmost). The second paradigm was doctrinal, whereby Chu imbued the *Great Learning* with independent classical status because of the text's clear definition and prescription of the goals, principles and procedures for moral self-cultivation and sociopolitical activism. Chow also shows how these paradigms of reading involved the use of two textual strategies: the assertion of "intellectual affinity" and the creation of "intellectual lineage." The former imagined the mutual identity of the text's messages and Confucius's teachings; the latter attributed the commentary to Confucius's disciple, Tseng-tzu, implying that the classic-commentary division mirrored the master-disciple relationship.

Chu's exposition of the *Great Learning* became orthodox and met no serious challenge until Wang Yang-ming's explicit plea for the return to the old version of the text when he published his *Old Edition of the Great Learning* (Ku-pen Ta-hsueh) in 1518. The circulation of Wang's *Old Edition* and the publication of Feng Fang's apocryphal stele edition had the cumulative effect of undermining the integrity of the official edition of Chu Hsi. Many modifications of the texts by sundry scholars appeared, based on the individuals' philosophic inclinations, no doubt also aided by the spread of printing technology. Finally, in the early Ch'ing, Ch'en Ch'ueh, in an effort to end the unruly motley of interpretations that had accrued around the Great Learning, condemned the classic as outright heterodox, a text written by neither Confucius nor his disciple Tseng-tzu, but one that was inspired by Ch'an Buddhism. Reminding one of the heresiographical strategies Henderson discusses in his chapter, Ch'en Ch'ueh, as Chow points out, used a reductionist strategy to reduce the entire text of the *Great Learning* to the heterodox teachings of Ch'an Buddhism.

Chow's highlighting of the hermeneutic "moments" of the *Great Learning* not only reveals the different discursive strategies employed, but also the fact that they were determined by the interpreter's and reader's beliefs and understanding of the Confucian tradition. A text passes through different hermeneutic moments as the boundary between canonicity and heterodoxy shifted.

On-cho Ng amplifies and extends Chow's findings in his pondering of the intimate relationship between hermeneutics and philosophy—the latter was often the domain within which the pursuit of and reflection on normative truths were undertaken. Through a detailed study of the exegetical efforts of an early Ch'ing Ch'eng-Chu scholar, Li Kuang-ti (1642–1718), Ng shows how the exegete's or interpreter's philosophical predisposition and preunderstanding guided his engagement with the classics, thereby collapsing the boundary between hermeneutics and philosophy. Ng's study provides an example of a rhetorical strategy orthodox Ch'eng-Chu heresiographers employed to attack Wang Yang-ming's teachings. In Li's case, his reading of the *Doctrine of the Mean* (Chung-yung) and the *Great Learning*, which involved textual rearrangement and emendation, was a function of his metaphysical understanding of human nature (*hsing*).

To demonstrate this nexus, Ng traces the contour of Li's philosophy, whose central premise was the assertion that human nature was the ontological hinge on which all Confucian meta-ethical arguments turned. In a way reminiscent of Ch'en Ch'ueh's identification of a specific idea with Ch'an Buddhism, Li's critique focused on refuting the Lu-Wang idea of the ontological centrality of the mind-heart (*hsin*). He affirmed the primacy of the innately good human nature as the underpinning of reality. Ng reveals the ways in which Li's hermeneutic rendering of the *Mean* and the *Great Learning* was strongly influenced by this philosophical thesis. In other words, Li, as a contingent historical agent with his particular philosophic preoccupation, sought a meaningful conflation of the past and present through his historically contextualized interpretation of the classics.

Ng further suggests that viewed in this light, classical exegesis in traditional China, in a general way, displays some interesting and revealing commonality with contemporary interpretive hermeneutics, inasmuch as both point to the ineluctable dialogical relations between the text and interpreter. The ending portion of Ng's essay addresses Li's hermeneutic endeavor in a comparative perspective by referring to the hermeneutic ideas and theories of Martin Buber, Hans-Georg Gadamer, and David Tracy. They all take the classics, or the scriptures, as the textual embodiment of a vital cultural tradition, the locus of their understanding. To all of them, exegesis is an interactive dialogue with a living past ensconced in the classics. The classics, because of their acknowledged essential perpetuity, offer a common context, a single cultural tradition, capable of absorbing and accommodating the diversity and historicity of their interpreters.

By casting Li Kuang-ti's hermeneutics in a comparative light, Ng contributes to a better understanding of Confucian hermeneutics, not as mere repetition of the classical words frozen in a timeless moment, but as a constant historical restating and reinterpretation of the classics' apparently transtemporal ideas. In the final analysis, according to Ng, the messages of the Confucian classics remained forever fluid. As long as those texts were read, the boundaries of their truth-claims would be constantly redrawn in accordance with the philosophical pre-understanding and preoccupation of the interpreters.

If the foregoing chapters all provide a horizontal perspective of the shifting of the boundaries of Confucianism, showing how the Confucian tradition engaged Buddhism and Taoism, and how varying internal orientations within this tradition did battles and cross-fertilized, Hsiung Ping-chen's essay asks us to take a vertical view of the Confucian literati and cast light on the middlebrow. She addresses the question of how self-criticism within an intellectual tradition could be tolerated. By focusing on one such character in the world of the Confucian middlebrow, T'ang Chen (1630–1704) of the early Ch'ing, she on the one hand delineates the real boundaries separating this group of literati from the elite in traditional Chinese society, and on the other, suggests that historians make a greater effort to appreciate the agency of the middlebrow in the making of the Confucian world.

Hsiung asks us to look beyond the texts of the Great Tradition and their authors, and examine the lives and thoughts of the less well-known followers of Confucianism. T'ang Chen and his family were socially and financially ruined during the Ming-Ch'ing transition. T'ang never did receive a sound classical education and endured much hardship. Throughout his life, he grubbed along with limited income from small landholding, temporary lowly administrative employment, small business, literary service and borrowing. At times, he starved. He can be regarded as a miserable failure in conventional Confucian terms. Moreover,

his brooding frustrations, compounded by the sense of personal failure and humiliation, fostered his alienation from dynastic politics and the sociopolitical order.
He became a bold critic of the existing system.

In his collected essays, the *Ch'ien shu* (Writings in Obscurity), T'ang
attacked the despotic nature of a political order in which authority was concentrated in the hands of one person, the emperor, summed up by his famous indict-
ment: "All kings and emperors are but bandits." He also criticized the oppression
of women and the pomposity of men, both results of a social order in which
women were treated as subservient. Nonetheless, T'ang considered himself an
authentic Confucian, once reporting to the local authorities that Confucius was
falsely and improperly worshipped as the God of the Earth in a small local
shrine. But perhaps because T'ang Chen, being a middlebrow Confucian, was
intellectually isolated and materially hard-pressed, he did tend to approach the
orthodox tradition individualistically, often yielding idiosyncratic ideas. As a
result, he found no audience, and was by and large excluded from the circles of
the elite literati such as Ku Yen-wu, who, as a contemporary of T'ang, was con-
trastingly blessed with connections and social networks available only to people
like himself.

But history provides an ironic twist and somewhat evens the score. A century after T'ang's son-in-law produced the first fifty copies of the *Ch'ien shu* in
memory of his father-in-law, a new generation of Confucian literati, interested in
statecraft, found T'ang's ideas on the political and social orders inspiring. The
compilers of the famous early-nineteenth-century work, the *Huang-ch'ao ching-
shih wen-pien* (Anthology of Essays on Statecraft of the Imperial Dynasty),
included no less than twenty-one essays out of T'ang's original ninety-seven, second in number only to Ku Yen-wu. The boundaries of Confucianism had shifted,
when domestic crises and looming foreign problems demanded new thinking.
What had been deemed impertinent in the seventeenth century was viewed with
enthusiasm in the nineteenth. T'ang's thought was finally embraced as a part of
the Confucian heritage.

Lauren Pfister, from a different vantage point, also leads us to a part of the
Confucian intellectual universe that is seldom visited, the part where Confucianism critically engaged Christianity. After the British had set up a colony in
Hong Kong in the mid nineteenth century, missionaries arrived. In 1843, a
young Scottish missionary James Legge (1815–97) met a minor Chinese official,
Lo Chung-fan (d. circa 1850). This meeting catalyzed in both men a certain
unique understanding of the Confucian classics and rituals, particularly the dis-
covery of a certain monotheism premised on the notion of Shang-ti (Lord-on-
High).

Lo left behind a commentary on the *Great Learning*, the *Explanations and
Discussions of the Old Text of the Great Learning* (Ku-pen Ta-hsueh chu-pien). As
some of the much better-known interpreters of this classic whom we have seen

above, Lo rejected both Chu Hsi's textual changes and his main interpretation of the work. But what is most remarkable about Lo's exegesis is his substantive claims about the nature of the Lord-on-High, who to him, is the "sovereign lord of creative transformation," the Way (*tao*) itself. It is only because of the indwelling presence of Shang-ti in the human heart that ultimate moral transformation is possible. Shang-ti, in fact, makes the human inner being a temple (*tien*), an idea of clear Christian origin, according to Pfister. In sum, Lo's hermeneutic interpretations of the *Great Learning*, although Confucian in many regards, are apparently heavily tinged by his nascent appreciation of an all-powerful being such as the Christian God, evidently a result of his study of the Christian Scripture. (Legge did inform us of Lo's knowledge of the Christian texts.) Lo, in essence, developed a systematic "Shang-ti-ist moral metaphysics," as Pfister describes it. James Legge himself was also prompted to speculate on the "monotheistic" tendencies in the Confucian traditions. In his study of the imperial prayers and worship of the Ming, Legge concluded that inhering in them was a form of ritual monotheism. He was the first missionary to translate the imperial prayers and unequivocally identify the spiritual being addressed in them with the Christian "God." Eventually, as a devout Christian, Legge nonetheless found much in common between Confucianism and Christianity. He declared that Confucius was his "Master," in the same way that Christ was "his Master and his Lord."

Pfister, using the case of Lo's and Legge's hermeneutics, takes issue with Max Weber's rather simplistic characterization of Confucianism in terms of its "relentless canonization of tradition," casting doubts on the tradition's flexibility. Lo's systematic development of a kind of "monotheism" is a good rejoinder. Furthermore, the fact that Legge succeeded in opening up a new understanding of Christianity for Confucian scholars and forged an accommodating approach to the Confucian traditions for Chinese Christians, demonstrates the fertile possibilities of cross-cultural boundary-crossing. Whereas Kai-wing Chow, in his essay, shows how the *Great Learning* moved through its various hermeneutical moments in the commentaries by Chu Hsi, Wang Yang-ming, and Ch'en Ch'ueh, Pfister reveals how the recognition of the notion of Shang-ti in the Confucian classic by Lo Chung-fan contributed to blurring the boundary between Confucianism and Christianity.

This collection of essays, thus, uses the variegated histories of Confucianism to interrogate the nature of Confucianism, a dynamic tradition constantly shifting its boundaries. It was constantly framed and reframed with the inevitable intervention of human agency.[11] Therefore, the history of Confucianism cannot be studied apart from the changing narratives (doctrinal, textual, hermeneutical, philosophical, and experiential) that were used to construct it. The chapters assembled here are less about the meanings of Confucianism than the means by which those meanings were manufactured. They thus show that Confucianism was never a formalism of ideas frozen in time, reified as immutable dogmas. Its very vitality, dynamism, and alas existence, depended on its remaking and re-inventing itself.

NOTES

1. David L. Hall and Roger T. Ames, *Anticipating China: Thinking through the Narratives of Chinese and Western Cultures* (Albany: State University of New York Press, 1995).

2. See for example his two anthologies of essays: *Confucian Thought: Selfhood as Creative Transformation* (Albany: State University of New York Press, 1985) and *Way, Learning, and Politics: Essays on the Confucian Intellectual* (Albany: State University of New York Press, 1993).

3. Wm. Theodore de Bary, *The Trouble with Confucianism* (Cambridge, Mass: Harvard University Press, 1991).

4. Thomas A. Metzger, *Escape from Predicament: Neo-Confucianism and China's Evolving Political Culture* (New York: Columbia University Press, 1977).

5. For a methodological perspective on interpreting Confucianism as a "philosophical system," see Anne D. Birdwhistell, *Li Yong (1627-1705) and Epistemological Dimensions of Confucian Philosophy* (Stanford: Stanford University Press, 1996), pp. 26–50.

6. Cf. Frank Kermode, *The Sense of an Ending* (Oxford: Oxford University Press, 1968).

7. Cf. Joseph Grigely, *Textualterity: Art, Theory, and Textual Criticism* (Ann Arbor: University of Michigan Press, 1995), pp. 1–10.

8. Michel Foucault, *The Archaeology of Knowledge*, trans. A. M. Sheridan Smith (New York: Pantheon Books, 1972), p. 172.

9. This is not the place to discuss the use of metaphors. Nonetheless, here, we do resort to the metaphor of boundary in order to illustrate the fluidity of the Confucian tradition. But we use the metaphor advisedly. Following Donald Davidson, we employ a metaphor, in this case, "boundary," to simply make us attend to some likeness between two or more things. The metaphor has no further meaning than its literal sense. It serves to draw attention to the sheer surface commonality or pattern of relationships and transformations, subsuming under it the diverse historical issues and subjects. It is a descriptive device to portray the movements, textual, doctrinal, or experiential, within Confucianism. It is also a prescriptive device to delimit the interpretive perspective. See Donald Davidson, "What Metaphors Mean," in his *Inquiries into Truth and Interpretation* (Oxford: Oxford University Press, 1984), pp. 246–47, 259–62.

10. On the multivocality of language, see M. M. Bakhtin, "Discourse in the Novel," in *The Dialogic Imagination: Four Essays*, ed. Michael Holquist, trans. Caryl Emerson and Michael Holquist (Austin: University of Texas Press, 1981).

11. We are here borrowing from both Jonathan Culler's and Derrida's notion of "framing," that is, on the act of reading a text in "context," such as all Confucian texts and doctrines were. But this notion of frame really transcends "context" in that, in Culler's words, "it reminds us that framing is something we do; it hints of the frame-up ('falsifying evidence beforehand in order to make someone appear guilty'), a major use of context; and it eludes the incipient positivism of 'context' by alluding to the semiotic function of framing in art, where the frame is determining, setting off the object or event as art, and yet the frame itself may be nothing tangible, pure articulation." See his *Framing the Sign: Criticism and Its Institutions* (Norman: University of Oklahoma Press, 1988), p. xiv. Derrida utters something similar: "It is the analytic which determines the frame as parergon, which both constitutes it and ruins it, makes it hold . . . and collapse. A frame is essentially constructed and therefore fragile: such would be the essence or truth of the frame. If it had any truth. But this 'truth' can no longer be a 'truth,' it no more defines the transcendentality than it does the accidentality of the frame. . . . Philosophy wants to arraign it and can't manage." See his *The Truth in Painting*, trans. Geoff Bennington and Ian McLeod (Chicago: University of Chicago Press, 1987), p. 73. For some elaboration of this idea, see Grigely, *Textualterity*, pp. 178–179.

2

A Problematic Model

The Han "Orthodox Synthesis," Then and Now

Michael Nylan

In late imperial China, the search for ideological order often reflected the desire for a strong political order; empire and orthodoxy were presumed to go hand-in-hand.[1] Hence, the Ch'eng-Chu masters' palpable distaste for Han Confucianism, which they found insufficiently "orthodox," being neither "unitary" nor "faithful" enough to the Master's precepts.[2] It is somewhat ironic, then, that such determined efforts to denigrate *all* of Han Confucianism may have lent it the essentialized air of a uniform entity, so much so that the most eminent Sinologists once spoke confidently of the Han "victory of Confucianism," a catchy Social Darwinist phrase, if one could figure out exactly what "victory" or "Confucianism" meant for the period. Slowly, recent scholarship has begun to chip away at the monumental facade presented by the supposed Han "victory" of a state-sponsored synthesis, showing that the "victory" was neither as complete nor as speedy as earlier envisioned.[3] Now, with a postmodern generation intent upon discerning suitably blurry boundaries for Ju belief and practice, it seems time to question that most cherished of historical assumptions regarding Han—the assumption that there was a recognizable Confucian synthesis, considered orthodox at the time but later dismissed as deficient.

The "victory" hypothesis imagined that Emperor Wu of Han (r. 140–87 B.C.), seeking ways to "rationalize" or "routinize" his charisma in the Weberian sense, decided to stake his particular claim to legitimacy on his control over canonical texts, instead of relying upon divine revelation, personal charisma, or brute force.[4] It argues that Wu-ti and his successors appointed scholars to *chih shu* ("regulate the texts"), with the idea of securing an imperial monopoly over classical learning and its bureaucratic proponents. Control by the center was then to be reinforced by the institution of an imperial academy staffed with scholars eager for imperial patronage. Founding a selective imperial academy, building up but setting limits on access to the imperial libraries, and staffing the bureaucracy with scholar-officials chosen by "Confucian" criteria—these were but three of the strong institutional measures designed to encourage strict adherence to Confucian norms among the subject population. According to the "victory" theory, after 135 B.C., classical learning was supposedly transmitted in a far more controlled fashion through the state's conferral of prescribed texts, through its rewards for model behavior, through long apprenticeship to state-approved masters, and through formal participation in a variety of state-sponsored rituals, including academic conferences. By this account, the "Confucian Classics" were "victorious" because the state had declared them the culminating revelation of the Tao operating in history, thereby securing early closure on the canon, which, in turn, inhibited potential challenges to an imperial interpretive monopoly.[5]

While such a theory certainly reflects the aspirations of a few Han emperors and their followers, as we can see from edicts and memorials, there are some grounds for regarding the conventional treatment of the Han orthodox synthesis with skepticism.[6] After all, the five fundamental premises that underlie the contention of a "Han synthesis" resulting in a "victory of Confucianism" can be challenged:

1. That we can easily identify who the Confucians really were, as a distinct group with a distinct ideology;
2. That the empire (i.e., its rulers and administrators), like the later Neo-Confucians, presumed an absolute need for a single ruling orthodoxy;[7]
3. That state sponsorship of Confucian activities was consistent;
4. That state sponsorship of Confucian activities was also effective, in that it led to markedly greater uniformity in thought and in practice; and
5. That this greater uniformity represented something quite distinct from what had existed in the pre-Han period.

Each of these five underlying premises is questionable, given present information.

Let me begin with the first assumption: that we can identify who the Confucians were. The "victory" hypothesis imagined a neat correspondence between Han Confucians and members of the "Ju" "school." But Han texts attached three logically separate meanings to the single Chinese word Ju:

1. "Classicist," meaning one who has mastered the classical precedents stored in ancient texts, along with the performance of antique rites and music;[8]

2. A "Confucian," defined for the sake of brevity in this paper as a "committed adherent of Confucius' Way of *jen* and the Five Relations," typically distinguished by their oppositional stances;[9] and

3. "Government official," actual or potential (*shih*).[10]

In the pre-Han period, of course, none of the texts (and very few of the practices) deemed "ancient" (i.e., "classical") had been identified as the exclusive intellectual property of Confucians.[11] Certainly, well into Western Han times, the corpus that we now call the "Confucian Classics" was regarded as the common literary heritage of *all* well-educated people, which explains why some Han writings identify opponents of the self-conscious followers of Confucius as "Ju."[12] Thus, Wu-ti's decision in 134 B.C. to limit the court academicians to specialists in the Five Classics in one important sense re-confirmed, rather than revolutionized, the pre-Han situation, as it made familiarity with, if not wholehearted devotion to, the Five Classics the standard preparation for most offices above the rank of clerk.[13] After all, the Ju had long been recognized as experts in diplomacy and religion, the two main concerns of state.[14]

The historian should at least consider, then, the proposition that the main significance of Han Wu-ti's decision lay not in a strict separation of Confucianism from rival "schools," but rather in the muddle begot by the implicit merging of no fewer than three competing definitions of Ju (classicist, Confucian, and government official).[15] The resultant confusion must have created problems for those living during the Han, as well as for the modern historian, for once a clear majority of aspirants and appointees to office were undeniably "Ju," the gate of state-sponsored "Confucianism" was opened wide to all manner of ethical, intellectual, and practical ideas promoted by well-meaning literati trained in the rhetorical arts, not to mention the various schemes of "vulgar Ju" (those who held the acquisition of factual knowledge or appointment to office above any moral consideration).[16] In consequence, modern historians find Han texts furnishing somewhat contradictory accounts of Ju thought and practice, which should hardly surprise us, given that the traditions, aims, and activities of each of the three Ju groups ("true Confucians," "classicists," and "career-bureaucrats") seldom coincided. That no absolute theoretical barrier prevented admission to Ju status (though the Han Ju were no less liable than we to be impressed by class and status indicators) only complicated matters further.[17]

Having satisfied ourselves that we cannot easily define the (good, bad, or typical) "Confucian" in Han, let alone the "proper Confucian" stance, we must search for indisputable evidence that the Han state aimed to promote a single orthodoxy in Han. Once again, the relevant evidence is not easy to find. We tend to gloss over the fact that Emperor Wu and his successors on the Han throne set up, on average, some fourteen different orthodoxies, one for each scholastic lineage representing one of several commentarial traditions favored for each

"Confucian" classic;[18] also, that even these state-approved scholastic lines failed to achieve an interpretive monopoly in its own area of Han classical studies. We also tend to forget that the inclusivist metaphor of "All roads lead to the Tao"[19] dominated intellectual discourse for much of the Han, until the virtual collapse of the empire in Eastern Han dramatized the court's inability to contain its presumably "Confucianized" subjects in some kind of unified order. The Han, after all, had prided itself on its firm refusal to adopt the top-down imposition of intellectual and political order associated with its predecessor, Ch'in; many felt that the Han founder, Kao-tsu, had won the empire because of his admirable flexibility in drawing upon the best of many approaches, rather than prescribing a single tactic for rule.[20] In any case, conventional wisdom held that political unity under just rulers would naturally lead to ideological unification, without psychological or physical coercion.

It would be folly to claim that there were no voices at court arguing for a well-defined orthodoxy; but surely it is telling that the most strident voices after Tung Chung-shu often belonged to the military families (often the *wai-ch'i* families) and their retainers, whose traditions stressing single-minded loyalty and the defense of Han against internal and external military threats, made them somewhat untypical of the general Han population as a whole and suspect to some Han literati in particular.[21] Basically, with no institutionalized religions or "barbarian" threats to challenge a nominally "Confucian" empire until very late in Eastern Han, the Han throne had no good reason to enforce a strict orthodoxy—and every reason not to.[22]

Next, we should ask whether the state sponsorship of Confucian activities was consistent. Again, the answer would be a negative one. Obviously, with classicists filling key posts in government, the state began to assess Ju mastery in systematic ways: through written and oral examinations; through periodic court debates; through essays, memorials, and declamations; and through formal recommendations attesting to exemplary ritual practice.[23] In theory, the state had a strong, vested interest in promoting the moral teachings associated with the "Confucian" canon as both sufficient and uniform.[24] But in practice, the state, made up of the Ju in its employ, seemed quite unable to come to any firm decision on how to achieve that uniformity. On the one hand, the Han throne and its officials understood the desirability of exerting some controls over classical instruction.[25] On the other hand, the Han throne, mindful of the fact that its legitimacy was ultimately dependent upon the good will of all three types of Ju, was loathe to invest too much authority in any single group of Confucian teachers or Ju bureaucrats, lest government advisors fall prey to one-sided preoccupations with abstract doctrine or a single faction gain too much power at court. (That, of course, had been Emperor Wu's primary motivation for favoring the Ju over the Huang-Lao adherents in the first place.) Meanwhile, the unquenchable thirst of a few Han emperors for miraculous new texts and new omens to justify Han rule prompted the further production of extracanonical and pseudocanonical texts. In truth, the state's theoretical need to strictly limit the number of interpretive traditions accorded serious consideration was always offset by its simultaneous intention to "weave a net [to capture all] omissions and *lacunae*" in the classical tradition.[26]

As a result, state sponsorship of the prolix "commentaries by chapter and verse" (*chang-chü*) attached to each of the Five Classics (whose explanations sometimes ran to some 20,000 characters for a short five-character phrase) alternated with equally pious assertions about the state's desire to promote "broad learning."[27] Throughout the Han, there were few signs that the state made more than half-hearted attempts to reduce the *chang-chü* to manageable proportions or to codify a single vision drawn from the unwieldy corpus of the Five "Confucian" Classics.[28] To the contrary, those attempting to elicit a unitary vision were apt to be charged with the crime of "creating" a new teaching, a prerogative reserved for Confucius and sage-rulers of the Han ruling in the Master's name.[29] Small wonder that the dynasty's scholars were frequently engaged in compiling lengthy anthologies, whose multiple entries made for "plausible deniability." In times of such unclarity, the search for balance (for reasons good and bad) was the order of the day.

The most staunchly "Confucian" texts (for example, Pan Ku's *Han shu*) place the blame for such lack of clarity squarely on the Han emperors, chastising many emperors for their signal lack of enthusiasm to create, then enforce, an ideological orthodoxy on a strictly Confucian model.[30] The very same texts tend to linger on events like that recounted in the opening passage of the *Hou Han shu*'s "Collective Biography of the Ju" (Ju lin lieh chuan). There we see Emperor Ming of the Eastern Han in A.D. 56 donning his "Communicating with Heaven" hat, prior to lecturing in all solemnity on the texts of the Five "Confucian" Classics, resolving textual problems, and promoting classical scholars on the basis of their adherence to classical precepts. While such passages verify the complex nature of Han court-sponsored "classicism,"[31] several important historical questions remain: What is the exact nature of the records that have been transmitted to us? Are they reliable enough or too polemical in nature?[32] How typical were "Confucian" activities for the two Han dynasties as a whole? What, specifically, was the quality and quantity of support for "Confucian" activities by each of the Han emperors? Put another way, how far, really, did the state's interest in promoting "Confucian" virtues go beyond the state's intention—not especially "Confucian"—to instill absolute loyalty in its subjects?[33]

Surely it is significant that the first committed "Confucian" emperor that comes to mind is the "usurper" Wang Mang—not a Han emperor at all—while the list of Han emperors said to be actively hostile to "Confucian" interests is, in fact, extensive, as it would have to include Wen-ti, Ching-ti, Hsüan-ti, Ch'eng-ti, An-ti, and most of the late Eastern Han emperors after Shun-ti (125–144).[34]

For most emperors (including the first grand imperial proponent of "Ju" classi-cism, Emperor Wu himself), the picture is decidedly mixed (i.e., sometimes pro-Confucian and sometimes anti-Confucian). Not surprisingly, then, numerous Han accounts tell of stark physical and intellectual declines in the main "Confucian" institutions, including the Academy; extant reports also reveal the frustration experienced by committed Confucians with many perceived "un-Confucian" activities of their emperors' highly placed, supposedly "Confucian" appointments.[35] That such reports date from the very moment of Emperor Wu's decision to patronize Ju and continue throughout Han history suggests, to say the least, a measure of imperial ambivalence toward Confucianism by Han rulers. Bluntly put, imperial attacks on renowned Ju leaders (e.g., the Partisans) and lack of institutional support for Confucianism surface nearly as often in the historical materials as imperial support.

Let us consider a fairly typical case, that of Emperor Chang (A.D. 76–88) of Eastern Han: The *Hou Han shu*'s "Collective Biography of the Ju" celebrates Chang-ti's decision to convene "all the Ju" at the White Tiger Pavilion in A.D. 79, to resolve doctrinal disputes in connection with the interpretation of the "Confucian" classics. But less than a decade later, in A.D. 86, Chang-ti grew annoyed with the Confucian scholastics. Angry that their deliberations never seemed to spark productive activity, he taunted them with a suitable classical allusion, "If a single K'uei was enough for [the sage-ruler] Yao, why should we need this throng of contending intellectuals?"[36] (Of this sea change in Chang-ti's attitude, by the way, the "Ju lin lieh chuan" says nothing.)[37]

Obviously, it is a well-attested fact that certain emperors, empresses, and ministers were anxious to promote Confucian values. And it is equally certain that several famous Han thinkers wished to forge an attractive "Han synthesis." The names of Tung Chung-shu, Yang Hsiung, and Cheng Hsüan spring immedi-ately to mind. But it is no less clear that such attempts at synthesis invariably failed, in part because there were at best only sporadic efforts by the state leaders to attend to "Confucian" projects and "Confucian" learning, in part because the pool of self-interested Ju was invariably so much larger in Han than the pool of committed Confucians, in part because of other factors. (But that is to get ahead of the argument. See below.)

Having demonstrated that state sponsorship of "Confucian" activities was inconsistent, it is time to ask whether in an identifiable era state sponsorship brought about appreciably greater uniformity in thought and in practice. What we have until late Han is a situation that essentially continues from the Warring States: adherence (nominal or real) to the slogan "employ the worthy" means that as the empire expands geographically, ever greater numbers of people—no longer just aristocrats—wish to demonstrate their acquaintance with "classical" (some now known to be pseudoclassical) texts and practices, so as to prove their employability and civil accomplishments. But an increase in sheer numbers of people claiming mastery of classical precedents apparently did little to facilitate the imposition or spontaneous formation of a single orthodoxy.

In 135 B.C., Tung Chung-shu had memorialized to Wu-ti, "At present teachers propagate strange principles; our fellow human beings hold to unusual practices; the many schools of thought have idiosyncratic methods and the conclusions to which they point are not identical."[38] Much later, after more than three centuries of imperial sponsorship of Confucian activities, Ts'ai Yung in A.D. 175 lodged a similar complaint in a memorial addressed to Emperor Ling (r. 172–177). According to Ts'ai, it was imperative to collate and standardize the texts of the Six Classics since *within the Confucian camp* "many errors have crept into the text, which have been wrongly interpreted by ordinary scholars, leading to confusion and befuddlement among younger students."[39] So, too, with practice. For instance, Ssu-ma Ch'ien's *Shih chi* compiled under Wu-ti presented an extensive panorama of acceptable behavioral models (many, such as the "knights errant," decidedly unorthodox). But centuries after that base line, an equally broad range of behavioral ideals appeared in Wang Ch'ung's *Lun heng* chapter categorizing distinct types of "worthies" (*hsien*).[40] One would think that some three hundred and fifty years of an imposed Confucian "synthesis" would have narrowed the range of acceptable models for theory and practice. Obviously, it did not, since even candidates for official preferment failed to accept the need to "maintain *chia-fa*" (i.e., keep strictly to standard interpretive traditions), though the Han government was paying the bills for the *po-shih* academics and their registered disciples.[41] What is still more striking is that a single synthesis never was achieved even in the select circles of dedicated Confucian "masters" working hard to distinguish their efforts, in the spirit of "renewing" Confucian teachings, from those of the "vulgar Ju." Even the self-identified Confucian masters of the Han period are best described as "eclectics," for lack of a more precise term.[42]

If polemical texts dating to Han can be believed, the state's failure to legislate Confucian morality was painfully obvious to many of its most eminent subjects. Even among self-conscious Confucians, as one Han text put it, "Each and every person had his own mind, and no two attained the Mean."[43] Again and again, contemporary texts inform us that "men all use their private judgement, right and wrong has no standard, and clever opinions and heterodox pronouncements have caused confusion among scholars."[44]

It may be suggested that there were four fundamental reasons why attempts at synthesis, even if they had been consistent, may have been doomed from the start. First, the Confucian project was at its base resistant to rule-based formulae. Second, the so-called "Confucian" scriptures, monumental texts of different dates addressing disparate topics in different styles and often conflicting messages, were by nature unamenable to tight control by the state, either at the theoretical or the practical level. (That is one reason why Chu Hsi advocated a curriculum based in the Four Books, a much smaller corpus more liable to unitary interpretation.) Third, the classical (and "Confucian") impulse to consult precedents entailed similar difficulties, as there were a host of competing models drawn from different eras and rival ideologies from which to choose. Fourth, the Confucian requirement that theory be adjusted to the needs of state, community, and family service meant that Confucian theory continually confronted a welter of practical considerations.

Let me begin with what some scholars have identified as the fundamental "problem" with Confucianism: the mysteries that lie at its heart.[45] Confucius had characterized himself as "unlike" other men in that he offered no rule-based formulae regarding right and wrong.[46] In line with Confucius, the Confucian tradition in Han embraced a number of moral quandaries, paradoxes, and polarities, all of which resulted from inexplicable mysteries that lay at the very center of the Han Confucian Way; no amount of painstaking explication by would-be rationalizers could excise these mysteries from the Confucian enterprise. Nine of the most important were:

1. In the sociopolitical realm the more you give away, the more you get. (The Han state, by the way, sought to institutionalize this paradox by devising a system of rewards for those who exhibited a remarkable capacity to *jang* ["yield"] in self-abnegation.)[47]

2. What is entirely natural and spontaneous (and thus by definition "good") is inadequate only in the single case of human beings. Humans, alone of all creatures, require a highly self-conscious form of patterning ("ritual") to counter their dangerous propensities toward imbalance.[48]

3. The full development of a person's individual nature and expressive powers depends, at least initially, upon strict adherence to the most conformist of activities: ritual.[49]

4. Many ritual acts prescribed in the Confucian classics are specifically designed to bridge the intrinsically unbridgeable gulf between good and evil, life and death—often by inversions of everyday experience, so as to convert a potential threat to the community into a protective force for the community.[50]

5. The full realization of human potential through total dedication to the arduous process of self-cultivation results in the acquisition of a "second nature" that is godlike in its transformative powers (as applied to oneself, as applied to others). What is most human, then, is also most divine (*shen*).[51]

6. The Confucian emphasis on the ritual implementation of integrity (*ch'eng*) pulls the individual both outward and inward: the person's salutary integration with Heaven-and-Earth corresponds to his signal achievement in unifying his own thoughts and deeds.[52]

7. The highest joy of the committed Ju, which rests in a perception of the true extent of the greatness of the Way, at the same time constitutes the committed Ju's deepest sorrow, for it inevitably entails a recognition on the Ju's part of the enormous gap that lies between its greatness and his pettiness, between his own halting efforts at self-cultivation and the effortless efficacy of the Way.[53]
8. Devotion to the Confucian Way represents the most profitable sort of activity in pursuit of the truly "good life," yet it has nothing to do with the pursuit of conventional profit.[54] Put another way, the Ju by pursuit of the Way may both improve and not improve his fate.[55]
9. The true sage at once engages in marvelous "creation" (*tso*) and faithful "transmission" (*shu*), through an intuitive process of "renewing the old."[56]

In a sense, these nine quandaries defined Confucianism in Han; it was to them that the best minds of Han continually returned. For instance, Yang Hsiung in his *Model Sayings*, positively embraces paradox, seeing in it the true source of the Mystery and the compelling intellectual and aesthetic power of Confucianism. Yet the sheer breadth of the Han vision, which strove to encompass the extrahuman world, as well as the human, in the utter perfection of the Great Peace, had Han Ju wrestling with more than the usual number of moral quandaries in a greatly expanded ethical universe. As the preferred "solution" to such quandaries rested, whatever the Han Ju said, upon individual understanding engendered by personal experience and taste, no final resolution in the form of rule-based notions was ultimately possible.

Insofar as scriptures (*ching*) are a special class of true and powerful words, whose very monumentality (presumably expressing a single, ultimate Truth) effectively blinds readers, early and late, to the quite astonishing range of possible relationships that people can enter into with such texts, we erroneously tend to assume literal, reverent reception of a "canon."[57] But in Han, widely different receptions of the Han "Confucian" canon were born from the widely varying interests and needs that individual persons brought to the Classics. A student at the Imperial Academy cramming for his qualifying examinations approached the canon quite differently from a local administrator intent upon modeling local institutions after those of antiquity. Those with interests in geography, in history, or in specific techniques (the rhetorical, the mathematical, the calendrical, the magical, the political), devotees of self-cultivation, and would-be office-holders alike sought information and answers in the esoteric and exoteric readings of the Classics.[58]

Looking backwards, later historians can reconstruct five fundamental kinds of reception and cultural use for Han scriptures, each of which enhanced the sacred character of the Classic, but entailed some change in its interpretation:

1. The informative, in which canonical texts shape and are shaped by one's understanding of the world and of history;
2. The transactive, in which recitation or reading of exact formulae preserved in the scripture allows direct communication with cosmic powers, which can be tapped for mundane and transmundane purposes;[59]
3. The legitimating, in which recovery or possession of a sacred text indicates Heaven's conferral of superhuman authority upon a specific person or dynastic line;
4. The transformative, in which the text facilitates a person's more profound entry into the Way by a process that is "sacred" by definition, since transformation invariably marks the locus of divine power in Han China;
5. The symbolic, in which the word or text comes to symbolize, even actualize the ultimate.[60]

To these complex, occasionally even contradictory modes of reception of the "Confucian scriptures," add two additional complications—first, that many of the "Confucian" texts in the absence of cheap paper and printing were taught orally and individually;[61] second, that Ju texts and textual practice, as dynamic agents of cultural change, themselves modified relations between throne and literati[62]—and it becomes nearly unthinkable that the Chinese state in antiquity could control the transmission of the Classics, even if it had identified this control as a top priority.

So, too, with all manner of past precedents. Even if the Ju as classicists, Confucians, and bureaucrats could plausibly be said to be in theoretical agreement about the necessity to uphold past precedents, there was always the troubling question of which set of past precedents to uphold: the legal precedents (Shang, Chou, or Han?), the bureaucratic precedents (Shang, Chou, or Han?), or the "Confucian" precedents imbedded in the Five Classics, each of which was frequently at odds with others in the same corpus. Take the case of Feng Yeh-wang, appointed as Supreme Commander General during the reign of Emperor Ch'eng. After the powerful General Wang had caused the summary execution of Feng's best political ally, Feng Yeh-wang grew sick with worry over his own career prospects. Feng then submitted a request for sick leave and returned "with his wife and children" to his home in Tu-ling in search of a cure. General Wang seized upon the irregularity, arguing that Feng should be impeached and charged with *lèse majesté*, since Feng had violated standard operating procedure when he forsook his bureaucratic post for personal reasons. A classical scholar, Tu Ch'in, who had "long admired the conduct and abilities of Feng" and his father, risked his own career as a member of General Wang's staff when he stepped forward to defend Feng. In order to succeed in his rhetorical defense, Tu found himself having to square three opposing standards for judgment: (1) bureaucratic precedent, which he conceded generally worked against Feng Yeh-wang; (2) legal statutes;

and (3) canonical precepts, both of which supported Feng's construction of his duty.[63] He argued:

> I have seen the statute that says, "Officials of 2,000 *picul* rank on leave are to submit their reports when passing by Ch'ang-an." It does not differentiate whether they are on home leave or sick leave. At present there are officials who believe that on home leave one may return home, but on sick leave one may not. That would be to have two sections in one statute. . . . Now [by General Wang's reasoning,] if one of the three highest officials in the land were to ask for home leave, that would be covered by the statute. But when an official who has been ill for a full three months takes sick leave, that would be a case of receiving imperial favor. Then [by the same logic,] statutory leave is permissible, but imperial favor is not, [which is an argument that] makes no sense.
>
> [Moreover] the tradition [based on the "Ta Yü mo" chapter of the *Documents*] says, "When it is doubtful whether a reward should be given, let it be given, so that one increases [the recipient's] sense of obligation and encourages merit. When it is doubtful whether a punishment should be given, let it be forsworn, so that one takes care in giving punishments. Cases where evidence is lacking are difficult to know." Now to set aside both the statute and precedent on the pretext of applying the law for *lèse majesté* is totally contrary to the principle that lenience is to be used in cases of doubt or insufficient evidence."[64]

The serious interpretive dilemmas that reportedly committed "Confucians" experienced in weighing opposing classical precedents are perhaps nowhere better illustrated than in three chapters (chaps. 3, 4, and 5 in the extant editions) of Ying Shao's *Feng su t'ung yi*. These chapters amply demonstrate the propensity of the Han literati, however well trained, to misconstrue classical precedents when evaluating conduct. Reputed "Confucian" exemplars, applauded by the members of their community and rewarded by the throne with high office, routinely engage in activity that is entirely contrary to basic Confucian precepts. Recipients of the "Filial and Incorrupt" title, for instance, refuse all contact with living parents; those awarded the title "Possessing the Way" ignore the standard Confucian mourning regulations in order to parade a close relation with an influential patron; and those commended for their humility compete aggressively for official preferment. So pervasive is bad judgment and bad conduct among the self-identified "Confucian" elites that un-Confucian activity has itself become a kind of precedent for thousands of followers and retainers.[65]

In retrospect, those who assume either for the Warring States or for modern times that the "marketplace of ideas"[66] is responsible for free and lively debate should, to be logically consistent, consider tracing the undeniable vigor of Han Confucianism to what many Confucians in Han times loudly bemoaned: the inherent dilemmas provoked by choosing between classical norms and models when applying them to Han political and social life, which made for lively debate over acceptable practice. For despite the inherent difficulties of reconciling opposing classical passages and precedents, by definition, the primary task of committed Han Confucians was to illustrate exemplary conduct—through their own conduct, and through their transmitted writings. Hence, we find numerous Han texts, among them Han Ying's *Han shih wai chuan*, Chia Yi's *Hsin shu*, and Liu Hsiang's compendia, the *Hsin yü* and *Shuo yüan*, illustrating classical precepts by reference to a host of historical and contemporary figures, so as to provide committed Ju with a sufficient number of didactic anecdotes from which to select more precisely analogous moral events. (Similarly, Han art propounded edifying moral lessons through its portraits of exemplary men and women, often accompanied by cartouches elucidating their exact moral significance.)[67] Clearly, for Han Ju, to know texts well was to apply them to real-life dilemmas. As one person put it, "To work hard at learning, intoning the *Odes* and the *Documents*—that's something any ordinary man can do."[68] More, much more, was demanded of the "true" Ju, in other words, than mere repetition and comprehension of the sages' phrases. Practice of the "canonical" Way and adherence to the former kings' institutions were needed.[69]

Variations in reception, always present in academic or court life, could only multiply exponentially when adjustments had to be made in the basic "Confucian" message to make it suitable for wider propagation.[70] Such adjustments were especially numerous when well-meaning Han officials faced the difficulty of applying classical norms and models to Han political and social life, especially in the many outlying and "uncivilized" areas, where "accommodation" could easily work in either direction (the official's "going native," the indigenous population's being sinified). In essence, Ju practice had to be revised when it was applied to routine, let alone crisis situations, in the administration of empire. While some Ju, admittedly, aspired to adapt the present to conform to an idealized past, their notions of the past tended to evolve in tandem with the unfolding historical and political situation in Han, so that they propounded ahistorical ideals with pseudohistorical arguments.[71]

Ju bureaucrat-heroes, the so-called "accommodating officials" (*hsün-li*), had their praises sung in the "Confucian" canon itself, as in the *Li chi*'s "Wang chih" section, in official biographies in the Han dynastic histories, and in unofficial accounts, such as the *Feng su t'ung yi*. These *hsün-li* were said to personify the Ju virtues of humaneness (*jen*), fairness (*p'ing*), public-spiritedness (*kung*), and reliability (*hsin*), while finding ways to use the authority of their offices to have Confucian systems of "rites and music" supplant indigenous cults and customs. The institution of "rites and music" (usually in the form of "ritual prohibitions"), for example, signified strict segregation of the sexes as a corollary to formal marriage relations; honor to the aged, the highly ranked, and the dead; the care of hapless widows, orphans, and childless; prohibitions against "excessive" expenditures on sacrifices, burials, or marriages, lest scarce local resources be wasted; and the encouragement of sedentary agriculture as "basic" economic activity, coupled with famine relief, to discourage vagrancy and crime. The establishment of these "Confucian" prohibitions, invariably accompanied by the institution of local schools and public commendations for local exemplars (the "Filial and Brotherly"; the "Diligent Farmers"), became the primary instrument available to paternalistic bureaucrats intent upon ordering the masses.[72]

Though it is often hard to reconstruct actual situations behind the flowery encomiums of the standard dynastic histories, it is evident enough that "accommodation" worked both ways. In order to "get [and retain] the hearts of the clerks and commoners," honest Ju officials anxious to convert the local populace to Confucian ways sometimes had to deviate from strict Confucian principles.[73] There are hints of this in the biography of one *hsün-li*, Wang Huan, who is said to "have worked hard to favor the common people."[74] And corroborating evidence comes from Ying Shao's (d. ca. A.D. 203) report on his own record as local prefect. As Ying tells it, in the area he administered, "every city, town, hamlet, ward and settlement" had erected a shrine to the deceased Liu Chang, king of Ch'eng-yang, a local hero credited with saving the Western Han house from usurpation. According to Ying, in the vicinity of all such shrines, "there was indiscriminate mixing of the sexes,... boiling and slaughtering [of sacrificial offerings], chanting and singing, with all in commotion for days on end until the people, deluding one another, claimed that the spirit was present."[75] Ying Shao promptly circulated an order to limit the "extravagant" and "excessive" sacrifices to "two sacrifices each year with a full set of sacrificial objects." But once the empire was not engaged in war on all three frontiers, Ying promised those in his jurisdiction that their "sacrifices would be reinstated in all their splendor."[76]

Even from Ying's rather self-serving account, we can sense the kind of give-and-take that characterized successful local rule, with state officials necessarily acceding to some local customs obviously contrary to good "Confucian" practice simply to keep the peace.[77] As Lu Chia (ca. 240–170 B.C.) had cautioned centuries before, "He who differs with the customs of the time will find himself isolated from [both] the lower officials and masses."[78] Repeated warnings in Ju texts against the naive official enforcing too many policy changes could easily justify acceptance of the local status quo.[79] While in theory the civilizing influence of the throne radiated outward in waves from the edifying example of the charismatic Son of Heaven, in reality, away from the court there was frequent contact with and acceptance of local practices, for obvious reasons. On three borders of the empire, the court-appointed prefect "ruling" vast outlying areas from his small, fortified office resembled nothing so much as a tiny island adrift in a sea of barbarians. And in over half the empire, Chinese and barbarians lived cheek by jowl.[80] Besides, given the rough equation of Ju and *shih*, Ju practice tended to be loosely defined as "acceptable practice among *shih* in power," giving ample reason for "exceptions" justified in the name of *ch'üan* ("weighing conflicting moral priorities" according to changing circumstances).[81]

If we grant the continual modification of multiple Ju discourses, one final question remains for modern historians to answer: Was there anything especially distinctive about the state-sponsored ideology in Han? Centuries before Han, a partial synthesis or discourse had emerged among prominent Warring States thinkers once conventionally depicted as arch enemies operating in separate "schools,"[82] people we now call, quite anachronistically, the Legalists, Taoists, Mohists, Confucians, and Yin-yang *chia*. Though theoretical consensus was limited to certain key assumptions about cosmic law, the operations of the human body, and the body politic, and some language used to describe the Good (despite disagreement on the particular meanings attached to that language), it was basically this partial synthesis, and *only* this synthesis, that prevailed in Han times.[83] Already in the Warring States, we learn, Ju beliefs and practices had proliferated among self-identified Confucian disciples, with serious rifts not only between idealists and materialists, but also between scholars emphasizing text-based erudition and those stressing the performance of classical rites and music.[84] These early pre-Han rifts could not heal in Han, if only because of the dramatic increase in the number of self-identified Ju after 136 B.C., each aware of the huge lacunae in extant traditions claiming descent from earlier times.[85] In response to these perceived gaps in classical knowledge, the process of gathering, compiling, interpreting, and inventing new "classical" materials proceeded in Han. Still, it is hard to point to many startling departures from the pre-Han discourse found in texts like the *Lü shih ch'un ch'iu*. Perhaps the main Han addition to the pre-Han consensus is the fairly widespread adoption on the part of Han Ju of those systematized Five Phases correlations associated with the earlier figure of Tsou Yen of the Warring States.

Some fine scholars in effect have argued that the Han synthesis can be characterized by what it lacks, when compared with Warring States discourse. Yuri Pines, for example, suggests that the Han discourse was distinctive in that it lacked a sharp antithesis between family and state that characterized the Warring States Legalists.[86] But other thinkers in the pre-Ch'in period, including the "Taoist" Chuang-tzu, had already forged a close analogy between family and state long before Han; this analogy the Ch'in in its stone steles strengthened, by its equation of filial piety, female chastity, and political loyalty.[87] Still, the apparent resolution of this perceived conflict was no resolution at all, for the tension between self, family, and state could never disappear entirely. As a result, the same tension came to be expressed in debates that took place *within* acceptable Ju thought, often through the use of terminology borrowed from the Chou;[88] while the code words for discussions sometimes changed, the fundamental nature of the explorations did not.[89]

Perhaps the most distinctive aspect of Han thought was this: During the Han certain committed Confucians faced what they knew to be an unprecedented situation. Long members of the "loyal" opposition operating as chief critics outside government, the Confucians by mid-Han times were in a position, as chief theoreticians defending the dynasty, to apply the precepts of Confucius and his main followers to everyday problems of administrative rule. Their initial elation was obvious (Typical was Ssu-ma Hsiang-ju's, "I passed through the Gate of Heaven, entered the Palace of God."), and though that initial elation gave way to discouragement, even despair (in some sooner than in others), the tone of Han thinkers is generally much more robust, optimistic,[90] and "muscular" than that of thinkers of late imperial China.[91] In essence, Han Confucians could not yet be sure that the Great Peace was not attainable in bureaucratic empire. Thus, Han Confucians who were far from insisting on the original goodness of human nature still presumed the ultimate goodness of human political culture. (Note the contrast with Neo-Confucian authors, who insisted on the ultimate goodness of human nature, despite its frailness, while positing a signal lack of goodness in aggregate human culture; they usually took a more pessimistic view of the possibilities of goodness to operate through dynastic history.) The relaxed Han conflation of "classicism" and "Confucianism" (in effect, an attempt to fit the entire historical past, in addition to scripture, under the rubric of "tradition"),[92] when combined with the Han preoccupation with finding parallels for the human order in the cosmic realm, meant that Han Ju busily set about sorting out all things "under Heaven," in the firm hope of attaining additional areas of consensus. Obviously, the urge to bring everything within the compass of system and order is the ideology of empire, but it was an empire to be built on refined categorical apprehension, rather than brute force enforcing a strict hierarchy.[93]

Many have mistakenly equated the inability of the Han Confucians to arrive at additional broad areas of consensus with a failure of imagination on the part of Han thinkers, being unmindful of the nature of Confucianism itself. A morality that emphasizes "graded love," suasive example, and the flexible adaptation of basic principles to specific cases may be slightly less interested in absolute consistency than social scientists brought up in another tradition. It was presumably this lack of interest, producing a large measure of flexibility, that may have, in turn, provided over time the most stable basis for an enduring system of bureaucratic empire. In any case, it is odd that many modern historians are content to adopt the positions of the very most conservative branches of Han Confucianism, assuming that bureaucratic totalism and ideological purity, hand-in-hand, constitute the primary good for both society and state. If that were true, then the signal failure of Han to develop a long-lasting orthodoxy might be considered to be "the trouble" with Han Confucianism. But surely it is also possible to see the incredible variation in acceptable Ju thought and practice, grounded in the Han readiness to admit a wide array of possible common goods and admirable virtues, as something that facilitated, rather than hampered, an effective sense of a shared Confucian past.

In summation, I would argue that none of the underlying premises of the so-called "Han synthesis" or "victory of Confucianism" holds up particularly well when subjected to the dispassionate light of modern historical inquiry. When our students (inadvertently echoing Chu Hsi) come to us with the frequent complaint that Han Confucianism is too messy to be called a synthesis, they are right; the paradigms of the "victory of "Confucianism" and the "orthodox" Han synthesis have probably outlived their usefulness both as teaching and learning devices. It seems that Han Ju thought and Han Ju practice were too varied, too volatile, and too elusive to be encapsulated within a neat formula, such as "orthodoxy" or "synthesis," despite—or because of?—a Confucian predisposition to favor unitary systems in principle. Above, I have purposely gone beyond Stuart Hampshire's *Innocence and Experience*,[94] which argues that there is something in the course of humanity that inevitably tends toward diversity; I argue that this impulse toward diversity was magnified when Confucians committed themselves to the project of applying the words of the Master to the vast operations of an imperial project.

But what does all this mean, then, when we come to consider Han Confucianism in light of Neo-Confucianism? Certain contrasts strike us immediately, beginning with the relation of the Ju to the state. For example, while the size of the Chinese empire was much bigger in post-Sung China than in Han, the degree of control over its subject population that the autocratic court could reasonably expect to exert—albeit indirectly, through local gentry—was far greater in late imperial China, in part because the "Confucianization" of the law, the "civilization" or Sinicization of the south (during the T'ang and Southern Sung, respectively),[95] better communications throughout the empire, and successive codifications of synthesized "Confucian" principles (first in the form of Wang An-shih's commentaries, then in the form of the Chu Hsi's) had paved the way for greater degrees of government control in late imperial China. At the same time, the ratio of court officials relative to the total population was considerably higher in Han, so that well-trained Han literati could reasonably expect to be employed by the state.[96] To the degree that their chances for appointment to office were significantly lower, Confucians in late imperial China were more likely to look beyond government employment for recognized signs of Ju accomplishment.

Turning to less obviously political matters, there are slightly different orientations in Han Confucianism and in later Ch'eng-Chu orthodoxy. Though Han Confucians and the Neo-Confucians operated in virtue-centered societies, as defined by the philosopher Alasdair MacIntyre,[97] their writings assigned different weights and sometimes even different content to the same virtues. The existence of a shared vocabulary and shared metaphors should not blind us to discontinu-ities behind the virtue-dominated thinking of Han and of late imperial China.[98]

In light of these continuities, several avenues in comparative thought seem worth exploration. First, the Han attempt to incorporate the entire historical past, in addition to scripture, as "tradition" presents a stark contrast with the later proposed rejection (led by Ch'eng-Chu adherents) of many aspects of tra-dition inherited by or from Han.[99] In a move that somewhat parallels the Protestant Reformation, some Neo-Confucian thinkers even called for the direct apprehension of the sages' intent without the mediation of established tradition.[100] This rejection of most of the past was accompanied by the recontex-tualization of the entire Confucian tradition through numerous anthologies and genealogies, what postmodern historians would recognize as the creation of "invented traditions."[101]

Second, Han thinkers, resisting some of the claims of the state, generally proposed rather reasonable definitions for filial piety, female chastity, and politi-cal loyalty. But later imperial China, probably in response to China's weakened military situation, propagated far stricter standards for these three virtues (seen as analogous)—and not only under the "barbarian" dynasties.[102]

Third, while Han "Confucian" classicism in its eclecticism undoubtedly embraced many rival Chinese traditions, so much so that no major Han thinker would escape the later charges that he was a Taoist, Sung and post-Sung "Confucianism" incorporated important notions from the non-Chinese (indeed, "Western") tradition of Buddhism, with the result that entirely new emphases, new language, and new theoretical constructions entered the hallowed "Confucian" tradition.[103]

Fourth, the new justification system of *li* and *ch'i*[104] proposed in Sung bears witness to a host of related changes, including an increasing emphasis on "inte-rior" virtue,[105] changes in assumptions about the senses' operation as they relate to virtue and the mind,[106] and the introduction of the idea of absolute transcen-dence or superordination.[107]

Fifth, while those who know Neo-Confucianism best are apt to emphasize the importance of its cosmological underpinnings (as these have been sadly neglected in the "rationalizing" accounts of some intellectual historians of China), surely their significance outside of state legitimacy theory pales in signif-icance when compared with Han beliefs, which simply cannot be imagined or articulated apart from continual reference to cosmic patterns. The Han Ju rou-tinely sought "proof" of excellence in extrahuman patterns which were regarded as infallible signs of the Tao. The dominant worldview of later imperial China is somewhat reduced, in that it becomes more preoccupied with a China-centered world that does not discount extrahuman patterns as evidence of the sublime but usually does not make such patterns its main focus.

This essay, chiefly in its last few pages, has suggested ample reasons for the "orthodox" Neo-Confucians' mistrust of Han Confucianism. At the same time, it also suggests that unless we are prepared to accept the Ch'eng-Chu views in their totality, we might do well to take a further look at the lessons that Han Confucianism can convey about the role of intellectual ferment, diversity, and inclusiveness in sustaining empires.

ABBREVIATIONS USED

CFL	Wang Fu, *Ch'ien fu lun* (Shanghai, 1978).
CHW	*Ch'üan Han wen*, ed. by Yen K'o-chün, in *Ch'üan Shang ku San tai Ch'in Han San kuo Liu ch'ao wen* (Peking, 1965), 5 vols.
CIS	*Chosho isho shosei*, ed. by Yasui Kozan and Nakamura Shohachi (Tokyo, 1971–), 6 vols.
CTYT	*Chuang tzu yin te* (Peking, 1947), supplement no. 20, Harvard–Yenching Institute Sinological Index series.
CYYT	*Chou yi yin te* (Peking, 1935), supplement no. 10, Harvard–Yenching Institute Sinological Index Series.
ECT	*Early Chinese Texts: A Bibliographical Guide*, ed. by Michael Loewe (Berkeley, 1993).
FSTY	*Feng su t'ung yi fu t'ung chien* (Peking, 1943), no. 3, Centre d'études sinologiques de Pekin series.
FY	Yang Hsiung, *Fa yen*, commentary by Li Kuei, in *(Hsin pien) Chu tzu chi ch'eng* (Shanghai, 1935; rpt., Taipei, 1978), II.
HHS	Fan Yeh, *Hou Han shu* (Peking, 1965), 6 vols.
HS	Pan Ku, *Han shu* (Peking, 1962), 8 vols.
HSWC	Han Ying, *Han shih wai chuan* (SPPY).
HTYT	*Hsün tzu yin te* (Peking, 1950), supplement no. 22, Harvard–Yenching Institute Sinological Index Series.
HY	*Hsin yü* (SPPY).
Ku	Mei-kao Ku, *A Chinese Mirror for Magistrates: The Hsin yü of Lu Chia* (Canberra, 1988).
LC	according to the H-Y index, *Li chi yin te*.
LH	*Lun heng chi chieh* (SPTK), annot. by Liu P'an-sui (SPTK ed.; Taipei, 1975), 2 vols.
PHT	*Po hu t'ung*, compiled by Pan Ku, in *Basic Sinological Series (Kuo hsüeh chi pen ts'ung shu)* (Taipei, 1968), LXVIII.
Restoration	Hans Bielenstein, *Restoration of the Han Dynasty*, in four parts in *Bulletin of the Museum of Far Eastern Antiquities* (as indicated).
SC	Ssu-ma Ch'ien, *Shih chi* (Peking, 1959), 10 vols.

SPPY	*Ssu pu pei yao* (Shanghai, 1927–35), 1372 *ts'e* (parts).
SSCCS	*Shih san ching chu shu*, comp. by Juan Yüan (Taipei, 1977, reprint of the 1815 imperial ed.), 6 vols.
SW	Hsü Shen, *Shuo wen chieh tzu fu chien tzu* (Hong Kong, 1966).
SY	Liu Hsiang, *Shuo yüan* (SPPY).
THC	*T'ai hsüan ching*, annot. by Ssu-ma Kuang (SPPY).

NOTES

1. Before Chu Hsi's definitive commentaries on the Classics, of course, there were those of Wang An-shih. The three-part definition of "orthodoxy" I borrow from James T. C. Liu, "How Did a Neo-Confucian School Become the State Orthodoxy"? *Philosophy East and West* 23.4 (Oct. 1973): 483–506: (1) the selection of one particular school or set of interpretations and commentaries as the official approved ones used in the civil service examinations; (2) official proclamation of the same in the name of the state, for presumed application throughout the government, not just the state examinations; and (3) other efforts, parallel to the state efforts, in getting the same to be accepted by the whole society, led by some elite and spreading downward among the common people.

I owe thanks to a number of people for helping me refine the arguments in this draft, including the editors of this volume, Anne Birdwhistell, Peter Nosco, Yuri Pines, Nathan Sivin, and Conrad Schirokauer.

2. See the opening paragraph of my "Han Classicists Writing in Dialogue about Their Own Tradition," *Philosophy East and West* 47:2 (April, 1987), 133–88.

3. Ch'ü Tung-tsu, for example, has shown that the Confucianization of Chinese law was a slow process completed only in the T'ang code of A.D. 653. See Ch'ü's *Law and Society in Traditional China*, p. 267f. A. F. P. Hulsewé, "Ch'in and Han Law," in *Cambridge History of China, Vol. 1: The Ch'in and Han Empires* (Cambridge, 1986), p. 543, shows that Confucian rules for marriage were not yet reflected in law. For example, in several cases Han women took the initiative to divorce.

4. Wu-ti was perhaps mindful of the enormous prestige accorded wealthy patrons of book collectors, including Lü Pu-wei in Ch'in, and aristocratic patrons, such as Liu An, King of Huai-nan; Liu P'i, King of Wu; and Liu Te, King of Ho-chien. Tung-fang Shuo remarked of such patron-collectors, "Those who gained the hearts of scholars became powerful while those who lost the scholars perished." See Ch'ü T-ung-tsu, *Law and Society*, pp. 127–30; 133–35; 188, 412–18.

5. To this end, they carefully reserved imperial favors for selected commentaries of the classics; they lectured on the classics while overseeing instruc-

tion at the Imperial Academy; they had scholars such as Liu Hsiang "regulate texts" (*chih-shu*) in the imperial collection; they actively discouraged private patronage; they convened periodic court conferences to establish norms and conventions.

6. Han scholarship today is free to consider something less like a jelled synthesis or set of dominant paradigms and more like contested "fields of cultural production" (adapting Bourdieu's terms), since Han Confucianism presented multiple sites of struggles whose perceived stake was "the power to impose the dominant definition of . . . the scholar." See Pierre Bourdieu, *The Field of Cultural Production: Essays in Art and Literature* (Cambridge, 1993).

7. Which the empire then either failed to attain (as Chu Hsi believed) or failed to sustain (following the dynastic histories' account).

8. HS 30.1728. See also SC 121.3115, which pits the Ju methods of governing (their "rites and music") against methods of governing by force. Ch'i and Lu, the early centers of Confucian learning, were particularly associated with *wen-hsüeh* (the study of texts and patterns) (SC 121.3117). The Confucian emphasis on ancient music was acknowledged at imperial performances staged in honour of Confucius, which supposedly played "the music of the Six Ages" (from the time of the Yellow Emperor down to the Chou). See HHS 79A.2562. This early emphasis on the educational role of music appears in HS 22, "The Treatise on Rites and Music."

9. The first part of this definition, possibly employed mainly for bibliographic and bureaucratic purposes, was needed once Emperor Wu desired to restrict his imperial patronage to the representatives of one faction at court. When "Confucian" rather than "classicist" is intended, Han texts most often contrast the Ju enterprise with that of thinkers we now dub Logicians and Legalists, for self-conscious adherents of Confucius, with their strong interest in statecraft, tried hardest to distinguish their positions from those of the Logicians, whose theories they saw as "unworkable," and from those of the Legalists, whose theories they saw as cruel and counterproductive. Some Han texts that we have for the reign of Wu-ti seem to collapse *hsing-ming* theories into "Legalism," the better to vilify them.

10. Kitamura Eiichi, "Sen Kan ni okeru reigaku no denju ni tsuite," *Ritsumeikan bungaku* 180 (1960), makes the important point that the Ju had long been recognized as experts in diplomacy and religion, the two main concerns of state. (See below.)

11. In writing "deemed . . . 'ancient'," I direct the reader's attention to Ku Chieh-kang's lesson: that certain stories, texts, scripts, and ideas labelled as "ancient" in Han (e.g., the "Yao tien" ch. of the *Documents*) were often quite new at the time; the label of "ancient" was applied, then, either because the sanction of hoary antiquity would help gain them widespread acceptance or because there was no "room" to admit them in the history of the recent past.

12. Because the Six Classics are the common intellectual property of all educated persons, HS 30 classifies them apart from the "Ju-chia" category. Thus, Ssu-ma T'an, a classicist with a known preference for Taoism, could write, "If only one could link up with the enlightened generations, ordering the *Changes*, continuing the *Spring and Autumn Annals*, and taking as basis the *Odes*, the *Documents*, the *Rites* and the *Music* texts!" (SC 130.3296). Later, the Yen t'ieh lun (BSS) 1.2.4 (Gale, 15), recording the Salt and Iron Debates of 81 B.C., shows opponents of the Ju shoring up their position by citing texts now considered "Confucian" (e.g., the *Odes*). Even more tellingly, the same text identifies as "Ju" some "thousand" advisors to King Hsüan of Ch'i at Chi-hsia, though these advisors reportedly included Tsou Yen, Shen Tao, and T'ien P'ien, thinkers assigned to the Yin/yang and Legalist, rather than Confucian, "schools" in standard bibliographies. See YTL 2.11.20–21 (Gale, 66–67).

13. In all this, it was the Ch'in and early Western Han that was anomalous, since their rulers' continual preoccupation with the urgent task of unifying the empire led them to neglect the peacetime advantages of bureaucratic Confucianism.

14. See note 10 above.

15. In any case, the specific idea of Ju as "Confucian" appears always to have been a subset of the general notion of Ju as "classicist." "Confucian" did not supplant "classicist" as both meanings of Ju implied an unusual dedication to the study of antiquity, a dedication marked by the punctilious performance of prescribed chants, songs, and dances by men in outmoded dress, but one that occasionally lapsed into a self-important antiquarianism easily satirized by contemporary utilitarian thinkers. Two incidents suggest the anti-utilitarian strain of the early Ju: (1) At the time of Liu Pang, the Ju in Lu, though surrounded by Kao tsu's troops, went on performing the ancient rites and music (SC 121.3115). (2) At the time of Wu-ti, Ju were asked to devise new court rituals for Han, but after "more than 10 years" they had not yet completed their task (SC 6.1397). For a standard description of the Western Han Ju, see YTL 4.19.37 (Gale, 123): the Ju "spread out their long robes and carried on their backs the ritual vessels and the *Odes* and *Documents* belonging to the family of Confucius" (describing K'ung Chia, who became advisor to Ch'en She). Even some Eastern Han masters, such as Han Jung, wore distinctive Ju robes (HHS 37.1250).

16. Histories of China have tended to ignore the degree of debate that was accepted practice, in part because a developed rhetorical tradition is usually presumed to be the exclusive property of the Greeks. The craft of speech (*yen-yü*) is one of the four subjects in the Confucian curriculum.

A general reliance on oral transmission (see below) probably facilitated the restatement of Confucian tenets in terms consistent with prevailing assumptions, according to Lü Ssu-mien, *Lü Ssu-mien tu shih cha chi* (Shanghai, 1982), 1:675–78. The relation between *fang-shih* and Ju in Han China, for example, may

be conceived in terms of successive waves of interaction between rival ritual traditions. See Ku Chieh-kang, *Han tai hsüeh shu shih lüeh* (rpt., Taipei, Ch'i-yeh,
1972). Archaeological evidence suggests an equally complex relationship
between the state-sponsored Confucian cults, justified by Ju academicians at
court, and the common religion. See Donald Harper, JAS (Feb. 1995): 156, on
the cult of T'ai Yi; Max Kaltenmark, "Les Tch'an-wei," *Han Hiue* 2 (1947):
363–73, passim. Derk Bodde cites evidence for the persistence of folk festivals
and folk beliefs (some dating from early Chou) into late Eastern Han, centuries
after the official adoption of Confucianism as state ideology. See Derk Bodde,
*Festivals in Classical China: New Year and Other Annual Observances during the
Han Dynasty, 206* B.C.–A.D. *220* (Princeton: Princeton University Press, 1975).

17. First, Han Confucians had inherited from Warring States and early
Western Han masters the notion that the potential community of Ju cut across
class barriers, linking All-under-Heaven "from the Son of Heaven on down to
the commoner." The correctness of this notion had been confirmed by the ascen-
sion of Liu Pang, a commoner, to the dragon throne. Second, so long as the centralized Han state professed its dedication to the principle of "Employ the
worthy," no single estate, class, or faction could be entirely secure in its monopoly over power, since even members of the imperial family, let alone well-connected bureaucrats, had to repeatedly demonstrate their worth by societally
accepted criteria, including divination and portent interpretation. Third, the
phrase "Employ the Worthy" implicitly conceded the existence of "*shih* in reclu-
sion" (*ch'u shih*) and private teachers as extragovernmental authorities whose
occasional resistance to joining the ranks of the Han bureaucracy called into
question more conventional definitions of "Ju."

See Patricia Ebrey, *Aristocratic Families of Early Imperial China: A Case Study
of the Po-ling Ts'ui Family* (New York, 1978), pp. 38–39, for the "relatively open"
attitude of even Eastern Han conservatives toward those who had mastered traditional learning and the Ju behavioral codes. Note that many Han Confucians
subscribed to notions encapsulated in the "Cycle of the Rites" chapter of the *Li
chi*, which described the ideal age as one in which class and familial divisions had
not yet arisen. See "Li yün," in *Li chi*, in SSCCS 2a.3a–3b (Legge, 1:364-66).

18. Note that since the prestigious posts of Academician (*po shih*) were
awarded to interpretive lines associated with recent masters, rather than to individual texts of the Five Classics themselves, it was clear that the authority of the
Han *ching* could never be single "either in purview nor in nature" (a characterization drawn from Levering, "Introduction," p. 16 n. 5). There is a related issue: To
students of Han history, nothing is more striking than the failure of Han Ju to
devise a formal convention by which to distinguish the Classics from the commentaries, traditions, and apocryphal materials associated with the Classics, even
when supplementary texts were known to be of recent date. It was very late in
Eastern Han before mechanical means (e.g., different colored inks, double

columns) were employed to visually separate commentary from the main text of the Classic.

19. HS 22.1027, where the "roads" belong to the Six Classics, later (e.g., in HS 30.1746) shown to be consonant with all learning. This metaphor reflected the widely held belief that disparate ideologies represented fragmentary offshoots from the holistic insights of Confucius, which perfectly reflected the Way of the Ancients (HS 30.1701). Cf. CYYT 46.Hsi B.3, which talks of "the same goal, [reached by] different paths; the single focus, [reached] by a hundred thoughts." Thus, HS 88.3598 tells us that the business of Ju is to *lun t'ung yi* ("discuss similarities and differences"), so that all lines of thought may be traced back to their common source. Hsü Kan in Eastern Han is one among many to offer his highest praise to those who can see what is common to different categories (chap. 8; Makeham, 150). Not coincidentally, the most characteristic form of literary expression in Han is the *fu*, of whose writers Ssu-ma Hsiang-ju remarked: "The mind of the *fu* writer encompasses the universe, and brings within view all things and people." See CHW 22.4b.

20. Hence, the *Shih chi* characterization of Han Kao tsu. Though it is difficult to quantify, the Han was characterized by what Charles Frankel (and Peter Nosco after him) have called in other contexts "cultural liberality" (meaning, culture was not perceived to be the monopolized prerogative of any particular class or group within society). See Nosco, *Remembering Paradise* (Cambridge, 1990), pp. 29–30.

21. In a most preliminary fashion, I have begun to explore an avenue of inquiry which so far links an emphasis on loyalty, filial piety, and female chastity with the *wai-ch'i* families engaged in the military. It was the "military guards" (*wu-shih*), for example, who are made familiar with the *Hsiao ching* (HHS 32.1126). Think also of Empress Dowager Teng's (d. A.D. 121) strong interest in staunching the "degeneration of [devotion to] the Five Classics," which she links with "a return to loyalty and filial piety" (HHS 10A.428); also, of Pan Ku and Pan Chao, author of *Nü Chieh*, a text that is notable for its somewhat straitlaced construction of Confucian gender types. The late synthesizing tendencies of Cheng Hsüan and of the Ching-chou school in late Eastern Chou may then be seen as an ideological response to the imminent military collapse of the empire. Centuries later, the strong emphasis on loyalty in the writings of Chu Hsi and many other Neo-Confucians, seems also to relate to the perilous military situation facing China and the Chinese.

22. Then, as the Han throne weakened, the Han rulers' ability to control literati dissent and curtail the proliferation of rival "truths" collapsed on the local level, along with the court's loss of political and military control. Accordingly, in the last decades of Western Han and again in the second century of Eastern Han, many classicists expressed outrage at the expected loss of their own power, which they had looked to the throne to preserve; for some, this outrage was exacerbated

by the prevailing belief that the truly Good cannot simply turn inward, because the people must be "awakened" to moral behavior by the exemplary conduct of members of the Ju political elite.

23. Though Emperor Wu had undoubtedly acted from self-interest, his decision in 136 B.C. to limit the assigned curriculum of the Imperial Academy to the Five Classics associated with the Ju had immediate consequences. Thereafter, the Ju were quick to acquire all the trappings of professionals: they proctored exams and manufactured lengthy "set texts" (the *chang-chü*) to prepare students to sit their exams; they try to reserve official posts for their members; they delineated scholastic affiliations, once again based on texts, though Ju learning prior to 136 B.C. had not been primarily text-based.

24. For the supposedly "simple" and "easy" message of the Confucian canon, see CYYT 39.Hsi A.1-5.

25. Hence, the power of Tung Chung-shu's totalizing vision of *ta yi t'ung* ("expanding the one rule"). See HS 56.2523; Wang Pao-hsüan, *Hsi Han ching hsüeh yüan liu* (Taipei, 1994), p. 185.

26. For the desire to fill in lacunae, see HHS 79A.2545. On the *chang-chü* and the standard arguments in favor of it, see HS 30.1723; HHS 44.1500. For complaints registered against those who only keep to "hair-splitting arguments" found in the *chang-chü*, see HS 30.1723. For *po hsüeh* as the indispensable condition of Ju, see *Li chi,* "Ju hsing," in SSCCS 59.8a. For "weaving the net," see HS 88.3621; HHS 79A.2546. Attempts to close the canon and rein in Ju scholars were continually countered by efforts to create the new scriptural or quasi-scriptural forms needed (*a*) to explicate portions of older texts whose universal significance had been lost as Chinese culture evolved, (*b*) to allow for the ongoing process of insight, and (*c*) to incorporate new concepts reflecting social realities that had not existed at the time when the older Classics had been written down.

If Eastern Han critiques are to be trusted, such contrary impulses undermined the very state, let alone its ability to foster or impose an orthodoxy: While the *chang-chü* had been expressly designed to curtail free-ranging or idiosyncratic academic interpretations, the mind-numbing memorization of the lengthy *chang-chü* commentaries reportedly hampered students from discerning any underlying meaning in the classics. Also, the many long years required to master the *chang-chü* stopped capable, but poor men from entering the Ju ranks. Thus, the empire's administration was too often left in the hands of the landed gentry—the group that could best afford to invest in education, but the group that was also the most likely to resist the throne's centralizing efforts. Likewise, the state's talk of "broad learning" undercut its ability to direct academic matters: Since many scholars had been appointed court academicians on the basis of their specialized learning in one particular classic, it became possible to consider scholars who held no government appointment (Cheng Hsüan and the Ching-chou scholars being two examples) as the equals or betters of those commended by the state administration.

27. For the critique of Confucians as "so broad" in their learning as to lack focus, see SC 130.3290. Cf. the related openness of the Confucian canon in Han times, as remarked upon by John B. Henderson, *Scripture, Canon, and Commentary: A Comparison of Confucian and Western Exegesis* (Princeton, 1991), p. 60. With supplementary materials cited as part of the main text, they quickly assumed quasi-scriptural or even scriptural status. Little wonder that quite late "traditions" attached to the *Ch'un Chiu*, *Rites*, and *Changes* enjoyed an authority equal to what we would now call the "canonical text." Naito Torajiro, *Shina Shigakushi* (Tokyo, 1948), pp. 86–90, sees the conflation of *ching* and *chuan* in a variety of Warring States texts, including the *Lao tzu*, *Mo tzu*, *Kuan tzu*, and *Han Fei tzu*. Han writers, then, would simply be continuing an earlier tradition. This openness presented challenges to pious followers of Confucius. For example, What was the proper sequence of canons and commentaries to be studied or the relative weight to be accorded each text? There was as yet no set course of study (a situation later remedied by Chu Hsi's proposal to elevate the Four Books to the highest rank in the Neo-Confucian curriculum), nor did there seem to be a decided preference either for specialization in a single "Confucian" classic or for "broad learning" (meaning, study of the Five Classics and the Hundred Thinkers).

Also, many Han classicists were students of the texts of the Hundred Thinkers (*pai-chia*). Lu Chia's (240–170 B.C.) comments are typical for the period: "Improving books do not necessarily arise from among Confucius' followers, just as medicine need not only come from Pien Ch'iao's prescriptions." See HY A.5a (Ku, 77). To contrast this assumption regarding the value of the Hundred Thinkers with later Neo-Confucian attitudes, see George Hatch, "The Thought of Su Hsun (1009–1066): An Essay in the Social Meaning of Intellectual Pluralism in Northern Sung" (Ph.D. thesis, University of Washington, 1972), p. 28. For the proper definition of the term *pai-chia*, see Jens Østergard Petersen, "Which Books Did the First Emperor of Ch'in Burn? On the Meaning of *Pai chia* in Early Chinese Sources," *Monumenta Serica* 43 (1995): 1–52.

Many Han *t'ung-Ju* ("polymath classicists") decided to study with a series of masters, each of whom specialized in one or more classics, as Cheng Hsüan (127–200) did. Another popular "solution" was to treat each of the Six Classics as elucidating one field of learning, which only in combination would illuminate the entire message of the former sage-kings. But a number of Han Ju masters felt that the best approach was to urge students to look beyond the welter of texts to find the right teacher or model (both signified by the character *shih*); without such a teacher-model, they argued, the beginning student could never assess wisely the texts and interpretation competing for attention in the marketplace. Yang Hsiung spoke for many when he wrote, "A marketplace with its noisy quarrels has innumerable different ideas contained in it. A book one scroll in length has innumerable different theories contained in it. For the market, one always sets up a balance; for the book, one always sets up a teacher. [This is the way to establish relative value.]" See FY 1.1.

28. For one example, see HHS 79B.2579, where an imperial order mandates that all repetitive material be deleted in a state-sponsored compilation of the *Ch'un Ch'iu*.

29. In the Analects 7.1, of course, Confucius says of himself that he is a "transmitter," not a "creator." In SC 130.3299–3300, however, Ssu-ma Ch'ien credits Confucius with "creating," rather than "transmitting," and takes Confucius' self-description to apply to his own task in writing the *Shih chi*.

The record is unclear with respect to Tung Chung-shu (who was thrown into jail for writing "nonsense"), but it is very clear that both Yang Hsiung and Wang Ch'ung felt the need to defend themselves against charges that they were "creating" new teachings. For Yang, see HS 87B.3576–79 (Knechtges, p. 54ff.); for Wang, see LH 84.

30. E.g., SW 15a.4a (postface), translated by Thern.

31. After all, Ming-ti wore clothes decorated with the sun and moon, gave audience to various lords in the Bright Hall, and then climbed the Numinous Terrace to closely observe the shapes of cloud portents. See HHS 79A.2545. Bright Hall and Numinous Terrace are translations for the Ming-t'ang and Ling-t'ai. Cf. HHS 48.1602, where the imperial patronage goes to preserving a variety of "venerable texts" (*shang shu*) not particularly associated with Confucian ethics.

32. In other words, the dynastic histories, especially the chapters devoted to the "Ju lin," tend to highlight the imperial sponsorship of Ju textual practice. However, they also provide evidence showing that the same emperor-patrons were less than dedicated or consistent patrons. See below, on Chang-ti.

33. I direct the reader's attention to the Han dynasty's well-meaning attempts to implement Hsün-tzu's policy prescriptions regarding a Confucian virtuocracy, attempts that had led, paradoxically, to the utter subversion of the one "crucial" "Confucian" virtue that the Han hoped to instill: loyalty to the state, anchored in respect for hierarchy. For more on this, see Nylan, "Confucian Piety and Individualism in Han," *Journal of the American Oriental Society* 116 (Jan.–March 1996): 1–27.

34. For example, An-ti (107–25) was reportedly too stingy to support academic pursuits, with the result that both the educational standards and the physical plant of the National Academy deteriorated. See HHS 78.1606, 109A.2547; Hans Bielenstein, *Loyang in Later Han Times*, p. 68ff. Of course, a comparable lack of support for specifically "Confucian" endeavors (especially textual practice) would not be found so regularly in late imperial China. After reading Charles Holcombe and David McMullen, it seems that imperial support for

Confucianism in Han was often at a level comparable with the supposed "Confucian Dark Ages" of the Wei-Chin and T'ang periods.

35. I am indebted to Stephen Durrant for proof of the questionable character of imperial patronage from Wu-ti's reign: SC 121 ("Ju lin lieh chuan") suggests that the majority of "successful" Ju in Ssu-ma Ch'ien's own time (as opposed to early Western Han) are anything but committed Confucians. Debate over the distinctions between the labels *su Ju* ("vulgar Ju") and *chen Ju* ("true Ju," restricted to "committed followers of Confucius") informs a number of Han texts, including Yang Hsiung's *Fa yen* and Wang Ch'ung's *Lun heng*. For the decline in studies at the Academy, see HHS 79A.2546–47.

36. HHS 35.1023, cited in ECT, p. 429. As the ECT entry notes, disdain for bookmen persisted unchanged for the next several decades.

37. Throughout Han, we see emperors turning away from the Ju (Confucians? classicists?), who seem unable to establish clear precedents for imperial activities. The Ju had first received favorable imperial notice when one of their number, Shu-sun T'ung (despite some opposition from a panel of Ju ritual experts), devised the splendid court ceremonials that allowed Emperor Kao tsu to finally sense the full measure of his imperial dignity. But committed Ju then angered Emperor Wu by their inability, "after more than a decade" of consultations, to put that knowledge of the classical precedents in service to the throne, so that suitable rituals could be devised for the most sacred *feng* and *shan* sacrifices to be offered by the emperor; stubbornly "objecting to any innovations," certain Ju were unwilling to countenance the emperor's wish to conflate reputedly ancient practices with rituals aimed to secure an elixir of immortality (SC 6.1397). Wu-ti in his anger blamed the Ju for paying too much attention to "grand antiquity" while neglecting the requirements of the present age (SC 6.1397). Cf. Huan T'an's criticism of Wang Mang in the *Hsin lun*, which says that Wang wished "to imitate antiquity in everything he did. He ignored things near and modern and chased after the remote past."

In the end, of course, more flexible (read: "opportunistic") ritual specialists were brought in to create for Wu-ti's pleasure a blend of old and new rituals, the object of whose worship was T'ai-yi, the Grand Unity, rather than Heaven. Thereafter, sacrifices to T'ai-yi became a kind of precedent for the Han house, for "members of [the ruling] family would not willingly discontinue the services they inherited from their forebears" (HS 25B.1258). But, this change was not to last. By 31 B.C., some fifty prominent Han Ju at court led by Kuang Heng persuaded Emperor Ch'eng to introduce major "reforms" that would redirect attention to Heaven and Earth. Passages drawn from two "Confucian" Classics, the *Li chi* and the *Odes*, were cited as "proof" of the new reforms' roots in ancient practice. See Loewe, *Crisis*, chap. 5.

38. HSPC 56.19a (trans. after Loewe [1994]).

39. HS 60B.1990.

40. LH 81.

41. See HHS 44.1500–1501, citing Hsü Fang's memorial for stricter controls on the Imperial Academy. It is possible that the linguistic shift from *shih-fa* to *chia-fa* represents the government's attempt to de-emphasize personal transmission so as to redirect attention on the textual transmission. It is also possible that this linguistic shift reflects a change in legal practice: In Eastern Han teachers are legally responsible for their registered disciples, as heads of households were responsible for members of their family, but I have to date found no evidence that this was so in Western Han times.

42. Han "Confucian" masters most often contrast the Confucian enterprise with that of thinkers we now dub Logicians and Legalists (see above). By contrast, Han Confucian masters seldom bothered to untangle the connections between their ideas and those put forward by thinkers we now call Mohist or "Taoist," Yin/yang or *hsing-ming* theorists, probably because many of their ideas had been absorbed into the broad stream of Confucian thinking. For one example of the Han incorporation of the Mohist term *po-ai* ("broad love") into "Confucian" theorizing, see Benjamin Wallacker, "Han Confucianism and Confucius in Han," *Ancient China: Studies in Early Civilization*, ed. by David T. Roy and Tsuen-hsuin Tsien (Hong Kong, 1978), pp. 215–28. Yang Hsiung's FY 4.10, 5.15 admits to adopting (*ch'ü*) aspects of the teachings of many other Warring States thinkers.

43. FSTY 4.31.

44. SW 15a.4a (postface), translated in K. L. Thern, *Postface of the Shuo wen chieh tzu, the First Comprehensive Chinese Dictionary* (Madison, 1956). Cf. Hsü Fang's famous memorial of A.D. 103, which insists that even the "erudites and students in the Academy . . . all speak from their own minds, with none following the authority of a school's teaching."

45. De Bary, like many conservative Confucian thinkers over the ages, seems to think that Confucianism "failed" when it failed to produce, then impose on China an orthodoxy of sufficient strength (sometimes akin to nationalism) to counter China's imperialist enemies in the nineteenth century. This is to skew the reading of all of Chinese history in favor of progressivist and counterprogressivist terms, a reading which sadly, if inevitably overlooks some of the most interesting aspects of Chinese thought.

46. *Analects* 18.8 (Waley, 222): "As for me, I am different from any of these [men of integrity]. I have no 'thou shalt' or 'thou shalt not'." *Analects* 11.22 also sanctions different applications of the same principle. Complicating the problem were words attributed to Confucius in *Li chi*, "Chi yi,"in SSCCS 47.6a (Legge, 2:214): "Should words be understood only in one way? Each saying has its own appropriate application!" In other words, ultimate truth lay beyond mere words (even the words recorded in the Classics), though the sages felt compelled to leave written records behind for their followers.

47. For the "Great Plan's" paradox, see Michael Nylan "The Shifting Center: The Original 'Great Plan' and Later Readings" (Nettetal, 1992), pp. 29–44. For the importance of *jang* as one of the chief political virtues in Han, see Nylan, "Confucian Piety." Cf. HY A.7a (Ku, 85); also HY B.3b (Ku, 110).

48. According to Confucians after Hsün-tzu, evil most often arises from the mind's tendency to "rationalize" selfish desires through a one-sided preoccupation with one abstract doctrine. In his chap. 3 ("Pu kou) and chap. 6 ("Fei shih erh tzu"), Hsün-tzu condemns those who hold onto one view while arbitrarily rejecting a hundred others. For comparable Han views, see, e.g., THC 16.App. 4; THC 54.App. 1.

49. On the noble man's duty to cultivate "what is singular to him," see LC 10.17; Legge, 1:402; LC 32.1, Legge, 2:300; LC 42.1; Legge, 2:413. For a discussion of Maspero's correction of Legge's mistranslation, see Riegel "Four Chapters," (1978), p. 87. Note the objections levelled against the standard translation of *hsing* as "innate nature," as summarized in David L. Hall and Roger T. Ames, *Anticipating China* (Albany, 1996), p. 188ff.

50. Hsün-tzu's chapter "On Ritual" (*Basic Writings*, p. 105) shows that ritual is designed to overcome gaps in the most appropriate and fitting fashion. For Han examples, see Derk Bodde, *Festivals*, on the No exorcism.

51. E.g., "The noble man says, 'Ceremonies and music should not for a moment be neglected by any one. . . . From them, . . . comes joy and then repose. The man in this constant repose becomes a sort of heaven, becomes a sort of god" (SSCCS 48.3b; Legge, 2:224).

52. See arguments in the "Doctrine of the Mean"; cf. HY A.6b (Ku, 83).

53. For further information, see Michael Nylan, "Han Classicists Writing in Dialogue," pp. 148–55. Yang Hsiung's appreciation of paradox may here be linked to Hsün-tzu's statement, "Every man who desires to do good does so precisely because his nature is evil" (HTYT 88.23.34; Watson, *Basic Writings*, p. 161).

54. See THC, "Introduction," part II.

55. The unresolved issue of the relation between fate and virtue was to become a central theme of many Han works, including Yang Hsiung's THC and Wang Ch'ung's LH.

56. For "renewing the old," see *Analects* 2.11. For "creating," see note 29 above. Talk of tension between "creating" vs. "transmitting" continues in Han, surfacing, for example, in Yang Hsiung's poem in defense of the THC and in LH 84.

57. Note that it is in the nature of Classics to be comprehensive enough in subject, varied enough in approach, and elliptical enough in phrasing to satisfy most readers who came to them with questions. See Alicia Ostriker's work on the necessary provocation and indeterminacy of sacred texts, such as the Old Testament. This section owes much to Miriam Levering's brilliant formulations

in *Rethinking Scripture*, the Introduction; and in "Scripture and Its Reception: A Buddhist Case." Thanks are also due to Raoul Birnbaum (and by the final draft, to Wu Hung's book), for ideas on "monumentality."

58. Though some Han Confucians, following Confucius and Hsün-tzu, assumed that human conduct presented the most important pattern for serious study, all categories of natural pattern (*wen*), human and nonhuman, as they related to the Classics were regarded as fit subjects of inquiry and expertise by Ju adherents, so long as they illuminated the ordered relations governing time and space. See Ku Chieh-kang, *Ch'in Han ti fang shih yu Ju sheng* (rpt., Shanghai, 1978).

The Ju master Yang Hsiung, himself an accomplished astronomer, warned against undue attention to astrology, for example, in FY 8.23. But the "Chung yung" argues that examining the patterns of Heaven-and-Earth (*wen-li*) improves the noble man's powers of discrimination. Contrast the range of inquiry by Han Ju with the arguments of Ch'eng Yi, who reasoned that since all *li* (inherent principles) are basically one, there is no reason for humans to "investigate things"; their task is simply to "arrive at" (i.e., to realize) their own inherent pattern.

59. Descriptions of Tung Chung-shu's teachings serve as reminders of the utterly sacred character of the Five Classics. Hidden away from the vulgar masses, Tung Chung-shu communicated the mysterious Way to members of his chosen circle, who would then pass on the basic substance of his meaning, if not the finer esoteric points, to lesser disciples. It should come as no surprise, then, that Tung Chung-shu is often depicted as a powerful magician. See, e.g., FSTY 9.73.

60. For the informative and symbolic, consider the "Great Commentary" to the *Changes*, which asserts that the *Changes* text faithfully "images" the entire course of Chinese history, while fully re-enacting the myriad changes in the phenomenal realms of Heaven-Earth-Man. For the transformative, remember the metaphor of the Five Classics as "doorway" through which the learned moved to reach the perfect insight that precedes self-cultivation. And for the legitimating, there is Wang Ch'ung's curious account of the excavation of Confucian classics from the wall of Confucius' old home; accompanied by the mysterious "sounds of strings and singing in the triumphal mode," the retrieval of the sacred texts reportedly conveyed "an auspicious omen" of Heaven's favor to Han. (See LH 61.409.) As the "Confucian" canon and its associated traditions in Han continually served religious, as well as secular, functions, all five modes and uses of canonical texts were in play during the period.

61. Note that in early China, the Five Classics scriptures were not texts to be read silently on one's own, but texts that gained lives of their own through oral-aural reception, in communities of scholars and office-holders (actual and potential). Silent reading was so unusual that the dynastic histories specially mention that it was Juan Chan's (fl. 307–312) habit. See Susan Cherniak, "Book Culture and Textual Transmission in Sung China," *Harvard Journal of Asiatic*

Studies 54 (June 1994); *Chin shu*, comp. by Fang Hsüan-ling (Peking, 1974), 49.1363. Anecdotes show Tung Chung-shu (?179–?104 B.C.) and Ma Jung (A.D. 79–166) teaching in much the same way: "His older disciples would pass on what they had learned to the newer ones, so that some of his students had never even seen his face." See SC 121.3127 (trans. after Burton Watson, *Records of the Grand Historian of China* [Columbia, 1971], 2:410); HHS 35.1207.

62. It would be naive to assume that textual practice classicism functioned either as passive reflector of societal change or as servile support to the Han throne. While the Han throne claimed to rule by virtue of its inculcation of Ju beliefs and implementation of Ju policies, three facts suggest the degree to which Han texts and textual practice contributed to changes in the course of Han history:

1. In building a tight analogy between filial piety and loyalty to the throne, Confucian theory paved the way for the process of reinfeudation that began in late Western Han when a series of underage, incompetent, or disinterested rulers ascended the Han throne. (As one text put it, "Of the most filial types of conduct, the highest is to secure a place for one's kin" [HHS 10A:412.]

2. Portent theories devised by classicists were frequently employed as potent weapons in the fight to curb imperial power, as Hans Bielenstein has shown.

3. Certain Ju scholars, on the basis of ancient or pseudo-ancient texts, directly challenged Han claims to an "eternal" Mandate when they calculated the duration of Han rule, or argued that the "true" successor to the "uncrowned king" would be found in Lu, the home state of Confucius, outside the Liu court entirely. Kan Chung-k'o and his followers, for example, predicted the imminent end to the Han Mandate.

For further information, see Loewe, *Crisis*, p. 279ff.; Gary Arbuckle, "Restoring Dong Zhongshu (BCE 195–115): An Experiment in Historical and Philosophical Reconstruction" (Ph.D. thesis, University of British Columbia, 1991), p. 359ff. For the *Kung-yang* scholars' attempt to locate the successor of the "uncrowned king" in Lu, see Wang Pao-hsüan, *Hsi Han*, p. 158ff. Classical scholars had always gotten themselves mixed up in questions of legitimacy. See SC 121.3122–23, regarding the argument of Masters Yüan Ku and Master Huang.

63. See HHS 48.1612–13. It was precisely this mess of contradictory precedents that Ying Shao attempted to order when he composed over 300 *p'ien* of legal works (no longer extant).

64. HS 79.3303–4.

65. As Ying writes, "It has come to the point where aggression is taken for upright behavior, and secretiveness is equated with righteousness, where crooked

behavior is taken for liberality, and falsehoods are equated with good reputation."
See FSTY 4.27.

66. This is not only a modern metaphor, but one used in Han times. See FY
1.1.

67. See Wu Hung, *The Wu Liang Shrine: The Ideology of Early Chinese
Pictorial Art* (Stanford, 1989), esp. appendix A.

68. HY A/10b (Ku, 96). Anxious to disprove early critiques of Ju as men
who "trust the past but disparage the modern," the Han Ju, upon assuming their
ranks within the political arena, generally contended for practical and theoretical reasons that accomplished Ju would always verify past principles by present
circumstances, mindful of Emperor Wen's (r. 179–57 B.C.) injunction: "Do not
discourse of high antiquity. May you [consider] what can be practiced today!"

69. FSTY *yi-wen* 2.94. According to the *Li chi*'s essay on "Ju Conduct," the
"true" Ju never prays to acquire many goods, but looks upon acquiring more correct behavioral patterns (*to wen*) as his chosen form of wealth. See *Li chi*, "Ju
hsing," in SSCCS 59.2b (Legge, 2:404). In considering who should qualify as a
"true" Ju, we must consider Hsün tzu (chap. 8), which attacks the "vulgar Ju" who
follow the ancient sage-kings, wore the old-style costume of the scholar, earn
money through their knowledge of ritual regulations, and study the classics in
utter ignorance of the underlying principles of ritual.

In Han, the vulgar Ju are said to have multiplied rapidly once the Ju
scholar Kung-sun Hung was elevated from commoner status to a post as one of
the emperor's three chief ministers: "Scholars throughout the empire, seeing
which way the wind was blowing, did all they could to follow his example."
See SC 121.3118 (trans. after Burton Watson in *Records of the Grand
Historian*, II, 398–99). Cf. FSTY *yi-wen* 2.99. For more on "vulgar Ju," see
Michael Nylan, "Han Classicists Writing in Dialogue about Their Own Tradition," pp. 148–55.

70. After all, there was some confusion in Han authoritative writings
about the degree to which the written word can be relied upon for guidance.
Admittedly, the praise and blame of the *Spring and Autumn Annals*, attributed
to Confucius himself, was said to reveal a perfect correspondence between
human event and moral language unsurpassed in human history. Nonetheless,
the Han "Great Commentary" to the *Changes*, also attributed to Confucius,
taught the fundamental inadequacy of spoken and written language: "Writing
does not capture as much as [verbal] phrases [presumably because spoken language, accompanied by gestures and changes in intonation, conveys meaning
better], just as phrases do not capture as much as ideas." In other words, ultimate truth lay beyond mere words, though the sages felt compelled to leave
written records behind for their followers. Complicating the "language problem" were more words attributed to Confucius, this time in one chapter of the

Li chi: "Should words be understood only in one way? Each saying has its own appropriate application!"

71. The phrasing of the later clause is borrowed from Nosco, *Remembering*, p. x, who uses it to describe eighteenth-century Japanese nativists. To give one example of evolving stances in response to historical change, let me chart, quite simply, the changes in standard "Confucian" economic proposals. In 81 B.C., the Salt and Iron Debates outlined the key economic objectives of the Ju during Western Han: (1) replacement of aggressive fiscal and diplomatic policies, including state monopolies on certain basic necessities, by "suasive government" designed chiefly to set moral patterns for those below; (2) frugality in government expenditures; (3) honoring agriculture as the primary occupation; and (4) taxing and apportioning of the land according to an equitable system. These policies, ostensibly designed to distinguish profit from the Right while protecting the "poor," suggest the Western Han Ju alliance with small-scale farmers and merchants, predicated on Ju support for the central government's plans to curtail the influence of local elites. (Not coincidentally, many prominent Western Han Ju came from relatively humble origins.)

By Eastern Han, the socioeconomic grounding for many Ju had shifted, so that increasing numbers of Ju came to depend upon gentry with land and education (rather than the throne) for their income and identity. As a result, most Ju came to accept the idea of large landholdings, lavish expenditures, and government monopolies on basic commodities, even when they entailed "families in government employ" competing openly with less-advantaged commoners for profit. See Francesca Bray, "The Agricultural Revolution," *Science and Civilisation in China*, vol. 6 (Cambridge, 1984), section 41, 529ff. Ch'en Ch'i-yün, "Han Dynasty China: Economy, Society, and State Power: A Review Article," *T'oung pao* 70 (1984): 127–48. For the quote, see HHS 43.1460. Therefore, by the end of the reign of Emperor Chang (r. 76–88), mixed reactions among the Ju to government monopolies had changed to general approbation (with a single protest coming from Chu Yün). Contrast HS 89.3624 and HHS 76.2459.

72. Such attempts to introduce salutary routines among the populace found their counterpart in the *hsün-li*'s continual insistence in his own administration that fairness guide all legal and bureaucratic procedures, especially in the case of the local tax and *corvée* assessments. In making local government both more just and more predictable, the goals of the *hsün-li* were to have the commoners identify with a bureaucratic state now more "attuned to peoples' hearts." The *hsün-li*'s success, then, lay in first, the replacement of the arbitrary exercise of power (by the gods, by local gentry, or by the local administration) with routine procedures, but more importantly, the personal gratitude (expressed as "love and respect") the local people bore their official for his tireless efforts.

73. See HS 89.3631. There is no need to mention here the manipulation and subversion of Ju norms by cynical souls intent upon getting or retaining power, the subject of numerous entries in the FSTY chaps. 3–5.

74. HHS 76.2470.

75. FSTY 9.69.

76. Ibid.

77. I put "Confucian" here in quotes to suggest that some of the practices and virtues associated with self-identified Confucians in Han do not date back to the time of Confucius.

78. HY A.8b (Ku, 89).

79. In early Han, such warnings were aimed against the policies of the First Emperor of Ch'in; in Eastern Han, against admirers of Wang Mang. For the benefits of "incremental change," see, e.g., THC 73.App. 2; CYYT 40.Hsi A.4. But accommodation, however well-meaning, could go too far. Therefore, HY A.8a (Ku, 88), speaks of conventionalists who "embracing the crooked, conform with the perverse." Cf. *Li chi*, "Ta hsüeh," in SSCCS 60.9b.

80. *Restoration*, part III, map 21.

81. For the contrary impulses to follow precedents and administer flexibly, see Hsing Yi-t'ien, *Ch'in Han shih lun kao* (Taipei, 1987), pp. 333–411. On the Han admiration for *ch'üan* ("weighing conflicting moral priorities"), see Li Hsin-li, *Ch'un Ch'iu Kung yang chuan yao yi* (Taipei, 1989), chap. 5; also, HY A.5 (Ku, 77), which advises the reader to "adapt to the world and weigh moral priorities."

82. Of course, it makes no sense to think of "schools" (*chia*) in the pre-Han or Han periods, if "schools" implies strict sectarian divisions between well-defined groups. Evidence for the pre-Han period shows that Warring States thinkers, aided perhaps by the linguistic overlap of key words in Chinese philosophy, borrowed from one another continually, apparently without fear of crossing potential lines between the various "scholastic lines" (*chia*) established by various thinkers. In postmodern terms, these schools partook of a common discourse. Such eclecticism continued apace in Han, long after Ssu-ma T'an's catalogue divided works in the imperial collection into six main sections. For this reason, aside from the dynastic histories, Han works typically do not lump individual thinkers together as members of the same *chia*; instead, thinkers are usually cited as individuals, even with the most self-conscious of the Han Confucian classicists (e.g., in Yang Hsiung's *Fa yen*). That may mean that outside of some academic circles far less emphasis was placed on the genesis and genealogies of teachers and teachings in Han than we are accustomed to from late imperial China. For the later Confucian genealogical emphasis, see Thomas A. Wilson, *Genealogy of the Way: The Construction and Uses of the Confucian Tradition in Late Imperial China* (Stanford, 1995), the main points of which have been summarized in Wilson's "Genealogy and History," pp. 3–33.

83. Note, for example, the use of the same language to describe the Good in Hsün-tzu (who equates it with ritual) and the Good in Lao-tzu (who equates it with the cosmic Tao), as recorded in HTYT 73.19.63 (Watson, 100); *Lao tzu*, chap. 77 (Lau, 139). Note also the decision by all Chinese thinkers to talk in terms of promoting what is *kung* ("in the public interest"), as against what is *szu* ("[merely] in the private interest"). Finally, all Warring States writings, not just those of Chuang-tzu, delight in describing the Good and the noble by means of paradoxes, as when a late passage in the *Analects* includes several passages describing the "noble man" in terms of paradoxes ("full yet empty," and so on). Of course, A. C. Graham in *Later Mohist Logic, Ethics, and Science* shows the pre-Ch'in Logicians, the late Mohists, and the Taoists sharing a common technical vocabulary and similar strategies of dialogic reasoning.

84. Ch'i and Lu, the early centers of Confucian learning, were particularly associated with *wen-hsüeh* (the study of texts) (SC 121.3117). But some Confucian masters won fame for their "countenance" (*jung*) and performance of the rites, rather than for textual erudition; see SC 121.3126.

85. At the beginning of Han, after centuries of war, Han classicists bemoaned the faulty nature of their two sources of authority: key texts were missing or nearly indecipherable (possibly through the Ch'in Burning of the Books in 213 B.C., but probably more importantly through the razing of the imperial capital in 207 B.C.), while key portions of the ancient systems of "rites and music" remained irrecoverable. Over the course of the Western and Eastern Han dynasties, Han classicists were to see further dramatic losses of respected "traditions" in the wars attending the "restoration" and downfall of the Han, losses that made it all the harder to definitely ascertain the correct Way of the Ancients.

86. Yuri Pines, private communication (dated November 16, 1996). I thank Dr. Pines for setting me this challenge.

87. CTYT 10.4.40-41 (Watson, 59-60).

88. See Michael Nylan, "Confucian Piety and Individualism," *Journal of American Oriental Society* 116 (Jan.–Mar., 1996), 1–27.

89. Perhaps because of our postmodern cynicism, we are much more likely to recall those situations where the same code words were applied to different situations. But the converse could also be true in Han, that an age-old problem would be treated with new terminology, in the hopes of resolving an issue.

90. For Ssu-ma Hsiang-ju, see the "Ta jen fu," in CHW 21.7a.8a. The Han Ju, for instance, seemed oddly confident that apparent contradictions within the tradition could eventually be resolved by disciplined exercises in public debate. The best of the Han Ju (e.g., Liu Hsiang, Hsü Shen, Pan Ku, Cheng Hsüan, Ying Shao) tackled with surprising openness the apparent (and real) contradictions in role models and in moral injunctions contained in the Classics. See FSTY, chap. 5, devoted to contradictory cases of behavior; WCYY; the *Lun heng*; and SY 11, entitled "Good Speech." See also FY 1.2, which assumes that with a good enough

teacher, the pupil can arrive at a standard by which to judge competing claims about goodness. Histories of China have tended to ignore the degree of debate that was accepted practice, in part because a developed rhetorical tradition is usually presumed to be the exclusive property of the Greeks.

91. The sense of newness that accompanied the Han experiments, which lent them an air of undoubted optimism, contrast sharply with the generally less sanguine search launched by self-identified Confucians in late imperial China for "the Way of antiquity," whose full glories were presumably too distant to recover. (Wang Yang-ming, among others, is an exception.) If art provides any insight into broader culture, the men of Han, even in the last days of the empire, faced the world with great exuberance, confident of their ability to manage it, in contrast to their moody later counterparts, who imagined themselves more tenuously positioned in an enigmatic reality.

92. Contrast this with the later proposed rejection (led by Ch'eng-Chu adherents) of many aspects of tradition inherited by or from Han. In a move that somewhat parallels the Protestant Reformation, some Neo-Confucian thinkers even called for the direct apprehension of the sages' intent without the mediation of established tradition. This rejection of most of the past, accompanied by the recontextualization of the entire Confucian tradition through numerous anthologies and genealogies, was predicated, of course, on a firm belief—utterly foreign to Han thinkers—that the operations of the sacred Tao were somehow discontinuous, in the sense that their transformative, moralizing effect had not informed the social realm of humans at all times in equal measure, letting culture and literary patterns (both *wen*) stray from the Path. Not only the Ch'eng brothers and Chu Hsi, but later critics as well (e.g., Li Yung) presumed the interruption of the Tao's transformative activities among men. Confucian thinkers in late imperial China debated whether this interruption of the Tao's operations resulted in inaccuracy in transmitted texts or a loss of moral knowledge. See Birdwhistell, *Li Yong*, pp. 43, 52ff.

This idea of the Tao's discontinuity by analogy presupposed a greater separation of ideas and language from dispositions to act, as well. Probably related to this is the unwillingness of many Neo-Confucians to grant that habituation to ritual forms can instill true goodness.

93. See Waiyee Li, *Enchantment and Disenchantment* (Princeton, 1993), p. 9.

94. Hampshire, *Innocence and Experience* (Cambridge, 1989).

95. For the Confucianization of the "law," see note 3 above. Contra W. J. F. Jenner, *The Tyranny of History: The Roots of China's Crisis* (London, 1992), p. 24ff. Jenner argues that the early imperial state was far more powerful, but in assessing degrees of relative power, he considers only the proportion of each farmer's time and taxes that the state could command.

96. David Knechtges (private communication, May 11, 1995) gives the size of the late Western Han court bureaucracy as 130,000, if accounts in the dynastic histories are to be believed, making the ratio of court officials to literati much higher in Han than in late imperial China. Meanwhile, the population of late imperial China continued to grow, until 19th c. Ch'ing China had a population about 7 times as great as the 60 million the Han had on its census books. Peter Bol, among others, has suggested that the Sung literati's recognition of their slim chances to be employed in public office was one factor leading them to completely redefine the term of *shih*.

Take the increased importance of the "private" arts: In the Han, art is primarily used for public instruction or for public display. I can find no suggestion that painting or calligraphy might advance or reveal self-cultivation. Many Neo-Confucians (though certainly not all), followed the suggestions of Su Shih and others in associating certain arts with specific virtues and the discipline of the arts in general with self-cultivation.

97. Alasdair MacIntyre, *After Virtue: A Study in Moral Theory* (Notre Dame, 1984), in which MacIntyre clarifies the distinction between rights-centered societies and virtue-centered societies.

98. There are a number of powerful metaphors from the pre-Han and Han period that continue in Neo-Confucianism, including the six treated in Donald Munro, *Images of Human Nature: A Sung Portrait* (Princeton, 1988): (1) the family network; (2) the stream of water; (3) the light source, usually a mirror; (4) the body; (5) plants; and (6) the ruler. But Munro demonstrates that these early images are handled quite differently in Chu Hsi's work.

In comparing the different weights accorded the "Confucian" virtues in Han times, one might point to the debates over the virtue of frugality in Han times, with some Han Confucians seeing in any "undue" stress on frugality the pernicious influence of the Mohists. See FSTY 2.13–16, for example, which argues against the popular admiration for frugality. The writings of the heirs to Chu Hsi, by contrast, generally focus on frugality (reflecting conquest of the desires, in addition to the admirable preservation of family property) as a "core value."

99. The relation of Han Confucianism to that of later imperial China is somewhat reminiscent of the relation of Catholicism (which accepts the authority of tradition on a par with scripture) to Protestantism (which minimizes the authority accorded tradition). Peter Bol's book traces a growing suspicion that the sacred Tao does not operate at all times within the human cultural realm.

100. For early calls, see e.g., Ssu-ma Kuang, *Ssu-ma Wen-kung chuan chia chi*, chap. 42, "Lun feng-su cha-tzu." Chu Hsi, of course, added the important proviso that the learner must accept the basic orientation of the Ch'eng brothers or lapse into dangerous heterodoxy. As Chu Hsi wrote, "Were it not for the Ch'eng brothers, no one would be able to receive the mind of the sages through their words." See Chu Hsi, *Ssu shu chi chu* (SPPY), 2a–3a. Regarding this desire for

direct apprehension of the Way, George Hatch writes, "Anyone claiming an affinity of mind with antiquity could assume the mission of social regeneration, and the ground of an incredible self-righteousness was laid." This led, according to Hatch, to all the interpretive anarchy implicit in the *fu-ku* ("return to antiquity") slogan. See the Hatch dissertation, "Su Hsün," p. 10.

101. Not only the Ch'eng brothers and Chu Hsi, but later critics as well (e.g., Li Yung) presumed the interruption of the Tao's transformative activities among men. Confucian thinkers in late imperial China debated whether this interruption of the Tao's operations was resulted in inaccuracy in transmitted texts or a loss of moral knowledge. See Birdwhistell, *Li Yong*, pp. 43, 52ff.

This idea of the Tao's discontinuity by analogy presupposed a greater separation of ideas and language from dispositions to act, as well. Probably related to this is the unwillingness of many Neo-Confucians to grant that habituation to ritual forms can instill true goodness.

102. Tung Chung-shu, whose legal judgments were considered authoritative in Han times, intended the legal definition of parent to depend less upon biological connections than upon the proper fulfillment of the parental role, in conformity with the Confucian doctrine of the Rectification of Names. As a result, parents "who did not act like parents" (whose "ties had been cut") were not owed filial obligations by their biological children. See Tung's *Ch'un ch'iu chüeh shih*, cited in Ma Kuo-han, 2:1180. Cf. *Shuo yüan* 6.1; 8.10b–11a, for statements that officials owe no obligations to rulers who do not act like rulers.

In contrast, post-T'ang "Confucian" thinkers referred continually to a forged *Classic of Loyalty* (falsely attributed to one of the Han classicists), which argued, "Even if a ruler does not act like a ruler, the subject may not but act like a subject. Even if the father does not act like a father, the son may not but act like a son." Chu Hsi's *Elementary Learning*, for example, urged total commitment to one's ruler, one's father, and one's husband. For more information, see J. Holmgren, "Myth, Fantasy or Scholarship: Images of the Status of Women in Traditional China," *Australian Journal of Chinese Affairs* 6: 147–70; and my book manuscript, tentatively entitled, *The Five "Confucian" Classics*; currently under reviews.

103. See Hall and Ames, *Anticipating China*, p. 210, which argues that early Confucianism succeeded to a large extent because of "its ability to accommodate within a ritually grounded society many of the profound elements of Daoism, Legalism, and Mohism"; this pattern of accommodation "would be repeated in Confucianism's gradual appropriation of Buddhist elements by its medieval adherents." I speak of Buddhism as a "Western" tradition, in part because its traditions (through Hinduism) relate more closely to traditions in the contemporary Mediterranean world than to traditions in East Asia.

104. Note the contrast between the Han emphasis on *wen* (complex relational patterns) and the later Confucian emphasis on *li*, often—though not always—to be read more as "fixed principles of order."

105. Peterson, "Pai chia," (1982), op. cit., suggests that the chief difference between the classical and medieval interpretations of *li* lies in the greater interiority of the latter. Early "Confucian" texts seldom concern themselves—even when talking of self-cultivation—with interior states or psychologizing, placing much greater emphasis on the quality of role performance as it relates to others and the necessary provision (whether "natural" or "artificial") of external signs. By "external signs," I refer to things as disparate as sumptuary regulations and heavenly portents.

Some prominent Han Ju disputed the very desirability and utility of inner vision. See, e.g., the controversy reported in Ts'ao Chih's "Pien tao lun," *Kuang Hung ming chi* 5.3a–b. Han Ju were inclined to condemn both solitary learning and the reclusive life. Han Ju would have been taken aback by Lo Ju-fang's (Ming dynasty) contention that it was a person's "true *hsin*"—not the practice of ritual—that induces the feelings of reverence and love that form the basis of all productive social life. See Yu-Yin Cheng, "Ethics of the Six Maxims (*Liu yü*) Redefined: Lo Ju-fang (1515–88) and His Restructuring of Community Convenants (*Hsiang-yüeh*)," paper presented at the annual meeting of the Association for Asian Studies, April 2–5, 1995, Washington, D.C.

In contrast, later Confucianism seems much more preoccupied with revised definitions of self-cultivation more dependent upon the purity and perfection of one's "quiet" inner state, on the priority of "reverential" mind over action. For example, most neo-Confucians insist that moral behavior depends upon having correct thoughts first; for Li Yong, see Birdwhistell, p. 122. Only in late imperial China, then—and not in Han—does "Confucian" society (facing "barbarian rule") grant the possibility that the need to maintain rigorous standards of self-cultivation can outweigh the need to engage in public service in times of peace. See Conrad Schirokauer, "Chu Hsi's Political Career: A Study in Ambivalence," in *Confucian Personalities*, ed. by Arthur F. Wright (Stanford, 1962), pp. 162–88.

106. The early canonical "Confucian" tradition portrays, of course, problems associated with overindulgence of the senses. Generally, however, it presumes that sensory experience and the mind form one interlocking, well-functioning system. Under Buddhist influence, however, Chinese thinkers increasingly accept the notion that sensory experience constitutes an inadequate guide to reason and that denial of sensory experience may be a good per se. See "Hung fan" chap. of *Documents*, para. 6 (Karlgren, 30). According to Don C. Wyatt, early Confucianism was a "sensationalist" philosophically because it "assumes that perceptions of the ordinary senses convey an accurate depiction of what is real," though it is clearly "anti-sensationalist" in the literary sense (i.e., it's against fanciful or rhetorical language). See Don C. Wyatt, "A Language of

Continuity in Confucian Thought," *Ideas across Cultures: Essays on Chinese Thought in Honor of Benjamin I. Schwartz*, ed. by Paul A. Cohen and Merle Goldman (Cambridge, 1990), p. 39.

107. Tao (and T'ien) in the writings of some, though not all, Neo-Confucian thinkers, becomes a fixed standard independent of human culture and society, much more remote from the present, natural world of Heaven-and-Earth. Peerenboom, *Lau* p. 76, describes early Confucianism as an ethical system that presupposes "the discretionary judgment of exemplary persons who create an emergent order from the particular context"; generally, it avoids appeals to universal or transcendent ethical principles, in a contrast to some later talk about *li*. Hall and Ames, *Anticipating China*, p. 233, suggest that early Chinese texts define "oneness" chiefly in terms of "continuity." It is possible that later imperial Chinese thinkers focused more on identity.

GLOSSARY

ch'eng	誠
ch'u shih	處士
chang-chü	章句
chia	家
chih shu	治書
ching	經
hsien	賢
hsing	性
hsun-li	循吏
po-ai	博愛
po-hsüeh	博學
po-shih	博士
shen	神
shih	士
t'ung-ju	通儒
wen	文

3

The Formulation of Early Medieval Confucian Metaphysics

Huang K'an's (488–545) Accommodation of Neo-Taoism and Buddhism

Yuet Keung Lo

A boundary marks outs a territory; it gives identity to an otherwise undifferentiated domain. Sometimes the demarcation itself actually lays claim to the ownership of the domain. The notion of ownership implies exclusivity; it excludes whatever lies outside the charted domain. An intellectual heritage or tradition is often carefully guarded, if not clearly defined, by ideological boundaries. These boundaries ensure the integrity of the tradition. But integrity does not necessarily imply that the tradition adheres to a form of essentialism that admits of no change over time. In fact, boundaries are hardly fixed for good; they often shift, and the fluidity of boundaries sometimes is precipitated, at least in part, by historical circumstances. Thus the fluidity of boundaries almost makes it impossible for a viable doctrine to endure over time without making any adjustment in response to changing circumstances. When the identity or essence of a doctrine changes, its boundaries shift accordingly. Alternatively, one may say that when the boundaries of a doctrine shift, its identity or essence inevitably redefines itself.

The survival and revival of the Confucian doctrine after the downfall of the Han dynasty in the early third century present an interesting case of the dynamic interplay between boundary shifting and philosophical regeneration of the Confucian doctrine vis-à-vis the multiple forces of Neo-Taoist and Buddhist philosophies. This paper argues that the momentous changes concomitant with the Han debacle provided the seismic impetus for recharting the domain of the Confucian doctrine. Boundaries do not shift in a vacuum; they shift partly in response to external stimuli. Through an examination of an emerging Confucian metaphysics as documented in Huang K'an's (488–545) *Lun-yü chi-chieh i-shu* (Subcommmentaries on the Collected Commentaries on the *Analects*), this paper further demonstrates how the Confucian doctrine accommodated foreign ideas from Neo-Taoism and Buddhism by realigning its doctrinal boundaries, and in the end gave fresh expression to a new metaphysics that would have been alien to Han Confucians.

HISTORICAL AND INTELLECTUAL BACKGROUNDS

Since Emperor Wu of Han adopted Tung Chung-shu's (179–104 B.C.) proposal to implement the Confucian ideology as state orthodoxy, the Confucian classics became the official curriculum for civil examinations while non-Confucian philosophies were accordingly denigrated. Thereafter, Confucian learning was given a utilitarian twist because it provided a ticket to officialdom. As a result, the study of Confucian classics flourished in the Han. A Confucian master would usually have thousands of disciples registered on his student roster. Even the barbarous Hsiung-nu nomads sent their people to study in the Han empire.[1] Indeed, the Han dynasty (206 B.C.–220 A.D.), as a whole, has been considered to be the heyday of Confucian learning.[2]

The prosperity of Confucian learning also found expression in the various commentarial traditions of each and every Confucian classic. Ironically, this very diversity of traditions also led to the waning of Confucian learning by the late Han. Commentarial traditions during the Han were strict and rigid; a student of one tradition was naturally obligated to carry on his master's tradition without adulterating it. An insulated tradition, to no one's surprise, tended to become ossified in time. Worst of all, the volume of elaboration of the meanings in a classic swelled horrendously over time. For instance, it was reported that one Confucian scholar expounded the meaning of the two-character title of the first chapter of the *Shang-shu* (Book of Documents) by using in excess of one hundred thousand words.[3] This hairsplitting tendency no doubt stunted the development of genuine Confucian scholarship. Moreover, beginning from the reigns of Emperors Huan (147–167) and Ling (168–188), Confucian scholars were incriminated in political struggles. Consequently, many of them were victimized, and the vogue of Confucian learning waned.

With the collapse of the Han empire, the two capital cities of the Han, the monuments of the cultural establishment, were devastated. Thus, the fall of the Han empire and the ossification of Han learning radically undermined the scholar-officials' erstwhile faith in Confucian thought as a guiding ideology. Indeed, Confucian learning was practically abandoned, and no sooner had the Han collapsed than the belief that Confucian learning was impractical prevailed.[4] According to one historical account, in the middle of the third century during the Wei period (220–264), only once did the Wei emperor summon senior Confucian scholar-officials to discuss the issue of the sacrificial altar for Heaven, and there were only a handful out of more than twenty thousand who would respond. Meanwhile, out of some four hundred junior scholar-officials, all but a dozen or so could barely hold a brush and write.[5] Such a miserable situation of the state of Confucian learning was at least partly attributable to Ts'ao Ts'ao (155–220), the de facto founding father of the Wei regime subsequent to the Han, who openly decried and condemned Confucian morality and single-mindedly advocated practical abilities and talents. Indeed, Tsao Ts'ao promoted the study of legalist philosophy.[6]

Experiencing decline in the late Han, Confucian learning in the third century was in need of a fundamental overhaul if it were to enjoy a revival. Furthermore, Tsao Ts'ao's open attack on Confucian learning also generated, albeit indirectly, the study of non-Confucian philosophies. The boundaries of Confucian learning thus became unstable and ambiguous. It was against this kind of historical and intellectual background that a new trend of academic learning began to emerge in the third century.

Long before the downfall of the Han dynasty, Confucian scholars had already begun to delve into the study of Taoism. The late Han Confucian master, Ma Jung (79–166), is a perfect case in point. Ma not only wrote a commentary on the Taoist classic *Tao-te ching*, but he apparently also led a life in accord with what he believed to be Taoist philosophy. Frustrated with Confucian philosophy, which emphasized social ethics and responsibilities, Ma converted himself to what he took to be a Taoist belief, the belief that an individual's life was of the utmost importance and personal freedom was more valuable than the entire world itself. Accordingly, as the *Later Han History* (*Hou-Han shu*) tells us, Ma indulged himself in various kinds of worldly pleasures, apart from, and in spite of, his teaching career as a past master of Confucian learning.[7] For Ma, there was apparently no doctrinal conflict between what to him were Confucian and Taoist philosophies. It must be emphasized that Ma's claim of Taoist philosophical justification for his pursuit of worldly pleasures is at least arguable, if not unacceptable. It is true that classical Taoism accords utmost importance to the personal self, yet it never endorses hedonism. Nevertheless, the fact that Ma Jung as a Confucian past master adopted Taoist philosophy and interpreted it in a way to justify his pursuit of worldly pleasures indicates that Taoism began to compete with Confucianism as a philosophical guide for life. But classical Taoism made a comeback only in a new hermeneutic mode after the fall of the Han dynasty, which precipitated the shifting of the doctrinal boundaries of Confucianism.

While many Confucian scholar-officials were ignorant as to how to hold a brush and write properly, a new philosophical concern began to consume the energies of the best minds in the third century. For instance, the aristocratic family of Hsün Hsü (163–212), who served as the prime counsellor to Tsao Ts'ao in the early third century, was famous for a host of virtuous and talented descendants. All of Hsün Hsü's sons were well known for their Confucian learning, except for Hsün Ts'an (ca. 203–231), who realized that the essence of the teachings of the sages could not possibly be recorded in the classics, which he considered nothing but "the chaff and leftovers of the sages."[8] Hsün Ts'an's view on language and Confucian classics is characteristically Taoist, and it is consistent with Wang Pi's (226–249) Neo-Taoist claim that language is inadequate in describing and capturing the essence of Tao. Yet, what is most important is that for Hsün Ts'an, the essence of Confucius's teachings lay in his views on human nature and the way of Heaven. Ts'an's new recognition of the essence of Confucius's teachings inevitably necessitated a shifting of the boundaries of the Confucian doctrine, and this boundary shift would in turn cause a broadening and deepening of the Confucian inquiries into matters related to human nature and the way of Heaven. It was no coincidence that such inquiries would later become the fundamental concerns of Neo-Taoist philosophy as well as early medieval Confucian thought.

The new philosophical concern in question was a persistent interest in exploring the ontology of the universe through writing commentaries on the Taoist classics like the *Tao-te ching* and the *Chuang-tzu*, as well as the Confucian classic, the *I-ching* (*Changes*). Of these commentaries, Wang Pi's *Lao-tzu chu* (Commentary on the *Lao-tzu*) and his *Chou-i chu* (Commentary on the *Changes*), along with Kuo Hsiang's (d. 312) *Chuang-tzu chu* (Commentary on the *Chuang-tzu*), were most popular and influential in their times as well as in later ages. These three texts were called the "Three Works on the Mysterious" (*san-hsüan*) in the early medieval period. The fact that the three texts from the Confucian and Taoist traditions were grouped together to form a unified project of philosophical inquiry suggests that the boundaries of both doctrines were sufficiently flexible for cross-fertilization. Another important figure in this collective project of ontological philosophizing was Ho Yen (190–249). He attempted to write a commentary on the *Lao-tzu*, but after reading Wang Pi's commentary on the same Taoist classic, he gave up his endeavor. Instead, he composed the "Tao-lun" (Treatise on Tao) to expound the fundamental concept of Tao in the *Lao-tzu*. The works by these three figures have been considered the basic core of a philosophy known as *hsüan-hsüeh* (the study of the mysterious) in the early medieval period, often called Neo-Taoism by modern scholars in the West.

Interestingly enough, these three major figures all wrote commentaries on the Confucian classic, the *Analects*. Ho Yen compiled the *Lun-yü chi-chieh* (Collected Commentaries on the *Analects*) which is still extant today. But the commentaries by Wang Pi and Kuo Hsiang unfortunately only survive in fragments which were partly incorporated into Huang K'an's *Lun-yü chi-chieh i-shu*.[9] Ho Yen's *Collected Commentaries on the Analects* in the early third century represented the first effort to compile scholarship on a Confucian text from various commentarial traditions. As noted above, commentarial traditions in Han times were strict and did not admit of deviation or incorporation of other traditions in general. Yet, by the end of the Han, Confucian masters began to widen their scope of learning; not only did many of them study Confucian classics from different lines of textual and exegetical transmission, but they also delved into non-Confucian philosophical works. The intellectual mind was broadened. Ho Yen's effort to bring together a number of commentaries from various traditions was simply an opportune move reflecting the temper of his time. The *Collected Commentaries* included the works of at least eight commentators and Ho Yen also occasionally inserted his own interpretations.

In the early fifth century, Chiang Hsi, whose thinking was essentially Taoist, also collected thirteen different commentaries on the *Analects* together, but unfortunately this work is long lost.[10] Then came Huang K'an who, on the basis of the works of Ho Yen and Chiang Hsi, incorporated at least thirty-one more commentaries in his *Subcommentaries on the Analects*.[11] Besides, Huang K'an did not mention the names of the commentators he cited in many instances. All in all, the number of commentaries cited by Huang K'an may very well exceed sixty. The fact that the *Analects* attracted so much scholarly and philosophical attention indicates that this little Confucian work won wide acceptance even in the days when Confucianism suffered considerably in the midst of the vogue of Neo-Taoism and Buddhism.[12] One of the reasons why the *Analects* was so popular in the early medieval period is that Confucius was considered to be the ideal sage by early medieval thinkers in general and by the Neo-Taoists in particular. Although most people would model after Chuang-tzu in their lifestyle, they did so only because the sagehood of Confucius was deemed to be too lofty and supreme for them to emulate.[13] Naturally the best way to approach Confucius was to study the *Analects*, in which Confucius's sagely personality and supreme virtues were well recorded.

HUANG K'AN THE SYNCRETIST

Huang K'an was a Confucian master in every sense of the word in his time. For one thing, his biography constitutes part of the "Biographies of Confucian Scholars" in the *Liang-shu* (Liang History).[14] He studied with Ho Yang (452–510), who himself was also a master in the Confucian classics. In the early sixth century when Emperor Wu of Liang established the imperial institutes for Confucian classics, Ho Yang was named Doctor of the Five Classics and subsequently wrote the *Wu-ching i* (Interpretations of the Five Classics). Ho was particularly known for his knowledge of Confucian rituals,[15] and in fact, the ritual systems of the Liang were primarily based on his ideas. Interestingly enough, in addition to his commentaries on the *Book of Rites* and the *Changes*, Ho Yang also wrote commentaries on the *Lao-tzu* and *Chuang-tzu*. Thus, he deserved to be regarded as a scholar in the Three Texts of the Mysterious. Indeed, about half of the Confucians scholars mentioned in the "Biographies of Confucian Scholars" in the Liang History were also known for their scholarship on Taoist and Buddhist texts.

Huang K'an was no exception. According to his biography, Huang completely mastered his teacher's scholarship and in particular, he was well versed in the *Li-chi* (Book of Rites), the *I-li* (Ceremonials), the *Chou-li* (Protocols of Chou), the *Classic of Filial Piety*, and the *Analects*. He began his official career as an assistant professor in the Imperial Academy and always attracted several hundred people to his lectures. In addition to his *Subcommentaries on the Analects*, Huang K'an also wrote the *Li-chi chiang-shu* (Commentarial Lectures on the Book of Rites) in forty-eight scrolls and the *Li-chi i-shu* (Subcommentaries on the Book of Rites), which were decreed to be stored in the Rare Books Section of the imperial library.[16] The *Subcommentaries* and the *Commentarial Lectures* as well as his *Subcommentaries on the Analects* were well respected and popular in his times.[17]

Huang K'an was also known for his filial piety. In the early medieval period, the Buddhist *Kuan-shih-yin ching* (Sutra of Avalokitesvara) was believed to have miraculous power, which could be invoked by simply reciting the sutra or even the very name of the bodhisattva Avalokitesvara. Stories about filial sons who recited the sutra to invoke power to cure or heal their parents' terminal infirmities or illnesses were widespread.[18] Huang K'an compared the *Book of Filial Piety* to the *Kuan-shih-yin ching*, and recited the Confucian classic twenty times every day.[19] A Confucian master notwithstanding, Huang's intellectual horizon was evidently broad enough to accommodate the Buddhist faith. Thus, it is no surprise that his *Subcommentaries* incorporates many non-Confucian interpretations. Indeed, in one place Huang K'an seems to have even considered Buddhism to be superior to Confucianism when he said that "the teachings of Duke Chou and Confucius concern only this life and know nothing about the previous and future lives."[20] For Huang, Confucianism seems to address problems pertaining to the "realm of form and vessel" (*hsing-ch'i*), and so he branded Confucianism as "outer teaching" (*wai-chiao*), as opposed to "inner teaching" (*nei-chiao*), which was implied to be Buddhism.[21] Huang's comparison of Confucian teachings and Buddhism indicates that he impartially acknowledged the inadequacy of Confucianism as he understood it. But it cannot be overemphasized that Huang did not recite the *Kuan-shih-yin ching*. Rather, he attempted to impute new religious significance to the *Book of Filial Piety* by reciting it twenty times every day —a practice that was hitherto unheard of.[22] Huang K'an remained in the end a Confucian.

The commentators cited by Huang K'an came from a variety of backgrounds.[23] There were Confucian scholars like his teacher Ho Yang, Yuan Hung (328–376), a Confucian historian, and Fan Ning (339–401), who wrote a famous commentary on the *Ku-liang chuan* (Ku-liang's Commentary on the Spring and

Autumn Annals) and was known for his diatribe against Neo-Taoism. Included were also Neo-Taoist thinkers like Wang Pi, Kuo Hsiang, Li Ch'ung, who himself compiled a collected commentary on the *Analects*,[24] and Yin Chung-k'an (336–399), who claimed that the base of his tongue would become stiff if he had not read the book of *Lao-tzu* for three days.[25] Most notably, however, there were also religious Taoists like Ku Huan (390–453) and Buddhist monks like Shih Pu-chih and Shih Hui-lin, as well as Buddhist laymen like Layman Shen. Judging from the number of citations and their philosophical nature, however, Huang K'an's *Subcommentaries* is predominantly Neo-Taoist in its orientation.[26] In what follows, based on the Neo-Taoist works mentioned above, I shall introduce some of the basic features of Neo-Taoist metaphysics that would have a bearing on the shaping of early medieval Confucian metaphysics.

THE METAPHYSICAL DUALISM IN NEO-TAOISM

The fundamental impact on the development of early medieval Confucian thought came from a Neo-Taoist ontology characterized by a metaphysical dualism. According to the Neo-Taoist ontology of Nonbeing espoused by Wang Pi and others, the origin of the universe is identified as Nonbeing from which the myriad things originate. Nonbeing and being are dichotomized, and this dichotomy, as will become clear, creates a metaphysical dualism of the transcendental and the phenomenal. Ho Yen's "Tao-lun" says, "Being (*yu*), in coming into being, is produced by Nonbeing (*wu*). Affairs (*shih*), as affairs, are brought into completion by Nonbeing."[27] Here, it is clear that Nonbeing is the origin of being; the former is ontologically superior to the latter. As the origin of being, Nonbeing has no predicates. It has no concrete form and thus cannot be identified by one particular name. In its formlessness and namelessness, Nonbeing is Tao in its completeness.[28] Although Tao, or Nonbeing, has no form or name, it brings forms into being and gives them a name corresponding to their finite existence. Tao "is able to make sounds and echoes brilliant, to cause material force (*ch'i*) and material objects (*wu*) to stand out, to embrace all physical forms and spiritual activity, and to display light and shadow."[29] Based on this ontology of phenomenal existence, a dichotomy of infinite Tao and finite beings/affairs is posited.

In Wang Pi's metaphysics, Nonbeing is also considered the ontological origin of the myriad things. In his commentary on chapter 40 of the *Lao-tzu*, Wang Pi says, "All things in the world come from being, and the origin of being is based on Nonbeing. In order to have being in total, it is necessary to return to Nonbeing."[30] Not only is Nonbeing infinite, but it is also timeless, as Wang Pi further emphasizes. Nonbeing underlies all beings, and in its absence, the myriad things will all disappear.

When Nonbeing gives rise to the myriad things, it not only justifies their existence, but also puts them in order. In this sense, Nonbeing is also called Principle (*li*) or Ultimate Principle (*chih-li*).[31] Nothing exists without Principle.[32] It is by Principle that all things can be understood[33] because Principle is manifested in the integrity and functioning of the myriad things.[34] Thus, in Wang Pi's formulation, there is a substance-function (*t'i-yung*) relation between Principle and the myriad things.[35] Principle exists in the transcendental realm and the myriad things in the phenomenal realm.

Principle not only guarantees the regularity and order of the phenomenal realm, but it also governs change, according to Wang Pi's essay and commentary on the *Changes*.[36] Although Principle manifests itself in the manifold phenomena such that each of them exists by virtue of a particular form of Principle, yet Principle transcends all ephemeral phenomena. It is one and universal. In spite of its particularity, each manifested principle in its concreteness is essentially the same. In his commentary on the *Changes*, Wang Pi sharply distinguishes Principle which is general, from facts, which are particular; but he insists that the general Principle can be discovered in any event.[37] Thus, there is a one-many relationship between Principle and phenomena/affairs.

In spite of their essential difference, the transcendental and the phenomenal are fundamentally two in one. The transcendental manifests itself through phenomena/affairs. Without phenomena, the transcendental would not be complete. Without the transcendental, phenomena are mere ephemeral changes whose appearance cannot even be explained. According to Wang Pi, there exists a substance-function relationship between the transcendental and the phenomenal; the former is the substance, the latter the function. Wang Pi's fundamental subscription to metaphysical dualism is best epitomized in his notion of the sage.

THE SAGE IN NEO-TAOISM

As mentioned earlier, Neo-Taoism as a new trend of thinking began to find its way to the intelligentsia when Confucianism was losing its grip in the early third century. In this period of philosophic transition, questions were inevitably raised about the relative supremacy of Confucianism and Taoism. When Wang Pi was barely twenty, P'ei Hui (ca. 209–250), who was versed in the study of the *Changes*, *Lao-tzu*, and *Chuang-tzu*, posed a long-pending question to him. P'ei asked,

> "Nonbeing is indeed that by which all things are sustained, yet the Sage (Confucius) was unwilling to vouchsafe any words on the subject. Lao Tzu, on the other hand, expatiated on it endlessly. Why?" To this Wang Pi replied, "The Sage *embodied* (*t'i*) Nonbeing. Furthermore, Nonbeing is not amenable to instruction. Therefore of necessity his words applied to Being. Lao-tzu and Chuang-tzu, not yet free of Being,

were continually giving instruction about that in which they felt a defi-
ciency."[38]

It is clear that Wang Pi honored Confucius as the Sage and considered the two
Taoist masters inferior to him on the basis of their inability to embody Nonbeing.
It is noteworthy that Wang Pi used the term "*t'i*" in two different but intimately
related senses. As a noun, *t'i* refers to both the ultimate ontic source of being and
value. As a verb, it refers to the process of the apotheosis of the sage who successfully emulates the virtues of the ultimately transcendent and embodies it in his
person. For Wang Pi the transcendent is anything but a hairsplitting verbal discourse; it is a spiritual life on a higher plane. Earlier we have seen that Hsün Ts'an
already noted that Confucius's words on human nature and the Way (Tao) of
Heaven, which were not vouchsafed, were indeed the essence of the sage's teachings. Here, again, P'ei Hui and Wang Pi also realized that the superiority of
Confucius over the two Taoist masters lay in his embodiment of Tao and his
understanding of human nature.

While Wang Pi emphasized the transcendence of Principle over phenom-
ena/affairs, Kuo Hsiang showed a special interest in the immanence of Principle
in every individual phenomenon.[39] Wang Pi used the term *t'ung-li* (general principle) when he stressed the universality of the single ultimate principle. In contrast, Kuo Hsiang introduced the notion of *ch'ün-li* (multitudinous principles) or
wan-li (ten thousand principles). Both terms, according to Ch'ien Mu, were
coined by Kuo.[40] Thus, while Wang advocated that all things are united in one
ultimate principle, Kuo maintained that "everything has its own principle,"[41] and
that "the multitudinous principles arise" from the myriad things.[42]

Since the multitudinous principles are immanent in beings themselves, a
split between the principle unique in every being and the phenomenal being
itself is theoretically impossible. Thus, Kuo Hsiang advocated a kind of harmonious relationship between Principle and phenomena, a relationship that is no
less dualistic in nature. The harmony between Principle and phenomena is characterized by the fact that every phenomenon is justified by virtue of its existence.
No existing phenomenon is illegitimate from the perspective of Principle.

The harmony between Principle and phenomena on the metaphysical level
had a tremendously important bearing on Kuo Hsiang's political philosophy. To
Kuo, the ideal person is a sage who is "sagely within and kingly without" and who
roams freely in both the transcendental and the phenomenal worlds. Indeed, the
transcendental realm is none other than the phenomenal realm. It is only the
unenlightened people who split the unity of Principle and phenomena into a
bipartite antinomy. The ideal person's attitude and perception that resulted from
his spiritual cultivation transcends this ordinary distinction. Thus, in the political arena, Kuo's sage pays attention to both withdrawal and participation; and in
fact, participation may perhaps even be superior to withdrawal at least in the
physical sense. The unity of participation and withdrawal occurs when the sage

actually takes part in mundane affairs but spiritually detaches himself from the gains and losses involved. By this standard, Kuo, like Wang Pi, did not consider the Taoist masters Lao-tzu and Chuang-tzu to be sages.[43] Instead, his sage was also Confucius. To be sure, Confucius was no hermit compared to the legendary Lao-tzu and the historical Chuang-tzu. Thus, contrary to the traditional Taoist eulogy of Hsü Yu, a hermit who, according to a legend in the *Chuang-tzu*, turned down the invitation to serve the state by the Confucian sage-king Yao,[44] Kuo Hsiang rated Yao above Hsü Yu on his merit of being "sagely within and kingly without."[45] Yao was a prime example of "governing by not governing and acting by not acting." His successful rulership did not depend upon Hsü Yu's alleged ability to assist him. Kuo then seriously challenged the notion of the sage sitting back in his transcendental cocoon without kingly merit in the phenomenal realm.:

> Are we to insist that a man fold his arms and sit in silence in the middle of some mountain forest before we will say he is practicing non-action? This is why the words of Lao-tzu and Chuang-tzu are rejected by responsible officials. This is why responsible officials insist on remaining themselves in the realm of action without regret. . . . For egotistical people set themselves up against things, whereas he who is in accord with things is not opposed to them. . . . Therefore he profoundly and deeply responds to things without any deliberate mind of his own and follows whatever comes into contact with him. He is like an untied boat drifting, claiming neither the east nor the west to be his own.[46]

It is not difficult to see that Kuo Hsiang attempted to strike a balance between a Taoist philosophy of social estrangement and the Confucian philosophy of social participation, thus collapsing the doctrinal boundaries of the two doctrines. In early medieval terms, it was known as the "unity of the teaching of names and spontaneity" (*ming-chiao yü tzu-jan ho-i*). This balance was reached and justified by the Neo-Taoist dichotomy of substance and function, a fundamental concept in the Neo-Taoist metaphysical dualism. Having the virtue of being "sagely within" is tantamount to having embodied substance, and having the merit of being "kingly without" is acquiring the ability to manifest the virtue of being "sagely within" in the human realm.

Because of his emphasis on the immanence of Principle, Kuo Hsiang, in spite of his contrasting Principle with facts,[47] perhaps did not contribute as much as Wang Pi to the construct of metaphysical dualism. His major contribution seems to have resided in his theory of self-cultivation as a gateway to absolute freedom. Kuo Hsiang's ideal person does not have a deliberate mind of his own. The ideal person's egoless mind will "penetrate to the utmost the perfect union of yin and yang and understand most clearly the wonderful principles of the myriad things. Therefore he can identify himself with changes and harmonize with transformations, and find everything all right wherever he may go."[48] Indeed, it is precisely in eliminating his deliberate mind and following his own self-nature in unison with the transformations of the myriad things that the ideal person can straddle both the transcendental and the phenomenal worlds and roam freely in them.[49] As will be discussed later, Kuo Hsiang's theory of emptying out one's egotistic mind was consistently incorporated into Huang K'an's *Subcommentaries on the Analects*, which also draws a distinction between the transcendental realm and the phenomenal realm.

REDRAWING BOUNDARIES TO ACCOMMODATE THE TRANSCENDENTAL

The development of early medieval Confucian metaphysics was made possible only because the Confucians, as represented by Huang K'an in his *Subcommentaries on the Analects*, were consciously aware of the distinction between a transcendental realm and a phenomenal realm, and they elaborated, in a concerted effort, the attributes of the two realms and the possible relationship between them. In drawing a distinction between the transcendental and phenomenal realms, the Confucians unmistakably owed their inspiration to the Neo-Taoists. In *Analects* 7.6, Confucius said, "I set my heart (*chih*) on the Way (*tao*), base myself on virtue, lean upon benevolence for support and take my recreation in the arts."[50] Ho Yen rejected all Han commentaries on this passage and introduced his Taoist interpretation. He glossed *chih* in its verbal sense as "to admire" (*mu*) and said that "Tao cannot be embodied, and therefore, one can only look up to it with admiration."[51] Now, it is well known that Confucius claimed that Tao is not far from man,[52] but Ho Yen gave Tao a new character — it is not within the reach of man, such that man "can only look up to it with admiration." Thus, Ho Yen did not read *chih* as "to set one's heart on" because "Tao cannot be embodied."[53] Since Tao is beyond the human realm, it is formless, as opposed to virtue, which, as Ho Yen claimed, "has a concrete form to rely on."[54] A distinction is drawn between the formless realm where Tao resides and the realm of form where virtues are concretized.

Although Ho Yen seems to have distinguished the formless from form, he himself did not explicitly describe Tao as formless. This point, rather, was spelt out in Huang K'an's subcommentary where he interprets Ho's statement "Tao cannot be embodied" to mean "Tao has no form."[55] It appears that Huang differs from Ho in that he might have claimed that Tao can be embodied while Ho claimed that this is not feasible. Indeed, Huang urges that Tao should be kept in one's mind all the time. Huang describes the attributes of Tao as follows: "Tao is that which pervades [everywhere] without being blocked. Being pervasive, Tao thus has no form. Therefore, man should always keep it in his mind with admiration. Even in a hurry he would not leave it momentarily."[56] The idea that Tao cannot be separated from man for a moment is of course Confucian.[57] Nevertheless, Huang's description of Tao and his new Confucian approach to Tao (by embodying) are by no means Confucian. Rather, they are directly borrowed from the Neo-Taoist Wang Pi.

In his commentary on the same passage, which was not explicitly quoted by Huang K'an, Wang Pi glosses the word Tao as follows: "Tao is the appellation for Nonbeing. There is nothing that it does not pervade and there is nothing that does not follow it. Therefore, [Nonbeing] is compared to a path (*tao*). Being tranquil (*chi-jan*), it has not a concrete body and cannot be represented by an image. Thus, Tao cannot be felt and *one can only keep it in mind with admiration*."[58] Thus, the conclusion may be drawn that Huang K'an instilled the Neo-Taoist notion of the ultimate Nonbeing into the Confucian notion of Tao. As a result, Huang began to draw a distinction between the formless Nonbeing and beings with concrete forms. This conclusion further points to the fact that under the influence of Neo-Taoism, Huang K'an as a Confucian would look back at his Confucian tradition differently; his new Confucian horizon was inclusive of a Taoist vision of metaphysics. For Huang K'an at least, the Confucian *Analects* needed to be reinterpreted.

The line between the formless and form is made even more clearcut in Huang K'an's subcommentary on *Analects* 2.9. Huang says, "What is above form and vessel (*hsing-ch'i*) is called Nonbeing. It is what the sage embodies. What is below form and vessel is called being. It is what the worthy possesses."[59] As noted earlier, Wang Pi ranked Confucius as the sage above the Taoist master Lao-tzu, and the very reason he did so was that Confucius was able to embody Nonbeing whereas Lao-tzu could only talk about it. In other words, Confucius operated at the level above form and vessel while Lao-tzu was confined to the level below form and vessel. Huang no doubt adopted Wang Pi's metaphysical dualism.

It is important to point out, however, that Huang did not necessarily consider Nonbeing as the ultimate accessible only to the sage. Rather, it is clear that he distinguished a metaphysical hierarchy of selfhood with the sage at the pinnacle. Though borrowing is difficult to ascertain, there is a striking similarity between Huang K'an's notion of metaphysical hierarchy of selfhood and a line of early medieval Chinese Buddhist thought that acknowledged gradual cultivation toward the goal of nirvana. Chinese monks like Chih Tun (314–366) and Seng Chao (384–414), both influential thinkers before Huang K'an's times, were two major proponents of gradual enlightenment. Both monks sequenced the process of enlightenment into ten stages, with the sixth stage as the watershed. Once a person reaches the sixth stage, he is said to have attained lesser enlightenment. Great enlightenment or nirvana is finally consummated when the person reaches the tenth stage. According to Seng Chao, the attainment of nirvana means that a person has acquired the transcendental body of the Buddha (*dharmakāya*) and entered the realm of Nonbeing. His mind cannot be fathomed by intellect, nor can his body be recognized through images. His achievement is "immeasurable," whereas a person whose attainment does not exceed the sixth stage is said to have "measurable" achievement.[60] The transcendental body of the Buddha in the realm of Nonbeing naturally calls for comparison with Huang K'an's notion of the sage who embodies the transcendental Nonbeing.

Earlier we have seen that Ho Yen interpreted "virtue" as something that "has a concrete form to rely on," but the distinction between the formless and form is only implicit there. With Huang's elaboration of "virtue" as "that which fulfills Principle through practicing concrete affairs," in contrast to his interpretation of Tao as "having no form," "concrete affairs" (having forms) and the formless Principle (Tao) are juxtaposed in contradistinction. Thus, for Huang, principle is formless, whereas affairs have forms.[61]

Furthermore, Huang asserted that the all-inclusive Principle exists prior to affairs, and affairs are the manifestations of Principle.[62] Based on this understanding, Huang saw new significance in the order of the title of the *Analects*, *Lun-yü*. *Lun* (discourse), as Huang interpreted it, refers to the exposition of the all-inclusive Principle, whereas *yü* (conversation) refers to the elaboration of the affairs that manifest the all-inclusive Principle.[63] *Lun* and *yü* thus form a one-many relation, and the *Analects* as a whole forms a one-many relation with all other Confucian classics. Indeed, Huang treated the *Analects* as the work that encompassed the teachings found in all Confucian classics.[64]

A NEW UNION OF HEAVEN AND MAN IN THE SUBSTANCE-FUNCTION DICHOTOMY

Having drawn the distinction between the transcendental realm and the human realm, Huang K'an next defined their relationship. Following Wang Pi again, Huang K'an considered the transcendental realm and the human realm to be intimately related. In fact, Principle, which resides in the transcendental realm, finds its expression in the human realm, while all the affairs in the human realm are governed by Principle. The two realms are thus mutually dependent upon each other. Yet, in order to make the claim that Principle and affairs are united and mutually dependent, Wang Pi had to assume that Principle is somehow immanent in affairs. As noted earlier, Kuo Hsiang single-mindedly advocated the immanence of Principle in the myriad beings. Indeed, Kuo's position might not have been so drastically different from that of Wang Pi, as traditional scholarship has us believe. Nevertheless, Wang Pi never mentioned the term *ch'ün-li* for "multitudinous principles" as did Kuo Hsiang, because his major interest was in *t'ung-li* (general principle). In his *Subcommentaries*, Huang K'an often introduces both the commentaries of Wang Pi and Kuo Hsiang, apparently in an attempt to bridge the gap between them.

In *Analects* 4.15, Confucius said to his disciple Tseng Ts'an, "Ts'an! There is one single thread binding my way together." . . . Tseng Tzu (Ts'an) said, "The way of the Master consists in doing one's best and in using oneself as a measure to gauge others. That is all."[65] Huang K'an interprets this to mean that "the way of Confucius's teaching is to unite the *ten thousand principles* (*wan-li*) in the world with *one single Tao* (*i-tao*)."[66] This interpretation is based on Wang Pi's commentary which Huang K'an quoted as saying, "Affairs have their resting place and Principle has unifying power. Therefore, as long as the resting place is obtained, although an affair may be complicated, it can be summed up with one single name. Similarly, as long as the unifying power gathers together, although Principle may be expansive, it can be summed up in the simplest terms."[67] Here, Wang Pi also explicitly contrasts Principle with affairs. Moreover, he further implies that Principle is necessarily found in affairs and affairs are governed by one single Principle.

When Huang K'an said that the way of Confucius's teaching is to unite the myriad principles in the world with one single Tao, he was indeed saying that every being has a principle that can be identified with the single universal Tao, which, as noted earlier, he already identified as Nonbeing. Every individual principle, like tributaries of a stream, is a particular derivation of the single universal Tao, which is comparable to the ocean. A formal relationship between the transcendental principle and the myriad things with their respective share of the principle was finally established. Such a relationship suggests that there is a one-many relation between the transcendental principle and the myriad things. As Huang K'an quoted Wang Pi as saying, "Once being able to fathom the ultimate of Principle, then there is nothing that cannot be united. Since this ultimate is so unique that there is not another like it, it is called one [as opposed to the myriad things]."[68] This one-many relation between the transcendental realm and the human realm indeed is what Wang Pi would call the substance-function relation.[69]

THE IDEAL PERSON IN EARLY MEDIEVAL CONFUCIAN METAPHYSICS

Since the transcendental and the human realms are united, the transcendental dualism espoused in Huang K'an's *Subcommentaries* naturally has a bearing on the early medieval Confucian concept of the ideal person. Being the ultimate origin of the myriad things, the transcendental Principle or Nonbeing is, above all, the ontic fount of human values. Nonbeing not only guarantees the order of things in the human world, but it also serves as an axiological model for human beings to emulate. Through a process of self-cultivation, human beings will eventually be able to act in accord with their comprehensive understanding of Nonbeing, allowing their self-nature to be one with Nonbeing. This ultimate apotheosis is called the embodiment of Nonbeing, and the ideal person who achieves this state of spirituality is considered to be the sage.

As pointed out before, Wang Pi ranked Confucius as the sage above the Taoist master Lao-tzu, and the very reason he did so was that Confucius was able to embody Nonbeing whereas Lao-tzu could only talk about it. By talking about Nonbeing, Lao-tzu was ironically attached to the realm of phenomenal beings nonetheless. Clearly, the transcendental Nonbeing supersedes phenomenal beings. This point, as we have seen, was further elaborated in Huang K'an's *Subcommentaries* when Huang defined "what is above form and vessel" as "Nonbeing," which the sage embodies, and "what is below form and vessel" as "being," which the worthies possess. In Huang K'an's mind, only Confucius's virtue was commensurate with the laurels of the sage. Even his best disciple Yen Hui could deserve only the name of a worthy.[70]

Huang K'an praised the greatness of Confucius, which was beyond any description and cannot be pinpointed with a particular laudatory appellation. Citing Wang Pi, Huang compared the greatness of Confucius to a piece of harmonious music that was composed of eight notes but by no means identified with any one of them.[71] Here, harmonious music is an analogy to Nonbeing, which is beyond any finite attributes; the sage is he who embodies Nonbeing and does not get himself attached to finite things. In *Analects* 7.38, it says, "The Master is cordial yet stern, awe-inspiring yet not fierce, and respectful yet at ease."[72] Huang K'an concluded that all these personal qualities were Confucius's virtues (te) which, as we recall, he interpreted to mean "that which fulfills Principle through practicing concrete affairs." In the case of Confucius, since he was able to embody Nonbeing, his virtues naturally manifested Principle to its fullest and were not confined to any specific moral excellence. Thus, Confucius was able to embody Nonbeing (Principle) and manifested it in the human arena. He thus straddled both the transcendental and the phenomenal realms. In Confucius, substance and function were united in harmony.

In singing praise of Confucius's moral transcendence, Huang K'an cites Wang Pi's Neo-Taoist commentary:

> Being cordial cannot be stern whereas being stern cannot be cordial. Being awe-inspiring, one's mind will be fierce and being fierce, one cannot be awe-inspiring. Being respectful cannot be at ease whereas being at ease cannot be respectful. These are the names of opposites. If one can be cordial yet stern, awe-inspiring yet not fierce, respectful yet at ease, one thus has the unnameable Principle to the fullest. Therefore in well-balanced seasoning the five flavors cannot be identified; in symphonic music the five tones cannot be distinguished. In centrality (*chung*) and harmony (*ho*) all qualities are encompassed and the five powers cannot be [specifically] named.[73]

Thus, it is clear that the early medieval Confucians represented by Huang K'an held Confucius in the highest esteem because of his moral transcendence, defined in Neo-Taoist metaphysical terms rather than traditional Confucian humanistic and moralistic terms.

Confucius was known for his versatility in teaching and enlightening his disciples of varying degree of intelligence. In Huang K'an's *Subcommentaries*, this versatility is attributed to Confucius's embodiment of Nonbeing, which enables him to respond to his external environment in the most appropriate way. Citing Miu Po, Huang K'an explains the altruism of Confucius as follows: "Responding to external beings without calculated choosing is called [following] the Way. Relieving the world without shirking is called the sage. When external beings are in trouble, one cannot help but come to their rescue; when Principle calls for it, one cannot help but respond."[74] Thus, to lead his disciples to pursue the Way is simply a natural, spontaneous self-realization of Confucius's sagehood.

Not only was Confucius given a Neo-Taoist aura as a sage, but he was also revered as if he were a Buddhist bodhisattva who adopted expedient liberative measures to stimulate and enlighten his disciples whenever the situation called for it.[75] According to Seng Chao, a bodhisattva possesses four fearless virtues: (1) capable of hearing and keeping the dharma and having absolute control over good and evil passions and influences; (2) capable of knowing the roots of intelligence and of sentient beings; (3) capable of overcoming and answering all sorts of intellectual challenges; and (4) capable of responding to questions posed to him and dispelling doubts.[76] By these standards, the Confucius as understood by Huang K'an is practically a bona fide bodhisattva.

Following the Taoist Li Ch'ung, Huang considered Confucius to be the sage whose mysterious understanding of Nonbeing was too subtle and profound for ordinary mortals to realize, yet he was never satisfied with his own personal transformation (*tu-hua*).[77] Rather, he would mingle himself with the rest of the world, trying to stimulate and encourage people to achieve their own transformation through the teachings pertaining to the realm of "form and vessel."[78] Like the Buddha, Confucius gave every seeker of truth a unique dose of medicine with regard to his particular illness.[79] In Huang's understanding, Confucius's responses to his disciples comprise the "affairs" that manifest his embodiment of Principle. The affairs, albeit different, are all "united" in the all-inclusive principle in that they equally illuminate it.

How is a person capable of embodying Nonbeing? To the Neo-Taoists, only the sage is capable of attaining such metaphysical transcendence and that is why they emulated only Lao-tzu and Chuang-tzu, who were still bound to the realm of phenomenal beings. The virtue of Confucius was simply too lofty to be emulated and thus Yen Hui was, instead, seated at the top of the echelon of Confucian exemplars because supreme as it was, Yen's spiritual accomplishment was within the reach of self-cultivation.[80] Early medieval Confucians, however, entertained a different view of emulation. Though they adopted the Neo-Taoist view of embodying Nonbeing, they did not believe that the embodiment of Nonbeing was accessible only to Confucius. It was learning that was most crucial in self-cultivation.[81] Sagehood was not a matter of fate. Rather, it was a process of understanding the all-inclusive Principle through self-cultivation. Most importantly, this lifelong process was open to anyone who was determined to set one's mind on learning. It appears that it is precisely the emergence of this Neo-Taoist-inspired metaphysics that filled up the theoretical vacuum in the early medieval Confucian justification for morality.

SELF-CULTIVATION AND THE DOCTRINE OF NO-MIND

For the early medieval Confucians, the goal of self-cultivation is sagehood characterized by the embodiment of Nonbeing. Sagely virtue needs to be nurtured within, and thus the sage embraces what lies within his physical form and is oblivious to what falls external to it.[82] Only when the sage cultivates his inner mind can he embody Nonbeing. In embodying Nonbeing the sage's mind is always empty without encumbrance. He can naturally make responses that befit the circumstances. On the other hand, the worthy is still bound to the realm of form and vessel. Unable to embody Nonbeing, he can simply emulate the sage in admiration, with his mind being intermittently empty.[83]

Boldly reinterpreting *Analects* 11.17, where Yen Hui was said to be constantly in dire poverty (*lü-k'ung*), Ho Yen first took *k'ung* (penniless) to mean "to be empty inside" (*hsü-chung*).[84] Second, he elaborated that Yen Hui's mind was not "empty" enough to understand the Way. Following Ho Yen's interpretation, Huang K'an first of all identified Yen Hui as a worthy rather than a sage, and he further noted that because Yen Hui could keep his mind empty only intermittently, the emptiness was not consistent, thus it is called "often empty" (*lü-k'ung*).[85] Elsewhere Huang further explained that the difference between Confucius the sage and Yen Hui the worthy lay in the fact that Yen could fully cultivate only his physical body whereas Confucius ventured beyond his physical form into his spirit (*shen*).[86] The distinction between body and spirit drawn here no doubt corresponds to that between the realm beyond form and the realm below form mentioned earlier. Thus, Yen Hui's spiritual accomplishment was limited and he naturally had difficulty in emulating Confucius.[87]

When the early medieval Confucians claimed that the mind was empty, they really meant that the mind was empty of desires. Indeed, Huang K'an identified Yen Hui's practice of "sitting in forgetfulness" (*tso-wang*) mentioned in the *Chuang-tzu* with the cultivation of emptiness in his mind.[88] Sitting in forgetfulness calls for setting aside benevolence and rightness, forgetting rituals and music, casting off the physical body, and doing away with the intellect.[89] This attempt at forgetting the totality of being, albeit marvelous, is nonetheless a form of attachment. Of course, the entire episode in the *Chuang-tzu* is fictitious, but to the philosophically minded Huang K'an, history and fiction could be blended together to form a philosophical syncretism. The historical Yen Hui whose mind, as Huang K'an interpreted it, was "often empty," was now identified as the fictional Yen Hui who, being a spokesman for Taoism, practiced sitting in forgetfulness. The religious Taoist Ku Huan noted that the worthy consciously aims at ridding the mind of desires and thus he is ironically bound to desires. On the other hand, since the sage has no desire whatsoever, he is truly desireless.[90] The attempt at ultimate forgetfulness and detachment no doubt resembles Kuo Hsiang's notion of absolute freedom noted earlier.

Truly desireless, the sage is said to have no mind — that is, having no deliberate mind of his own. Wang Pi once explained that the sage shares all human feelings with his fellow beings, yet he is able not to get attached to things or humans he interacts with.[91] Kuo Hsiang also held the view that the sage has feelings but can keep them under the control of Principle. And when one's feelings are guided by Principle, the sage is able to comply with his nature so that his spiritual intelligence will shine forth.[92] Human nature is essentially tranquil. When Nonbeing is embodied, the sage is attached to neither sorrow nor joy, and yet he can always respond situationally with the appropriate sentiment.[93] As Kuo Hsiang succinctly puts it, the sage "wails as other people wail and he grieves as other people grieve. This is because a person with no feeling has transformed himself with all beings."[94] What Kuo actually means here is that the sage has no deliberate mind. Thus, he has no feeling that attaches to and craves for things. The sage "interacts with the world without a deliberate mind of his own."[95] The line between deliberate mind and nondeliberate mind also demarcates Confucius's sageliness from Yen Hui's worthiness.[96]

It is probable that Huang K'an's theory of no mind also reflected the Chinese Buddhist theory of self-cultivation, most notable in the commentaries by Kumarajiva and his student Seng Chao on the *Vimalakīrtinirdeśa*. To begin with, Kumarājīva identifies the mind as the basis of virtues. The mind is the agent of virtues.[97] Thus, all cultivation naturally starts with the care for the mind. According to Kumarajiva, the Buddha's mind is free of discrimination and distinction-making.[98] Similarly, Seng Chao claims that the sage's mind should always be free of defilements (*wu-hsin*); only then can the sage treat everything equally as empty. If a mind has deliberative intention, it is then subject to limitations. Being confined, the mind will not be able to treat things equally as empty,[99] because it will then wallow between conventional truth and falsehood.[100] The sage should treat things as they are. Beauty and ugliness, if such distinguishing attributes ever exist, belong to things themselves; they have nothing to do with our judgment.[101] All illusory perceptions come from the working of our mind.[102] When our mind becomes attached to phenomena, we will become bound to them. As soon as our mind becomes untainted again, all the bonds will be released.[103] Thus, the sage's mind should not be attached to anything, because he, having reached the tenth stage of enlightenment, has a mind that transcends the notions of self and other. [104] Only then will the myriad phenomena be equally illuminated without the mind's having retained anything.[105]

Despite this similarity, the early medieval Confucian doctrine of no mind differs from the Chinese Buddhist counterpart in that while the Buddhist doctrine is predicated on the belief in the emptiness of phenomena, the Confucian doctrine is firmly grounded on the Neo-Taoist theory of embodying Nonbeing. As long as the sage embodies Nonbeing in a state of no mind, even desire, let alone feeling, is not considered to be intrinsically bad. Occasionally, desire is deemed undesirable because it is believed to be capable of misguiding feeling and leading it astray from human nature. Thus, a strong emphasis on nurturing human nature so as to ward off feeling and desire is sometimes evident. With this emphasis, the early medieval Confucian doctrine retained its integrity in spite of its shifting doctrinal boundaries.

The foregoing analysis of Huang K'an's formulation of Confucian metaphysics shows that when philosophic boundaries shift, they often do so to include and assimilate rather than exclude and dissociate from a new domain. It should be noted that the shifting of the Confucian doctrinal boundaries in this case was not forced upon the Confucian thinkers by anyone; it was rather much like a self-realigning process that constantly redefined the essence of what the Confucian doctrine was over time under given historical circumstances. Boundaries in the end are perhaps meaningless as a distinction-making device because as a human construct, they are ultimately the handmaiden for the exigencies intrinsic to any vibrant and thriving doctrine.

NOTES

1. Fan Yeh (398–445), *Hou-han shu* (Later Han History), "Ju-lin chuan" (Biographies of Confucian Scholars), quoted in P'i Hsi-jui, *Ching-hsüeh li-shih* (History of Scholarship on the Confucian Classics), with Chou Yü-t'ung's annotations (Shanghai: Chung-hua, 1959), 114.

2. P'i, *Ching-hsüeh li-shih*, 101–40. Specifically, P'i considers the period from 48 B.C. to the end of the Han the pinnacle of Confucian learning.

3. Huan Tan, *Hsin-lun*, quoted in P'i, *Ching-hsüeh li-shih*, 134.

4. Ch'en Shou (233–297), *San-kuo chih*, *chuan* 16, quoted in P'i, *Ching-hsüeh li-shih*, 141. We do not mean to say that Confucianism as a way of thinking and a guiding principle of living completely lost its grip on the people. There were still people who remained upright and saw their mission in maintaining the Confucian order of morality. See, for example, Yü Chia-hsi, *Shih-shuo hsin-yü chien-shu* (Peking: Chung-hua shu-chü, 1983), 6; Richard B. Mather, *A New Account of Tales of the World* (Minneapolis: University of Minnesota Press, 1976), 5.

5. *San-kuo chih*, *chuan* 13, quoted in P'i, *Ching-hsüeh li-shih*, 141.

6. Ho Ch'i-min, *Wei-Chin ssu-hsiang yü t'an-feng* (Taipei: Hsüeh-sheng shu-chü, 1976), 41–44.

7. Wang Hsien-ch'ien, *Hou-han shu chi-chieh*, 5 vols. (Peking: Shangwu yin-shu-kuan, 1959), *chuan* 50a, 3:2111–12.

8. See Yü Chia-hsi, *Shih-shuo*, 200; Mather, 96.

9. Wang Pi's commentary is called *Lun-yü shih-i* (Clarification of the Doubts in the *Analects*) and Kuo Hsiang's commentary is called *Lun-yü t'i-lüeh* (The Skeletal Gist of the *Analects*); both are listed in the bibliographical section in the Sui-shu (Sui History).

10. Chiang Hsi's collected commentary, also known as *Lun-yü chi-chieh*, was recorded in the bibliographical section of the *Sui History*.

11. Actually thirty-three commentators were cited by name in Huang K'an's *Subcommentaries*. However, two of them, namely, Cheng Hsüan (127–200) and Wang Su (195–256), were also cited by Ho Yen. Yet, this is not to say that Huang K'an's citations from these two commentators are identical with those cited by Ho Yen. On the other hand, four of the thirteen commentators were not, at least explicitly, cited by Huang K'an in his *Subcommentaries*.

12. For a detailed but by no means complete list of early medieval commentaries on the *Analects*, see the bibliographical section in the *Sui History*.

13. Yü Chia-hsi, *Shih-shuo*, 109; Mather, *New Account*, 54.

14. Yao Ssu-lien, *Liang-shu*, 3 vols. (Peking: Chung-hua shu-chü, 1973), *chuan* 48, 3:680–81. See also Huang's biography in Li Yen-shou's *Nan-shih*, 6 vols. (Peking: Chung-hua shu-chü, 1978), *chuan* 71, 6:1744.

15. Ho Yang's grandfather was also known for his scholarship on the *Book of Rites*, the *Ceremonials* and the *Protocols of Chou*, and he was said to have transmitted the scholarship of his family. See Yao Ssu-lien, *Liang-shu*, *chuan* 48, 3:672. See also *Nan-shih*, *chuan* 62, 5:1507.

16. Both texts were recorded in the bibliographical section in the *Sui History*.

17. *Nan-shih*, 6:1744.

18. For samples of these miraculous tales from the early medieval period, see Robert Ford Campany, "The Earliest Tales of the Bodhisattva Guanshiyin," in Donald S. Lopez Jr., ed., *Religions of China in Practice* (Princeton, N.J: Princeton University Press, 1996), 82–96.

19. Huang K'an wrote a subcommentary on the *Book of Filial Piety*. See Wu Ch'eng-shih, *Shih-wen hsü-lu shu-cheng* (Peking: Chung-hua shu-chü, 1986), 138. Earlier we have seen that Chang Jung demanded to have a copy of *Book of Filial Piety* and *Lao-tzu* placed in his left hand and a copy of the *Lotus Sutra* placed in the other hand. Chang was also known for his filiality in his times. *Nan-shih*, 3:836. It should be noted also that the *Kuan-shih-yin ching* is in fact a chapter singled out from the *Lotus Sutra*. Meanwhile, the religious Taoist Ku Huan, who was indeed also a professor of Confucian classics, reportedly preached the *Lao-tzu* to

dispel animal spirits and advised sick people to sleep by the *Book of Filial Piety* to cure their ailments. See Ku's biography in *Nan-shih, chuan* 75, 6:1874–75. Thus, it is probable that early medieval thinkers saw a certain kind of affinity among the three classics from different traditions.

20. Huang K'an, *i-shu,* 11.11, 6:7a.

21. Ibid., 6:6b. The distinction between "inner" (*nei*) and "outer" (*wai*) with the former being superior undoubtedly comes from the early medieval hierarchy of *fang-nei* (within the realm of form) and *fang-wai* (beyond the realm of form). Ironically, the inner teachings are meant to liberate one beyond the realm of form. Huang K'an's admiration for the sage roaming beyond the realm of form encouraged him to radically reinterpret *Analects* 14.46. The passage in question mentions a figure named Yuan Jang who sat with his legs spread wide. Taking it as an offense of propriety, Confucius reprimanded him by calling him, among other things, a "pest (*tse*)." But Huang K'an's commentary praises Yuan Rang and calls him "a sage beyond the realm of form" (*fang-wai chih sheng-jen*). Meanwhile, Confucius is considered "a sage within the realm of form" (*fang-nei chih sheng-jen*) who always concerned himself with rituals and edification. See ibid., 7:45b. Compare Huang K'an's *Subcommentary on the Book of Rites* where he also praises Yuan Jang as the "supremely sagely person." See *Li-chi Huang-shih i-shu* (Master Huang's Subcommentary on the *Book of Rites*) in Ma Kuo-han, ed., *Yü-ha-shan-fang chi-i-shu* (Hunan: Hsiang-yuan-t'ang edition, 1884), vol. 32, 198b. Huang's comment easily reminds us of Juan Chi (210–263), who defiantly decried Confucian ritualism by saying "Were the rites established for people like me?" See Yü Chia-hsi, *Shih-shuo,* 731; Mather, *New Account,* 374. And in the eyes of his contemporaries, Juan Chi was a man beyond the realm of form (*fang-wai chih jen*). Yü Chia-hsi, *Shih-shuo,* 734; Mather, 375.

22. For this reason, the Confucius as understood by Huang K'an was probably not the same one who he called "the sage within the realm."

23. For a brief introduction to the biographies of the commentators, see Wu Ch'eng-shih, *Shih-wen hsü-lu shu-cheng* (Peking: Chung-hua, 1986), 147–53.

24. Li's commentary was known as *Lun-yü chi-chu* in a seventh-century bibliography. See Wu Ch'eng-shih, *Shih-wen hsü-lu shu-ch'eng,* 144.

25. Yü Chia-hsi, *Shih-shuo;* 242, Mather, *New Account,* 124. It must also be noted that Yin was also known for his understanding of Buddhist philosophy in his time. For instance, see Yü Chia-hsi, *Shih-shuo,* 214; Mather, 104.

26. Chiang Hsi, the compiler of a subcommentary before Huang K'an, was cited most often (93 times) and we can tell from his commentaries that Jiang Hsi was a Neo-Taoist thinker. The Neo-Taoist Li Ch'ung came second with 63 citations and the Confucian Fan Ning followed with 48 citations. It is by no means insignificant that Wang Pi was cited 42 times as the fourth most frequently cited commentator.

The *Lun-yü chi-chieh i-shu* was influential in the early medieval period and was carried to Japan during the T'ang dynasty. In the Sung dynasty the *Subcommentaries* became a substantial blueprint for the official commentary on the *Analects*, the *Lun-yü cheng-i* (The Orthodox Commentary on the *Analects*) by Hsing Ping (932–1010). The *Subcommentaries*, however, was lost around the thirteenth century. When the Neo-Confucian notion of lineage transmission of doctrinal orthodoxy was firmly established and Chu Hsi's (1130–1200) commentaries on the *Four Books* were finally made the core of curriculum studied by candidates for civil service in the thirteenth century, Huang K'an's *Subcommentaries* simply fell into oblivion. It was not until the eighteenth century that the work was brought back from Japan and called for new attention in China.

27. Cited by Chang Tsan (fl.317) in his commentary on the *Lieh-tzu*. See Yang Po-chün, *Lieh-tzu*, 11.

28. "Tao-lun," cited in Yang Po-chün, *Lieh-tzu*, 11.

29. Ibid.

30. Wing-tsit Chan, *Source Book*, 323.

31. For a good discussion of Wang Pi's idea of Principle, see Ch'ien Mu, *Chuang-Lao t'ung-pien* (General Studies of *Chuang-tzu* and *Lao-tzu*) (Kowloon: Hsin-ya yen-chiu-so, 1957), 346–53. See also Ariane Rump (in collaboration with Wing-tsit Chan), trans., *Commentary on the Lao Tzu by Wang Pi*, Monographs of the Society for Asian and Comparative Philosophy no.6 (Hawaii: University of Hawaii Press, 1979), xi–xvi.

32. Lou Yü-lieh, *Wang-Pi chi*, 2:591.

33. Ibid., 1:34 (chap. 15).

34. Ibid., 1:117–18 (chap. 42), 1:126 (chap. 47).

35. In his commentary on chapter 38 of *Lao-tzu*, Wang Pi first proposed the concepts of *t'i* (substance) and *yung* (function) in the history of Chinese thought. There *t'i* is identified with Nonbeing. See Wing-tsit Chan, *Source Book*, 323. For a discussion of Wang Pi's understanding of the substance-function dichotomy, see Ch'ien Mu, *Chuang-Lao*, 379–84.

36. Wang Pi's commentary on the *ch'ien* hexagram, Lou, *Wang-Pi chi*, 1:216.

37. Ariane Rump and Wing-tsit Chan, *Commentary on the Lao Tzu*, xii.

38. Yü Chia-hsi, *Shih-shuo*, 199; Mather, *New Account*, 96. The translation is slightly modified. Emphasis is mine.

39. See Kuo's commentary on the *Chuang-tzu*, chap. 2, Kuo Ch'ing-fan, *Chuang-tzu chi-shih*, 2 vols. (Taipei: Shih-chieh shu-chü, 1971), 1:85.

40. Ch'ien Mu, *Chuang-Lao*, 365.

41. Kuo Ch'ing-fan, *Chuang-tzu*, chap. 2, 1:84.

42. Ibid., chap. 12, 1:406.

43. In the preface to his commentary on the *Chuang-tzu*, Kuo Hsiang decried Chuang-tzu as a man who understood "the way of sagely within and

kingly without" and yet "was unable to embody it." And the Sage is certainly not someone who talks about Tao in the transcendental realm without embodying it in the phenomenal realm. Kuo Ch'ing-fan, *Chuang-tzu*, 1:5.

44. Ibid., chap. 1, 1:22–24.

45. Hsiang Hsiu, another prominent commentator on the *Chuang-tzu*, criticized Hsü Yu as "timid, pusillanimous" and "not worthy of much emulation." See Yü Chia-hsi, *Shih-shuo*, 79; Mather, *New Account*, 40.

46. Kuo Ch'ing-fan, *Chuang-tzu*, 1:24.

47. Kuo Ch'ing-fan, *Chuang-tzu*, chap. 2, 1:22, chap. 11,1:400.

48. Wing-tsit Chan, *Source Book*, 328.

49. Ibid., 333.

50. D.C. Lau, trans., The *Analects* (Harmondsworth, U.K.: Penguin Books, 1979), 86.

51. Huang K'an, *I-shu*, 7.6, 4:3a.

52. For example, see *Analects*, 7.30.

53. Contrary to Ho Yen, Wang Pi claimed that the sage is able to embody Nonbeing. This is one of the important differences between Ho Yen and Wang Pi in their philosophy of Nonbeing.

54. Huang K'an, *i-shu*, 7.6, 4:3a.

55. Ibid., 4:3b.

56. Ibid., 4:3b. See also 14.7, 7:21b–22a.

57. See, for instance, the first chapter of the *Doctrine of the Mean*.

58. Wang Pi, *Lun-yü shih-i* (Clarification of Doubts in the Analects). See Lou Yü-lieh, ed. (with annotations), *Wang-Pi chi chiao-shih*, 2 vols. (Peking: Chung-hua shu-chü, 1980), 2:624.

59. Ibid., 1:23b.

60. Li I-cho, ed., *Wei-mo-chieh ching chi-chu* (Taipei: Lao-ku ch'u-pan-she, 1983), 27. See also pp. 20, 22.

61. Huang K'an's notion of *shih* includes both affairs/events and objects. See Huang K'an, *i-shu*, 3.15, 2:13b.

62. Wang Pi obviously held the same belief when he said the sage's mind knows the truth prior to his empirical experience. See ibid., 2.4, 1:19b–20a.

63. Ibid., preface to Huang's *Subcommentary*, 3b.

64. Ibid., commentary on the title of the first book, 1:1a.

65. Lau, *Analects*, 74.

66. Huang K'an, *i-shu*, 4.15, 2:31a.

67. Ibid.

68. Ibid., 4.15, 2:31b.

69. See Wang Pi's commentary on chapter 38 of the *Lao-tzu*. He says, "Although [Heaven and Earth] are engaged in great undertakings and have great wealth in possessing the myriad things, each thing still has its own character without being self-sufficient and comprehensive. Therefore, Heaven by itself

cannot carry [the myriad things], earth by itself cannot cover [the myriad things], and man by himself cannot provide for himself sufficiently. Although the myriad things themselves are valuable, nonetheless they rely on Nonbeing to function, and they cannot dispense with Nonbeing as their substance." See Lou, *Wang-Pi chi*, 1:94.

70. Citing Miao Po who said Yen Hui could embody the truth pertaining to the realm of form and vessel, Huang K'an justified his claim that Yen Hui was only a Confucian worthy, not a sage. See Huang K'an, *i-shu*, 2.9, 1:23b.

71. Ibid., 9.2, 5:2b. It should be noted that this musical analogy probably comes from the second chapter of the *Chuang-tzu*.

72. Lau, *Analects*, 91.

73. Huang K'an, *i-shu*, 7.37, 4:21b. The five powers refer to metal, wood, water, fire, and earth. It should be noted that the Neo-Confucian Ch'eng I defined *chung* as in the title of the *Doctrine of the Mean* (*chung-yung*) as "not being one-sided." In Wang Pi's conception, *chung* represents a metaphysical ultimate which is full of infinite potentialities. See also Wang's commentary on *Lao-tzu*, chap. 5. *Chung* is also an ideal virtue to Kuo Hsiang; see Kuo Ch'ing-fan, *Chuang-tzu*, chap. 2, 1:68, chap. 3, 1:116, 3:117, chap. 4, 1:163. Huang K'an interpreted *chung-ho* (centrality and harmony) as "the way of ancient kings whose Principle is supremely good." See Huang K'an, *i-shu*, 6.27, 3:38a. It is noteworthy that when centrality and harmony were given a metaphysical dimension in the early medieval period, they were then used to interpret Confucius's personal name, Chung-ni. For instance, Liu Hsien of the Ch'i dynasty (479–502) interpreted *chung* as centrality and *ni* as harmony, and because Confucius had the virtue of centrality and harmony, so he was called Chung-ni. See *Hsiao-ching Liu-shih shuo* (Liu's Interpretation of the Classic of Filial Piety), in Ma Kuo-han, *Chi-i-shu*, vol. 47, 36a.

74. Huang K'an, *i-shu*, 6.26, 3:37b.

75. Ibid., preface to the *Subcommentary*, 1a–3b.

76. See Seng Chao's commentary on the *Vimalakīrtinirdeśa* in Li I-cho, *Wei-mo-chieh ching*, p. 24. Elsewhere in the commentary, Seng Chao notes that the Buddhist dharma is not confined to any particular phenomenon. The Wonderful King of Dharma expounds on it in accord with the intellectual proclivity of his audience. See ibid., p. 50.

77. The idea of *tu-hua* is distinctive in Kuo Hsiang's Neo-Taoist philosophy.

78. Huang K'an, *i-shu*, 2.4, 1:20a.

79. Ibid., 2.8., 1:23a.

80. In the early medieval period, in fact, Yen Hui was always revered as the model of the highest virtue possible. Confucius was simply beyond the reach of ordinary mortals. For instance, see Yü Chia-hsi, *Shih-shuo*, 107; Mather, *New Account*, 52–53.

81. Incidentally, the early medieval Chinese Buddhists also considered learning to be the basis of practices that ultimately lead to pure nirvana. See, for instance, Seng Chao's commentary on the *Vimalakīrtinirdeśa* in Li I-cho, *Wei-mo-chieh ching*, chap. 1, pp. 60, 67.

82. Huang K'an's subcommentary on *Analects* 4.9 where he relies on the Taoist Li Ch'ung's interpretation. See Huang K'an, *i-shu*, 2:29a.

83. Ibid., 11.17, 6:11a.

84. Ibid., 6:10b.

85. Ibid., 6:11a.

86. Ibid., 11.8, 6:5b. The difference between what lies within the physical body and what lies outside it is also mentioned in the *Chuang-tzu* (chap. 5), and Kuo Hsiang's commentary on that passage also emphasizes the inner virtue within because Principle does not reside in the physical body. See Kuo Ch'ing-fan, *Chuang-tzu*, 1:201, 1:208. To Kuo Hsiang, the inner virtue is the master to which the physical body should be subservient. Ibid., 1:211.

87. See Sun Cho's (314-371) commentary on *Analects* 9.10, quoted by Huang K'an. Huang K'an, *i-shu*, 5:9b–10a.

88. Ibid., 11.17, 6:11a.

89. Kuo Ch'ing-fan, *Chuang-tzu*, chap. 6, 1:284.

90. Huang K'an, *i-shu*, 11.17, 6:11a. This distinction between being desireless and willingness to be desireless is similar to the Buddhist distinction between being in nirvana and willingness to attain nirvana. For instance, see Tao-sheng's (363–434) commentary on the *Vimalakīrtinirdeśa* in Li I-cho, *Wei-mo-chieh ching*, chap. 3, 134.

91. See T'ang Yung-t'ung, "Wang-Pi sheng-jen yu-ch'ing-yi shih" ("An Explanation of Wang Pi's Theory of the Sage Having Feelings"), in his *T'ang Yung-t'ung hsüeh-shu lun-wen chi* (Collection of Scholarly Works by T'ang Yung-t'ung) (Peking: Chung-hua shu-chü, 1983), 254–63.

92. See Kuo Ch'ing-fan, *Chuang-tzu*, 2:617, 2:1091.

93. Miu Po's commentary on *Analects* 11.9, cited in Huang K'an, *i-shu*, 6:5b.

94. Kuo's commentary on *Analects* 11.9, cited in Huang K'an, *i-shu*, 6:5b. See also Kuo's commentary on the *Chuang-tzu*, chap. 6, 1:245–46.

95. Huang K'an, *i-shu*, 15.25, 8:11b.

96. Kuo's commentary on the *Chuang-tzu*; see Kuo Ch'ing-fan, *Chuang-tzu*, chap. 5, 1:221.

97. Li I-cho, *Wei-mo-chieh ching*, chap. 1, 48.

98. Ibid., chap. 1, 52.

99. Ibid., chap. 1, 55.

100. Ibid., chap. 1, 59.

101. Ibid., chap. 1, 61.

102. Ibid., chap. 1, 82.

103. Ibid., chap. 1, 59.
104. Ibid. and chap. 1, 10.
105. Ibid., chap. 1, 52.

GLOSSARY

ch'i	氣
chi-jan	寂然
Chiang Hsi	江熙
Ch'ien Mu	錢穆
chih	志
chih-li	至理
Chih Tun	支遁
Chuang-tzu chu	莊子注
ch'ün-li	群理
chung	中
chung-ho	中和
Chung-ni	仲尼
Fan Ning	范寧
fang-nei	方內
fang-nei chih sheng-jen	方內之聖人
fang-wai	方外
fang-wai chih sheng-jen	方外之聖人
ho	和
Ho Yen	何晏
Hou-han shu	後漢書
Hsiang Hsiu	向秀
hsing-ch'i	形器
hsü-chung	虛中
hsüan-hsüeh	玄學
Hsün Hsü	荀勖
Hsün Ts'an	荀粲
Huang K'an	皇侃
I-ching	易經
i-tao	一道
Ku Huan	顧歡
Ku-liang chuan	穀梁傳
Kuan-shih-yin ching	觀世音經
Kuo Hsiang	郭象
Lao-tzu chu	老子注
li	理
Li-chi chiang-shu	禮記講疏
Li-chi i-shu	禮記義疏

Li Ch'ung	李充
Liang-shu	梁書
Lü-k'ung	屢空
Lun-yü chi-chieh	論語集解
Lun-yü chi-chieh i-shu	論語集解義疏
Ma Jung	馬融
ming-chiao yü tzu-jan ho-i	名教與自然合一
mu	慕
Nan-shih	南史
nei-chiao	內教
P'ei Hui	裴徽
san-hsüan	三玄
Seng Chao	僧肇
Shang-shu	尚書
shen	神
shih	事
Shih-Hui-lin	釋惠琳
Shih P'u-chih	釋普智
Sun Cho	孫綽
tao	道
"Tao-lun"	道論
Tao-te ching	道德經
te	德
t'i-yung	體用
Ts'ao Ts'ao	曹操
tse	賊
tso-wang	坐忘
tu-hua	獨化
Tung Chung-shu	董仲舒
t'ung-li	通理
wai-chiao	外教
wan-li	萬理
Wang Pi	王弼
wu	無
Wu-ching i	五經義
Yen Hui	顏回
Yin Chung-k'an	殷仲堪
Yuan Hung	袁宏

4

Military Governance versus Civil Governance

A Comparison of the Old History and the New History of the Five Dynasties

Tze-ki Hon

THE HISTORIOGRAPHIC PROBLEM OF THE T'ANG-SUNG TRANSITION

In the study of Sung China (960–1279), experts in the field tend to see the period as part of a long process of change dating back to the T'ang (617–907). This six hundred years of change, or the T'ang-Sung transition, is considered to have fundamentally altered political, social, and intellectual life in medieval China. Politically, building on G. William Skinner's findings, many Sung experts view the period as a continuation of the weakening of the Chinese state as Chinese society became increasingly variegated. For these Sung specialists, this weakening of the Chinese state may have begun in the mid-T'ang, but the process definitely quickened when the Sung court was moved in 1127 from K'ai-feng (in the Eastern Yellow River basin) to Hang-chou (in the lower Yangtze River area).[1] For many scholars, the relocation of the Sung court signifies the further disintegration of the national polity and the concomitant rise of the local gentry as the real power-holders.

Socio-economically, the T'ang-Sung transition was equally dramatic. Based on Japanese scholarship, many students of the Sung describe the period as one characterized by rapid technological and commerical progress. There occurred rapid urbanization, the rise of a monetary economy, the development of new staple and commercial crops, and a vast increase in population.[2] Thus the social structure of China and the contents of Chinese lives were greatly transformed during these six hundred years.

Correspondingly, intellectual changes took place during the T'ang-Sung transition. These included the rise of the ancient prose style, the revival of classical studies, the emergence of civil culture, and the genesis of Neo-Confucianism. Moreover, these intellectual changes were not isolated events. They were the literati's attempts at redefining themselves in response to sociopolitical changes, and each of the literati's self-redefinitions altered the criteria by which the Chinese leadership was measured.[3]

Seeing development from a broad perspective, Sung experts in general give preference to continuity over ruptures. Despite all the resemblances between the early T'ang and the Sung, there was a two-hundred-year gap between 760 and 960, when state and society in China underwent dramatic changes. The mid-T'ang crisis, beginning with the Rebellion of An Lu-shan (755–63), ushered in a period of military governance in northern China, one that did not end until the establishment of the Sung dynasty in 960. This military governance, a combination of Central Asian nomadism and the T'ang system of military governorship (*chieh-tu shih*), gradually displaced the early-T'ang civil governance. This process took several steps. It began with dividing the mid-T'ang empire into the military zone in the northeast and the civil zone in the central and southern part of the country. This bifurcation of China led to what historian Ch'en Yin-k'o calls the condition of "one dynasty, two states" (*yi-ch'ao liang-kuo*).[4] Then the process continued with the expansion of the military zone at the expense of the civil zone, finally reaching a point in the late T'ang, around the time of the Huang Ch'ao rebellion from 875 to 884, when the military governors displaced the T'ang court as the de facto rulers of China. This process reached its climax when the military governor of Ho-nan, Chu Wen (r. 907–912), brought the T'ang dynasty to its end in 907. The fall of the T'ang signaled the beginning of a period of fifty-three years of total military control of the body politic of China, known in history as the Five Dynasties period (907–960).[5]

THE NORTHERN SUNG PROJECT

By highlighting this two-hundred-year period of rupture in the T'ang-Sung transition, it is not my intention to deny resemblances between the early T'ang and the Sung. Indeed, in many respects the early T'ang and the Sung were similar—the pen controlling the sword, and the center over the periphery. Rather, my intention is to underscore the originality of the first few generations of the Northern Sung rulers and literati, who were committed to terminating military governance. To me, the resemblances between the early T'ang and the Sung were not repetitions by chance. They were the results of a partnership between the Northern Sung rulers and literati to recreate a civil governance that had lost its appeal for some time. In this process of recreating a civil governance, the Northern Sung rulers and literati certainly took the early-T'ang model seriously.

But they also intended to go beyond the early-T'ang model to make sure that the new civil governance would not eventually produce military domination as the early T'ang did.

This Northern Sung project of recreating a civil governance was easier said than done. Much rebuilding had to take place to break down the military establishment, particularly the military governance at the center and military practices in society. In terms of putting an end to military governance, the first two Northern Sung emperors—T'ai-tsu (r. 960–976) and T'ai-tsung (r. 976–997)—had made decisive moves to centralize military power in their own hands. Themselves career military officers before coming to the throne, the two emperors made three major changes in their reigns. First, immediately after the Sung was established, all the major generals were persuaded to give up their military power. Second, the military establishment was completely overhauled in such a way that the best army in the country was stationed around the capital, K'ai-feng, leaving the more feeble and the less trained units in the provinces. Third, all the top military positions were filled by civil ministers, setting the stage for the civil to dominate the military.[6]

Although, thanks to the concerted efforts from above, military governance had been structurally demolished in the first three to four decades of the Sung, many military practices and military values remained dominant in society. It took another half a century, through the reigns of Jen-tsung (r. 1024–63) and Shen-tsung (r. 1068–85), for a new civil culture to be fully developed. Those sixty years from 1024 to 1085 have long been regarded as the high point of the Northern Sung. In thought, the first generation of the *Tao-hsueh* (Learning of the Way, or more commonly called Neo-Confucianism) scholars, including Chou Tun-i (1017–73), Chang Tsai (1020–77), Ch'eng Hao (1032–85) and Ch'eng I (1033-1107), began to make their marks in the intellectual landscape. In politics, the two major Northern Sung political thinkers, Wang An-shih (1021–86) and Ssu-ma Kuang (1019–86), initiated wholesale reforms according to their own visions of society. In the arts, poet Su Shih (1037–1101), writer Ou-yang Hsiu (1007–70), and painter Kuo Hsi (ca. 1020 – after 1090) completed their masterpieces. Although it would be an exaggeration to characterize the mid Northern Sung as a complete break with the early Northern Sung, substantial differences are evident in the values and social practices of these two periods.

TWO ACCOUNTS OF THE FIVE DYNASTIES

One difference between the early Northern Sung and the mid Northern Sung can be seen in their interpretations of the history of the Five Dynasties. A period of fifty-three years of political disunity preceding the establishment of the Sung dynasty, the Five Dynasties were controversial to the Northern Sung literati. The Five Dynasties were controversial partly because they involved the question of

what to inherit and what to abandon from that period of disunity. But the controversy went even further. Any account of the Five Dynasties had to explain
why three out of the five dynasties (i.e., Later T'ang, Later Chin, and Later Han)
were founded by the Sha-t'o Turks, who had been present in China for centuries
as T'ang military officers. Some of the Sha-t'o Turks even carried the T'ang royal
family name, Li. In short, any account of the Five Dynasties had to include an
appraisal of the T'ang political structure, as well as military strategy and ethnic
policy.

In the standard twenty-four dynastic histories (*erh-shih-ssu shih*), we have
two accounts of the Five Dynasties from the Northern Sung, namely, *The Old
History of the Five Dynasties* (*Chiu Wu-tai shih*) by Hsueh Chü-cheng (912–981)
and *The New History of the Five Dynasties* (*Hsin Wu-tai shih*) by Ou-yang Hsiu
(1007–1072). These two histories of the Five Dynasties were separated by sev-
enty-nine years—the *Old History* finished in 974 and the *New History* completed
in 1053. While the *Old History* is known for its lengthy accounts and factual
details, the *New History* is famous for its didacticism and its eloquent style of writing. While the *Old History* treats all the five short-lived dynasties as distinct
political entities by offering a separate book (*shu*) for each dynasty, the *New
History* sees the five dynasties as a continnum sharing a common ethos. And
whereas the *Old History* gives a relatively positive reading of the Five Dynasties as
a period with its own unique way of ordering the world, the *New History* condemns the Five Dynasties as a dark moment in Chinese history characterized by
political chaos and moral degeneration.[7]

Seen with our historical hindsight, these differences between the two histories of the Five Dynasties seem more ideological than historiographic. They
involve judgment and perspectives, more than style and emphasis. Like the first
generation of the Northern Sung literati, Hsueh Chü-cheng, the author/compi-
lor of the *Old History*,[8] saw the history of the Five Dynasties not as distant events
but as lived experiences. Having served as an official in four out of the five dynasties, Hsueh understood not only how government was run in the Five Dynasties,
but also why civil officials of one dynasty joined another without remorse.
Accepting the military over the civil as given, Hsueh did not see the Five
Dynasties as disorderly; he held that there was a discernable rule governing the
coming and going of dynasties.

Seventy years later, when Ou-yang Hsiu composed the *New History*, the
sociopolitical environment in the Northern Sung had changed. In Ou-yang's
time, militarism had long become obsolete, and the literati had transformed
themselves into the new ruling class. With a civil government firmly in the
hands of the literati and a civil culture based on Confucian ethics widely spread,
Ou-yang looked at the Five Dynasties as a historical other to reflect upon the present. In writing another account of the Five Dynasties, Ou-yang's goal was not to
search for more details about the period, but to draw moral lessons from it to edu-

cate his contemporaries. Consciously modeling his *New History* after the *Records of the Grand Historian* (Shih chi), Ou-yang wanted his work to be didactic, clarifying the fundamental principles of rulership and moral cultivation.[9]

In what follows, I will elucidate the ideological differences between the two histories of the Five Dynasties by contrasting how the two authors dealt with the following four issues: (1) the Mandate of Heaven, (2) the Sino-Khitan relationship, (3) kinship based upon adoption, and (4) the moral mission of a Confucian scholar. These four issues, corresponding to the four levels of self-cultivation in the *Great Learning* (Ta Hsueh),[10] were fundamental to defining human boundaries from the Confucian perspective. These four issues addressed the complexity that Confucian literati might encounter when they harmonized the human realm with the natural realm (*ping t'ien hsia*), managed the government as officials (*chih kuo*), gave order to their families (*ch'i chia*), and cultivated themselves as moral persons (*hsiu shen*). These four issues—interlocked like four concentric circles centered upon an individual and extending outward to family, state, and the cosmos—encapsulated the Confucian vision of integrating self-learning with family, government, and human destiny.

Interestingly, the literati in early Northern Sung and mid Northern Sung understood this Confucian vision differently. They each had their own way of defining themselves as Confucian scholars. They drew different boundaries between individual, family, government, and human destiny. Although they all called themselves *shih* (learned persons steeped in Confucian learning), the literati in the early Northern Sung and mid Northern Sung differed both in their conceptions of Confucian learning, and in their strategies for practicing their learning.

THE MANDATE OF HEAVEN

To narrate a period in which dynastic changes took place once every ten to fifteen years, it is not surprising to find that both Hsueh Chü-cheng and Ou-yang Hsiu devoted a considerable amount of space to discussing the Mandate of Heaven. If indeed it was Heaven that gave an emperor the right to rule, according to the conventional Chinese way of legitimizing a regime,[11] then Hsueh and Ou-yang had a difficult task in explaining why Heaven had changed its mandate so frequently.

To Hsueh, what was heavenly could not really be divined by humanity. Human beings were forever barred from understanding the intents of Heaven in appointing an emperor. What human beings did and could know was the manifestations of the heavenly will, that is, the portents. When such auspicious portents as dragons, fragrant smoke, colored clouds, rare animals, and good dreams did appear, they related the heavenly will to the future ruler. Conversely, if such inauspicious portents as eclipses, droughts, locusts, and weird animals occurred, they indicated that Heaven was not pleased with the current emperor. Either drastic reform was in order, or a new dynasty would soon be founded.

By resuscitating the Western Han theory of portents, Hsueh did not intend to bring back Han customs. What he wanted to show was that for whatever reasons Heaven did give and withdraw its mandate five times during the Five Dynasties. As mentioned above, Hsueh wrote one book (*shu*) for each dynasty, treating all five dynasties as equally legitimate. At the beginning of each book, Hsueh always began with an elaborate report of the appearance of portents, indicating that heaven did give sufficient signs to show its will. The prime example of Hsueh's reportage of portents is his biography of the first emperor of the Later Liang, Chu Wen (r. 907–912). Unlike the other four first emperors in the Five Dynasties who replaced dynasties which lasted no more than twenty years, Chu Wen distingished himself as the military warlord who formally ended the three hundred years of T'ang rule. The natural question for Hsueh was why Chu Wen was chosen by Heaven to undertake this significant task of establishing a new dynasty replacing the T'ang.

To Hsueh, Chu Wen's success was due less to his military skills than to his readiness to respond to heavenly signs. In Chu's early life, Hsueh reported that dragons appeared many times both in his dreams and in broad daylight to indicate that Heaven had chosen him to be the next emperor. At one point, an astrologist came forward to announce that a re-alignment of the planets assumed the shape of a Chinese character that resembled Chu Wen's family name.[12] For this reason, Hsueh did not see Chu Wen as usurping the T'ang right to rule. Similar to Yao's abdicating and turning his throne over to Shun in Chinese mythology, the T'ang emperor simply complied with the heavenly will by transmiting his right to rule to Chu Wen. To illustrate this point, Hsueh included in his narrative Chu Wen's first imperial edict, where he announced in majestic language his right to rule:

> Emperors are appointed by Heaven, with the responsibility for enlightening the world [literally, the four oceans, *ssu hai*], honoring Heaven above, and benefiting the people below. In the transition from an old [authority] to a new [authority], one can ascertain the heavenly mandate in advance by consulting the calender and numerology. For founding a new dynasty and establishing a long-lasting government, one can tell with high accuracy in [hexagram] diagrams and fortune-telling lines. When the heavenly mandate descends upon you, there will be corresponding auspicious portents. . . . The T'ang emperor knew that the vitality [of the dynasty] was exhausted, and that the time allotted [to the dynasty] had come to an end. Having consulted the oracle bones and the bronzes to ascertain the heavenly will, the T'ang emperor transmitted the right to rule [to me] by passing the imperial sword and the imperial zeal.[13]

Turning to Ou-yang Hsiu, we find a different way of understanding the Mandate of Heaven. Taking the Mencian view, Ou-yang believed that it was humankind who granted the right to rule to an emperor, not Heaven. In his usual didactic tone, Ou-yang announced to his reader: "Alas! Although one may call the principle (*li*) of prosperity and decay the heavenly mandate, it is actually human affairs."[14] For Ou-yang, the Mandate of Heaven was just another way of saying how effective the human order was. If the human order was sound, the dynasty flourished and the people were content. If the human order no longer worked, the dynasty decayed and the people rose to found a new dynasty. In the entire process, there was nothing mysterious. The process was governed by a clear priniciple, that is, the people had the right to replace an irresponsible government. And the Mandate of Heaven was the mandate of the people who demanded a good government and a good life.

From this perspective, Ou-yang argued that there was no Mandate of Heaven in the Five Dynasties. The reason for the rapid change of government in the Five Dynasties was that none of the emperors was capable of establishing a stable government based on the Confucian five cardinal human relationships (namely, emperor and minister, father and son, husband and wife, older brother and younger brother, and friend and friend). For Ou-yang, this total collapse of Confucian order was what made the Five Dynasties a chaotic period. He wrote:

> Alas! Morality, humanity and righteousness are that which [a ruler] employs to administer a state. Laws and institutions are that which [a ruler] employs to make the state long-lasting. Since ancient times, it has been that chaos and dissolution of states occur after laws and institutions have degenerated. Degeneration and chaos beget each other. When institutions no longer exist, then the process of decay intensifies and chaos occurs. This is what ought to happen. This is [what we find] in the Five Dynasties.[15]

On the surface, Ou-yang seemed to repeat something that had been known to Confucian scholars for centuries. Back in the third century B.C. Mencius had announced: "Heaven does not speak. It simply signified its will through [the ruler's] conduct and handling of affairs. . . . Heaven sees as my people see, Heaven hears as my people hear."[16] But by re-affirming the importance of human factors in the mandate of heaven, Ou-yang in effect repudiated the passive view of political legitimacy advocated by Hsueh Chü-cheng. Instead of letting Heaven decide who would be the ruler, Ou-yang argued that there was a bond between the ruler and the ruled—the ruler would rule so long as he was a good ruler, and the ruled would accept the government so long as the ruler ruled properly. Thus political legitimacy was a human decision worked out between all parties involved. Human beings always had the capabilities to determine their destiny.

By emphasizing the importance of hierarchy and reciprocity in human bonds, Ou-yang made the civil code of behavior the guiding principle in ordering society. Instead of sorting out winners and losers in battlefields as in the case of Chu Wen, Ou-yang saw negotiation and compromise in a host of binary human relationships as the proper way for resolving conflicts. For this reason, Ou-yang did not recognize the Five Dynasties as legitimate governments. He called them "chaotic" (luan) because they had forsaken the civil code of behavior.

SINO-KHITAN RELATIONSHIP

The Sino-Khitan relationship was a sensitive issue in the Northern Sung, because the Khitan was a major foreign threat. A tribal state based in Manchuria, the Khitan (or Liao) shared a long border with the Northern Sung from the Yellow Sea to the upper elbow of the Yellow River. A major bone of contention between the two states was the sixteen prefectures in Hopei ceded to the Khitan in 937 by Shih Ching-t'ang (r. 937–942), the first emperor of the Later Chin. The sixteen prefectures were strategically important to the Sung in its defense of the North China plain. To recover the lost territories, Emperor T'ai-tsung twice personally led military campaigns against the Khitan in 979 and 986. Both campaigns, however, failed miserably. Finally, after years of war, the Northern Sung found no other way but to accept the existing boundary by signing the treaty of Shanyuan with the Khitan in 1004.[17]

To both Hsueh Chü-cheng and Ou-yang Hsiu, the task of narrating the loss of the sixteen prefectures involved an assessment of the historical figure Shih Ching-t'ang, and the nature of the Sino-Khitan relationship. Assessing the latter was particularly important, for it was tantamount to establishing a definition of China. Acutely aware that Northern Sung China was a part of the multistate system, Hsueh and Ou-yang had to define China by delineating its nature, its jurisdiction, and its boundary vis-a-vis the Khitan tribal state.

To Hsueh, Shih Ching-t'ang had his reasons for ceding the sixteen prefectures to the Khitan. First of all, Shih Ching-t'ang was literally put on the throne by the Khitan. A Sha-T'o Turk himself, Shih Ching-t'ang sought help from the Khitan in his rebellion against the Later T'ang. Not only did the Khitan respond to Shih's request with unexpected swiftness, but also the Khitan King personally led his best army to fight for Shih. To express his gratitude, Shih agreed to cede territories and pledged to be a son of the Khitan king.

In Hsueh's account, we find a heart-warming passage describing how thankful Shih Ching-t'ang was toward the Khitan king:

> That evening [of the hsin-chou day of the ninth month in 936], the emperor [Shih Ching-t'ang] left the north gate [of K'ai-feng] to meet with the Khitan king. The Khitan king held the emperor's hands and said: "I regret not meeting you earlier." Then, they discussed forging a

father-son relationship. . . . At the beginning, the emperor did not form any alliance with the Khitan. Since Mo-ti [Li Ts'ung-k'o of the Later T'ang] had pressured him to do things against his will, the emperor dispatched his trusted man Ho Fu [to see the Khitan king], bringing along with him [the imperial] sword as a symbol of trust. [The Khitan king] responded to the request and personally led an expedition. [The expedition] proceeded with lightning speed. This is indeed the will of Heaven.[18]

It is revealing that Hsueh did not condemn Shih Ching-t'ang for forging a father-son relationship with a foreigner. Unlike later historians, Hsueh did not think that Shih's "family" relation with the Khitan would bring an inferior status to China. As a matter of fact, in the *Old History* Hsueh had reported many cases where strangers of different ethnic backgrounds forged a father-son relationship. Known as "joining the hearts by sharing the same family name" (*shih hsing i chieh ch'i hsin*), this practice of strangers' forging a father-son relation could be traced back to the seventh century when a large number of Sha-t'o Turks were given the Li royal family name for their loyalty to the T'ang court.[19] For Hsueh, who had served in all three Sha-t'o Turk dynasties in the Five Dynasties (Later T'ang, Later Chin, and Later Han), China was hardly ethnically homogeneous. In the Five Dynasties, family and polity were defined more by efficacy and mutual pledge than by ethnicity and bloodline.

Turning to Ou-yang Hsiu, again we find a different picture. We do not find any discussion of the practice of "joining the hearts by sharing the same family name." Instead, we find Ou-yang's spending a considerable amount of time pondering the ways to deal with the barbarians (*yi-ti*). When Ou-yang was writing the *New History* in the 1040s and 1050s, the Khitan was not the only foreign threat to the Northern Sung. The Hsi Hsia, the Tangut tribal state based in the northwestern Yellow River valley, had superseded the Khitan as the most deadly threat to the Northern Sung.[20] Facing two foreign threats simultaneously, it is not surprising to find that Ou-yang was acutely sensitive to the unity and security of China. Unlike Hsueh, Ou-yang consciously separated the Northern Sung from other foreign states.[21] One of the hidden agendas in Ou-yang's didacticism in the *New History* was to educate his contemporaries about what constituted China as a culturally and historically unique entity.

Commenting on Shih Ching-t'ang's "family" relation with the Khitan, Ou-yang made known what he saw as the evils of the barbarization of China:

The Five Dynasties were a chaotic period full of wars and bandits. It was a time when rituals and music were destroyed, the three bonds (*san kang*) and the five constancies (*wu ch'ang*) were terminated, and the institutions and writings of the ancient emperors were entirely swept aside. . . . As barbarians, the [Shih] family of [Later] Chin usurped the right to rule the world. Kao-tsu [Shih Ching-t'ang] made [the Khitan king] Yeh-lu Te-kuang his father. Ch'u-ti [Shih Ch'ung-kuei] treated [Yeh-lu] Te-kuang as his grandfather by addressing himself as grandson. At the same time [Ch'u-ti] named his own father as his official. These practices were so bizarre that they did not follow human principles.[22]

To Ou-yang, the period of the Five Dynasties was chaotic not just because of the collapse of the Confucian sociopolitical order. More importantly, the period was disorderly because of the barbarization of China, which led to a loss of self-identity among the Chinese. Shih Ching-t'ang and Shih Ch'ung-kuei of the Later Chin (936–946) were a case in point. (See appendix I.) To Ou-yang, as Sha-t'o Turks, they were wrongly allowed to assume important military positions in China. Worse still, they were given the chance to rule China for a considerable length of time, turning it from a settled civilization into a tribal state.

Of the two Later Chin emperors, Shih Ch'ung-kuei (r. 942–946) was even worse. Succeeding Shih Ching-t'ang as the second emperor of the Later Chin, Shih Ch'ung-kuei continued to pledge "family" relationships with the Khitans by honoring the Khitan king Yeh-lu Te-kuang as his "grandfather." (Yeh-lu Te-kuang was the same Khitan king with whom Shih Ching-t'ang had pledged a father-son relationship.) To express his preference for the pledged family relation over the bloodline family relation, Shih Ch'ung-kuei consigned his own father to a minor official post. For Ou-yang, the case of Shih Ts'ung-kuei showed that it was efficacy rather than propriety, self-serving rather than communal interest, that people in the Five Dynasties valued in family relationships. In this sense, the period of the Five Dynasties was indeed a dark moment in Chinese history. It was the time when China had lost its essence of being the Middle Kingdom—the perfect ordering of human relationships based on bloodline.

To Ou-yang, it was not coincidental that there were so few Confucian virtuous persons in the Five Dynasties. Writing with a strong ironic overtone, Ou-yang explained why the "Chapter on One Virtuous Deed" (*I hsing chuan*) was composed:

> In the chaotic period of the Five Dynasties, an emperor was not an emperor, a father not a father, a son not a son. Even the human bonds governing older brother and younger brother, and husband and wife were greatly destroyed. The principle of Heaven was almost terminated. During this time, there might be someone in a remote village who made a name in the world by cultivating himself in filial piety. Unfortunately, there were few records left behind. Searching through books to look for references to these people, I could only locate one person. His name was Li Tsu-lun. Hence I composed the "Chapter on One Virtuous Deed."[23]

Since China had been so militarized and tribalized in the Five Dynasties, it did not surprise Ou-yang Hsiu to find few virtuous persons in that period. What worried Ou-yang, however, was that the task of rebuilding the Confucian sociopolitical order and revitalizing the Confucian spirit of communal sharing had to be laborious and time-consuming.

KINSHIP BASED UPON ADOPTION

As mentioned above, in the Five Dynasties, the practice of "joining hearts by sharing the same family name" was quite commonplace. The implication of this practice was that once pledged, the two strangers would treat each other as father and son. The adopted father would regard his adopted son as if he were his son by blood, giving him all the family privileges and property inheritance. Likewise, the adopted son would regard his adopted father as if he were his real father, cutting all connections with his blood father.

This practice of forming kinship based upon mutual consent was popular among the military generals in the late T'ang and the Five Dynasties. The practice was a means for the military generals to build up an elite army known as the "Army of the Adopted Sons" (*I er chün*). Personally loyal to the military generals, the "Army of the Adopted Sons" was the military general's core army in battle and his administrators in occupied territories. Related as lords and vassals, the military generals and the "Army of the Adopted Sons" pledged to share whatever they gained in conquest.[24]

Familiar with this practice of adoption, Hsueh Chü-cheng was not surprised to find that many emperors in the Five Dynasties were adopted sons and stepbrothers. A case in point was Li K'o-yung's family, who founded the Later T'ang (see Appendix II). The ancestors of Li K'o-yung, originally the Sha-t'o Turks, were given the Li royal family name after participating in T'ang T'ai-tsung's expedition to Korea.[25] Later, Li K'o-yung became a prominent military officer in north China after helping the T'ang court in suppressing the Huang Ch'ao rebellion. In 923, Li K'o-yung's eldest son Li Ts'un-hsü founded the Later T'ang. After Li Ts'un-hsü's death, the Later T'ang continued for three more emperors (Li Ssu-yuan, Li Ts'ung-hou, and Li Ts'ung-k'o), the last two of whom were stepbrothers.[26]

In Hsueh Chü-cheng's account, there is a passage describing how the third emperor, Li Ssu-yuan (r. 926–933), rationalized in 925 his decision to succeed his deceased stepbrother Li Ts'un-hsü (r. 923–926). As an adopted member of the Li family, Li Ssu-yuan's decision involved two parts: (1) how he claimed to inherit his stepbrother's throne; (2) after coming to the throne, whether he would establish a new dynasty or continue the imperial line of the Later T'ang. Hsueh's passage goes as follows:

> The emperor [Li Ssu-yuan] said: "I had served Hsin-tsu [Li K'o-yung's father] since I was thirteen years of age. Since then, I have been

treating the [Li] family like my blood family. I had also served Wu-
wang [Li K'o-yung] for thirty years by helping him resolve problems,
bearing the gusty wind and pouring rain, and risking my life in combat. [In the process] I had experienced all the danger and borne all
the hardship. The enterprise of Wu-wang is my enterprise; the world
ruled by earlier [Li] emperors is my world. Hence it is rightful for me
as a younger brother to succeed my deceased older brother [Li Ts'un-
hsü]. It will deviate from the rites and conventions if members of the
same family adopt a different [dynastic] name. Whether the future
will flourish or decline, I will take full responsibility for the Li family.
I have decided not to accept the suggestion [to establish a new
dynasty].[27]

The heart of Li Ssu-yuan's argument was that one's kinship was not given by
birth, but earned through sharing hardship together to achieve a common goal.
Having been adopted into the Li family in adolescence, Li Ssu-yuan regarded
himself as a full-fledged member of the Li family. Moreover, he had worked very
hard to contribute to the family. Therefore he found himself qualified to succeed
his deceased stepbrother, and he would prove his loyalty to the Li family by continuing the dynastic line of the Later T'ang.

Turning to Ou-yang Hsiu, we find another picture. Not only was Li Ssu-
yuan's argument seen as an excuse to usurp the throne, but also the entire practice of adoption was criticized for causing the barbarization of China. To
Ou-yang, politically the barbarization of China in the Five Dynasties took the
form of militarizing and tribalizing the Chinese state, and socially barbarization
assumed the guise of dissolving the Confucian family system. In addressing this
barbarization of Chinese society, Ou-yang writes:

Alas! When the world is in decline and the human bonds have
degenerated, the principle of delineating close and distant relatives
no longer functions in its normal way. Wars occur among members of
the same family, and strangers pledge to become fathers and sons. In
the fifty years from Kai-ping [the early years of the reign of Chu Wen
of Later Liang, 907–909] to Ch'ien-te [the final years of Shih-tsung of
Later Chou, 954–959], there were five dynasties run by people of
eight families. Among the eight families, three of them were related
by adoption. All this happened because [the people in the Five
Dynasties] banded together for conquering the world. They also
banded together for gaining fame and reward, and for winning high
positions in government and in the military. Taking advantage of the
time, they banded together in pursuit of their own interests.[28]

To Ou-yang, kinship based upon mutual consent was built upon a marriage of
convenience. Formed to achieve a common goal, the kinship based on mutual

consent randomly included people from different backgrounds. This kinship was formed out of calculation rather than love, and out of immediate interests rather than long-term considerations. Once the common goal had been reached, such kinship would have difficulty in continuing unless a new common goal was found.

To prevent the barbarization of Chinese society from happening, Ou-yang defined a new set of kinship boundaries. To him, bloodline provided the foundation for a more stable and long-lasting kinship. Not only did a bloodline kinship present clearer distinctions in human relationships, it also prescribed a well-defined code of behavior regulating human emotions and resolving human conflicts. For this reason, Ou-yang Hsiu wrote a special chapter on the family system in the Five Dynasties. The chapter was called the "Chapter on Family Members" (*Chia jen chuan*). Explaining the purpose of the "Chapter on Family Members," Ou-yang wrote:

> Alas! The way of ordering one's family has to be proper. Through rituals one distinguishes [the high and the low] and clarifies subtle [human] sensitivities. In the Five Dynasties, the way enabling an emperor to be an emperor, an official to be an official, a father to be a father, and a son to be a son, had gone astray. The distinctions were lost between lineage temples and the imperial palaces, and between human beings and ghosts. The Five Dynasties was indeed a chaotic period, not frequently seen in history.[29]

By arguing for a re-ordering of the family system according to bloodline and Confucian hierarchy, Ou-yang wanted to replace the kinship based upon mutual consent with the kinship based upon biological ancestry.

THE MISSION OF A CONFUCIAN SCHOLAR

Both Hsueh and Ou-yang agreed that in the Five Dynasties military officials performed much better than civil officials. In general, military officials were brave in combat, responsible for their specific tasks, and clear on where their loyalty lay. In contrast, the civil officials were selfish and calculating. They did whatever they could in pursuit of fame, wealth, and security. They were always the ones who initiated palace coup d'états, and the first group to justify the new regime with majestic terms.

But Hsueh and Ou-yang disagreed on one civil official, Feng Tao (882–954). Like Hsueh, Feng Tao served in four out of the five dynasties. Feng Tao had a good relationship with all major military leaders, so much so that despite rapid dynastic changes, he always found a way to remain in power. According to one account, even the Khitan king was so fond of Feng Tao that he had asked him to serve in his government, though Feng tactfully rejected the offer. Other than being good at winning the trust of the military leaders, Feng Tao was also capable of linking the military with the civil. He was particularly good at remonstrating with the military leaders in humble and yet clear language mixed with military metaphors. Apparently, Feng Tao was the subservient civil official par excellence in the Five Dynasties.[30] For Hsueh and Ou-yang, what was controversial about Feng Tao was the extent to which he personified the Confucian Way, and was worthy enough to be called a Confucian scholar.

In Hsueh's narrative, Feng Tao's career was given a positive reading. Not only did Hsueh speak highly of Feng Tao's delicate balancing act between the military and the civil, he also endorsed Feng Tao's claim that he had done his best as a true Confucian in the Five Dynasties. Commenting on Feng Tao as a historical figure, Hsueh emphasized two points:

> What [Feng] Tao had done exemplified the standards of ancient gen-
> tlemen. What [Feng] Tao had achieved in submitting to [leaders] ful-
> filled the demanding task of a major official.[31]

By emphasizing that Feng Tao's subservience was fulfilling his responsibility as an official, Hsueh judged Feng on the basis of a submissive official's (ch'en) serving a dominating emperor (chün), the first relationship in the Confucian Five Cardinal Relationships. To Hsueh, after heaven had made its view known regarding who was the Son of Heaven, an official had to follow the Mandate of Heaven by serv-ing wholeheartedly the Son of Heaven. Thus, there was nothing wrong with Feng Tao's being subservient.

Nor was Feng Tao's serving four different dynasties morally wrong. Himself having served in four dynasties, Hsueh commented favorably on a group of Later Liang civil officials who joined the Later T'ang government. Hsueh compli-mented them for rendering a high quality of service to both governments as "a steadfast palm tree [which] does not change in the four seasons, and a broken jade [which] can stand a hot fire."[32] As secondary players in politics, the best civil offi-cials could do in the Five Dynasties, according to Hsueh, was to serve responsibly any government that happened to have the Mandate of Heaven.

Turning to Ou-yang Hsiu, we again find a different view. Feng Tao became the prime target in Ou-yang's condemnation of unethical Confucian scholars. Compared with Hsueh's account of Feng Tao, Ou-yang's was brief on biographi-cal details but lengthy on the significance of Feng Tao's being a fake Confucian. In his usual didactic tone, Ou-yang condemned Feng for being shameless:

> Having read Feng Tao's self-glorifying account in his *Preface to an
> Ever-happy Old Man*, I find him shameless. One can tell how shame-
> less the society was at that time. In the Five Dynasties, I can only find
> three persons with full integrity, and fifteen civil officials who died
> for their government. But there were many strange people wearing

Confucian gowns and claiming to learn from the past. They received a high salary and served in the government, but they never made sacrifices for the sake of righteousness and loyalty. Instead, only the military officers and soldiers made sacrifices. It seems that there was no Confucian scholar [in the Five Dynasties].[33]

To Ou-yang, the case of Feng Tao was revealing. It revealed how serious the barbarization of China had become. Not only had the barbarization of China corrupted the Chinese state and the Chinese family, it had also corrupted the scholars, the self-proclaimed custodians of Confucian culture. Even if both the Chinese state and society were corrupted, there was still hope that a cultural reawakening might occur in the Five Dynasties through the sheer inspiring examples of a few true scholars. But since the scholars were also as corrupted as Feng Tao, Ou-yang found the Five Dynasties to be utterly hopeless.

Particularly important to Ou-yang was what Feng Tao's example might have meant to his mid–Northern Sung readers. If Feng Tao could be called a Confucian, the Northern Sung project of rebuilding a civil governance would only be empty rhetoric. What the Northern Sung literati were rebuilding would have been nothing but a continuation of the Five Dynasties system. To Ouyang, his critique of Feng Tao was not only a critique of him as a person, but also a critique of the feckless Confucian scholars who had yielded to the military state.

EARLY– AND MID–NORTHERN SUNG: A PARTING OF WAYS

These two different readings of the history of the Five Dynasties reveal to us the different intellectual milieux in the early Northern Sung and the mid Northern Sung. As I have argued, this intellectual change was brought about by a shift from military governance to civil governance in the early part of the eleventh century. This intellectual change not only gave rise to a new historical perspective to retrieve meanings from the past, but more importantly, it occasioned a sincere attempt to redefine the Confucian sense of boundaries with respect to individual, family, government, and human destiny. In their readings of the history of the Five Dynasties, Hsueh Chü-cheng and Ou-yang Hsiu presented two different sets of criteria in an attempt to delineate the boundaries of these four core Confucian issues.

For Hsueh Chü-cheng, who was preoccupied with the question of finding a suitable role for civil officials to perform in a military state, the boundaries of the four essential Confucian concerns had to be redefined in order to suit the needs of the military rulers. He took for granted the values of efficacy and expediency in a military state. He worked hard to create a civilian ethical code that would allow the civil officials to serve responsibly the military rulers—the true rulers of China. In contrast, Ou-yang Hsiu was consciously making a distinction between a military governance and a civil governance. He wanted to paint a black-and-white picture, where the virtues of civil rule were contrasted with the drawbacks of military rule. In Ou-yang's mind, there was no middle ground between civil rule and military rule. The four cardinal Confucian principles, with their distinct boundaries, were the cornerstones of civil governance, of which the civil officials must take charge.

In sum, within the boundaries drawn in Confucian terms, there were inscribed visions of a human community in which individuals were linked to family, government, and the universe, but they were inexorably elastic, ultimately depending on one's conception of what an ideal Confucian society should be. The disparate ways Hsueh and Ou-yang negotiated the boundaries of the four paramount Confucian concerns tell us a great deal about how differently society was envisioned in the early and mid Northern Sung.

APPENDIX I: LIST OF RULERS OF THE FIVE DYNASTIES

Later Liang (907–922)
    Chu Wen (T'ai-tsu), 907–912
    Chu Yu-kuei (Ying-wang), 912–913
    Chu Yu-chen (Mo-ti), 913–923

Later T'ang (923–935)
    Li Ts'un-hsu (Chuang-tsung), 923–926
    Li Ssu-yuan (Ming-tsung), 926–933
    Li Ts'ung-hou (min-ti), 933–934
    Li Ts'ung-k'o (lu-wang), 934–937

Later Chin (936–946)
    Shih Ching-t'ang (Kao-tsu), 937–942
    Shih Ts'ung-kuei (Ch'u-ti), 942–946
    [Interegnum: Khitan Liao Yeh-lu Te-kuang (T'ai-tsung), 946–947]

Later Han (947–950)*
    Liu Chih-yuan (Kao-tsu), 947–948
    Liu Ch'eng-yu (Yin-ti), 948–950

Later Chou (951–960)
    Kuo Wei (T'ai-tsu), 951–954
    Ch'ai Jung (Shih-tsung), 954–959
    Ch'ai Tsung-hsun (Kung-ti), 959–960

(*Sha-T'o Turks)

APPENDIX II: LI K'O-YUNG'S FAMILY OF THE LATER T'ANG

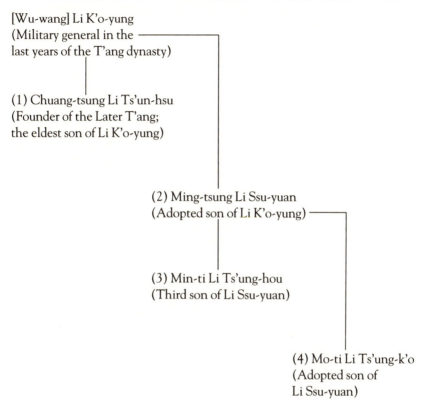

[Wu-wang] Li K'o-yung
(Military general in the
last years of the T'ang dynasty)

(1) Chuang-tsung Li Ts'un-hsu
(Founder of the Later T'ang;
the eldest son of Li K'o-yung)

(2) Ming-tsung Li Ssu-yuan
(Adopted son of Li K'o-yung)

(3) Min-ti Li Ts'ung-hou
(Third son of Li Ssu-yuan)

(4) Mo-ti Li Ts'ung-k'o
(Adopted son of
Li Ssu-yuan)

NOTES

1. Robert Hartwell, "Demographic, Political, and Social Transformation of China, 750–1550," *Harvard Journal of Asiatic Studies* 42 (1982): 365–442; Robert Hymes, *Statesmen and Gentlemen: The Elites of Fu-chou, Chiang-hsi, in Northern and Southern Sung* (Cambridge: Cambridge University Press, 1986).

2. Robert P. Hymes and Conrad Schirokauer, ed., *Ordering the World: Approaches to State and Society in Sung Dynasty China* (Berkeley: University of California Press, 1993), p. 3.

3. This argument is given a cohesive articulation in Peter Bol, *This Culture of Ours: Intellectual Transitions in T'ang and Sung China* (Stanford: Stanford University Press, 1992). Bol argues that from the T'ang to the Sung, the constitution of the literati had been thrice redefined. Although the term for the literati remained *shih* throughout the T'ang and the Sung, Bol points out that the criterion for *shih* had been changed. In the early T'ang *shih* were the

aristocrats from wealthy families; in the Northern Sung they were the bureaucrats armed with reform ideas; and in the Southern Sung they were the gentry
who had firm control of local property. See *This Culture of Ours*, pp. 32–75.

4. See Ch'en Yin-k'o, *T'ang-tai cheng-chih shih shu-lun kao* [A Preliminary
Study of the Political Institutions in the T'ang Dynasty] (Hong Kong: Chung-
hua shu-chu, 1974), pp. 1–49. See also Edwin G. Pulleyblank, "The An Lu-shan
Rebellion and the Origins of Chronic Militarism in Late T'ang China," in John
Curtis Perry and Bardwell L. Smith, eds., *Essays on T'ang Society: The Interplay of
Social, Political and Economic Forces* (Leiden: E. J. Brill, 1979), pp. 32–60; C. A.
Peterson, "Court and Province in Mid- and Late T'ang," in Dennis Twitchett,
ed., *The Cambridge History of China*, vol. 3 (London: Cambridge University
Press, 1979), pp. 464–560.

5. The Five Dynasties period includes five northern dynasties and ten
southern kingdoms. The five dynasties were the Later Liang, Later T'ang, Later
Chin, Later Han, and Later Chou. (For a list of rulers of the Five Dynasties, see
Appendix I.) The ten kingdoms were Wu, Nan T'ang, Wu-Yueh, Min, Nan
Han, Ch'u, Early Shu, Later Shu, Nan P'ing, and Pei Han. For a brief history of
the five dynasties and the ten kingdoms, see Cheng Hsueh-meng, *Wu-tai shih-
kuo shih yen-chiu* [A Study of the Five Dynasties and the Ten Kingdoms]
(Shanghai: Shanghai Jen-min ch'u-pan she, 1991).

6. Fang Hao, *Sung Shih* [History of Sung] (Taipei: Chung-hua wen-hua
ch'u-pan shih-yeh wei-yuan-hui, 1954), pp. 1–66.

7. For a comparison of the two histories of the Five Dynasties, see Chao I
(1727–1814), *Nien-er shih cha-chi* [Notes on the twenty-two histories]
(Shanghai: Commercial Press, 1937); Wang Ming-sheng (1722–97), *Shih-ch'i
shih shang-ch'ueh* [Critical Comments on the Seventeen Histories] (Shanghai:
Commercial Press, 1937); Wang Gungwu, "Some Comments on the Later
Standard Histories," in Donald D. Leslie, Collin Mackenas, and Wang Gungwu,
eds., *Essays on the Sources for Chinese History* (Columbia: University of South
Carolina Press, 1973), pp. 53–63; reprinted in Wang Gungwu, *The Chineseness
of China* (Hong Kong: Oxford University Press, 1991), pp. 11–21.

8. For the process and materials used in the compilation of the *Old
History*, see Wang Gungwu, "The *Chiu Wu-tai Shih* and History-Writing during
the Five Dynasties," *Asia Major*, new series, 6, part one (1957): 1–22; reprinted
in Wang Gungwu, *The Chineseness of China*, pp. 22–40.

9. See Wu Chiang et al., eds., *Tseng-ting Ou-yang wen-chung kung nien-
p'u* [An Enlarged Yearly Account of Ou-yang Hsiu] (Chao-t'ai chung-shu edition), 9a–10b; Chang Shun-hui, ed., *Chung-kuo shih-hsueh ming-chu ti-chieh* [An
Introduction to Famous Chinese Historical Works] (Peking: Chung-kuo ch'ing-
nien ch'u-pan-she, 1983), pp. 138–42.

10. For a translation of the *Great Learning* and an informed discussion of the various levels of self-cultivation expounded in the text, see Wm. Theodore de Bary et al., *Sources of Chinese Tradition*, vol. 1 (New York: Columbia University Press, 1960), pp. 113–17.

11. See de Bary, *Sources of Chinese Tradition*, vol. 1: 1–14.

12. *Chiu Wu-tai shih* (Peking: Chung-hua shu-chu, 1976), p. 46.

13. *Chiu Wu-tai Shih*, pp. 47–48.

14. *Hsin Wu-tai shih* (Peking: Chung-hua shu-chu, 1974), p. 397.

15. *Hsin Wu-tai shih*, p. 514.

16. de Bary, *Sources of Chinese Tradition*, vol. 1: 96.

17. Herbert Franke and Denis Twitchett, eds., *The Cambridge History of China*, vol. 6 (London: Cambridge University Press, 1995), pp. 108–11.

18. *Chiu Wu-tai shih*, p. 985.

19. On the characteristics of the Sha-t'o Turks and their relationship with the T'ang and the Five Dynasties, see Wolfram Eberhard, *Conquerors and Rulers: Social Forces in Medieval China*, second, revised edition (Leiden: E. J. Brill, 1965), pp. 140–71.

20. *Cambridge History of China*, vol. 6: 154–214.

21. Sensitive to the vulnerability of Sung China, some scholars have insightfully placed the Northern Sung in a "multistate system." For their arguments, see articles by Wang Gungwu and Tao Jing-shen in Morris Rossabi, ed., *China among Equals: The Middle Kingdom and Its Neighbors, 10–14th Centuries* (Berkeley: University of California Press, 1983), pp. 47–86.

22. *Hsin Wu-tai shih*, pp. 187–88.

23. *Hsin Wu-tai shih*, pp. 369–70.

24. For details, see Wang Gungwu's case study of Chu Wen in *The Structure of Power in North China during the Five Dynasties*, pp. 47–78.

25. *Chiu Wu-tai shih*, p. 331.

26. *Chiu Wu-tai shih*, pp. 1067–1129.

27. *Chiu Wu-tai shih*, pp. 490–91.

28. *Chiu Wu-tai shih*, p. 385.

29. *Hsin Wu-tai shih*, p. 173.

30. For a biography of Feng Tao and a an assessment of him as a preserver of culture in the Five Dynasties, see Wang Gungwu "Feng Tao: An Essay on Confucian Loyalty," in Arthur F. Wright and Denis Twitchett, eds., *Confucian Personalities* (Stanford: Stanford University Press, 1962), pp. 123–45; reprinted in Wang Gungwu, *The Chineseness of China*, 41–63.

31. *Chiu Wu-tai shih*, p. 1666

32. *Chiu Wu-tai shih*, p. 860.

33. *Hsin Wu-tai shih*, p. 611.

GLOSSARY

An Lu-shan	安祿山
Chang Tsai	張載
ch'en	臣
Ch'en Yin-k'o	陳寅恪
Ch'eng Hao	程顥
Ch'eng I	程頤
chia-jen chuan	家人傳
ch'i-chia	齊家
chieh-tu shih	節度使
chih kuo	治國
Chiu Wu-tai shih	舊五代史
Chou Tun-i	周敦頤
Chu Wen	朱溫
Ch'u Ti	出帝
erh-shih-ssu shih	二十四史
Feng Tao	馮道
Hang-chou	杭州
hsin-ch'ou	辛丑
Hsin Wu-tai shih	新五代史
hsiu-shen	修身
Hsueh Chü-cheng	薛居正
Huang Ch'ao	黃巢
K'ai-feng	開封
Kuo Hsi	郭熙
Li K'o-yung	李克用
Li Ssu-yuan	李嗣源
Li Tzu-lun	李自倫
Li Ts'un-hsu	李存勖
Li Ts'ung-hou	李從厚
Li Ts'ung-k'o	李從珂
Liao	遼
luan	亂
Ou-yang Hsiu	歐陽修
p'ing-t'ien-hsia	平天下
san-kang	三綱
Sha-t'o	沙陀
shih	士
shih-hsing i chieh-ch'i-hsin	錫姓以結其心
Shih Ching-t'ang	石敬塘
Shih Ts'ung-kuei	石從貴

shu	書
Ssu-ma Kuang	司馬光
Ta Hsueh	大學
Tao-hsueh	道學
Wang An-shih	王安石
wu-ch'ang	五常
Yeh-lu Te-kuang	耶律德光
i-ch'ao liang-kuo	一朝兩國
i-er chun	義兒軍
I-hsing chuan	一行傳

5

Strategies in Neo-Confucian Heresiography

John B. Henderson

Chinese religious and philosophical thinkers are sometimes celebrated for their syncretic genius, for their ability to build bridges between various traditions, as opposed to digging ditches around them.[1] Examples of syncretic enterprises, of attempts to reconcile key aspects of two or more religious traditions, appear in almost every era in the history of Chinese thought from the Han through the Ch'ing. However, the contour of most intellectual landscapes is such that ditches, as well as bridges, are sometimes called for, and boundaries demarcated. Perhaps the most prominent delineators of such boundaries in premodern Chinese intellectual history are Neo-Confucian scholars of the Ch'eng-Chu persuasion who sought to distinguish the Tradition of the Way (*Tao-t'ung*) from various heterodoxies and heresies (*i-tuan*), ranging from Buddhism and Taoism to various renegade forms of Confucianism.

Such a demarcation of boundaries between orthodoxy and heresy was not, however, a very straightforward enterprise, characterized by a simple act of categorization or condemnation. It entailed the invention and application of a number of heresiographical strategies or arguments that in the aggregate mapped out the contours of heresy, showing both its relationships with orthodoxy and its internal divisions and gradations. These strategies appear prominently in antiheretical writings of several great religious traditions, not just that of orthodox Neo-Confucianism of the Ch'eng-Chu school. Their wide distribution points to the existence of a universal grammar of heresiography, the "science of the errors of others."[2]

Paradoxically, the first of our heresiographical strategies for mapping the phenomenon of heresy appears to entail an erasure of boundaries between orthodoxy and heresy, not their demarcation. This strategy is, in a nutshell, the reduction of heresy to orthodox terms. That is, the orthodox heresiographer does not recognize that the alleged heretics might march to the beat of a different drummer, that they might inhabit an intellectual or spiritual realm distinct from that of orthodoxy. Chu Hsi (1130–1200), for example, reduced the errors of the Buddhists and Taoists to their alleged partial understanding of the principles enunciated in the Confucian *Great Learning*, remarking that "the learning of the Buddha and Lao-tzu desires to 'advance its knowledge' but does not know that 'the investigation of things' is the means whereby one advances knowledge."[3] The early Ming scholar Hu Chü-jen (1434–84) also reduced heresy to the status of a familiar doctrinal error, thus domesticating it even as he expelled it from the circle of orthodoxy. The trouble with heretics, he remarked, was their separation of *hsin* (heart-mind) from *li* (pattern-principle).[4] And the seventeenth-century scholar Chang Li-hsiang (1611–74) similarly argued that "The Buddhists speak of heart-mind apart from human nature; therefore they tend toward wildness and dissipation. They speak of human nature apart from heart-mind; therefore they reach emptiness and extinction."[5] Chang also accused Chu Hsi's rival, Lu Hsiang-shan (1139–92), of one-sidedly recognizing only the first half of the orthodox Neo-Confucian philosophical formula: "principle is one; but its particularizations are diverse."[6]

Heresy, in other words, resides in a partial, one-sided, or isolated apprehension of orthodox truth. It is an incomplete or biased version of orthodoxy. This sort of heresiographical reductionism thus deprives heresy of its autonomy, its language, and its problematic, to say nothing of its historical context. Far from delineating a clear boundary between the realms of orthodoxy and heresy, it makes it difficult to imagine an intellectual or spiritual universe apart from the orthodox one.

When Neo-Confucian heresiography does admit the existence of a context for heresy, it is not so much that of history as of other heresies. This brings up a second major strategy for the mapping of heresy, one that requires more elaboration than the first, namely the schematic relating of heresies to one another. This sort of schematization elides not only the historicity of heresy, but also its complexity, confirming the general principle enunciated by a modern student of social deviance that "Ideological systems describing, explaining, and justifying one's own behavior tend to be detailed and subtle . . . , those describing other people's are often shallow and simplified."[7]

Perhaps the oldest schematizing device used by Neo-Confucian heresiographers for relating heresies to one another is their pairing of heresies as complementary opposites centered on an orthodox middle way. The locus classicus for this sort of arrangement is Mencius' coupling of Yang Chu's egotism with Mo-tzu's indiscriminate altruism, which was cited by such major Neo-Confucian authorities as the Ch'eng brothers.[8] Later Neo-Confucian writers applied this sort of dualistic pairing of heretical opposites to other heresies and heterodoxies as well. The prominent Ming heresiographer, Ch'en Chien (1497–1567), for example, remarked that of those who reject Ch'eng-Chu orthodoxy, "the lofty enter into Buddhism and Taoism while the lowly incline toward utilitarianism."[9] A scholar of the Ch'ing era, Yang Ming-shih, posed a similar dichotomy, accusing Han and T'ang Confucians of "stagnating in [their concern with] the external while forgetting the internal," and Buddhists of "concentrating on the internal while ignoring the external."[10] Here again, heresy is characterized by partiality or one-sidedness, as compared to the comprehensiveness of orthodoxy.

Aside from constructing binary oppositions, the most prominent means by which Neo-Confucian writers schematically related heresies to one another and to orthodoxy was by arranging them in hierarchies. Ch'eng-Chu scholars keyed these hierarchies to various scales, one of which was by the degree to which the various heresies harmed the orthodox Way. According to Ch'eng Hao (1032–85),

> The harm of Yang [Chu] and Mo[-tzu] is greater than that of Shen-tzu and Han-tzu [two ancient Legalist philosophers], and the harm of the Buddha and Lao-tzu is greater than that of Yang and Mo. . . . Since the shallowness and crudeness of Shen-tzu and Han-tzu is obvious, Mencius only refuted Yang and Mo because of their deluding the world to a greater extent. The words of the Buddha are near to the truth, and thus cannot be matched by Yang and Mo. That is why they are so harmful.[11]

Hu Chü-jen arrayed Lao-tzu, Chuang-tzu, and Buddhism in a similar hierarchy of harmfulness (or perhaps of outrageousness), as follows:

> Although Lao-tzu goes against the Way of the Sages, he does not dare to insult the Sages. Chuang-tzu does insult the Sages. But although he insults the Sages, he does not dare to insult the cosmos. The Buddha, however, insults the cosmos.[12]

In addition to rating their degree of harmfulness, scholars of the Ch'eng-Chu school also ranked heresies and heretics by the order in which the wayward were apt to be converted either from or to them. A canonical adumbration of this second sort of hierarchy of heresy appears in Mencius: "Those who desert the Mohist school are sure to turn to that of Yang; those who desert the Yang school are sure to turn to the Confucianist. When they turn to us we simply accept them."[13] Later Ch'eng-Chu scholars, however, commonly reversed the direction of such conversion sequences, primarily to show how an innocent indulgence in relatively minor heresies might lead one down the slippery slope to entrapment in a major one. Thus Ch'en Chien warned that the road to Ch'an led through Chuang-tzu.[14]

A final device for schematically relating heresies to one another did not distinguish between these heresies dualistically, hierarchically or otherwise, but rather reduced them to a common denominator of error. This particular heresiographical strategy may also be traced back to the first great Confucian heresiographer, Mencius. Although Mencius criticized his two major opponents, Yang Chu and Mo-tzu, for going to opposite extremes, he also criticized them together "because in his mind they had both made a similar kind of mistake," namely arguing for "moral judgments based upon calculations of *li* (benefit)."[15] If Mencius provided a precedent for finding a common point of error behind diverse heresies, he also furnished a memorable reductionist trope, based on a parable in which Mencius asked a king whether or not soldiers who fled only fifty paces from the scene of a battle were more meritorious than those who fled a full hundred paces (Mencius 1A.3). Later heresiographers such as Chu Hsi and Lu Lungch'i (1630–92) cited this parable to argue that divergent heresies were pretty much the same in order of merit (or demerit).[16]

Later Ch'eng-Chu scholars gave different accounts of just what was the common point on which supposedly divergent heresies converged. The most attractive possibility was selfishness, cited by Chu Hsi and some of his successors as the common failing of both the utilitarians on the one hand and the Buddhists and Taoists on the other.[17] According to Ch'en Chien, the heretical schools "all negate the naturalness of heavenly principles. They are as one in proceeding from the machinations and manipulations of selfish knowledge."[18] Some later heresiographers, however, mysteriously neglected to specify the common point on which all heresies converged, as illustrated in the following statement by Li Kuang-ti (1642–1718): "Chuang-tzu and Lao-tzu would extinguish the teaching, the Buddhists the Way, and Ch'an the moral nature. But their understanding is as one."[19]

Besides reducing all heresies to a common doctrinal or moral point, Neo-Confucian heresiographers also reduced them to one another, but particularly to the canonical ur-heresies condemned by Mencius, those of Yang Chu, Mo-tzu, and Kao-tzu, the heresiarchs. As in other matters heresiographical, Chu Hsi set the Neo-Confucian precedent for this identification by likening major "heretics" of his own era, Wang An-shih (1021–86) and Su Shih (1037–1101), to Mo and Yang, respectively.[20] But Chu also likened Mo-tzu's teachings to those of the Buddhists, indicating perhaps that Chu used Mo more as an all-purpose heretical trope than as the basis for an exercise in comparative philosophy.

In any case, Chu's identification of latter-day heretics with the heresiarchs, Yang and Mo, resounded down through the Neo-Confucian tradition, all the way to the nineteenth century. The sixteenth-century heresiographer Feng K'o (fl. 1562) accused Wang Yang-ming of promoting Mo,[21] while the seventeenth-century philosopher Huang Tsung-hsi (1610–95) remarked that Buddhism was nothing more than a deepening of Yang and Mo. Indeed, Huang went so far as to claim that "from ancient times to the present, all harm stemmed from Yang and Mo."[22] The nineteenth-century neo-orthodox heresiographer Fang Tung-shu

(1772–1851) observed that "the people of our age who refute the Buddhists assimilate the Buddhists to Yang and Mo," while conservative scholars of the late Ch'ing likened even the new Western learning of that era to that of Yang and Mo.[23]

In sum, Neo-Confucian heresiographers' identification of the canonical ur-heresies with those of their own day allowed them to discredit the latter all the more totally by equating them with those that had already been most thoroughly and authoritatively condemned. Moreover, if heresy was indeed all of a piece, like a monolith, then the study of its newer forms could have held little attraction or interest.

However, Neo-Confucian heresiographers did not in all cases simply reduce latter-day heresies to their ur-heretical archetypes. In some cases, they presented them as combinations or composites of several earlier heresies. This heresiographical strategy had the obvious polemical value of presenting the most objectionable contemporary heresy as a monstrous amalgamation of all past heresies, as the epitome of heretical evil. For many Neo-Confucian scholars of the Sung era, this epitome was embodied in Buddhism, which combined the errors of the ancient heterodox philosophers. In a notable anticipation of Chairman Mao's pronouncement of policy during the Great Leap forward, Chu Hsi stated that the Buddhists of his own time walked on two legs, Yang Chu and Mo Ti.[24] The Ming heresiographer, Feng K'o, specified just how Buddhism had combined these two ancient heresies:

> Alas! Mo [taught the doctrine of recognizing] no father. As for the Buddha, he rejected his kin and lived as a hermit, saying [that one should] leave home. Is this not the negation of one's father? Yang [taught the doctrine of recognizing] no lord. As for the Buddha, he abandoned other people and stood alone, saying [that one should] leave the world. Is this not the negation of one's lord? Yang's "negating one's lord" does not necessarily entail negating one's father. And Mo's "negating one's father" does not necessarily entail negating one's lord. Yet the Buddha combined the two negations, thus joining Yang and Mo in one person. If Yang and Mo are like wild beasts, then what of one who unites them?[25]

Later Ch'eng-Chu scholars, particularly Li Kuang-ti, repeated the accusation that the Buddha combined the most objectionable points of Yang and Mo, though Li also charged him with having amalgamated two forms of Taoism.[26]

Among all the forms of Buddhism, Neo-Confucians of the Ch'eng-Chu school singled out Ch'an as the most harmful to the Confucian Tao. The Ming-era heresiographer Huang Wan (1480–1554) wrote that "of all the heresies, none is greater than Ch'an. Ever since the study of Ch'an has flourished, the Way of the Sages has daily become more chaotic and confused."[27] His close contemporary Chan Ling proclaimed that "Ch'an is the heresy of heresies."[28] According to Huang Chen, the reason why Ch'an was the "heresy of heresies" was because of its combinatory character. It incorporated the comic absurdities of the Taoist philosophers, Chuang-tzu and Lieh-tzu, into Buddhism.[29] Ch'an, like Buddhism in general, was a syncretic heresy, only more so.

From the point of view of many late Ming and Ch'ing scholars, the most syncretic, as well as the most threatening heretic of all was a nominal Confucian, Wang Yang-ming (1472–1528). Wang's learning may have been distantly derived from a quasi-Confucian source, Lu Hsiang-shan. But "generally speaking, [Wang] had consistently rebelled on those points on which [Lu] Hsiang-shan was in accord with the learning of the sages, and had consistently extended those points on which [Lu] Hsiang-shan had been close to the learning of Ch'an."[30]

But the gravity of Wang Yang-ming's heresy did not spring simply from his veering much closer to Ch'an than had his Confucian predecessors. It also arose from his having devised an even more comprehensive summa of heresies than appeared even in Ch'an and other forms of Buddhism. According to Hsiung Tz'u-li (1635–1709), Wang managed to combine the learning of Ch'an with the perverse practice of the hegemonists, even throwing in the classical philosopher Kao-tzu for good measure:

> Wen-ch'eng's (= Wang Yang-ming's) learning was mixed with that of Ch'an. Wen-cheng's practical undertakings were purely those of the hegemonists. . . . He strung the two together, [and with his teaching on] human nature's being neither good nor evil, distinctly followed the example set by Kao-tzu.[31]

Like Confucius himself, Wang thus composed a complete concert, albeit of the licentious songs of Cheng rather than the refined music of Shao.

In the same treatise, *A Record of Defending the Way* (Hsien-tao lu), Hsiung also credited (or discredited) Wang with synthesizing another pair of heresies and heretics, those of Kao-tzu and the Northern Sung literatus, Su Shih (= Su Tung-p'o):

> Kao-tzu only wished to smash Mencius' [teaching on] "goodness"; and Tung-p'o only wished to smash Master Ch'eng's [teaching on] "reverence." But when Yang-ming's sayings became current, then both "goodness" and "reverence" were shattered together in one fell swoop.[32]

So convincing was this heresiographical portrait of Wang as the syncretic epitome of error that its effects outlived the demise of imperial China. As late as the 1970s, Chinese Marxist historians accused Wang of having diabolically combined two primary heretical roles (though from a Marxist rather than Neo-Confucian perspective), those of priest and executioner.

The latter half of the Ming era was indeed one of the most syncretic ages in Chinese intellectual history. It was an era in which the "Unity of the Three Teachings" movement flourished, and in which leading Confucian thinkers sometimes expressed sympathy for Buddhist and Taoist ideas and practices. The heresiographical works composed by orthodox Ch'eng-Chu scholars of the sixteenth and seventeenth centuries could not help but reflect this legacy. But this does not necessarily mean that these heresiographers' "take" on mid- and late-Ming syncretism was very accurate or perceptive. First, the heresiographers accused late Ming Confucians of having synthesized the ideas and practices of semilegendary heresiarchs, such as Kao-tzu, Mo-tzu, and Yang Chu, with whom they had little or no connection, intellectual or otherwise. Second, the orthodox polemic against late Ming Confucian syncretists followed a negative and reductionist approach, accusing them of having smashed this or that orthodox teaching in favor of its heretical obverse to form a perverse mirror image of orthodoxy. The resulting caricature bore little resemblance to the true face of late-Ming syncretism. It also exaggerated its power and influence. Following in the footsteps of Mencius, who hyperbolically remarked that all the world had turned to either Yang or Mo (Mencius 3B.9), late-Ming heresiographers presented themselves as a sort of righteous remnant alone in a Philistine wilderness. Ch'en Chien, for example, lamented that "in today's world, everyone reveres and believes in the school of Lu [Hsiang-shan]; and I alone reject it."[33]

However rare the appearance of resolute Confucians and however tenuous the tradition of the Way, in every age a master heresiographer had arisen to expose the errors of each new heresy and restore the boundary between orthodoxy and heresy. According to Ch'en Shou-ch'i (1771–1834), "Of old, Confucius abhorred the local hypocrites, Mencius refuted Yang and Mo, Han Yü refuted the Buddhists, and the Ch'engs, Chang [Tsai] and Chu Hsi refuted Ch'an."[34] The mid-Ch'ing scholar Ch'en Tzu matched heresiographers and heresiarchs of more recent times as follows:

> Heaven gave birth to Tzu-ching [Lu Hsiang-shan] at the time when [the Sung dynasty] moved to the South. When [Lu] threw the tradition of learning into chaos . . . , then [Heaven] had to give birth to Chu Hsi in order to connect with the tradition of Confucius and Mencius. Heaven gave birth to [Wang] Yang-ming in the late Ming era. When [Wang] conflated Buddhism with Confucianism with [his teaching that] "the streets are filled with sages," then [Heaven] had to give birth to [Chang] Yang-yüan (= Chang Li-hsiang) in order to continue the tradition of Ch'eng and Chu.[35]

However, these master heresiographers' redemarcation of the boundary between orthodoxy and heresy was no simple task, particularly in view of the seductive subtlety and subterfuge of heretics, especially of those like Lu Hsiang-shan and Wang Yang-ming who claimed to be Confucian. According to Lo Ch'in-shun (1465–1547), Lu had "outwardly eschewed the name" of Ch'an while he "inwardly employed its substance."[36] The orthodox early-Ch'ing scholar, Lu Lung-ch'i, saw a larger long-range pattern, even a sort of conspiracy, behind such heretical dissimulations:

> Among Han and T'ang Confucians, those who venerated orthodox scholarship only respected Confucius and Mencius. When the Way of Confucius and Mencius was respected, then the words of the [hetero-dox] hundred schools of philosophy were obliterated. From T'ang times onward, heretics and crooked scholars, knowing the Confucians' respect for Confucius and Mencius, all relied on Confucius and Mencius to broadcast their own theories. When we talked of Confucius and Mencius, they also talked of Confucius and Mencius. Thus scholars were not able to distinguish the right and wrong of the matter. When Ch'eng and Chu came forth and venerated the orthodox while refuting the heterodox, then the Way of Confucius and Mencius was once again glorified, and thus the whole world respected it. But from Sung times onward, heretics and crooked scholars, knowing the Confucians' respect for Ch'eng and Chu, all relied upon Ch'eng and Chu to broadcast their own theories. When we talked of Ch'eng and Chu, they also talked of Ch'eng and Chu. Thus scholars were again not able to distinguish the right and wrong of the matter. As Ch'eng and Chu spoke of "heavenly principle," they also spoke of "heavenly princi-ple." Although the name of "heavenly principle" was the same, what it referred to was [as distant from one another] as Heaven and Earth.[37]

Lu went on to assert that even staunch adherents of orthodoxy found it difficult if not impossible to detect heresy when it masqueraded as orthodoxy. Small wonder that orthodox heresiographers like Ch'en Chien proclaimed that it was better to be openly heretical, like the Ch'an masters, than to attempt to conceal one's heresy, like Lu Hsiang-shan.[38]

From the point of view of orthodox Ch'eng-Chu scholars, heresy's capacity to disguise its true face increased over time, as heresies became increasingly subtle and difficult to recognize.[39] As Ch'eng Hao remarked, "The reason why the Way is not glorified is that heresy harms it. In the past, this harm was proximate and easy to recognize. But now the harm is deep and difficult to distinguish. In the past, misleading people took advantage of their confusion and ignorance. Now, infiltrating them depends on their cleverness."[40] The progress of Buddhism in China was a case in point:

> In the past there was also a time when Buddhism flourished. But it still only exalted image worship, so the harm it did was very small. But the fashion today is to first speak of human nature, destiny, the Way, and

its virtue, which first and foremost stimulates the knowledgeable. Thus the more clever are one's mental faculties, the deeper one sinks.[41]

The Ming heresiographer, Ch'en Chien, saw the history of heresy's sub-tilization as a multistage process that extended over a longer period of time:

Now from the decline of the Chou [dynasty] down to the Warring States era, although there were different heresies in the world, such as those of Yang, Mo, Shen, and Han and the like, their theories were still shallow and not enough to deeply delude people. Proceeding to the Eastern Han era, Buddhism entered China. And proceeding again to the [era of the] Northern and Southern dynasties, Bodhidharma came from the west to transmit Ch'an. His discussion on "illuminating the mind and seeing the nature" to begin with was enough to snow clever scholars. And the likes of his [seeing the amoral] "original counte-nance" was enough to confuse the truth of the *Doctrine of the Mean's* "not yet expressed" [part of the moral mind]. Alas! Ch'an Buddhism's proximity and resemblance [to the Confucian Way] is already enough to delude people. And how much weightier is [Lu] Hsiang-shan's change of appearance (without changing the reality), borrowing from Confucian books to paper over the cracks in Buddhist learning![42]

Orthodox early Ch'ing scholars echoed their Sung and Ming predecessors' pronouncements on the greater subtlety of latter-day heresies. Ku Yen-wu (1613–81) remarked that whereas "the [heretical] 'pure talk' of the past spoke of Lao-tzu and Chuang-tzu, the pure talk of the present speaks of Confucius and Mencius."[43] And Chang Li-hsiang complained that whereas "the heresies of the past were outside the orthodox Way, the heresies of the present are within the orthodox Way."[44] Finally, a prominent Korean scholar, Yi I (1536–84), also argued that heresy had become more and more subtle and perfidious over the course of Chinese history, culminating in Ch'an.[45]

But the greatest damage to the Confucian Way was caused not by Ch'an, but by the crypto-Buddhists, Lu Hsiang-shan and Wang Yang-ming, who claimed to be Confucians. Of the two, Ch'en Chien regarded Lu as the more harmful to the Way because of his greater skill in concealing his Ch'an. In contrast, Wang Yang-ming's Ch'an was more obvious.[46] On the other hand, Lu Lung-ch'i saw Wang as the greatest threat to the Way not only because of the subtlety of his heresy, but also because he really did have some good points about him that moved others to accept his teachings.[47] In other words, the subtlety of heresy might even extend to a partial apprehension of the orthodox Way, as well as an artful imitation of it, which made it all the more difficult to draw a boundary between the two.

The subtlety of heresy, moreover, was matched by the precariousness of orthodoxy, rendering the boundary problem even more acute. As the oft-quoted sentence from one of the apocrypha to the *Classic of Changes* remarks, an infinitesimal error at the beginning will lead to an infinite error by the end.[48] According to Ch'eng I (1033-1107), the heresiographical genius of Mencius lay in his ability to extrapolate the dire end results of the relatively small errors committed by Yang and Mo:

> Yang Chu originally studied rightness and Mo-Tzu originally studied co-humanity [both of which were primary Confucian virtues]. But since what they studied was slightly biased, its outcome [eventually] reached the [extreme] point of denying fathers and lords. Mencius wanted to rectify the original source [of this outcome]. Therefore, he extrapolated to that [extreme] point.[49]

In attempting to emulate Mencius's perceptive foreknowledge of monstrous future heresies that might eventually develop from slight perturbations in contemporary orthodoxy, Neo-Confucian heresiographers cultivated a sort of paranoid style of heresiography. For the apparent absence of clear boundaries between orthodoxy and heresy meant that the latter might be found in the very heart of orthodoxy. This enemy within might even go unrecognized until some great disaster overtook the country, such as the decline and fall of the Ming dynasty and the Manchu conquest of the 1640s. Only then would the extent of the harm wrought by this philosophical fifth column be fully palpable.

However, inasmuch as orthodox Ch'eng-Chu scholars frequently depicted heresy as stemming from a partial or one-sided apprehension of orthodox truth, they themselves were in a way responsible for inserting heresy in the heart of orthodoxy. Had they made more of an attempt to understand various "heresies" on their own terms, and not as some narrow expression or deviant variation of orthodoxy, then it would perhaps have been easier to draw a clear boundary between orthodoxy and heresy. But the ability to recognize a universe of discourse apart from our own is a rare talent, as much for modern scholars as for premodern heresiographers.

NOTES

1. Richard J. Smith, *Fortune-tellers and Philosophers: Divination in Chinese Society* (Boulder, Colo.: Westview Press, 1991), p. 51.

2. Steven M. Wasserstrom, *Between Muslim and Jew: The Problem of Symbiosis under Early Islam* (Princeton: Princeton University Press, 1995), p. 154.

3. Chu Hsi, "Ta Chiang Te-kung," in Wang Mou-hung, "Chu-tzu lun-hsüeh chieh-yao yü," in *Chu-tzu nien-p'u* (Taipei: Shang-wu, 1971), p. 350.

4. Hu Chü-jen, *Chü-yeh lu* (Taipei: Shang-wu, 1966) 1.2.

5. Chang Li-hsiang, *Pei-wang lu*, in Morohashi Tetsuji et al., eds., *Shushigaku taikei* (Tokyo: Meitoku Shuppansha, 1974) 11:383.

6. Yang Hsiang-k'uei, *Ch'ing-ju hsüeh-an hsin-pien*, vol. 1 (Chinan: Ch'i-Lu shu-she, 1988), p. 641.

7. Erich Goode, "On Behalf of Labeling Theory," in Henry N. Pontell, ed., *Social Deviance: Readings in Theory and Research* (Englewood Cliffs, N.J.: Prentice Hall, 1993), p. 101.

8. Ch'eng I and Ch'eng Hao, in Chu Hsi, ed., *Erh-Ch'eng yü-lu*, (Taipei: Shang-wu, 1966) 16.261.

9. Ch'en Chien, *Hsüeh-pu t'ung-pien* (Taipei: Shang-wu, 1966), 12.160.

10. Yang Ming-shih, in T'ang Chien, *Ch'ing hsüeh-an hsiao-chih* (Taipei: Shang-wu, 1969) 7.204.

11. Ch'eng Hao, quoted in Chu Hsi, ed., Chiang Yung, annot., *Chin-ssu lu* (Taipei: Kuang-wen, 1972 reprint) 13.1.

12. Hu Chü-jen, *Chü-yeh lu* 7.81.

13. *Mencius* 7B.26, trans. in D. C. Lau, *Mencius* (Harmondsworth, U.K.: Penguin Books, 1970), p. 199.

14. Ch'en Chien, *Hsüeh-pu t'ung-pien* 3.24.

15. Philip J. Ivanhoe, *Ethics in the Confucian Tradition: The Thought of Mencius and Wang Yang-ming* (Atlanta: Scholars Press, 1990), p. 9.

16. Wing-tsit Chan, *Chu Hsi: New Studies* (Honolulu: University of Hawaii Press, 1989), p. 452, citing Chu Hsi's *Wen-chi* 54:8a–b; Lu Lung-ch'i, *Wen-hsüeh lu* (Taipei: Shang-wu, 1966) 3.25.

17. Wm. Theodore de Bary, *The Message of the Mind in Neo-Confucianism* (New York: Columbia University Press, 1989), p. 3.

18. Ch'en Chien, *Hsüeh-pu t'ung-pien* 6.69.

19. Li Kuang-ti, *Jung-ts'un yü-lu* 20.11, in Wang Yün-wu et al., eds., *Ssu-k'u ch'üan-shu chen-pen, chiu-chi* (Taipei: Shang-wu, 1979 reprint), vol. 198.

20. Peter K. Bol, "Chu Hsi's Redefinition of Literati Learning," in Wm. Theodore de Bary and John W. Chaffee, eds., *Neo-Confucian Education: The Formative Stage*, (Berkeley: University of California Press, 1989), pp. 161 and 183; Daniel K. Gardner, *Learning to Be a Sage: Selections from the Conversations of Master Chu, Arranged Topically, by Chu Hsi*, translated with a commentary by Daniel K. Gardner (Berkeley: University of California Press, 1990), pp. 68–69.

21. Chan, *Chu Hsi: New Studies*, p. 469.

22. Huang Tsung-hsi, *Meng-tzu shih-shuo* 3.5b, in *Li-chou i-chu hui-k'an*, vol. 2 (Taipei: Lung-yen ch'u-pan she, 1969 reprint).

23. Fang Tung-shu, "Pien tao-lun," in *Shushigaku taikei* 11:428; Hsiao Kung-ch'üan, "Sheng-chiao yü i-tuan," in Hsiao, *Chi-yüan wen-lu*, in *Hsiao Kung-ch'üan hsien-sheng ch'üan-chi* (Taipei: Lien-ching ch'u-pan shih-yeh kung-ssu, 1983), 9:48–49.

24. Chu Hsi, *Chu-tzu yü-lei*, quoted in Chiang I-pin, *Sung-tai ju-shih t'iao-ho-lun chi p'ai-fo-lun chih yen-chiu* (Taipei: Taiwan Shang-wu, 1988), p. 7.

25. Feng K'o, *Ch'iu-shih pien*, pp. 49–50, in Araki Kengo et al., eds., *Kinsei Kanseki sokan, shiso sanhen* (Tokyo: Chubun Shuppansha), vol. 15.

26. Li Kuang-ti, *Jung-ts'un yü-lu* 20.10b and 20.22a.

27. Huang Wan, *Ming-tao pien* (Beijing: Chung-hua shu-chü, 1983) 1.2.

28. Chan Ling, *I-tuan pien-cheng*, pp. 9–10, in Araki Kengo et al., eds., *Kinsei Kanseki sokan, shiso zokuhen* (Tokyo: Chubun shuppansha), vol. 5.

29. Huang Chen, *Tung-fa chiang-i*, in Huang Tsung-hsi and Ch'üan Tsu-wang, eds., *Tseng-pu Sung-Yüan hsüeh-an* (Taipei: Chung-hua shu-chü, 1970) 86.3a.

30. Lei Pa, quoted in Kao Ling-yin and Ch'en Ch'i-fang, *Fu-chien Chu-tzu-hsüeh* (Fuchou: Fu-chien jen-min ch'u-pan she, 1986), p. 464.

31. Hsiung Tz'u-li, *Hsien-tao-lu*, in Hsü Shih-ch'ang, ed., *Ch'ing-ju hsüeh-an* (Taipei: Shih-chieh shu-chü, 1979 reprint) 38.14a.

32. Ibid. 38.8b.

33. Ch'en Chien, *Hsüeh-pu t'ung-pien* 3.35.

34. Ch'en Shou-ch'i, "I-li pien," from *Tso-hai wen-chi* 3, quoted in Ch'ien Mu, *Chung-kuo chin san-pai-nien hsüeh-shu shih* (Taipei: Taiwan Shang-wu, 1968), 2:567.

35. Ch'en Tzu, postscript to *Yang-yüan hsien-sheng nien-p'u*, in T'ang Chien, *Ch'ing hsüeh-an hsiao-chih* 11.379.

36. Lo Ch'in-shun, *Knowledge Painfully Acquired: The K'un-chih chi by Lo Ch'in-shun* 2.41, translated, edited, and with an introduction by Irene Bloom (New York: Columbia University Press, 1987), p. 140.

37. Lu Lung-ch'i, "Hsüeh-shu pien, shang," in *Lu Chia-shu hsien-sheng wen-chi* (Taipei: Taiwan Shang-wu, 1965) 1.10.

38. Ch'en Chien, *Hsüeh-pu t'ung-pien* 5.91.

39. Wm. Theodore de Bary makes a similar point in *The Message of the Mind*, p. 116.

40. Ch'eng Hao, in Chang Chiu-shao, *Li-hsüeh lei-pien* 8.2a, in *Ssu-ku ch'üan-shu chen-pen, liu chi*, vol. 186; also (slightly modified) in Ch'en Chien, *Hsüeh-pu t'ung-pien* 6.116.

41. Ch'eng I and Ch'eng Hao, *Erh-Ch'eng yü-lu* 1.19.

42. Ch'en Chien, *Hsüeh-pu t'ung-pien*, "T'i-kang," p. 2.

43. Ku Yen-wu, "Fu-tzu chih yen hsing yü t'ien-tao," in *Yüan-ch'ao pen Jih-chih lu* (Taipei: Ming-lun ch'u-pan she, 1970) 9.196.

44. Chang Li-hsiang, in *Ch'ing-ju hsüeh-an hsiao-chih* 1.9.

45. Martina Deuchler, "Reject the False and Uphold the Straight: Attitudes toward Heterodox Thought in Early Yi Korea," in Wm. Theodore de Bary and JaHyun Kim Haboush, eds., *The Rise of Neo-Confucianism in Korea* (New York: Columbia University Press, 1985), pp. 394–95.

46. Ch'en Chien, *Hsüeh-pu t'ung-pien* 9.122.

47. Lu Lung-ch'i, *San-yü-t'ang jih-chi* (Taipei: Shang-wu, 1965) B.93.

48. *I-wei t'ung-kua yen* 5a, in *I-wei*, ed. Wang Ch'ien-yü (Pan-ch'iao: San-ts'ai shu-chü, 1978 reprint), p. 205.

49. *Erh-Ch'eng yü-lu* 11.172. Also translated in Ivanhoe, *Ethics in the Confucian Tradition*, p. 23.

GLOSSARY

Ch'an	禪
Chan Ling	詹陵
Chang Li-hsiang	張履祥
Chang Tsai	張載
Chang Yang-yuan	張楊園
Ch'en Chien	陳建
Ch'en Shou-ch'i	陳壽祺
Ch'en Tzu	陳梓
Cheng	鄭
Ch'eng	程
Ch'eng-Chu	程朱
Ch'eng Hao	程顥
Ch'eng I	程頤
Chu Hsi	朱熹
Fang Tung-shu	方東樹
Feng K'o	馮柯
Han-tzu	韓子
Han Yü	韓愈
Hsien-tao lu	閑道錄
hsin	心
Hsiung Tz'u-li	熊賜履
Hu Chü-jen	胡居仁
Huang Chen	黃震
Huang Tsung-hsi	黃宗羲
Huang Wan	黃綰
i-tuan	異端
Kao-tzu	告子
Ku Yen-wu	顧炎武
li (principle)	理
li (profit)	利
Li Kuang-ti	李光地
Lieh-tzu	列子
Lo Ch'in-shun	羅欽順
Lu Hsiang-shan	陸象山
Lu Lung-ch'i	陸隴其
Mo Ti	墨翟

Shao	韶
Shen	申
Shen-tzu	申子
Su Shih	蘇軾
Su Tung-p'o	蘇東坡
Tao-t'ung	道統
Tzu-ching	子靜
Wang An-shih	王安石
Wang Yang-ming	王陽明
Wen-ch'eng	文成
Yang Chu	楊朱
Yang Ming-shih	楊名時
Yi I	李珥

6

"Goodness Unbound"
Wang Yang-ming and the Redrawing of the Boundary of Confucianism

Kandice Hauf

The boundaries of Confucianism constantly shifted according to the individual Confucian's response to intellectual and socioeconomic changes. By the sixteenth century, not only did the orthodox teachings of Confucians of the Sung dynasty (960–1279) not represent an unbroken transmission, but over the course of three hundred years, they had undergone many recreations by individual thinkers in unique contexts.[1] Such was the case for Wang Yang-ming (1472–1529). His inclusive definition of Confucianism differed from that of the leading Sung synthesizer of Neo-Confucianism, Chu Hsi (1130–1200), evolved in stages in response to his own personal development, and expanded the boundaries of Confucian thought and practice for himself and his followers. First, I explore the issue of the boundaries of Confucianism by examining in general, Wang's notions of Confucianism in relation to Chu Hsi's teachings, Buddhism and Taoism. Next, in particular, I analyze Wang's expansion of Confucianism in practice through his experience with non-Han peoples. The focus is on his appropriation of the Kweichow Miao's popular cult of Hsiang by re-inscribing a Confucian meaning on this local religious practice. Finally, I consider the question of intellectual boundaries in terms of the use of physical space by evaluating the use Wang and his followers made of Buddhist and, to a lesser extent, Taoist establishments, such as shrines, temples and monasteries.

It is common knowledge that Wang Yang-ming was a pivotal thinker of the Ming. He was not the first or only person to question the sterility he saw in Ch'eng-Chu orthodoxy, that is, the officially sanctioned teachings of Chu Hsi and Ch'eng I, but Wang was able to clearly present a comprehensive philosophical alternative which he exemplified in his own life. Moreover, he inspired numerous disciples who accepted his ideas and continued his teachings after his death in 1529. Wang Yang-ming was not very interested in abstract definitions,[2] but in concrete results. To a certain extent we may say that for Wang the end justified the means in his attempt to open up sagehood through "goodness unbound," that is, the recovery of the innate moral knowledge (*liang-chih*) he taught was present in each person. For Wang, Confucian boundaries were fluid. He dealt not only with setting boundaries, but also with removing and shifting boundaries. He implied that innate moral knowledge gave him, and ultimately everyone, the autonomy to judge what was of value in alternate spiritual traditions, and therefore, the ability to transcend the boundaries between sage and commoner, and between Confucianism, Buddhism, and Taoism. His redefinition of Confucianism was governed by several factors, including the stages of Wang's own personal intellectual development, and the social roles that he assumed at various junctures in his life.

REDRAWING THE BOUNDARY OF CONFUCIAN ORTHODOXY

Wang Yang-ming came to view himself as an orthodox Confucian. To uphold this view he had to reconcile his philosophy with that of Chu Hsi and Ch'eng I, recognized as orthodox in the Ming, and to evaluate his attitude toward Buddhism and Taoism. As a *chin-shih* of 1499 and an official, Wang was expected to have mastered the Ch'eng-Chu interpretations which the state had adopted as the standard to be tested in the civil service examinations.[3] For many years Wang studied Chu Hsi and tried, but failed, to put Chu's method of self-cultivation, the investigation of things (*ko-wu*), into practice. Chu taught that principles should be sought in external things, but Wang came to the conclusion that principles were situated internally within the mind. As we will see in the next section of this chapter, Wang's years in Lung-ch'ang, Kweichow were important ones for him to test and expand his own philosophy. There he had an enlightenment experience, realizing that principle (*li*) was found in the mind (*hsin*). This contrasted with Chu Hsi's view that principle was found in nature (*hsing*). Though rejecting both Chu's method and object of self-cultivation, Wang satisfied his claim to orthodoxy in his own mind by concluding that Chu Hsi eventually arrived at ideas similar to his own. Wang's main statement of this is his essay "Chu Hsi's Final Conclusions Arrived at Late in Life," written in 1515 and published in 1518.[4] Wang presented himself here as part of the orthodox transmission of Confucianism by developing his own interpretation of the transmission of the Way (*tao-t'ung*).[5] He wrote that the transmission of the Way first went from Confucius to Mencius. It was revived in the Sung dynasty by Chou Tun-i (1017–73) and Ch'eng Hao (1032–85), and was further developed by Chu Hsi and his followers who, however, fragmented the teaching so much that it had disintegrated.[6] It was implicit in Wang's argument that he had recovered the transmission of the Way, and his disciples indeed hailed him as the contemporary recoverer of the Way in their own interpretations of the transmission of the Way.[7] Wang had accepted his first disciple in 1505, and through his students and publications of his writings, his teachings were becoming well known and controversial in the 1510s. Many contemporary Confucians criticized him as having misrepresented Chu Hsi.[8] In a letter of 1520 to a critic, Lo Ch'in-shun (1465– 1547), Wang stated his belief that the Way belonged to all and that the words of Chu Hsi, and even of Confucius, needed to be evaluated for their contemporary relevance:

> The Way is public (*kung*) and belongs to the whole world, and the doctrine (*hsüeh*) is also public and belongs to the whole world. They are not the private (*ssu*) properties of Master Chu or even Confucius. They are open to all and the only proper way to discuss them is to do so openly.[9]

Wang's reinterpretation of Confucianism did not eclipse state-supported Ch'eng-Chu Confucianism. However, for about a century, the numerous followers of Wang's teachings played a lively and important role in China's cultural life.[10] In large part in reaction to the logical extremes to which the T'ai-chou school of Wang followers pushed his ideas, the seventeenth century witnessed a conservative turn away from Wang.[11] In the late Ming, Wang was often criticized, as in these harsh words of the Tung-lin scholar Kao P'an-lung (1562– 1626): "Not satisfied with remaining as an adherent of Buddhism and Taoism, Yang-ming was determined to usurp a position in the orthodox Confucian line."[12] Despite criticism, Wang and his followers believed he was an orthodox follower of Confucius.

In agreement with Kao P'an-lung's accusation, many Ming Confucians decided that Wang was heterodox. During his lifetime some of his students did not pass the examinations when they espoused his interpretations.[13] In 1521 Wang's teachings were criticized as heterodox and were the reason for his not being given a post.[14] In late 1528, Wang was very ill and started home from his final post in Kwangsi without waiting for official permission. He did not reach his home in Chekiang, but died in Kiangsi in January 1529. After his death, the Minister of Rites accused him of heterodoxy and deserting his final office.[15] Therefore, posthumous honors were not given, and his earlier titles were taken away. Only in 1567 did the new emperor grant him a posthumous title (*Wen-ch'eng*, completion of culture), and restore Wang's other titles to him and to his son.[16] From 1572 to 1573 there was a debate in court over the question of Wang's inclusion in the Confucian temple.[17] In 1573 Wang's inclusion was approved, but the actual installation came only in 1584 after the death of its main opponent, Grand Secretary Chang Chü-cheng (1525–82).[18] Enshrinement in the Confucian temple, an honor bestowed on only four men during the Ming, conferred orthodox status on Wang. As we have seen, his followers had already considered Wang a teacher of orthodox Confucian learning through their own interpretation of the transmission of the Way.[19] After 1584, Wang officially became part of the state religion and was worshipped in all Confucian temples throughout China.

Enshrinement in the Confucian temple did not protect Wang from posthumous criticism. One of Wang's most prominent critics was the Ch'ing scholar Ku Yen-wu (1613–82), who blamed the fall of the Ming dynasty on what he interpreted as the useless speculation on mind and inattention to statecraft that Wang Yang-ming's teachings supposedly encouraged in his followers.[20]

CROSSING THE BOUNDARIES BETWEEN CONFUCIANISM, BUDDHISM, AND TAOISM

Influenced by the religio-philosophies of both Buddhism and Taoism, their teachings figured most prominently in Wang's intellectual universe. In fact, Wang was seen to be so influenced by Buddhism that many accused him of being a Ch'an Buddhist rather than a Confucian. Tu Wei-ming writes of Wang's life as one comprising seven main wrenching episodes, one of which was "his abortive attempt to find a meaningful life in either the Taoist cult of longevity or the Ch'an Buddhist practice of spiritual detachment during his self-imposed moratorium in his early thirties."[21] It should, however, be noted that Wang Yang-ming was not a glaring exception in this regard. Much of the reevaluation and restoration of Confucianism had been attempted with the impetus generated by the strength and appeal of immortality and the transcendent ideal in Buddhism and Taoism from the late Han through the T'ang. On the nature of the challenge to Confucians in the T'ang-Sung period, Yü Ying-shih has written:

> It is then quite clear that the Neo-Confucian breakthrough would not be complete unless and until the Neo-Confucians succeed in developing a metaphysical vision of the transcendent reality of their own that can take the place of Ch'an Buddhism. In other words, the vital area in which Neo-Confucianism must compete with Ch'an Buddhism was not this world but the other world. For, as we have seen above, the Ch'anists had been willing all along to cede this world to the Confucians. It was for this reason, I believe, that the Sung Neo-Confucians, from Chou Tun-yi onward, set as their central task the metaphysical construction of the Confucian other world culminating in the idea of the Heavenly Principle.[22]

With the development of Neo-Confucianism, there was unquestionably a certain blurring of the metaphysical boundaries between the Buddhists, Taoists, and Confucians. Although the transcendent aspect of Confucianism was greatly strengthened in the Sung, Ming Confucians continued to find philosophical relevance and personal consolation in Buddhism and Taoism. In addition, in the Ming, there was so much borrowing and appropriation of terminology between the various traditions that elements from these two religio-philosophies were often considered as just shared parts of a common Chinese heritage. For example, Ming literature is rich in Buddhist and Taoist ideas, allusions, and themes.[23] Images and architecture from Buddhism and Taoism dotted the Chinese landscape.[24] The ninth-century suppression of Buddhism broke its political power, but Buddhism continued to play a vibrant role in T'ang-Sung society.[25]

On the other hand, from the late T'ang onwards, a sharp sense of boundary began to develop to separate Confucianism from Buddhism and Taoism. Chu Hsi strongly criticized Buddhism, starting from the major criticism that Buddhists were selfish (*ssu*) in devoting themselves exclusively to self-cultivation, rather than serving the world.[26] He included his contemporary Lu Hsiang-shan (1139–93) as a culprit who committed the Buddhist error of identifying principle with the mind. Ch'eng-Chu followers in the Yüan and early Ming on the whole became even more anti-Buddhist than the Sung founders of Neo-Confucianism.[27] When Wang Yang-ming propounded his philosophy of the mind in the mid Ming, even though he did not associate himself closely with Lu, the similarities in their basic orientation meant that others would link them together. Critics of Wang, using the precedent of Chu's labeling of Lu as Ch'an, also branded Wang a Ch'an Buddhist.

Under the Ming dynasty, institutional Buddhism continued, but was not very dynamic until it underwent a revival in the late sixteenth and early seventeenth centuries.[28] The Ming founder had been an orphan who had become a monk in order to survive. As emperor, however, he established regulations to limit the number of both Buddhist and Taoist monasteries and clergy, although these were not always or consistently enforced.[29] Several Ming emperors were patrons of Buddhism or Taoism.[30] Wang Yang-ming, therefore, grew up in a society where Buddhism, Taoism, and Confucianism had amalgamated to a great extent. Buddhism and Taoism had great personal relevance for Wang, and he spent years studying them both. Later in his life, he realized the social relevance of Confucianism. He then criticized Buddhism and Taoism as too selfish because they did not advocate ordering the world. However, he continued to advocate taking from Buddhism and Taoism what he found helpful. In the course of applying his philosophy in teaching and practical statecraft, Wang distinguished among the three ways of thinking, but found transcending grounds to teach an ecumenical approach.[31]

It is well known that Wang Yang-ming studied Taoism as a young man. An often repeated tale about him is that when he was sixteen, he spent his wedding night conversing with a Taoist priest about immortality.[32] Taoist longevity techniques might have appealed to Wang in part because he suffered from poor health throughout his life. There was some family tradition for his interest in popular religious techniques, as Wang's great-great-grandfather had been a recluse skilled in divination.[33] However, Wang's father, the first-place *chin-shih* of 1481, appeared to have been a stern Confucian official who eschewed Buddhism and Taoism.[34]

Even while in office, Wang continued to meet with Taoist hermits.[35] In his teaching Wang used Taoist terms.[36] Wang met his students where their interests and concerns were. In one exchange, Wang replied to his disciple's question by using Taoist terms:

> Innate moral knowledge is one. Its active function is called the spirit, its pervasion the *ch'i*, and its condensation the essence. . . . If you are clear about my theory of innate moral knowledge, then questions of this kind will be solved without further explanations. Otherwise, there will still be a lot of things such as the "Three Passes," the "Seven Rounds," and the "Nine Turns" mentioned in your letter which remain undefined and uncertain.[37]

Wang uses the Taoist terms metaphorically to refer back to his all-encompassing philosophy of innate moral knowledge. But at the end of his reply, Wang warned his students not to delve more deeply into Taoist teachings. This exchange demonstrates that Wang and his students were familiar and at home with Taoist terminology. In one essay, Wang even uses the line from the *Chuang-tzu* about no longer needing the fish trap once the fish are caught to introduce his approach to the five classics. He uses this to emphasize that the classics do not need to be studied every day, but should be used as general reference material.[38] On other occasions when Wang uses anecdotes from the *Chuang-tzu*, he does so to criticize Taoism. After all, the Taoist classics, the *Chuang-tzu* and the *Lao-tzu*, were also classics of Chinese literature and formed part of the mental universe of all educated Chinese.[39] Rather than proving that Wang was a Taoist at heart, his use of Taoist terms and images simply shows that he was willing to meet his students on their own terms, and to employ all the resources of Chinese culture to convey his message.

Wang Yang-ming readily admitted that he studied Taoism for the attainment of longevity until he was in his thirties. In his early thirties Wang removed himself from the world to practice Ch'an Buddhist detachment and Taoist longevity techniques.[40] Wang was under pressure from himself, his family, and his society to succeed in a public career, and this withdrawal functioned as safety valve and nourishment. As his contemporary and friend Chan Jo-shui wrote in his funerary epitaph, Wang had gone through five "falls" before returning to Confucianism: "His fourth was in the art of pursuing immortality, and his fifth was in Buddhism. Only in the year 1506, did he return to the correct teaching of the sages."[41] Wang returned to office in 1504 and concentrated more on Confucianism as the ideology of his profession and as personal philosophy, but without entirely eschewing Buddhism and Taoism.

Wang Yang-ming's ecumenical approach can be seen in the question he wrote for the Shantung provincial civil service examination of 1504. This act was significant as it marked Wang's return to office. As a *chin-shih* and an official, Wang was expected to have mastered the Cheng-Chu Confucianism supported by the state as orthodoxy. Wang's examination questions are significant documents for understanding his thinking about the Confucian heritage and statecraft, about the subjects students and future officials should know and the way they should think. After receiving the *chin-shih* degree in 1499 (on his third attempt), Wang served in minor posts until 1502. From 1502 to 1504 he was in retirement studying Taoism and Buddhism. In 1504, at the age of thirty-three, Wang once again had a government post. One of his duties was to oversee the Shantung provincial examination. This location had a powerful resonance for Wang as it was the birthplace of both Confucius and Mencius. After questions on specific texts, (the *Four Books*, the *Book of Changes*, and the *Spring and Autumn Annals*), Wang set several essays under three standard categories. Under the category of current topics (*ts'e*), Wang posed five questions. The second question in this set concerned Buddhism and Taoism. In order to show more precisely the content and tone, the entire text of this examination question is quoted here:[42]

> Buddhism and Taoism's damage to the world did not occur in one day. More than one person has attacked them, but still we have not gotten rid of them. Does that mean that their way is something we cannot eliminate? Or, is there something wrong with the method of removal? Or, is it that even though we do not eliminate them, they are not a real threat to the world?
>
> Today's Buddhists and Taoists are vulgar, base, shallow, and inferior. Even in their basics their falseness is not difficult to see. Why, then, would Master Ch'eng[43] compare them to Yangism and Mohism,[44] as being close to Principle? Does this mean that in the beginning they had validity, but current practitioners exemplify the dregs of the original teachings?
>
> We do not have a verifiable history of the transmission of the Buddhist sutras. But, in the case of Confucius's contemporary Lao-tzu, Confucius asked him about ritual, and never said one word to attack his faults.[45] However, later generations exclude and ignore him [Lao-tzu]. Why is this?
>
> Yang [Chu's] egoism (*wei-wo*) and Mo [-tzu's] universal love (*chien-ai*) undoubtedly are not the Way. Comparing them to later generations who are greedy, rash, shameless, or selfish, is there not a difference between them? Mencius considered them as denying fatherhood (*wu-fu*) and denying rulership (*wu-chün*), and, therefore, equivalent to

beasts.[46] Later Han Yü[47] considered that the damage of Buddhism and Taoism was greater than of Yangism and Mohism. So, [if they are lower than beasts], to what are they equivalent? I do not know if today there are representatives of "universal love" and "egoism." If there are, should they be eliminated? Can we learn from them? If today we do not see any actual Yangists and Mohists, then the damage is limited to Buddhism and Taoism. But, are there other vexations in addition to Buddhism and Taoism? Or, is there nothing else to be worried about?

There are people who declare that something is right, but do not know the reason it is right, or criticize something as false, but do not know the reason why it is false. They echo opinions in order to get along with people. I am deeply troubled by this. Therefore, I implore you gentlemen to make a profound analysis of this.

Wang Yang-ming's criticisms here were aimed at two targets. One was contemporary Buddhists and Taoists who "are vulgar, base, shallow, and inferior." They therefore did not represent the two spiritual systems which actually had some truth claims at their beginning. Wang stated this most clearly as regards the "father" of Taoism, Lao-tzu, when he wrote that "Confucius asked him about ritual, and never said one word to attack his faults." The other, more fundamental criticism here, was aimed at contemporary Confucians. Wang knew, and expected the candidates to know, the history of the critiques of heterodoxy in Chinese history. However, particularly in their role as examination candidates, Wang urged the students to think for themselves and not just "echo opinions in order to get along with people." Wang dedicated himself to the quest for sagehood and tried to convince his students that rather than examination success, sagehood was the ultimate goal. In the pursuit of sagehood they needed to be able to think for themselves.

In his commentary that followed this examination question, Wang was critical of how Taoism developed after Lao-tzu. Taoism was found wanting for excessive emphasis on the self and lack of concern for ordering the world. In this commentary Wang wrote:

> I do not know much about Buddhism, but Lao-tzu was well known for his knowledge of ritual. He was the one our teacher asked about ritual. Therefore, as a human being he was definitely not of low rank. Is his cultivation of the body and nourishment of the nature in order to seek harmony with the Way initially so different from Confucius's [ways]? However, they [Taoists] only concentrated on the self, without a thought for the world or the state. Then they became different from our teacher's [teachings].[48]

Wang continued by referring to Confucius's saying concerning why the Way was unclear or not carried out. He concluded, "Alas, although the Way is one, people vary and are wise, ignorant, worthy, and unworthy. This is the reason why there is the bad result of going too far or not far enough. This is also the reason why heterodoxy arises."[49] Frequently in Wang's writings, there was the acknowledgment that people were at various levels of intellectual development and intelligence, and so they would approach the Way in different ways. But no doubt, Wang saw Confucianism as the most complete philosophy that encompassed both internal cultivation and external application, thereby canvassing even the concerns of Buddhism and Taoism. Therefore, what he advocated was that people not waste time arguing with Buddhists and Taoists or calling them heterodox, but focus on strengthening their understanding and application of an expanded Confucianism.

Wang and his students studied and appreciated Buddhism and Taoism, developing relationships with practitioners of these religions. These two traditions enriched their interpretation of Confucianism, but their dominant self-identification was Confucian. Their argument was not with the original truth claims of these alternate systems of thought, but with the abuses of contemporary adherents. Wang railed against their vulgarity and shallowness in his examination essay discussed above. In a similar manner, Wang's first generation follower, Nieh Pao, criticized contemporary Buddhists and Taoists in a memorial he wrote while serving as censor of Fukien, 1525–28. Nieh wrote that Buddhists and Taoists in Fukien made up fewer than one percent of the population, but owned two percent of the property, not to mention their immorality: "These days Buddhists and Taoists have a lot of land, and their granaries are very full. They have money, are proud, and do bad deeds. They eat well, act immorally, and break their own rules."[50] Nieh urged the court to enforce statutes issued in 1452 and 1470, which stipulated that smaller Buddhist and Taoist establishments be restricted to owning sixty *mou*, and larger ones one hundred *mou* of land. Nieh suggested that amounts over this be given to tenants to produce grain, so that the tax revenue from this could be used to build granaries and provide public relief.[51] But like his teacher, Nieh Pao also found personal meaning in Buddhism and Taoism. He built on Wang's teaching of the extension of innate moral knowledge (*chih liang-chih*) to develop an inner-directed method of self-cultivation based on meditation.[52] Like Wang, Nieh Pao would also criticize Buddhism and Taoism by separating these two traditions' useful teachings from the unworthy actions of their contemporary practitioners.

WANG YANG-MING AMONG THE NON-HAN PEOPLES

Between the years of 1508 and 1510, Wang had his first opportunity to test the utility of Confucianism among non-Han peoples. In 1506 Wang had been flogged and imprisoned for standing up to the powerful eunuch Liu Chin (d. 1510).[53] In 1507, he was demoted to the lowly position of post-station head in

Lung-ch'ang, Kweichow. Arriving in this hardship post in 1508, Wang had to forge connections with the local, non-Han people in order to survive. Wang referred to these people as *Man, I,* or *Miao.* This was consistent with traditional nomenclature that often imprecisely referred to all southern tribes as Man or Miao. In modern secondary literature these peoples are referred to as Miao.[54] The same ideograph for Miao, apparently designating a non-Chinese people, occurred in legends about the ancient sage kings Yao and Shun.[55] However, since the name did not reappear in texts until the Yüan dynasty, it is difficult to equate the earlier and later uses of the name.[56] E. G. Pulleyblank wrote that "[i]n spite of the discontinuity in nomenclature, one can confidently connect the later Miao-Yao with the various Man peoples who lived in the Yangtze watershed in Chou and Han times and who are first described in some detail in the *Hou-Han shu.*"[57]

In evaluating Wang Yang-ming's relation to non-Han peoples, two complementary contexts need to be considered. The first is the ongoing Confucian project to sinify peoples on the borders of China proper by educating them to adopt Confucian ritual practices. This is the kind of activity that Chu Hsi was engaged in while serving in Fukien. A related part of this project was bringing non-Han peoples under government control.[58] During the Han dynasty, there was considerable economic and political expansion into present-day southern China.[59] In the Three Kingdoms period (221–317), Chu-ko Liang, from his base in Szechwan, extended his control southward into parts of Kweichow, becoming "the first to bestow hereditary ranks and Chinese family names on tribal chieftains."[60] In the Kweichow local gazetteers, Chu-ko Liang is honored for fair treatment of the non-Han peoples. In fact, he and Wang Yang-ming are viewed as the two major cultural heroes of the area.[61] Control of Kweichow was sporadic and incomplete until, in the thirteenth century, the Yüan dynasty incorporated much of the southwest into its empire.

The Ming made Kweichow a separate administrative unit. In 1413 it finally became a province, and a permanent grand coordinator was designated in 1449.[62] The Ming dynasty inherited and then consolidated a Yüan system of aboriginal offices (*t'u-ssu*) for governing tribal peoples, particularly in Szechwan, Yunnan, and Kweichow.[63] Tribal peoples the government saw as trustworthy were granted hereditary positions to help in the government of the local area. Around Lung-ch'ang the two powerful families who served as native officials were the Sung and the An.[64] From the 1500s on, this system was used in relatively assimilated areas where there was a combination of aboriginal and Chinese officials who were under the Ministry of Personnel. When Wang Yang-ming served in Lung-ch'ang the *t'u-ssu* system was in operation. He, as a centrally appointed civil official from outside the province, served with non-Han officials from the local area. In contrast, in less assimilated areas, the court designated tribal chiefs as aboriginal officials (*t'u-kuan*) who were placed under the jurisdiction of the Ministry of War, but as long as they kept order they "retained full customary control over their subjects," in the words of Charles O. Hucker.[65] This latter designation afforded the non-Han peoples more autonomy. There were proposals during the Ming to eliminate the *t'u-ssu* and *t'u-kuan* systems and uniformly impose the *chün-hsien* (prefectures and counties) organizational structure of local administration on minority areas. The *chün-hsien* system was the centralized, bureaucratic political system in the rest of Ming China.[66] After the suppression of a rebellion in Kweichow in the later sixteenth century, a censor proposed establishing the *chün-hsien* system, but the Grand Coordinator was more convincing in arguing that the non-Han people were unwilling to be placed under the new system, so the *t'u-ssu* system continued.[67] The frequency of rebellions in Kweichow through the nineteenth century indicated the reluctance of the local people to be colonized by the Chinese.[68] While serving at his final post quelling a rebellion in Kwangsi in 1527–28, Wang memorialized in support of restoring the *t'u-kuan* system there to govern the non-Han people. He wrote that the rebels had sent in their confession and were willing to surrender, but wanted their grievances to be heard in hopes of receiving imperial grace. They complained that since they had been placed under more direct government control, officials had opened up territory and imposed communal groups (*li*) that had been harmful to local customs. Hence, the area became unstable and rebellious. Wang agreed with the local leaders that the best course would be to return to the *t'u-kuan* system. He urged the emperor to stop the military action, mollify the local people, and, thus, manifest his benevolence.[69]

Ming attitudes toward the non-Han people were often negative. The characters used to refer to them usually contained radicals relating to animals. The less assimilated were described as "raw" (*sheng*), in contrast to the more sinified, who were "cooked" (*shu*).[70] The late Ming official Chang Chü-cheng expressed this negative view of "barbarians" and compared them to animals in a letter on frontier relations:

> Just like dogs, if they wag their tails, bones will be thrown to them; if they bark wildly, they will be beaten with sticks; after the beating, if they submit again, bones will be thrown to them again; after the bones, if they bark again, then come more beating. How can one argue with them about being crooked or straight or about the observation of law?[71]

Thus, Chang had a harsher view of non-Han peoples than Wang, and failed to see their transformability as Wang did.

Wang had several posts that brought him into contact with non-Han peoples. In addition to Kweichow, this included service in Kiangsi, 1517–21, and Kwangsi, 1527–28. In all these areas, Wang established schools for the purpose of "using Chinese culture to transform the non-Han" (*yung Hsia pien i*).[72] What was his general attitude toward non-Han peoples? Wang took part in the general "civilizing" project that Chinese officials carried out when posted to areas where many minorities lived. While in Kweichow, Wang described the non-Han peoples as being rough in their improper behavior, but concluded that this did not damage their internal character. Wang saw the transformability of the non-Han peoples and did not express the harsh view that, for instance, Chang Chü-cheng embraced. To commemorate a study that the non-Han people built for him in Lung-ch'ang, Wang wrote an essay in which he explained why he named it the "How Can It Be Vulgar Pavilion" (*Ho lou hsüan*). He began the essay with the classical reference for his choice of name, which was a passage in the *Analects* that stated that Confucius wanted to live among the nine non-Han peoples (*I*). When he was asked if he would mind their vulgarity, Confucius replied that if a gentleman (*chün-tzu*) were to live among them, how could there be any vulgarity (*ho lou chih yu*)?[73] Wang wrote that he named his studio to show his agreement with this sentiment. In this essay he described the people as follows:

> These non-Han peoples (*I*) are like unpolished jade and unplaned wood. Even though they are rough and sharp, naughty and stubborn, there is still room for awl and ax. Therefore, how can we call them vulgar? The non-Han of today worship shamans and serve ghosts, blaspheme ritual and let their emotions rule, which does not accord with the Mean and is not properly disciplined. Eventually they could not help but be called vulgar. . . . However, this does not damage their essence. Truly, if a gentleman lives among them, they will change when he transforms (*hua*) them.[74]

In this essay Wang recorded the fact that these non-Han people did not follow accepted Chinese rituals, but this did not harm their essence, which would make it possible and indeed easy for a gentleman to transform them. He ended the essay on a modest note, stating that he was not such a gentleman, but was merely one who was waiting for such a man to arrive.

In another essay written while he was in Kweichow, Wang commemorated the rebuilding of a monastery and the addition to it a three-story hostel. He related how the local people used to go to this monastery during festivals to worship and celebrate until it fell into disrepair. Wang quoted the man in charge of the renovation to the effect that the Miao did know the rites of respect for the ruler and love for superiors, but they, unfortunately had not had a chance to practice them.[75] Again we see that Wang saw these people as having the capability of a moral life; they just needed a way according to which to practice it. Wang did not compare the non-Han people to animals. He established schools and other institutions in Kweichow, Kiangsi, and Kuangsi in order to transform them through education.

One of the educational techniques that Wang used to communicate with commoners was songs. Music always played an important, if still not well understood, role in Chinese ritual and culture. As an important part of ritual, it was linked with governing and claims to political legitimacy.[76] Music was often mentioned in the Confucian classics.[77] Wang recommended including singing in the primary school curriculum that he wrote in Kiangsi in 1518.[78] In the stratified world of Ming China, it was difficult to have communication across barriers of class and gender. Songs were a possible way to bridge this gap.[79] In one of Wang's recorded conversations he discussed the importance of music with his students, and proposed using it as an educational tool.

> If we want to return people's customs to simplicity and purity, we must take the theatrical music of today, eliminate all the depraved and licentious words and tunes, and keep only the stories about loyal ministers and filial sons, so that everyone among the simple folk can easily understand them, and their innate knowledge can unconsciously be stimulated into operation.[80]

Wang tried to improve the atmosphere in Lung-ch'ang by teaching songs to those around him.[81] More than twenty years after Wang served there, another civil servant in Kweichow, Wang Hsin, reported that he heard songs with a Yüeh (Wang's home of Chekiang) accent. When he asked the local people about this, they replied that this was part of the continuing influence of Wang Yang-ming in Lung-ch'ang.[82]

Today in Kweichow, one scholar condemns the "feudal" past when Han chauvinism was prevalent, while applauding Wang for a more tolerant attitude toward minorities. He lists four reasons that might help explain Wang's openness. First, he grew up in a scholarly family steeped in Confucian teachings. He taught that everyone had innate moral knowledge, so he did not discriminate. Second, Wang's traumatic experiences and suffering in his political career changed his mentality, and allowed him to be more sympathetic to the common people. Third, practical need was a factor in that while in exile the only way for Wang to survive was to cooperate with the locals. Finally, in his interaction with the locals, Wang became familiar with their plain virtues, which compelled him to get rid of his prejudices toward them.[83] In any case, the point is that Wang sought to expand the cultural boundary of the Han to include the I.

The two most powerful native officials that Wang came in contact with were from the An and the Sung families. Wang corresponded with An Kuei-jung, a native official from Shui-hsi, an area close to Lung-ch'ang. The An family had come into prominence when An Lung-fu received an official title in the *t'u-ssu* system in 1442. An Lung-fu did not have a son, so after his death the title was inherited by his nephew An Kuan, who passed the title on to his son An Kuei-jung.[84] An Kuei-jung asked Wang Yang-ming to write an essay commemorating the renovation of a local shrine to Hsiang, the evil stepbrother of the mythical sage king Shun.[85] In the myths of the Shang that informed the Chou texts, Sarah

Allan has identified Shun as a high ancestor of the Shang dynasty.[86] He was
described in human terms as " the son of a blind man; his father was stupid, his
mother was deceitful, (his brother) Hsiang was arrogant."[87] Mencius recorded
that Hsiang attempted daily to kill Shun, but that rather than banishing him,
Shun made him a prince because, as Mencius explained, a benevolent man must
love his brother.[88] In his essay Wang wrote that the shrine was located on Ling-
po Mountain and that those living around the mountain treated Hsiang as a god
(*shen*). When he asked the local people why they wanted to renovate it, they
replied that they did not know when the shrine began, but that at least from their
great-grandfathers' generation they had honored the god and made sacrifices
there. Therefore, they maintained it and did not dare to abolish it. Wang
recorded his response to this history: "Hsiang's way was to be unfilial as a son and
arrogant as a younger brother. There was worship of Hsiang in the T'ang dynasty,
but people abolished it. Somehow it has flourished in this place. This is absurd!"
        All that Wang could discover from the Man was that they had worshipped
at the Hsiang shrine for at least three generations. The legend of King Shun had
played an important role in eastern China, but also in parts of the South.[89]
According to Wolfram Eberhard, the evil stepbrother Hsiang became associated
with a rain god, and in the Han dynasty there was a shrine dedicated to Hsiang in
Kwangsi.[90] In the South, elephants (the character for Hsiang is the same as that
for elephant), were important in local history and religion.[91] Sarah Allan has
found that one of the motifs on Shang dynasty bronzes was the elephant. This
also appears on oracle bones as one of the animals hunted by the king. "The elephant may have had some special meaning: the brother of Shun . . . was called
Hsiang, meaning 'elephant.' Elephants were buried sacrificially at Yin-hsu. . . .
[T]he enormous size and strange trunk of the elephant are beyond the bounds of
normal reality and may have given the animal a supernatural aura."[92] Therefore,
it is possible that worship of Hsiang was initially worship of elephants.
        In his essay Wang seemed only to think of Hsiang as the evil stepbrother,
and therefore, tried to understand why such an unfilial and unbrotherly person
would be worshipped. He posited several different reasons. First he stated that the
people who worshipped Hsiang were actually worshipping the sagely Shun.
Then, he cited a statement in the *Book of History* that declared that harmony was
attained. Wang implied that this referred to Shun and meant that Hsiang had
been transformed by Shun, because if he was still unfilial, harmony would not
have been attained. Wang then argued that Shun enfeoffed his brother, but sent
officials to actually regulate the state. Because Hsiang allowed these officials to
govern, Wang asserted that this demonstrated that Hsiang had been transformed.
Therefore, he could benefit people who commemorated him after his death.
People in the T'ang were thinking of the early life of Hsiang when they abolished
shrines to him. But, argued Wang, these non-Han peoples worshipped Hsiang
because of whom he became through transformation. Wang concluded, "From

this I became full of the belief in the goodness of human nature. There are no people in the world who are not transformable. . . . If the gentleman cultivates his virtue to its utmost, then even such an unbenevolent person as Hsiang is still transformable." Rather than treating the worship of Hsiang as a "profane cult" (*yin-tz'u*) to be destroyed and replaced with a more appropriate Han Confucian model, Wang was able to expand the boundaries of Confucianism to include this local cult as a model of the transformability of all people. Thus, in this essay we see Wang's attempt to understand the local people by not dismissing their beliefs out of hand. It was a clear statement of his acceptance of the basic goodness of all people, and their potential for transformation. It required a gentleman who had cultivated himself to the full, such as Shun, to uncover the goodness in people. This was the task that Wang also set for himself.

The reasons for Wang's approval of this shrine were complex and open to conjecture, but show an inclusive approach. Wang was new to the area, had arrived as an exile, and served in a lowly post. He needed to gain the support of the non-Han officials, so he would want to comply with An's request to write an essay. He also needed the support of the local people in order to succeed, and even to survive.[93] At first Wang was not convinced of the acceptability of a shrine to Hsiang, but after interviewing people and thinking it over, he decided that he could appropriate this local cult. By presenting Hsiang as an example of transformation, Wang re-inscribed a Confucian meaning on a questionable shrine. He gave Hsiang an improved persona so that he could serve as a moral exemplar. In this case, Wang expanded the boundaries of his interpretation of Confucianism in order to reach the uninitiated.

INTELLECTUAL BOUNDARIES AND THE USE OF PHYSICAL SPACE

Wang Yang-ming often visited, stayed at and taught in Buddhist temples. According to Wing-tsit Chan this totaled forty temples in eight provinces, with his longest stay lasting eight months when he was thirty-two and still immersed in Buddhism. Usually he stayed for a short time of one to two weeks, but when he was 42, 48, and 54, he stayed for a month at a time.[94] Japanese scholars have made the case that this shows his great interest in Buddhism, but this activity has to be seen in the larger context of travel, tourism, and self-cultivation in the Ming.[95] Confucian literati would usually not be in the same category as pilgrims.[96] It was common for literati to travel, visit temples, and use them as guesthouses and meeting places. The fact that many temples were in mountainous and scenic locations only added to their appeal. As Timothy Brook has shown, there was also a lack of large buildings for gatherings in the Ming, so temples and monasteries were appropriated for public use.[97] In his plan for the organization of community covenants in Kiangsi, Wang proposed using temples as meeting places.[98] Here is an example of temples' being used as inns. It was recorded that in 1523, so many people flocked to see Wang in his home of Yü-yao, Chekiang, that the Buddhist temples could not accommodate them all.[99] Obviously, it was commonplace for people to stay in Buddhist temples in their travels.

The use of Buddhist and Taoist religious establishments as meeting places had occurred before the Ming. The Northern and Southern Sung Confucians met in temples. For example, in 1175 Chu Hsi and Lu Hsiang-shan took part in the famous debate on their differences concerning self-cultivation at the Goose Lake Monastery in Kiangsi. Note must also be made of the use of Buddhist monasteries as libraries and study centers for individual scholars from the third century until the Confucian revival in the tenth and eleventh centuries. From the Sung period onwards, there was the development of Confucian study facilities in academies. This growth was facilitated by the increase in publication and affordability of books for private libraries. The Ming was especially an active period of academy building, often on the model of Buddhist monasteries.[100] Many of these were built in scenic, quiet, and secluded locations that would help literati concentrate on self-cultivation. Confucians were building their own educational and spiritual architecture,[101] partly on the model of the Buddhists. It is difficult to state with certainty the impact that meeting in Buddhist (and occasionally Taoist) temples had on Confucian practice. The atmosphere produced by the art, music, incense, costumes, and rituals must have been compelling. Confucian rituals and ritual paraphernalia at shrines and academies did come to resemble those in Buddhist services. An example of the use of Buddhist architecture for non-Buddhist purposes was the building of large numbers of pagodas in the Ming and Ch'ing dynasties, which were constructed for the purpose of improving the geomantic configurations of the area. Some were built as shrines dedicated to the success of local literati in the civil service examinations. These towers, especially prevalent in southern China, were called wen-feng-t'a.[102]

At times, Buddhist temples were taken over for Confucian meetings and even turned into academies. An example of such encroachment[103] took place at Ch'ing Yuan, a mountainous area southeast of the prefectural capital of Chi-an, Kiangsi, where Wang taught. There, his first-generation disciples established a Yang-ming Academy. Ch'ing Yuan, as well as other locations in Kiangsi, had well-developed Ch'an Buddhist establishments dating from the T'ang dynasty.[104] A preface to the Ch'ing Yuan Mountain Gazatteer emphasizes that the Buddhist and newer Confucian establishments coexisted in harmony.[105] The local history and a second-generation Wang follower from Chi-an, Lo Ta-hung (chin-shih, 1586), give a more contested history to the use of Buddhist buildings. Inspired by Wang's example of teaching when he was in Kiangsi, two of his disciples began lecture-discussion meetings in a Buddhist temple on Ch'ing Yuan. "Considering this a suitable place to gather like-minded friends, they did not think of establishing a permanent place to meet."[106] By the late Ming, there was enough support for the Buddhists and once again, their spaces were clearly delineated.[107] Lo Ta-hung gave this report on the history of the "Former Worthies' Shrine," established to honor Wang Yang-ming and four of his first-generation disciples from Chi-an:

> Later, some local scholars wanted to promote our teaching, so they built a "Former Worthies' Shrine" on the right side of a Buddhist monastery. Those who criticized this said that if you treat this as an ancient Buddhist temple then it lacks something, and if you consider it as a Confucian temple then it appears that you are placing the Confucians on one side. There are errors in both ways. Now, local official Kuo has followed public opinion and has restored the ancient temple, torn down the old hall, and returned all the land to the Buddhists at Ch'ing Yuan. Then, he rebuilt the "Former Worthies' Shrine" and a meeting hall in front of the mountain. Men who are concerned for our Confucian school complained that the "Former Worthies' Shrine" had been established for a long time and then all of a sudden it was washed away. It is as if we are promoting Buddhism and slighting Confucianism. This is not right.[108]

In any case, the point is that Confucians encroached on and shared space with Buddhists. This was often done peacefully. Another example was Lo Hung-hsien's building a school in the countryside of Chi-an in 1546. As a follower of Wang Yang-ming, he nevertheless invited a monk named Ming-kuo to join him there when he opened the school, and the monk also became the abbot of the K'ai-shan temple.[109]

To conclude, we have seen how Wang Yang-ming expanded the boundaries of Confucian doctrines and practice in three areas. First, in the area of doctrine, Wang departed from Ch'eng-Chu orthodoxy, and with his inclusivist approach, erected his own conception and version of Confucianism, accommodating Buddhism and Taoism. Second, in the domains of both doctrine and practice, Wang's administrative and bureaucratic dealings with the non-Han peoples, and his re-inscription of Confucian meanings on a Miao shrine amply show the practical and doctrinal elasticity of Confucianism in action. Third, in the realm of practice, there was the physical breaching of boundaries as evidenced by the liberal use of Buddhist and Daoist establishments. Throughout his life, Wang reinterpreted the Confucian heritage and redrew its boundaries both in response to his own evolving spiritual development and as an answer to the need of bringing the Confucian message to as many people as possible.

NOTES

1. This is the thesis of Wm. Theodore de Bary, *Neo-Confucian Orthodoxy and the Learning of the Mind-and-Heart* (New York: Columbia University Press, 1981).

2. On Wang's tendency to equate many concepts, including *tao, liang-chih,* and *t'ien-li,* see David S. Nivison, "Protest against Conventions and Conventions of Protest," in Arthur F. Wright, ed., *The Confucian Persuasion* (Stanford: Stanford University Press, 1960), pp. 177–201.

3. The Ch'eng-Chu interpretations were accepted as state ideology from 1313 to 1905. In spite of this, the Ming founder established some religious pluralism and interest in alternate traditions. See Romeyn Taylor, "Official and Popular Religion and the Political Organization of Chinese Society in the Ming," in Kwang-Ching Liu, ed., *Orthodoxy in Late Imperial China* (Berkeley: University of California Press, 1990), pp. 126–57.

4. See the translation of the preface to this document in *Instructions for Practical Living and Other Neo-Confucian Writings by Wang Yang-ming,* trans. Wing-tsit Chan (New York: Columbia University Press, 1963), pp. 263–67.

5. The idea of an interrupted transmission of Confucianism that was then recovered by an exceptional individual began with Han Yü (768–824), who stated that the Confucian Way stopped being handed down after Mencius. See his "What Is the True Way?" (*Yuan Tao*) in Wm.Theodore de Bary, Wing-tsit Chan and Burton Watson, eds., *Sources of Chinese Tradition,* vol. 1 (New York: Columbia University Press, 1963), pp. 376–79.

6. Wang presents his "spiritual autobiography" in the preface cited above in *Instructions,* pp. 263–67.

7. See, for example, Lo Hung-hsien (1504–64), *Nien-an Lo hsien-sheng wen-chi,* Ssu-k'u ch'uan-shu chen-pen (Taipei: Shang-wu yin-shu kuan, 1974) 11/p.54b.

8. For the major criticisms see *Instructions,* 263 n. 3.

9. Ibid., no. 176, p. 164. On Lo Ch'in-shun, see L. Carrington Goodrich and Chaoying Fang, eds., *Dictionary of Ming Biography, 1368–1644* (New York: Columbia University Press, 1976), pp. 972–74, hereafter cited as DMB. See also Irene Bloom, *Knowledge Painfully Acquired: The K'un-chih Chi by Lo Ch'in-shun* (New York: Columbia University Press, 1987). Although Wang works to reconcile his teachings with those of Chu Hsi, there is a sense in his mature teaching that he believes he is beyond adherence to any humanly designated standard of orthodoxy. As in this quote, he teaches that students should question any authority, even Confucius, if it does not conform to their own standard (*liang-chih*) when put into practice.

10. On the various groups of Wang followers during the Ming, see Huang Tsung-hsi, *Ming-ju hsüeh-an* (Taipei: Shih-chieh shu-chu, 1973). Wang's teachings continued to have some influence during the Ch'ing dynasty, and their value was greatly appreciated by several twentieth-century reformers. The influence of Wang's ideas was considerable in Korea and Japan.

11. On the T'ai-chou men, named for the home of their spiritual leader Wang Ken (1483–1541), see DMB, 1382–85, and Wm. Theodore de Bary,

"Individualism and Humanitarianism in Late Ming Thought," in Wm. Theodore de Bary, ed., *Self and Society in Ming Thought* (New York: Columbia University Press, 1970), pp. 145–247. The Manchus' need to be perceived as "orthodox" also influenced this shift away from interest in Wang Yang-ming.

12. Julia Ching, *To Acquire Wisdom: The Way of Wang Yang-ming* (New York: Columbia University Press, 1976), p. 189, quoting the *Ming-ju hsueh-an* 58.32a. On Kao, see DMB, pp. 701–10. The Tung-lin scholars criticized Wang for questioning both the authority of the classics, and Chu Hsi's interpretations. Others who accused Wang of using the legitimacy of Chu to present his own doctrine are listed in *Instructions*, p. 263 n. 3.

13. For example, Wang's teachings were criticized in the 1523 *chin-shih* examinations. See Julia Ching, *To Acquire Wisdom*, p. 48.

14. Ibid., p. 33.

15. Ibid., p. 34.

16. DMB, 1415.

17. See Hung-lam Chu, "The Debate over the Recognition of Wang Yang-ming," *Harvard Journal of Asiatic Studies* 48.1 (1988): 47–70.

18. Ibid., p. 68. On Chang Chü-cheng see DMB, pp. 53–61.

19. Wm. Theodore de Bary makes the point that there were two forms of orthodoxy practiced in late imperial China: that conferred by the state, and that conferred by the actions of Confucians in local schools. See his *Neo-Confucian Orthodoxy and the Learning of the Mind-and-Heart* (New York: Columbia University Press, 1981), p. xi.

20. Ku Yen-wu, *Jih-chih lu* (Taipei: Commercial Press, 1965) 6.8.121.

21. Tu Wei-ming, *Neo-Confucian Thought in Action: Wang Yang-ming's Youth, 1472–1509* (Berkeley: University of California Press, 1976), p. 4.

22. Yü Ying-shih, "Intellectual Breakthroughs in the T'ang-Sung Transition," manuscript, p. 21.

23. For a late Ming example, see Judith Berling, "Religion and Popular Culture: The Management of Moral Culture in *The Romance of the Three Teachings*," in David Johnson et al., eds., *Popular Culture in Late Imperial China* (Berkeley: University of California Press, 1987), pp. 188–218.

24. On Buddhist art, see Marsha Weidner, "Buddhist Pictorial Art in the Ming Dynasty," in Marsha Weidner, ed., *Latter Days of the Law: Images of Chinese Buddhism, 850–1850* (Honolulu: University of Hawaii Press, 1994), pp. 51–87.

25. See the articles in Patricia Ebrey and Peter Gregory, eds., *Religion and Society in T'ang and Sung China* (Honolulu: University of Hawaii Press, 1993).

26. *Reflections on Things at Hand, The Neo-Confucian Anthology Compiled by Chu Hsi and Lü Tsu-ch'ien*, Wing-tsit Chan, trans. (New York: Columbia University Press, 1967), p. 282. For a list of Chu Hsi's criticisms of Buddhism, see Wing-tsit Chan, *A Sourcebook in Chinese Philosophy* (Princeton: Princeton University Press, 1963), pp. 572–87.

27. Timothy Brook, *Praying for Power: Buddhism and the Formation of Gentry Society in Late-Ming China* (Cambridge, Mass.: Harvard University Press, 1993).

28. Ibid., pp. 3–4, and Chun-fang Yü, *The Renewal of Buddhism in China: Chu-hung and the Late Ming Synthesis* (New York: Columbia University Press, 1981), pp. 2–3

29. Chun-fang Yü, 144–52.

30. Ibid., pp. 153–54, lists these eight patrons of Buddhism and two of Taoism between 1402 and 1620. In his article on Taoist influences on Ming Confucianism, Liu Ts'un-yan mentions three emperors who were patrons of Taoism. See his "Taoist Self-Cultivation in Ming Thought," in de Bary, *Self and Society*, pp. 291–330.

31. Some of Wang's late-Ming followers went further to embrace "Three Teachings are One" syncretism.

32. *DMB*, p. 1408, and the *nien-p'u* (biographical annals) of Wang Yang-ming for the year 1488, in *Wang Yang-ming ch'uan-chi* (Shanghai: Ku-chi ch'u-pan-she, 1995).

33. Tu Wei-ming, *Neo-Confucian Thought in Action*, p. 15 n. 8, states Wang was an expert in the *Book of Changes*.

34. Ibid., considers the importance of this father-son relationship, and Wang's possible rebellion against his successful father.

35. Ibid., pp. 52–53, citing the *Nien-p'u* for 1501.

36. Liu Ts'un-yan, pp. 291–330, demonstrates that Ming thinkers used Taoist terminology, including Wang in *Instructions for Practical Living*.

37. Cited in Ibid., p. 308. Translation slightly modified.

38. Wang Yang-ming, "On the Five Classics," in *Kuei-yang fu-chih*, 1850 ed., 11:3a–3b.

39. Kwang-Ching Liu writes that the *Three-Character Classic*, a primer that gained currency in the thirteenth century, recommends the study of the *Lao-tzu* and *Chuang-tzu* in addition to Confucian classics such as the *Four Books* and the *Classic of Filial Piety*. See his "Socioethics as Orthodoxy," in Kwang-Ching Liu, *Orthodoxy*, pp. 83–84.

40. Tu Wei-ming, *Neo-Confucian Thought*, p. 4.

41. Quoted in Julia Ching, *To Acquire Wisdom*, p. 100. On Chan Jo-shui, see DMB, pp. 36–42.

42. Wang Yang-ming, *Wang Wen-ch'eng kung ch'uan-shu*, Ssu-pu pei yao ed. (Shanghai: Chung-hua shu-chu, 1934), 31b. 33a–34b (question), 31b.34b–38a (commentary).

43. Probably Ch'eng Hao (1032–85).

44. Founded by Warring States thinkers Yang Chu (4th century B.C.), and Mo Tzu (479?–381? B.C.).

45. Wang follows the unverified story of a meeting between Confucius and Lao-tzu as it first appeared in Ssu-ma Ch'ien's *Shih-chi*.

46. *Mencius*, 3.2.99, in *Four Books*, trans. James Legge (Taipei: Ta-shen shu-chu, 1975).

47. Han Yü (768-824) is the famous T'ang critic of Buddhism and Taoism who advocated a restoration of Confucianism.

48. Wang Yang-ming, *Wang Wen-ch'eng kung ch'uan-shu* 31b.35b–36a. The "teachings" are enumerated as the eight stages set out at the beginning of the *Great Learning*.

49. Ibid., 31b.34b.

50. Nieh Pao, "Nieh Chen-hsiang chi," in Ch'en Tzu-lung et al., eds., *Huang Ming Ching-shih wen-pien*, fascimile reproducation of the Ch'ung-chen edition (Taipei: Kuo-lien t'u-shu, 1964) 222.10a–10b.

51. Ibid. 222.11a.

52. See my "The Jiangyou Group: Culture and Society in Sixteenth Century China" (Ph.D. dissertation, Yale University, 1987).

53. DMB, pp. 941–45.

54. I visited this area in Kweichow in July 1996 and found that the majority of the population is designated as part of the Miao national minority.

55. E. G. Pulleyblank, "The Chinese and Their Neighbors in Prehistoric and Early Historic Times," in David N. Keightley, ed., *The Origins of Chinese Civilization* (Berkeley: University of California Press, 1983), p. 425.

56. Ibid.

57. Ibid., p. 426.

58. See Lien-sheng Yang, "Historical Notes on the Chinese World Order," in John K. Fairbank, ed., *The Chinese World Order: Traditional China's Foreign Relations*. (Cambridge, Mass.: Harvard University Press, 1968), pp. 20–33, and Richard Von Glahn, *The Country of Streams and Grottoes* (Cambridge, Mass.: Harvard University Press, 1987). Von Glahn examines the "civilizing" of Szechwan in the Sung dynasty. For demographic information on immigration into non-Han areas, see James Lee, "The Legacy of Immigration in Southwestern China, 1250–1850," *Annales de Demographie Historique* (1982): 279–304.

59. Yü Ying-shih, *Trade and Expansion in Han China: A Study in the Structure of Sino-Barbarian Economic Relations* (Berkeley: University of California Press, 1967).

60. Inez de Beauclair, *Tribal Cultures of Southwest China*, Asian Folklore and Social Life Monographs, vol. 2 (Taipei: Orient Culture Service,1970), p. 11.

61. *Kuei-chou t'ung-chih*. It must be considered that the writers of the gazetteers were likely Han Chinese.

62. Charles O. Hucker, "Governmental Organization of the Ming Dynasty," *Harvard Journal of Asiatic Studies* 21 (1958): 1–66.

63. Charles O. Hucker, *A Dictionary of Official Titles in Imperial China* (Stanford: Stanford University Press, 1985), p. 78. On the *T'u-ssu* system in Kweichow, see *Ming shih* (Taipei: Ting-wen shu-chu, 1975) 316.8167–99.

64. These two families and their rivalry in the sixteenth-century rebellion mentioned above are discussed in the *Ming shih* 316.8170–71. On the An and Sung, see also "Preface to the An Family Geneology," 23.579, and "Preface to the Sung Family Records," 23.582, in the Wan-li edition of the *Kuei-chou t'ung-chih* (rpt., Peking: ku-chi ch'u-pan-she, 1991). On the An and Wang Yang-ming, see the K'ang-hsi edition of the *Kuei-chou t'ung chih* 30.39b–40b.

65. Hucker, *Dictionary*, p. 78.

66. Ibid., p. 201.

67. *Ming shih* 316.8171.

68. On the mid-nineteenth-century rebellion, see Robert D. Jenks, *Insurgency and Social Disorder in Guizhou: The "Miao" Rebellion, 1854–1873* (Honolulu: University of Hawaii Press, 1994).

69. Wang Yang-ming, "A Memorial to Report the Pacification of T'ien-chou and Ssu-en," 13th day, 2nd month, 1528, *Wang Yang-ming ch'üan chi* 14.467–76 (especially 467, 468, 472, 473).

70. Norma Diamond writes that this distinction is applied to the Miao in the 1558 *Yen-chiao chi wen* (notes on the southern frontiers). See his "Defining the Miao: Ming Qing, and Contemporary Views," in Steven Harrell, ed., *Cultural Encounters on China's Ethnic Frontiers* (Seattle: University of Washington Press, 1995), p. 100.

71. Quoted in Lien-sheng Yang, "Historical Notes on the Chinese World Order," in Fairbank, *The Chinese World Order*, p. 31.

72. This is in the first line of Wang's proposal that schools be built in Kwangsi in 1528. *Wang Yang-ming ch'üan chi* 18.631.

73. *Analects* 9.13, in *Four Books*, trans. Legge.

74. Wang Yang-ming, "On the Ho lou Pavilion," in *Wang Yang-ming ch'üan-chi* 23.890–91.

75. Wang Yang-ming, "On Restoring the Yüe-t'an Monastery and Erecting a Hostel," in ibid. 23.896.

76. For ancient China, Kwang-chih Chang has shown the links to the ancestors and claims to legitimacy validated, in part, through ritual. See his *Art, Myth and Ritual: The Path to Political Authority in Ancient China* (Cambridge, Mass.: Harvard University Press,1983), especially pp. 80–81.

77. See Walter Kaufmann, *Musical References in the Chinese Classics* (Detroit: Information Coordinators, 1976). In recent years there has been increasing interest in music in Chinese history.

78. *Instructions*, pp. 182–86.

79. The role of music in mitigating the difficulty of communication with superiors is raised, but mostly in terms of social criticism, in Bell Yung et al., eds, *Harmony and Counterpoint: Ritual Music in Chinese Context* (Stanford: Stanford University Press, 1996).

80. *Instructions*, p. 233. Other references to music are on pp. 234 and 235.

81. *Nien-p'u*, Spring of 1508, in *Wang Yang-ming ch'üan chi*.

82. Kuo Ch'ang-chih, "Wang Yang-ming yü Kuei-chou hsiao-ssu min-tzu," in Wang Hsiao-hsin, ed., *Wang Yang-ming yü Kuei-chou* (Kuei-yang: Kuei-chou jen-min ch'u-pan-she, 1996), p. 184.

83. Chu Wu-yi, "Wang Yang-ming te min-tzu chi ch'i i-i," in ibid., pp. 190–91.

84. *Ming shih*, 316.8.170.

85. Unless otherwise noted, the following is based on Wang Yang-ming's essay, "On the Shrine to Hsiang" (*Hsiang-tz'u chi*), in *Kuei-chou t'ung-chih* 1697: 34.38a–38b; and in *Wang Yang-ming ch'üan chi* 23.893–94. Wang returned to the story of Shun and Hsiang later in discussions with his students in *Instructions*, 232.

86. Sarah Allan, *The Shape of the Turtle: Myth, Art and Cosmos in Early China* (Albany: State University of New York Press, 1991), p. 62. Also helpful is Eduard Erkes, "Zur Sage Von Shun," *T'oung Pao* 34 (1938): 295–333.

87. Allan, *Shape*, p. 62, quoting from Karlgren's translation of *The Book of Documents*, p. 4, paragraph 12.

88. *Mencius*, D. C. Lau trans. (London: Penguin, 1970) 5A.3.

89. Wolfram Eberhard, *Lokalkulturen im Alten China*, Part 2: *Die Lokalkulturen des Südens und Ostens* (Peking: The Catholic University, 1942), p. 268. Eberhard states that Shun had close connections especially with Hunan and Kwangsi.

90. Ibid., p. 267. Eberhard states that in 1942 there was a shrine to Hsiang in Kuei-yang.

91. Ibid., pp. 262–71.

92. Allan, *Shape*, p. 164.

93. Eventually, the local non-Han people built a house for Wang. See *Kuei-chou t'ung-chih* 1697.

94. Wing-tsit Chan, "How Buddhistic Is Wang Yang-ming?" *Philosophy East and West* 12.3 (Oct. 1962): 203–15.

95. For an example of the record of self-cultivation in travel writing, mentioning numerous temples visited, see a piece by Wang's disciple Lo Hung-hsien (1504–64), "A Winter's Journey to Nanking," in *Nien-an Lo hsien-sheng wen-chi*, in *Ssu-k'u ch'uan-shu chen-pen*.

96. On pilgrimage, see Susan Naquin and Chun-fang Yü, eds., *Pilgrims and Sacred Sites in China* (Berkeley: University of California Press, 1992). Ann Waltner has written on the late Ming literati who were supporters of the female Taoist T'ang Yang-tzu, in her "T'ang-yang-tzu and Wang Shih-chen: Visionary and Bureaucrat in the Late Ming," *Late Imperial China* 8.1 (June 1987): 105–33.

97. Brook, *Praying for Power*, passim.

98. *Instructions*, p. 300.

99. Ibid., p. 245.

100. On the Buddhist influence on academies, see John Meskill, *Academies in Ming China* (Tucson: University of Arizona Press, 1982), pp. 1–2, 9–11, 14, 45–46, 49, 107, 109–10.

101. On the building of shrines to Confucian worthies in the Ming, see Kandice Hauf, "Shrines to Wang Yangming," paper presented at the annual meeting of the Association for Asian Studies, April 1996.

102. Liang Ssu-ch'eng, *A Pictorial History of Chinese Architecture*, Wilma Fairbank ed. (Cambridge: MIT Press), p. 154.

103. A counterexample is Chiu-hua shan, Anhui, a Buddhist center where Confucian buildings were made into places of Buddhist worship.

104. For a discussion of the Ch'an establishments and a map of their locations in the T'ang and Five Dynasties (907–960), see Suzuki Tetsuyu, "Kosei chiho ni okeru Zenshu kakuha no tenkai" (The Development of Individual Ch'an Sects in Chianghsi). See also, *Ch'ing Yuan shan-chih*, 1669 ed., especially chapter 2 which contains biographies of Ch'an masters in Ch'ing Yuan from the T'ang dynasty through the early Ch'ing.

105. Third preface to the *Ch'ing Yuan shan-chih*.

106. Lo Ta-hung, from "Lo Ta-hung's Discussions from the Hall of Ch'an Talks," in *Chi-shui hsien-chih* 66.34b–35a.

107. Brook, *Praying for Power*, writes about the increased patronage of monasteries as a late Ming phenomenon.

108. Ibid. This restoration should be viewed in the context of the increase in local elite patronage of Buddhism in the late Ming.

109. *Chi-an fu-chih*, 1875 ed., 37.74b.

GLOSSARY

An Kuei-jung	安貴榮
Chan Jo-shui	湛若水
Chang Chü-cheng	張居正
Ch'eng Hao	程顥
Ch'eng I	程頤
ch'i	氣
Chi-an	吉安
chien ai	兼愛
chin-shih	進士
Ch'ing Yuan	青原
Chou Tun-i	周敦頤

Chu Hsi	朱熹
Chu-ko Liang	諸葛亮
Chuang Tzu	莊子
chün-hsien	郡縣
chün-tzu	君子
Han Yü	韓愈
hsiang	象
hsin	心
hsing	性
hsüeh	學
I	夷
Kao P'an-lung	高攀龍
ke-wu	格物
kung	公
Lao Tzu	老子
li (Principle)	理
li	里
liang-chih	良知
Liu Chin	劉瑾
Lo Ch'in-shun	羅欽順
Lo Hung-hsien	羅洪先
Lo Ta-hung	羅大絃
Lu Hsiang-shan	陸象山
Lung-ch'ang	龍場
Man	蠻
Miao	苗
Mo Tzu	墨子
mu	畝
shen	神
sheng	生
shu	熟
Shui-hsi	水西
Shun	舜
ssu	私
tao	道
tao-t'ung	道統
t'ien li	天理
ts'e	策
t'u-kuan	土官
t'u-ssu	土司
Tung-lin	東林
tz'u	祠
Wang Yang-ming	王陽明

wei-wo	為我
Wen-ch'eng	文成
wen-feng t'a	文風塔
wu-chün	無君
wu-fu	無父
Yang Chu	楊朱
yin-tz'u	淫祠
yung Hsia pien I	用夏變夷

7

Between Canonicity and Heterodoxy

Hermeneutical Moments of the Great Learning (*Ta-hsueh*)

Kai-wing Chow

THE FLUIDITY OF CANON

The Ch'ing scholar Kung Tzu-chen (1792–1841) once said, "In times subsequent [to antiquity], commentaries were regarded as Classics, notes as Classics, ordinary texts as Classics, writings of the various philosophers as Classics; and when people were still not satisfied, they treated the menial (*yü-t'ai*) as Classics."[1] Kung's remark needs some elaboration in order to introduce the theoretical issues that this paper will address, namely, the idea of "fluidity of canonicity" in studying Chinese classical texts, and the role of textual criticism in creating, shifting, and removing imagined boundaries in discourse. What were the criteria for placing a text within the boundary of an intellectual school? How were the boundaries imagined and of what were they constituted? Commentaries and notes on a particular Chinese classic are generally easy to identify because in most cases, there are external texts of reference whose canonical status was either taken for granted or sanctioned by the imperial state. The commentaries written by K'ung Ying-ta (547–648) on the Five Classics and Chu Hsi's (1130–1200) commentaries on the Four Books are good examples. But it is less evident when a text was reclassified as a Confucian Classic. The major theoretical issue this paper proposes to address is the ways in which scholars in the late Ming and early Ch'ing identified a text as Confucian. What were the assumptions and strategies employed in such efforts? This paper tackles the specific questions of how a text attained canonicity and what caused the boundary of a canon to shift. I will argue that the characterization of a text as a forgery or as heterodox were two of the common discursive strategies scholars employed to create a boundary to exclude texts containing ideas with which they strongly disagreed.

THE QUESTION OF TEXTUAL UNITY: FROM CHAPTER TO INDEPENDENT TREATISE

As John Henderson points out, unlike most canonical traditions, the Confucian canon was notable "in the extent to which it remained open, resisting final fixation or complete closure."[2] The Confucian canon had been more fluid because in part Confucianism did not assume institutional form as a church. The political idioms it provided for legitimating dynastic regimes constituted only part of its vast range of teachings. Insofar as the legitimacy of a regime was not questioned, there was no need to impose a rigid system of exposition on the Confucian Classics. Without institutional control over doctrines, the Confucian canon remained relatively open. Only when the central meanings were fixed by reading-control devices such as commentaries or annotations, and when the hermeneutical principles were enforced by institutional sanctions would a text become "frozen" in its meanings. But it could become fluid again when the reading or institutional controls were removed or weakened.

What constitutes a text as distinct from a book is itself a subject of great debate. The controversy in part stems from the fact that a text is conceived of as a body of writing whose boundary is a function of the criteria with which the unity or coherence is defined. One salient characteristic of a text is its textual instability. It multiplies through copying and printing. The multiple existences of a text passing through the hands of countless copyists, editors, and printers create numerous problems for scholars and editors aiming at identifying and restoring the "original" text. The history of the changing status of the "Great Learning," one of the most important texts of the Four Books, provides an excellent case for examining the question of the instability of a text and the question of how boundaries of a canon shift.

In this essay, the change in the status of a text in discourse is referred to as the "moment" of the text, signifying the fluidity of its discursive status, rather than its true, objective identification as a canon as such. To use the term "moment" is to avoid organizing the different variations of a text into a rigid schema of development. In textual studies there are two commonly held views: first, a text once created will degenerate through various kinds of corruption; second, a text can be eventually restored to its original version by editing out mistakes and making corrections or additions.[3] These two processes, it is often believed, operate at the textual level. But the techniques and methods of textual criticism are validated by a set of hermeneutical principles, which are the rules that define the validity of evidence, the proper procedures for editing, and the appropriate methods of proof. It is in fact impossible to speak of an independent system of textual criticism devoid of any hermeneutical principles. The hermeneutical level is intimately linked to the textual level. As will be shown, the methods of textual criticism often operate within the parameters set by some hermeneutical principles. When hermeneutical principles change, the findings of textual criticism will change. The discursive status of a text will change in accordance with the changing criteria of validity sanctioned by new hermeneutical principles.

CANONIZATION OF THE GREAT LEARNING IN THE SUNG

Since the Sung period the Great Learning had been one of the Four Books that formed the core texts of the Tao-hsueh (Learning of the Way, or commonly, Neo-Confucianism) school.[4] The Four Books provided the hermeneutical principles for reconfiguring the relative importance of individual Confucian Classics. The Great Learning was originally the forty-second chapter of the Book of Rites when the Confucian Classics first assumed the discursive status of canon in the Han period.[5] Its emergence as a major treatise in the Neo-Confucian tradition began when it figured prominently in the criticism of Buddhism in Han Yü's (786–824) writings.[6] But its status as a chapter continued well into the Sung dynasty. But the text as a separate treatise began to assume increasing importance in the Northern Sung. As early as 1030 it was given as a gift from the emperor to successful examination candidates in the highest-level examinations.[7] Ssu-ma Kuang (1019–86) had written a commentary on both the Great Learning and the Doctrine of the Mean. His commentary is perhaps the first one ever written on the Great Learning as an independent treatise.[8] From the Northern Sung on until the early Ch'ing, it enjoyed the status of a unified treatise independent of the Book of Rites. But it was again relegated to its previous status as a chapter and was even dismissed as a text of heterodox origin in the early Ch'ing.

The elevation of the Great Learning to a separate Confucian canonical text in the Sung period went through three steps. First, a dubious link between the text and Confucius himself was initially suggested by Ch'eng I (1033–1107) and Ch'eng Hao (1032–85). Second, later in the Southern Sung, based on Ch'eng I's view, Chu Hsi (1130–1200) divided the text into the classic proper and the commentary section. Finally, passages in the classic proper were attributed to Confucius and the commentary to his disciple Tseng-tzu. The three procedures in turn were justified in terms of two discursive strategies which may be described respectively as "intellectual affinity" and "intellectual lineage."

Both Ch'eng I and Ch'eng Hao regarded the text as the "bequeathed teachings" (i-shu) of Confucius. To claim that the Great Learning embodied the personal teachings of Confucius was to imagine an "intellectual affinity" between the ideas in the text and those of Confucius. By identifying some cognate ideas in the Analects, the Ch'eng brothers constructed an intellectual affinity between the *Great Learning* and the *Analects*. Even though most of the basic interpretive and philosophical ideas about the *Great Learning* had been suggested and laid down by the Ch'eng brothers, they did not explicitly attribute them to Confucius and his disciple. It was Chu Hsi who once explicitly said it was Confucius who wrote the text and that it was transmitted by his disciples who further elaborated on the idea of the "great learning."[9] It was also Chu Hsi who created two reading paradigms for subsequent interpretations of the text. The first is a paradigm about the structure of the text. Following the Ch'eng brothers, Chu Hsi treated the chapter as the writing of Confucius. But unlike them, Chu divided the chapter into two parts: the classical text proper (*ching*) and the commentary (*chuan*). By identifying portions of the text as the personal writings of Confucius, Chu Hsi both elevated the text and left the question of the "authenticity" of the text open. Part of the *Great Learning* text was now accorded a higher status than its moment as a chapter in the *Book of Rites*. By encircling a part as the commentary and attributing it to Confucius's disciple Tseng-tzu, Chu Hsi explained and justified the presence of a commentary as an integral part of the Classic. To attribute the commentary to Confucius's disciple Tseng-tzu was a crucial attempt to forestall its potential rejection as an erroneous addition by a person whose Confucian identity was open to question. The master-disciple relationship performed a crucial role in keeping the *Great Learning* intact while providing the needed space for the textual reconfiguration that Chu Hsi felt compelled to make. Asserting a master-disciple relationship, that is, constructing an "intellectual lineage," was an easy way to establish intellectual affinity without arousing suspicion.

Imagining intellectual lineages has been a universal strategy for creating distinct intellectual identities. By attributing the commentary part to Confucius's disciple Tseng-tzu, Chu continued to draw implicitly on the belief in intellectual lineage as a criterion for conferring canonicity on the "commentary" part. By clearly identifying a part of the chapter as the actual remarks of Confucius and the rest as commentary by his disciple, Chu created a new "textual paradigm" for reading the text that was to dominate Neo-Confucian scholarship until the late Ming. The status of the chapter as an authentic Confucian text hinged upon Chu's "Classic-commentary" scheme, which became the hermeneutical principle of the Neo-Confucian tradition. The creation of this paradigm was important as the canonical status of the *Book of Rites* was called into question by the Tao-hsueh scholars in the Sung. Most of the chapters in the *Book of Rites* were dismissed as writings of Han scholars who were criticized for making serious mistakes in their transmission and exegetical endeavor.[10] As we shall see, later efforts aiming at undermining the status of the *Great Learning* focused precisely on rejecting such an internal distinction based on Chu Hsi's paradigms. In any case, the partition strategy of "classic-commentary" was crucial to Chu Hsi's reconfiguration of the text and to his adding the supplementary section in the commentary (*pu-chuan*), which, he argued, had been lost amid transmission.

The second paradigm that Chu Hsi created was doctrinal in nature. To him, the *Great Learning* clearly defined the goals, principles, and procedures for moral cultivation and for the fulfillment of the social and political obligations of a Confucian. He stipulated the "Three Cardinal Principles" (*san kang-ling*) and "Eight Headings" (*pa t'iao mu*) as the central teachings of the *Great Learning*.[11] The Three Cardinal Principles are: "manifest one's illustrious virtues" (*ming ming te*), "renew the subject" (*hsin min*), and "stop where supreme goodness is attained" (*chih yü chih-shan*). The Eight Headings are: *cheng-hsin* (rectifying the mind-heart), *ch'eng-i* (making the will sincere), *ko-wu* (investigating things), *chih-chih* (extending knowledge to the utmost), *hsiu-shen* (cultivating the self), *ch'i-chia* (bringing order to the family), *chih-kuo* (ruling the country), and *p'ing tien-hsia* (achieving peace among all-under-Heaven). According to Chu, all the "Three Cardinal Principles" and "Eight Headings" were clearly explained, except the sections on *ko-wu* and *chih-chih*. He thought that since each of the "Three Cardinal Principles" and "Eight Headings" had explanatory comments except for the *ko-wu*, the commentarial part of the *ko-wu* must have been lost amid transmission. Therefore, based on his own understanding of the text and his conception of its "perfect" edition, he offered to fill the gap with his own commentary. This resulted in his producing the famous "supplementary commentary" (*pu-chuan*) on the *ko-wu chih-chih* passage (investigation of things and the extension of knowledge to the utmost). Chu Hsi's "supplementary commentary" and his paradigms were fully articulated in the commentary he wrote for the *Great Learning*.

CRITICS OF THE CANONIZATION OF THE *GREAT LEARNING*

Chu Hsi's commentaries on the Confucian Classics were made the official texts in the civil service examinations from 1313. With the blessing of the imperial state, the moment of the Four Books as the cardinal Confucian texts became frozen. Minor incidents of dissension were not enough to pose a serious challenge to Chu Hsi's paradigms until the sixteenth century when the decanonization process took great strides. But actually the seed of the decanonization of the *Great Learning* had already been sown in Chu Hsi's time, a result of conflicting interpretations of the treatise. The philosophical battle between Chu Hsi and Lu Hsiang-shan (1139–93) was conducted on grounds of their contending interpretations of the *Great Learning*. The term that lay at the heart of the debate was "*ko-wu*." Chu Hsi favored an intellectualist or discursive approach to the term *ko-wu*, or investigation of things, whereas Lu championed an intuitive approach. By stressing the need to examine knowledge as much as possible, both moral and non-moral, Chu Hsi imposed a great demand on his disciples and followers. Lu's intuitive approach encouraged moral effort and introspection, relegating the pursuit of discursive knowledge to secondary importance. The disagreement between Chu Hsi and Lu Hsiang-shan was reduced to insignificant bickering by Lu's disciple Yang Chien, who simply rejected the *Great Learning* as a Confucian text. His opposition to the text was based on his reading that the text contained ideas incompatible with those of Confucius himself.[12] This strategy of denial was one of the most frequently used weapons in intellectual debates over exposition of texts. Yang's strategy involved three parts: first, a reductionist approach to the text and Confucius's ideas; second, a contrast of the selected ideas, and finally, dismissing the text's ideas as incompatible with Confucius's. As we shall see, the same strategy was used again by Ch'en Ch'ueh (1604–77) in the early Ch'ing.

WANG YANG-MING AND THE OLD TEXT OF THE *GREAT LEARNING*

The Ming dynasty inherited the examination system of the Yuan and continued to use Chu's commentaries in the examinations. Through his commentary, Chu Hsi's exposition of the *Great Learning* became the dominant view in the Ming. A few dissenting voices did little to undermine Chu's paradigms. The debate between Chu Hsi and Lu Hsiang-shan remained a scholarly issue in private circles. The greatest challenge to Chu Hsi did not come until the sixteenth century when Wang Yang-ming (1472–1529) criticized him for misunderstanding the meaning of the idea of *ko-wu chih-chih* (investigation of things and extension of knowledge to the utmost). The explanation Chu Hsi advanced in his commentary called for a rigorous investigation of things, which was essential to moral cultivation. In Wang's view, the lack of focus in Chu's intellectualist program of moral cultivation would only lead the literati astray. Dissatisfied with Chu's intellectualist approach to moral cultivation, Wang set out to challenge Chu's classic-commentary paradigm, in whose terms Chu's interpretation and his addition of the Supplementary Commentary on *ko-wu chih-chih* were justified.

In 1518 Wang published the *Old Edition of the Great Learning* (Ku-pen Ta-hsueh) and a collection of Chu Hsi's letters to his disciples, which Wang gave the title "*Chu-tzu wan-nien ting-lun*" (Definitive Ideas of Chu Hsi in the Last Years of His Life). The first work provided the textual foundation for his own interpretation of the term *ko-wu* in the *Great Learning*. The second work was published to forstall any attack on his view as heterodoxy by showing how Chu Hsi in his later life had already come to the same understanding of the term *ko-wu* as he did.[13]

As the forty-second chapter of the *Book of Rites*, the *Old Edition* of the text was not separated into the classic proper and the commentary, nor was the text divided into chapters and verses (*chang* and *chieh*). Wang Yang-ming argued that Chu Hsi had taken liberty in rearranging and dividing the text into chapters and verses in accordance with his own emphasis on the intellectual pursuit of knowledge. He lamented that the sage's meaning was lost as the text was divided into chapters and verses.[14] What he found in the *Old Edition* was a textual order that supported his reading that stressed "sincerity in one's thought"and "investigation of things" in the mind.[15]

The "rediscovery" of the *Old Edition of the Great Learning* was crucial to Wang's attempt to discredit Chu Hsi's exposition of the text. By denying the existence of a distinction between a classic proper and a purported commentary in the text, Wang meant to criticize Chu Hsi for tampering with the classic. Chu Hsi would be protected from the accusation of meddling with the classics, if indeed the part he changed was only a commentary as he asserted. But the strategy Chu Hsi used to demote the status of part of the text of the *Great Learning* into commentary was employed by Wang Yang-ming to restore it back to the status of a classic. By showing that in the *Old Edition*, the section on "*ko-wu chih-chih*" written by Chu Hsi served no function because the section on *ko-wu chih-chih* had not been lost, Wang Yang-ming could now claim that his interpretation of the meaning of *ko-wu chih-chih* was correct because it was based on the original, untampered text. It should be noted that of the two paradigms that Chu Hsi created, Wang had only discredited the "classic-commentary" paradigm of the textual structure. He did not challenge the "doctrinal structure" paradigm. He continued to speak of the "Three Cardinal Prinicples" and "Eight Headings" of the *Great Learning*.

In Wang's time, an ordinary literatus only studied Chu Hsi's edition of the *Great Learning* and had no knowledge of its previous status as a chapter in the *Book of Rites*.[16] This ignorance was due to the fact that Chu's commentary was printed with the text of the *Great Learning*, and the *Complete Compendium of the Four Books* simply deleted the text from the *Book of Rites*. When Wang Yang-ming printed the *Old Edition*, even officials renowned for their scholarship did not believe the existence of such a version with the *Great Learning* as one of the chapters of the *Book of Rites*. However, Wang Yang-ming's appeal to the *Old Edition of the Great Learning* soon won many supporters for his interpretation, even though there were some who were less impressed with the way he utilized a textual argument to promote his own philosophy. For instance, Lo Ch'in-shun (1465–1547), a staunch exponent of Chu Hsi's teachings, did not regard the *Old Edition* as adequate evidence for disputing Chu's exposition of the term *ko-wu* and likewise the Classic-commentary paradigm. After reading the *Old Edition of Great Learning* and *Definitive Ideas of Chu Hsi as Developed in His Later Life*, Lo wrote a letter to Wang in 1520. He pointed out that the stress Chu Hsi put on "broad learning" (*po-hsueh*) was in perfect accord with Confucius's teaching in the *Analects*.[17] The strategy Lo used here was to appeal to the word of Confucius himself and to a specific teaching as the criterion for determining the correct interpretation of the text. But, in response, Wang Yang-ming also appealed to the authority of Confucius. He said, "The *Old Edition of the Great Learning* is the original version transmitted from generation to generation in the Confucian school. Master Chu, suspecting that errors and gaps had crept in, corrected and amended it. But I believe that there have not been any errors and gaps. That is why I followed the Old Edition completely."[18] He continued to criticize Chu Hsi for tampering with the classic with his editorial reconfiguration of the text. He opined, "By what authority did Chu Hsi decide that this paragraph should be here and that one should be there, that this part had been lost and should be provided for . . . ? Are you not taking too seriously my divergences from Chu Hsi but not seriously enough Chu's rebellion against Confucius?"[19] On the surface, Wang appealed to the authority of Confucius. He was actually making his argument on the very assertion that Ch'eng I and Chu Hsi made about the authorship of the *Great Learning*. Wang did not challenge Chu Hsi's attribution of the text to Confucius but his editorial divisions and interpolation.

When Wang questioned Chu Hsi's authority in separating the *Great Learning* into chapters and verses and his inclusion of his "Supplementary Commentary," he was not making a plea for adhering to tradition. One easily recalls that it was Wang who said:

> If [words] are examined in the mind and found to be wrong, then even if they have come from [the mouth] Confucius, I dare not accept them as correct. How much more so for those which have come from people inferior to Confucius! If [words] are examined in the mind-heart and found to be right, then even if they have come from [the mouth] of mediocre people, I dare not regard them as incorrect. How much more so for those which have come from Confucius?[20]

It is clear that in his defense of his new interpretation of the *ko-wu* passage, he was using a criterion he thought his critic would not question. But for his own divergence from Chu Hsi, or even Confucius, his own mind would be sufficient in justifying any change to the text. In this case, his position was not very different from that of Ch'eng I and Chu Hsi, who believed that with the understanding of the heavenly prinicples, they were qualified to make any change to correct or improve the texts through reconfiguration, deletion, and addition.

The philosophical argument for moral intuitionism that Wang Yang-ming formulated did gain popularity as a result of the publicity he had created for the *Old Edition of the Great Learning*. Ironically, the mounting pressure to accept Wang's exposition based on the *Old Edition of the Great Learning* facilitated the wider circulation of a new version of the *Great Learning*—the *Shih-ching Ta-hsueh* (the *Great Learning* inscribed on a stele).

BETWEEN SANCTIONED CHANGES AND FORGERY

Wang Yang-ming's argument for returning to the *Old Edition of the Great Learning* was further strengthened when Feng Fang (*chin-shih.*1523) circulated a text called the *Great Learning on the Stele* (*Shih-ching Ta-hsueh*). The common belief in the ease with which a text was corrupted as a result of copying mistakes not only enabled many to justify changes in terms of correcting transmittal mistakes, but also facilitated acceptance of sanctioned changes as attempts to restore the "original" and "untampered" text. As I will show, the line between forgery and sanctioned change is extremely fine. The question of what constitutes a forgery is in fact similar to the question of what consitutes a Confucian text.

The last one hundred years of the Ming regime witnessed rampant forgeries of all sorts. Fake books, paintings, silver and bronze vessels flooded the market of connoisseur goods.[21] One of the falsified texts that added fuel to the debate over the editions of the *Great Learning* was the new modified version, the *Great Learning on the Stele* that Feng Fang created. Feng was a versatile scholar famous for his ability to imitate different styles of calligraphy. He inherited from his father a rich library including many rare editions. Following Wang Yang-ming, with the Stele edition, Feng wanted to challenge Chu Hsi's textual paradigm of separating the text into the classic proper and the commentary. In the Stele edition, there was no additional section to explain the headings of *ko-wu* and *chih-chih*. There was also much reshuffling of passages in the Stele edition. This reconfiguring of the text was not entirely new, for the Ch'eng brothers and Chu Hsi had made their own configurations. In a way resembling Chu Hsi's creating of the supplementary section on *ko-wu chih-chih*, Feng inserted a passage from the *Analects*.[22] It was the famous question Yen Yuan posed to Confucius on the meaning of "humaneness" (*jen*). The choice of the passage suggests Feng's own interpretation of the central teachings of Confucius. The strategy he used was again based on the belief in intellectual affinity between disciple and Confucius. In the case of Chu Hsi, it was Tseng-tzu, and in Feng's case, it was Yen Yuan. Neither claim, however, was based on external evidence.

Feng went one step further than Chu Hsi; he undertook the task of manufacturing some external evidence. At the same time that he revealed the possession of the Stele edition of the *Great Learning*, he also fabricated a few historical accounts in order to lend credibility to the Stele edition. He claimed to have discovered a copy of the Stele version of the *Great Learning* inscribed on stone tablets by imperial order during the Ching-ho reign of the Wei dynasty (220–265). This is a somewhat puzzling move because there was no such reign in the Wei period. In other words, why would he refer to a nonexistent reign if his goal was to infuse an aura of authenticity? In any case, to add further credibility to the text, he also identified those scholars responsible for the inscriptions. As an expert in emulating calligraphical styles, Feng wrote the Stele edition in the *chuan*-style calligraphy, endowing it with a veneer of historical authenticity.[23]

As early as 1562, the Stele edition began to circulate in Feng Fang's circle of friends, including the renowned scholar Cheng Hsiao (1499–1566). Cheng learned of the Stele version from Feng Fang himself. Another well-known scholar, Wang Wen-lu (1503–86), based on the edition he got from Feng Fang and on the references to this work in the writings of Cheng Hsiao, became convinced of its authenticity. Thereupon in 1564, he published the text.[24] With the blessing of scholars such as Cheng Hsiao and Wang Wen-lu, the Stele version of the *Great Learning* began to appear in various printed texts and rapidly attained popularity.[25] The Stele edition drew support from both exponents of Chu Hsi's and Wang Yang-ming's learning. The success of the text was due in part to the desire to settle the controversy over the "correct" interpretation of the phrase *ko-wu chih-chih*. The solution of this textual problem would, it was hoped, resolve the contest of interpretations about the approach to Confucian ethics. The second reason for its popularity perhaps had to do with the appeal to an unexamined belief in the reliability of text inscribed on stone, a belief rendered all the more powerful as there was a growing awareness of the various editorial and printing mistakes that resulted from the rapid expansion of commerical printing in the late Ming period.

But how is the Stele edition different from the other modified editions? As pointed out above, Feng inserted the passage on *jen* (humaneness) from the *Analects*. His goal in doing so was to underscore "self-cultivation" (*hsiu-shen*) as the central message of the text. Like Chu Hsi's "Supplementary Commentary," the insertion was a result of Feng's own interpretation of the ethical message of the *Great Learning*. As we have seen, scholars beginning with the Ch'eng brothers had made various changes to the textual order of the *Great Learning*. Most changes involved reconfiguring the constituent parts of the text, that is, moving words and phrases around and adding or excising verses. But in most cases, when the reasons for making the changes were clearly explained, the text would not be treated as a forgery. Chu Hsi was criticized for filling the perceived gap with his own "Supplementary Commentary" (*pu-chuan*) on the "investigation of things." But he was not accused of forging a text. What made the case of the Stele Version of the *Great Learning* stand out was that the changes made were not explained at all. They were assumed to be the restoration of the original. Unexplained changes based on putative rediscoveries could certainly be construed as an act of forgery in strictly textual terms. However, on the hermenutical level, it was no different from the additional section Chu Hsi authored in order to articulate his emphasis on "investigation of things." The main difference between the insertion of passage in Chu Hsi's edition and Feng's Stele version is this: whereas in the former, there was explicit justification for modification and addition, in the latter, there was none. Furthermore, Chu Hsi did not fabricate historical accounts as external evidence to support his claim.

For some, the appearance of the Stele version was a timely solution to the heated debate between supporters of Wang Yang-ming and defenders of Chu Hsi. Many followers of Wang Yang-ming seized the opportunity to promote his ideas. Keng Ting-hsiang (1524–96), Chao Ta-chou, and Kuan Chih-tao (1537–1608) enthusiatically promoted the *Old Edition*.[26] Some, however, see the appearance of the Stele version as a weapon for a counterattack on Wang Yang-ming's interpretation. In 1584 Tang Po-yuan (1540–89) submitted a memorial to the emperor condemning the *Old Edition*. Instead, he recommended the distribution of the Stele version to all government schools.[27] Even learned scholars like Ku Hsien-ch'eng (1550–1612) and Liu Tsung-chou (1578–1645) were attracted to the Stele text.[28] The Stele version of the *Great Learning* was consequently extensively quoted and reproduced in many commentaries on the text. In Chang Tzu-lieh's *Ssu-shu ta-ch'uan pien* (Disputations on the Complete *Four Books*), several versions of the *Great Learning* were included for the readers to compare. The Stele version was one of them.[29] A more dramatic consequence of the great appeal of the Stele version and the stories invented by Feng Fang was the writing of an examination question based on it, by Chiang Hsing-wei in the last years of the Chung-chen reign (1628–44).[30] Despite its popularity, the sudden appearance of the Stele version of the *Great Learning* did not receive universal acceptance. A few incredulous scholars suspected forgery by the discoverer Feng Fang. Ch'en Yao-wen, an expert in textual criticism, expressed doubt about the dubious origin of the text.[31] Hsu Fu-yuan and Wu Ying-pin were also among the few who were suspicious of the Stele version.

Regardless of the question of the text's authenticity, the circulation of the Stele version and the *Old Edition* in their printed forms had the cumulative effect of undermining the integrity of the official edition. They prompted ever more modifications of the text by sundry scholars based on different interpretive justifications. Liu Tsung-chou, a foremost exponent of Wang Yang-ming's teachings, sadly lamented the profusion of confusion as a result of the emergence of large numbers of modified editions based on different interpretations of the *Great Learning*. Kao P'an-lung expressed his anger and frustration in his remark that in the present time, everyone created his own edition of the *Great Learning*.[32] But perhaps it was Kuo Tzu-chang who made one of the most trenchant comments on the nature of the bone of all the contentions surrounding the *Great Learning*. He commented that the *Great Learning*, as a chapter of the *Book of Rites*, is not divided into sections and verses. To him, although the stele version of the *Great Learning* differed from both the *Old Edition* and the official edition based on Chu Hsi's changes, there was one central message of the text, that is, *ko-wu*, investigation of things. As long as the meaning of *ko-wu* was understood, discrepancies in the three versions did not matter.[33] This remark by Kuo touches upon an important issue in textual studies—not every word in the text counts. What matters here for Kuo is the meaning of *ko-wu*. Differences in other parts of the *Great Learning* are insignificant as long as the purport of the term and idea of *ko-wu* is brought to light. It is important to note that Kuo was one who actually had reservations about the Stele version, but he nonetheless accepted it on philosophical grounds.

FROM FORGERY TO HETERODOX TEXT: CH'EN CH'UEH'S CRITIQUE

The controversy and confusion over the various versions of the *Great Learning* continued to rage in the wake of the Manchu conquest. The debate took a drastic turn when Ch'en Ch'ueh (1604–77), a student of Liu Tsung-chou, condemned the text of *Great Learning* itself as outright heterodox, regardless of the various editions and versions. With the rise of Confucian purism, Ch'en was among the few who advocated a thorough cleansing of Confucian texts of heterodox ideas and terms.[34] His radical view immediately caused commotion among Liu's students. Though a student of Liu, Ch'en was repelled by the syncretic tendencies characteristic of many of Wang Yang-ming's followers in the late Ming. He was particularly critical of what he believed to be the central message of the text—the stress on knowlege at the expense of neglecting moral practice. To Ch'en Ch'ueh, this was clearly a teaching of Ch'an Buddhism.[35] To him, the teaching of *chih-chih*, "extension of knowledge," had two problems: first, the belief that once one knew the moral principles, there was no more to know; second, knowing was sufficient without practice.[36]

The strategies or textual methods Chen used to discredit the *Great Learning* involved both ordinary methods of textual criticism and interpretive devices. Ch'en declared that the *Great Learning* was written by neither Confucius nor his disciple.[37] He tried to prove that there was no evidence for attributing the *Great Learning* to Confucius. Nor was there any reference to the title *Ta-hsueh* in other Confucian texts such as the *Spring and Autumn Annals*, the *Book of Odes*, and the *Book of Documents*. Ch'en then explained how Ch'eng I and Chu Hsi contributed to turning this heterodox text into the most important text of Confucianism. Ch'en first pointed out that Ch'eng I's claim that the *Great Learning* was a "bequeathed work" of Confucius was groundless.[38] Ch'en argued that except for three direct quotations of the words of Confucius and Tseng-tzu, there was no other evidence for the claim that the entire text represented Confucius's and Tseng-tzu's ideas.[39] Furthermore, unlike the *Doctrine of the Mean* there is no mention of the title *Great Learning* in other Confucian texts.[40] What contributed to the popularity of the text was its promotion by the emperor of the Sung dynasty.[41] Ch'en's explanation actually referred to the important role that institutions and political power played in conferring canonicity on texts.

The strategy Ch'en employed is commonly used to establish or deny intellectual affinities between texts and a set of ideas. By arguing that there was no trace of the idea in the most important sources of Confucius's ideas, Ch'en was discrediting the *Great Learning* as a Confucian classic. Ch'en identified the idea of *chih-chih* (knowing where to stop) in the text as the cardinal teaching of the text, and argued that the idea could only be a heterodox teaching incompatible with the teachings of Confucius. To Ch'en, only Ch'an Buddhism advocated instant enlightenment, and the term *chih-chih* in the *Great Learning* signified a similar idea. According to Ch'en, the learning of a Confucian gentlemen (*chün-*

tzu) ended only with death.[42] The idea that once there was understanding, there was no more to know was nothing but Ch'an Buddhism. But the characterization of the idea of *chih-chih* as one similar to Chan Buddhism's advocacy was clearly Ch'en's own reaction against Chu Hsi's interpretation of the term. Ch'en was fully aware that removing the Confucian status from the *Great Learning* would eliminate the source for all the controversy about the textual and edition problems that had occupied scholars since Wang Yang-ming's promotion of the *Old Edition*. Even though Ch'en was deeply committed to Wang Yang-ming's teaching of the "unity of knowledge and practice" (*chih-hsing ho-i*), he was not concerned about the impact of his textual surgery on Wang's learning. His radical approach toward the *Great Learning* had much to do with his own moral philosophy, which underscored moral practice and ritual practice.[43]

How justified is Ch'en's rejection of the *Great Learning* as a Ch'an Buddhist text? The only evidence Ch'en presented was the view that *chih-chih* (knowing where to stop) was a Ch'an teaching. This argument does not sound convincing in terms of the meager amount of evidence marshalled in its support. But it is not that much different from the assertion made by Ch'eng I and Chu Hsi about the authorship of the *Great Learning*. Both used a similar method of asserting an intellectual link between a person and a text or a teaching. In the case of Ch'eng I and Chu Hsi, they attributed the text to Confucius and his disciple. The *Great Learning* was represented as a canonical text, presumably retrieved from among the writings of Han dynasty scholars. While disputing Chu Hsi's interpolation and editorial changes, Wang Yang-ming continued to accept the intellectual link Chu and Ch'eng I had asserted between Confucius and the text. But this link was rejected by Ch'en Ch'ueh who instead argued for the existence of a link between Ch'an Buddhism and the text. Neither Ch'en nor Chu presented any compelling evidence for such a link. The classification of the *Great Learning* as a Confucian canonical text hinged upon those claims. Feng Fang's insertion of a passage by Yen Yuan into the Stele version clearly was a common strategy used to identify the intellectual orientation of a text. The creation of a clear boundary for a text is a reductionist process that suppresses its heterogeneity and complexity so as to arrive at a manageable set of fixed ideas. The same method is used to eliminate a text from an intellectual tradition by labeling it a heterodox text or forgery.

To conclude, the choice and use of techniques of textual criticism to establish authorship, to restore the original form, and to distinguish the intellectual identity of a text, are often guided by hermeneutical principles grounded in contesting ideologies. The textual paradigms of Chu Hsi, Wang Yang-ming's reestablishment of the *Old Edition*, and the reconfiguration of the *Great Learning* under the label of the Stele version by Feng Fang, all exemplify discursive strategies for the advancement of their own beliefs, their reading of a text, and their understanding of the Confucian tradition. The case of Ch'en Ch'ueh's rejection

of the *Great Learning* as a Confucian text clearly shows that the imagined boundaries, or more precisely the markers or signposts of intellectual affinity and lineage, were grounded on a series of strategies. These hermeneutical strategies fix
authorship to a set of highly selected ideas or values through a series of reductionist attempts that eliminate or deny the fluidity, heterogeneity, and complexity of
a text. We see these strategies employed at various hermeneutical moments of
the *Great Learning*: as a Confucian canonical text, as a forgery, and as a heterodox
text that smacked of Ch'an Buddhism. The hermeneutical moments of the *Great
Learning* arose as the boundary between canonicity and heterodoxy inexorably
shifted.

NOTES

1. Kung Tzu-chen, *Kung Tzu-chen ch'uan-chi* (The Complete Works of
Kung Tzu-chen) (Shanghai, Jen-min ch'u-pan she, 1975), p. 38.

2. John Henderson, *Scripture, Canon, and Commentary: A Comparison of
Confucian and Western Exegesis* (Princeton: Princeton University Press, 1991), p.
49.

3. For a discussion of European views, see Susan Cherniak, "Book Culture
and Textual Transmission in Sung China," *Harvard Journal of Asiatic Studies* 35.1
(1994): 79–82.

4. The elevation of the *Four Books* into the Confucian canon in the Sung
was anticipated by the T'ang scholar Ch'uan Te-yu. David McMullen, *State and
Scholars in T'ang China* (Cambridge: Cambridge University Press, 1988), pp.
96–97.

5. For discussion of the sources and general nature of the Confucian classics in the pre-Han period, see Henderson, *Scripture, Canon, and Commentary*,
chapter 1.

6. Lin Ch'ing-chang, *Ch'ing-ch'u ti chun-ching pien-wei hsueh* (A Study of
the Critical Examination of Falsified Classical Texts in the Early Ch'ing)
(Taipei: Wen-chin ch'u-pan-she, 1990), p. 359. Huang Chin-hsing, "Li-hsueh,
k'ao-chu hsueh, yü cheng-chih: i Ta-hsueh kai-pen ti fa-chan wei li-cheng"
(Neo-Confucianism, Textual Criticism, and Politics: the Development of the
Revised Editions of the *Ta-hsueh* as an Example), *Bulletin of the Institute of History
and Philology* (Academia Sinica) 60, pt. 4 (1989): pp. 889–90.

7. Ibid.

8. Huang Chin-hsing points out that the *Great Learning*, contrary to conventional accounts, might have been published as a separate treatise prior to Ssu-
ma Kuang's commentary. But Ssu-ma's commentary may still be the first
commentary on the *Great Learning* as an independent text. "Li-hsueh k'ao-chu
hsueh yü cheng-chih," pp. 889–90.

9. Chu Hsi, Chu *Wen-kung wen-chi* (hereafter CWKWC) 13:749. But when he wrote the preface for his commentaries on the Four Books, he retreated from the confident tone regarding the text's authors.

10. Chu Hsi, *Chu-tzu yü-lei* (Peking: Chung-hua shu-chu, 1986), 6: 2193.

11. Chu Hsi's notion of the presence of the "Three Cardinal Principles and Eight Headings" might have been borrowed from Lin Chih-ch'i (1112–76).

12. See Lin Ch'ing-chang, *Ch'ing-ch'u ti chun-ching pien-wei hsueh*, p. 361.

13. Julia Ching, *To Acquire Wisdom: The Way of Wang Yang-ming* (New York: Columbia University Press, 1976), p. 79. *Chu Hsi wan-nien ting-lun* (Definitive Ideas of Chu Hsi in His Later Life) immediately provoked attack from supporters of Chu Hsi. They accused Wang of mistaking Chu's view in his middle period as that in his later period. According to Wing-tsit Chan, in terms of the dating of the letters, Wang Yang-ming's claim is defensible. But his choice of letters, however, is not representative of Chu's view. For he presents only thirty-four pieces out of over 1,600 letters. See Wing-tsit Chan, "Ts'ung Chu Hsi wan-nien ting-lun k'an Yang-ming chih yü Chu Hsi" (The Relationship between Wang Yang-ming and Chu Hsi as Seen in the Essay "Definitive Ideas of Chu Hsi in His Later Life"), in *Chu hsüeh lun-chi* (Collected Essays on the Study of Chu Hsi) (Taipei: Hsueh-sheng shu-chu, 1982), pp. 358–61.

14. Wang Yang-ming, "Preface to the Old Edition of the *Great Learning*," in *Wang Yang-ming Ch'uan-chi* (Complete Works of Wang Yang-ming) (Hong Kong: Kuang-chi shu-chu, 1959), p. 58.

15. Wang Yang-ming, *Ch'uan-hsi lu*, in *Wang Yang-ming Ch'uan-shu*, p. 4.

16. Mao Ch'i-ling, *Ta-hsueh cheng-wen* (Verifying the text of the *Great Learning*), Ssu-k'u ch'uan-shu, *chen-pen*, ser. 9, vol. 65, 1.1b–2a.

17. Lo Ch'in-shun, *K'un chih chi* (Knowledge Painfully Acquired), appendix, Ssu-k'u ch'uan-shu, vol. 714, 1a–2a.

18. Ching, *To Acquire Wisdom*, p. 101.

19. Ibid., p. 102.

20. The translation is based on Julia Ching, who has modified Wing-tsit Chan's. Ching, *To Acquire Wisdom*, p. 102. Wang Yang-ming, *Instructions for Practical Living and Other Neo-Confucian Writings*, Wing-tsit Chan trans. (New York: Columbia University Press, 1963), p. 159.

21. Craig Clunas, *The Superfluous Things: Material Culture and Social Status in Early Modern China* (Urbana and Chicago: University of Illinois Press, 1991).

22. See Liu Ssu-yuan, *Ta-hsueh ku-chin pen t'ung-k'ao* (A Comprehensive Study of Ancient and Contemporary Editions of the *Great Learning*), in *Chung-kuo tzu-hsueh ming-chu chi-ch'eng* (Collection of Famous Writings of the Miscellaneous Philosophies in China), vol. 15 (Taipei: Chung-kuo tzu-hsueh ming-chu chi-ch'eng pien-yin chi-chin-hui, 1971), 3.2a. See Li Chi-hsiang, *Liang-Sung i-lai Ta-hsueh kai-pen chih yen-chiu* (A Study of the Various Corrected

Editions of the *Great Learning* since the Sung) (Taipei: Hsueh-sheng shu-chu, 1988), pp. 145–54.

23. The handcopied edition was written in the *kai* style. But later there were printed editions written in *chuan* and *li* styles. See Mao Ch'i-ling, *Ta-hsueh cheng-wen*, 2.4b–6b.

24. Lin Ch'ing-chang, *Ch'ing ch'u ti chun-ching pien-wei hsueh*, pp. 413–16.

25. Li Chi-hsiang, *Liang-Sung i-lai Ta-hsueh kai-pen chih yen-chiu*, pp. 145, 157–58. For example, the Stele edition was printed in the collectanea *Shuo fu*. See Yao Chi-heng, *Ku-chin wei-shu k'ao* (A Study of Falsified Texts in the Past and Present), in *Chung-kuo hsueh-shu ming-chu* (Famous Writings in Chinese Learning) (Taipei: Shih-chieh shu-chu, 1960), p. 6.

26. Li Chi-hsiang, *Liang-Sung i-lai Ta-hsueh kai-pen chih yen-chiu*, pp. 137–41.

27. Mao Ch'i-ling, *Ta-hsueh cheng-wen*, 2.3b. See also Huang Chin-hsing, "Li-hsueh k'ao-chu hsueh yü cheng-chih," p. 905

28. Li Chi-hsiang, *Liang-Sung i-lai Ta-hsueh kai-pen chih yen-chiu*, pp. 141–42.

29. Chang Tzu-lieh, *Ssu-shu ta-chuan pien*.

30. Mao Ch'i-ling, *Ta-hsueh cheng-wen*, 2.6b.

31. Mao Ch'i-ling quoted Ch'en Yao-wen's remarks in *Ching-tien ch'i-i*. See Mao, *Ta-hsueh cheng-wen* 2.3a–b.

32. Liu Ts'ung-chou, *Liu tzu ch'uan-shu* 36.1b., quoted in Huang Chin-hsing, "Li-hsueh Kao-chu hsueh yü cheng-chih," p. 907.

33. *Ch'ing-lei kung i-shu* (Bequeathed Writings of Kuo Tzu-chang) (Ming edition, no place, no date) 15.9b–10a.

34. Kai-wing Chow, *The Rise of Confucian Ritualism in Late Imperial China: Ethics, Classics, and Lineage Discourse* (Stanford: Stanford University Press, 1994), pp. 47–48.

35. Ch'en Ch'ueh, *Ch'en Ch'ueh chi* (Collected Works of Ch'en Ch'ueh) (Peking: Chung-hua shu-chu, 1979), p. 557. This work is hereafter cited as CCC.

36. Ch'en Ch'ueh, CCC, p. 586.

37. Ch'en Ch'ueh, CCC, p. 552.

38. Ch'en Ch'ueh, CCC, p. 562.

39. Ch'en Ch'ueh, CCC, pp. 557–58.

40. Ch'en Ch'ueh, CCC, p. 563.

41. Ch'en Ch'ueh, CCC, p. 562.

42. Ch'en Ch'ueh, CCC, p. 554.

43. Chow, *The Rise of Confucian Ritualism*, pp. 47-48.

GLOSSARY

ch'eng-i   誠意
ch'i-chia   齊家

Cheng Hsiao	鄭曉
cheng-hsin	正心
Chiang Hsing-wei	蔣星煒
chih yü chih-shan	止於至善
chih-chih	致知
chih-chih	知止
chih-hsing ho-i	知行合一
chih-kuo	治國
ching	經
Ching-tien ch'i-i	經典稽疑
Chu-tzu wan-nien ting-lun	朱子晚年定論
chuan	傳
Ch'uan-hsi lu	傳習錄
chuan-t'i	篆體
hsin-min	新民
hsiu-shen	修身
Hsu Fu-yuan	許孚遠
i-shu	遺書
k'ai-shu	楷書
ko-wu	格物
ko-wu chih-chih	格物致知
Ku-chin wei-shu k'ao	古今偽書考
Ku-pen Ta-hsueh	古本大學
li-shu	隸書
Lin Chih-ch'i	林之奇
Liu Ssu-yuan	劉斯原
Lo Ch'in-shun	羅欽順
ming ming-te	明明德
pa t'iao-mu	八條目
p'ing t'ien-hsia	平天下
po-hsueh	博學
pu-chuan	補傳
san kang-ling	三綱領
Shih-ching Ta-hsueh	石經大學
Shuo fu	說郛
Ta-hsueh ku-chin pen t'ung-k'ao	大學古今本通考
Tseng Tzu	曾子
Wang Wen-lu	王文祿
Wu Ying-pin	吳應賓
Yao Chi-heng	姚際恆
Yü-t'ai	輿臺

8

Negotiating the Boundary between Hermeneutics and Philosophy in Early Ch'ing Ch'eng-Chu Confucianism

Li Kuang-ti's (1642–1718) Study of the Doctrine of the Mean (Chung-yung) and Great Learning (Ta-hsueh)

On-cho Ng

> There's another rendering now; but still one text. All sorts of men in one kind of world, you see.
>
> —Melville, *Moby Dick*

Our wariness toward broad generalizations notwithstanding, it is easy to agree with Roger Ames's remark that "the dominant Chinese philosophic tradition has tended to be commentarial rather than systematic, with philosophers reinterpreting the classical core in order to accommodate changing historical circumstances."[1] In a slightly different vein, while examining comparatively the varied exegetical traditions in different cultures, John Henderson informs us that in imperial China, the grounds for the contest and affirmation of truths were the classics. Flowing out of the classical hermeneutic wellspring, in the form of the commentary and annotative exegesis, was a mainstream in Chinese intellectual history.[2] Steven Van Zoeren, in his detailed study of the history of the interpretation of the *Classic of Odes*, arrives at the conclusion that "the interpretation and exegesis of canonical texts were occasions for normative, political and speculative teaching and thinking."[3] All these authors' remarks suggest that there was a close interrelationship between exegetical endeavor and philosophic excogitation, but since neither Henderson nor Van Zoeren are specifically concerned with this question, their studies understandably stop short of revealing just how

165

Confucian hermeneutics generated and expressed reflective thinking about questions of reality and existence.

In this essay, through an examination of some of the exegetical efforts of an early Ch'ing Ch'eng-Chu scholar, Li Kuang-ti (1642–1718), I aim to show how the exegete's (and hence the interpreter's) philosophical predispositions and pre-understanding guided his interaction with classical texts. Kuang-ti is chosen as the example here for two reasons. First, under the aegis of the K'ang-hsi emperor (r. 1662–1722), Li Kuang-ti, recognized as one of the foremost proponents of the Ch'eng-Chu school, was given the task of organizing the compilation of this school's important works. He was, in essence, assigned the illustrious role as the imperial interpreter of orthodoxy, devoted to consolidating and promoting the *tao-t'ung* (lineage of the Way) as defined by Chu Hsi.[4] Unfortunately, Kuang-ti has not received much scholarly attention, largely because Ch'ing learning as a whole has been studied in terms of the so-called *ching-shih* (practical statecraft) and *k'ao-cheng* (evidential stuides) orientations, the supposed intellectual *leitmotif* of the age. To focus on some of Kuang-ti's exegetical efforts is to rescue from relative obscurity the learning of this important court-intellectual of the early Ch'ing period, whom Wm. Theodore de Bary rightly describes as "the most important figure in the formulation of the official orthodoxy of the Ch'ing."[5] Second, despite Kuang-ti's avowed allegiance to Ch'eng-Chu tenets, he did not refrain from critiquing Chu Hsi's earlier exegeses on the *Mean* and *Great Learning*. His reading of the two texts, which involved their textual rearrangement and emendation, was integrally a function of the ordering power of the principal assumptions and views of his philosophical world. Thus, by examining Kuang-ti's endeavors, one catches a clear glimpse of the fluid nature of Confucian hermeneutics, even within the boundary of an acknowledged orthodoxy.

I will further suggest that, viewed in this light, classical exegesis in traditional China in a general sense may not be all that different from contemporary interpretive hermeneutics, inasmuch as both point to the interpenetration of the text and the interpreter. Needless to say, the differences are also legion and crucial. On a general level, it can be argued that the Confucian exegetical project is an illustration of the "hermeneutical axiom," that is, the contention that all thought involves interpretation and is relative to the contingent context of particular historical forces and factors, including the interpreter's preunderstanding and predisposition.[6] But Confucian exegesis certainly did not cast doubt on classical truth itself, even though it might critically evaluate some of the sources in which this truth was supposedly expressed; nor did it claim to be anything more than the retrieval and reassertion of such truth. Therefore, two caveats are in order. First, in this essay, hermeneutics in Confucian terms refer specifically to the study of the classics, although in illustrating the pursuit of such study, references will be made to the larger question of hermeneutics as the philosophy of interpretation. Second, it should be noted that in Confucian hermeneutics, the ultimate universality of the values embodied in the classics was taken for granted, not subject to questioning in relativistic terms. Thus, although individual authorial imprints and historicocultural conditions did yield interpretive latitude, the timeless authority of the classical texts themselves furnished the unshakable bedrock of the hermeneutic order. In contrast, certain contemporary hermeneutic assumptions would have been anathema in the Confucian scheme of things, namely, that words refer merely to other words, without general referential capacity; that texts are stormy linguistic seas in which truths and meanings are easily adrift; that meanings must be endlessly deferred along a string of signifiers; and that the self, both from the author's and reader's standpoints, is insubstantial at best, an ideological construction at worst. Such tenets are particularly pronounced in French poststructuralist hermeneutics, where the distrust of the explicit meanings of words effectively means the end of the communicative power of the canons with regard to the delivery of truths and traditional values. Furthermore, the French mode of interpretation views tradition as something to be overcome and surmounted, insofar as most of the ideas embraced by the past thinkers were anchored on the false consciousness of foundationalism. In the final analysis, the engagement with texts breeds merely self-referential paradoxes incapable of supporting any truth-claims.[7]

My comparative perspective is, therefore, better served by German hermeneutics, which,[8] while acknowledging the incompleteness and ephemerality of apprehending human knowing through texts, affirm the meaningfulness of words as interpretations and expressions of truth.[9] In particular, I will refer to Martin Buber's and Hans-Georg Gadamer's hermeneutic arguments and principles. Both stress the interactive import of and, in the words of Nathan Scott Jr., the "dialogical approaches" to reading the classics as a way to engage human responsibility, understanding, and eventually liberation.[10] Fruitful comparisons may also be drawn between Confucian hermeneutics and David Tracy's Christian hermeneutics within the domain of what he calls "systematic theology," in that the latter is premised on the conviction that "no classic can be reduced to mere privacy."[11] Tracy's thesis "is that what we mean in naming certain texts . . . 'classics' is that here we recognize nothing less than the disclosure of a reality we cannot but name truth."[12] As "truth," the classics are in effect "public" and even "transcultural," embodying both "an excess and a permanence of meaning that later generations must retrieve."[13] But such retrieval must be a result of critical and rigorous interpretations on the part of the textual interrogator with his or her particular historical understanding. As interlocutors with the classics, the interpreters ineluctably bring into the conversation their preunderstanding.[14]

These hermeneutic approaches refuse to superannuate past traditions ensconced in the classics but instead seek a meaningful conflation of the past and present by seeing the timelessness of the classics in relation to their temporal manifestations in the present historical contingencies. To put it another way, the truth that issues forth from the classics is indeed mediated by interpretation and therefore contextualized, but its truth-value is not at all threatened by such interpretive contextualization. The classics, because of their essential perpetuity, offer a common context, a single cultural tradition, which is capable of absorbing and accommodating the diversity and historicity of their interpreters. By casting Li Kuang-ti's exegetical endeavors in a comparative light, this essay hopes to contribute to a better understanding of Confucian hermeneutics, not as mere repetition of the classics frozen in a timeless moment, but as constant historical restating and reinterpretation of the classical texts' apparent transtemporal claim. In other words, the Confucian quest for truths within the hermeneutic boundary involved constant remapping of the textual landscape with the intrusion of philosophical interlopers.

BASIS OF LI KUANG-TI'S HERMENEUTICS:
PHILOSOPHY OF HUMAN NATURE

A brief word on Kuang-ti's philosophy is in order. To be sure, in general, Kuang-ti endorsed Ch'eng-Chu teachings. But he diverged from them in one significant regard—his philosophy was premised on the ontological primacy of the Heaven-endowed nature (hsing), and not principle (li): "Nature is the master; principle is its tributary."[15] Thus, in contrast to the well-known Ch'eng-Chu dictum that "principle is one, but the manifestations are varied" (li-i fen-shu), Kuang-ti maintained instead that "the diverse varieties of the myriad things are ultimately nothing but the completion of their immanent nature."[16] Why was there such a reassertion of human nature? It may be argued that Kuang-ti's metaphysical refocusing was a continuation of the late Ming Ch'eng-Chu scholars' effort to take issue with the Wang Yang-ming school's definition of original substance (pen-t'i) as beyond good and evil (wu-shan wu-o). As Mou Tsung-san points out, conceptions of human nature (hsing) in the Confucian tradition were not piecemeal philosophical analysis of a problem of humanity. They were doctrines that responded to questions of ultimate reality. For human nature was the whole of reality. Referring to the Doctrine of the Mean, Mou explains: "Hsing was that which flowed down from the reality mandated by Heaven and was fully embodied in the self." Thus, the locus of one's transcendence was found in self-awareness and the moral-ethical deeds that stemmed from such awareness: "Since nothing was outside of the 'reality of the self's nature' (hsing-t'i), the cosmic order was the moral-ethical order; the moral-ethical order was the cosmic order."[17] While the Confucian thinkers saw the everyday world as one fraught with uncertainties and one that demanded their ceaseless acts to do good, they were certain that the universe embodied and manifested in the authentic nature of the self was enlivened with moral inclinations.[18] Thus, within the Confucian definition of the vital reality of every life, there was, to borrow Ortega y Gasset's argument, a "certainty of faith" (*creencia*) in nature's innate goodness or moral creativity. *Creencias*, in Ortega's terms, are ideas and conceptions of reality that have become identified with reality; they are "not ideas which we *have*, but ideas which we *are*."[19] The conception of *hsing* as the encapsulation of Heaven's nature was not a mere explanation of reality with the tentative quality of a philosophical speculation; it was engagement with ultimate reality itself. Such a conception was not a contingent statement of truth, but a collective faith, a part of reality with which Confucians must reckon.

As a result, the Confucian philosophical speculation on human nature was a self-referential activity—discourses on *hsing* were ideally instances of *hsing*'s own meaning. Not unlike the Socratic dictum that philosophy merely explained what was known, in the Confucian scheme of things, to learn was to bring to light what the authentic self already knew.[20] Every thought and every act that followed were at once involved in presumptions of the fundamental reality of our nature. Learning was practice; knowing was acting.[21] To the extent that epistemology was ontology, pursuing false learning, such as misconstruing the nature of human nature, meant not only misrepresenting the truth of reality; it was also in itself a violation and corruption of reality. For in the process of learning to know *hsing*, we also turned inward to cultivate our nature, and in so doing, we at once humanized and cosmicized our being.

Thus, when the latter-day followers of Wang Yang-ming in the late Ming propounded the idea of nature's being beyond good and evil, they were seen by many Confucian literati, led by the Ch'eng-Chu inspired Tung-lin scholars such as Ku Hsien-ch'eng (1550–1612), not only as mere exponents of ideas but as destroyers of *creencias*, of parts of reality. Such destruction was readily evidenced by dynastic weakening, a direct consequence of the misapprehension of human nature, which in turn led to spiritual degeneration and moral anarchy. As scholars sought to extirpate the flawed understanding of human nature that bred the spiritual-psychological plague of ethicomoral relativism and the sociopolitical scourge of dynastic decline, they also positively reformulated a view of human nature to renew the unalienable *creencias* underlying the Confucian order.

This is not the place to discuss in detail the Tung-lin partisans' philosophical positions. It suffices here to note that, to combat relativism, they began with the reassertion of the certainty of faith in human nature as the innately good and morally creative reality. To forestall pure philosophizing about *hsing*, they further reaffirmed it as the inexorably good ontological foundation of state and society. Knowing nature involved the simultaneous working out of its potentialities. No person, even with the Heaven-endowed virtues and power, was an eternal person. He/she must constantly act in concert with the changing circumstances as he/she sought to know and contemplate truth and reality.[22]

Li Kuang-ti inherited this late Ming Ch'eng-Chu philosophical agenda. He emphasized the paramount importance of the nature of humanity (*jen-hsing*), which replicated the comprehensive goodness of Heaven-and-Earth. In other words, the universal nature of Heaven-and-Earth found full manifestation in the goodness of humanity.[23] It is, therefore, precisely in the primacy of Heaven-conferred nature that one finds the central reference point of Kuang-ti's thought.

Kuang-ti took such great pains in establishing Heaven-conferred nature as the ontological fulcrum on which the universe moved because of his foremost goal of achieving practicality in philosophy by pegging it to the immediate human experience. The ultimate reality of nature of Heaven-and-Earth, ontologically speaking, found expression in human nature; experientially speaking, it was revealed and expressed in that which existed and took place in the human community. The innately good human nature served as the key to transforming morally the state and society.[24]

Kuang-ti wanted to show the transposition of Heaven-and-Earth's qualities into ethicomoral virtues as they were brought to bear on the human community. Dwelling on the suprahuman world held no fascination for him. Thus, Kuang-ti felt that the notion of principle intimated no immediate connection with the human world. It detracted from practical confrontation with problems of the here-and-now: "Not knowing that principle is human nature, [one] seeks the transcendent abstruse principle, falling short in pursuing quotidian practicality. Drowning in the deluge of principle, one is ignorant of the fountainhead."[25]

In brief, the metaphysical category of principle created a gaping chasm between that which was putatively ultimate, and ordinary life as it was. The notion of the primacy of human nature, in contrast, conveyed a sense of immediacy and urgency. Reality was defined in terms of human nature and resulting human actions, which could not be dissolved in and accounted for by transcendental idealities. Heaven's endowment created no human perenniality. Goodness (*shan*) was not some eternalized human condition; it had to be realized and completed with human beings' incessant efforts, encapsulated in the pursuit of the Mean (*chung*), or that which was central. People were vessels of goodness from Heaven, but it was their responsibility to realize this quality by constantly embracing the virtues of humanity and righteousness in life, just as they could not for a moment dispense with food and clothing.[26]

Armed with this fundamental philosophical assertion of the centrality of human nature, Kuang-ti sought to remedy what he saw as the principal problem of the Ming world of thought, that is, the lack of certitude in the fundamentally moral and good nature. As Huston Smith reminds us, in any culture that set great store in traditions, when "people want to know where they are—when they wonder about the ultimate context in which their lives are set and which has the final say over them—they turn to their sacred texts."[27] So Kuang-ti did and accordingly confronted the classics. In other words, Kuang-ti, as the interpreter bound by the contingent needs of his own time, struggled to understand the classics anew. The problem of interpretation of the classics had to take on added significance and importance when the interpreter, such as Kuang-ti, perceived his own time to be a period of cultural crisis, still grappling with the pernicious legacy of Wang Yang-ming's thought.[28] He was therefore prompted to take issue with Chu Hsi, the sage whom he regarded as the transmitter of true Confucian learning. He did not hesitate to critique Chu's hermeneutics of the classics, which had in themselves achieved canonical status. He further substantiated his disagreement with Chu's exegesis by proffering his own interpretations. I will focus on Kuang-ti's hermeneutic endeavors with respect to two of the Four Books, that is, the *Doctrine of the Mean* (Chung-yung) and *Great Learning* (Ta-hsueh), the two canonical texts that were supposed to have encapsulated the philosophical truths of the ancient sages.

LI KUANG-TI'S HERMENEUTICAL INTERPRETATIONS OF THE *CHUNG-YUNG* (DOCTRINE OF THE MEAN) AND *TA-HSUEH* (GREAT LEARNING): CRITIQUE OF CHU HSI'S COMMENTARIES

Because of Kuang-ti's advocacy of the primacy of human nature, which was in effect his hermeneutic preunderstanding or expectation, he had to understand the classics differently from the original authors and their earlier audience. Inevitably, he found Chu Hsi's exegesis on the *Chung-yung* (Doctrine of the Mean) and *Ta-hsueh* (Great Learning) unsatisfying. Chu Hsi had compiled the *Chung-yung chang-chü* (Chapters and Verses of the *Doctrine of the Mean*) in thirty-three chapters, in which he accepted Ch'eng I's definition of the notions *chung* and *yung*:

> Master Ch'eng said, "By *chung* (central) is meant what is not one-sided, and by *yung* (ordinary) is meant what is unchangeable. *Chung* is the correct path of the world and *yung* is the definite principle of the world." This work represents the central way in which the doctrines of the Confucian school have been transmitted. Fearing that in time errors should arise, Tzu-ssu wrote it down and transmitted it to Mencius.[29]

Following Ch'eng I's renditions of the eponymous key words, Chu's *Chung-yung chang-chü* aimed at expounding the "path" of "centrality" and the "principle" of "ordinariness," regarded by Tzu-ssu (492–431 B.C.), Confucius's grandson, as the "central way" (*hsin-fa*) of the Confucian tradition. The division of the text into thirty-three chapters would faithfully and strategically convey the "central way" that was originally transmitted by Tzu-ssu.[30]

However, Chu Hsi himself did not consider his exegetical interpretation and textual arrangement as the last word. In fact, he bemoaned the painstaking and ever-changing process of engaging the classics, whose meanings remained tantalizingly elusive. Specifically with regard to the *Mean* and *Great Learning*, he lamented:

> [My exegeses] on the *Great Learning* and *Mean* were repeatedly revised, failing in the end to reach the point where revisions could no longer be made. Recently, [my work] on the *Great Learning* appears to have few problems. [Its] meanings and principles are best explained in lectures. But once [they] are committed to paper and brush, [I] feel that [I] have not arrived at even the most basic. Even if they are discussed adequately, there is no brilliant [insight]. Now, in order to probe the heart-felt messages of the sages, we can only look at them on paper. How can we see the very bottom? Once I think about this, I always close my books in dismay.[31]

Here, Chu alluded to the ultimate insufficiency of words as means to apprehend the sages' truths. Yet, one had no choice but to resort to and rely on texts and their *chang-chü*, the verses and sentences. Chu, with an obvious tone of regret and resignation, explained at once the inadequacy and indispensability of textual manipulation; hence his writing the *Chung-yung chang-chü*:

> Whenever I study the text [of the *Mean*], I rashly use my own ideas to divide it up into verses and sentences. But since, as Master Ch'eng claimed, it was that by which the central way of the Confucian school was transmitted, I wonder deep down if [its meaning] can be pursued through verses and sentences. But it is also known that one who studies the classics can only get through to their meanings by way of their words. Therefore, I dare to apply my own understanding to it [the *Mean*] as a way of studying and thinking.[32]

Thus, Chu did not mince words in describing his interaction with the classics as an ongoing dynamic process, redolent with ambivalence and uncertainty. While the ultimate value of the classics as the repositories of truths was an absolute given, interpreting them was a protean and tentative exercise.

Insofar as studying the Classics never meant foreclosing the experience of them, there was forever room for exegetical maneuver. Thus, a devout Ch'eng-Chu follower such as Li Kuang-ti would take issue with Chu Hsi's rendering of the *Mean*. Kuang-ti, in an essay on the *Chung-yung*, began by first criticizing Ch'eng I's definition, which furnished the basis for Chu Hsi's own understanding of the *Mean*:

> Master Ch'eng used [the ideas of] not being one-sided and not leaning toward one direction, of the correct path, and of the definite principle to interpret and explain the two terms of *chung* and *yung*. [They are] certainly intriguingly fine. But in speaking of the path and

principle, there should be added the idea of origin. Human nature is the origin of the path and principle.[33]

Through such hermeneutic redefinition, Kuang-ti affirmed the ultimacy of human nature and accordingly lay bare the significance of the *Doctrine of the Mean* as he saw it. In a nutshell, to Kuang-ti, the full import of the entire text could be comprehended if this opening line was understood: "What Heaven mandates for humanity is called human nature."[34]

In another essay on the *Mean* that he completed in 1710, Kuang-ti again attempted to explicate the central meaning of this canon in terms of the ontological primacy of human nature (*hsing*); nature, in a nutshell, is coeval and mutually identified with heaven (*t'ien*) and the supreme ultimate (*t'ai-chi*):

> *Hsing* . . . refers to that which is imbued in humanity, but speaking in terms of heaven, that would be called "mandate" (*ming*), a term which honors Heaven. . . . There is what is called Heaven's virtue (*t'ien-te*) or Heaven-and-Earth's virtue (*t'ien-ti chih te*). Such virtue is human nature. . . . Therefore, there is what is called the oneness of the principles of Heaven and Earth, and of Heaven and humanity. Human nature is the supreme ultimate. In the movement and stillness of the supreme ultimate is seen our sentiments (*ch'ing*) and mind-heart (*hsin*). But is it not called nature but the supreme ultimate? It is also a term honoring Heaven.[35]

With his avowed faith in the enveloping human nature as the source of all beings and meanings, Kuang-ti expatiated and amended some of Chu Hsi's annotations in the *Chung-yung chang-chü*. A case in point is Chu's explication of this verse in the *Chung-yung*: "The Way cannot be separated from us for a moment. What can be separated from us is not the Way." In order to stress the omnipresence of the Way both in spatial and temporal terms, Chu asserted that "nothing is without [the Way], and not a moment is without [the Way]." Kuang-ti proffered his interpretation of Chu's statement. According to Kuang-ti, many scholars thought that what Chu was saying was that all things had "the self-evident principle" (*tang-jan chih li*) or "the self-evident pattern" (*tang-jen chih tse*). For instance, a table had the principle of table, a chair that of chair, speech that of speech, dining that of dining, and so forth. They were wrong:

> [Chu's statement] that nothing does not have [the Way] refers to the fact that one has the immanent virtue of discussing human nature. It is so with everyone. . . . His [Chu's] saying that not a moment does not have [the Way] refers to the fact that the mind's substance is in motion all the time. Since everyone has it and every moment has it, [the *Doctrine of the Mean* says] that [the Way] cannot be separated [from us] for a moment. If it is separated [from us] for a moment,

human nature will be terminated and the mandate of Heaven will be extinguished."[36]

In brief, the Way in the *Doctrine of the Mean* was, in itself, nothing but the eternal and omnipresent human nature.

Kuang-ti also criticized Chu Hsi for presenting a truncated view of the Way (*tao*) from the twenty-second chapter onward: "From the chapter 'Only those who are most sincere can develop their nature to the utmost' (*chih-ch'eng chin-hsing*) onward, Master Chu artificially separates the way of Heaven (*t'ien-tao*) from the way of humanity (*jen-tao*). It is not quite appropriate or proper."[37] Chu Hsi identified human nature with the Way of Heaven, and so only the sages could fully extend human nature and eradicate selfish desires. Being at one with Heaven, the sages' moral force would emanate outward and transform the people, creating the "way of humanity." Kuang-ti countered this view by rhetorically asking: "When speaking of Heaven's way, and the rise and fall of the country, can it be said that those below the great sages cannot know the way? . . . Originally, these were not exclusively the business of the sages."[38] Kuang-ti held that the *Mean's* idea of "developing nature to the utmost " should be viewed with reference to the holistic notion of "the myriad things as one body" (*wan-wu i-t'i*). In other words, "all human nature is good." Selfishness, moral transgressions and folly were all results of "not exhausting nature to the utmost. . . . As one becomes aware of this in oneself, one also becomes aware of this in others. . . . To develop exhaustively nature is to develop to the utmost the nature of others and things."[39]

Since Kuang-ti placed no great store on Chu Hsi's goal of transmitting the so-called "central way" of Tzu-ssu, even though he subscribed wholeheartedly to Chu's notion of a "lineage of the Way" (*tao-t'ung*), he presented his own version of the Mean, the *Chung-yung chang-tuan* (Chapters and Sections of the Mean). In this 1716 text, Kuang-ti came up with his own arrangement of the original classic, dividing it into twelve chapters in order that he could best highlight human nature as the central theme of the Mean. He explained the organization of this work:

> The first chapter is a general introduction, the last chapter is a general conclusion. In between, the first five chapters elaborate and illuminate the origin and development of human nature, the Way (*tao*) and teaching (*chiao*). The following five chapters elaborate and illuminate the practice and function of extending centrality and harmony."[40]

In fact, in writing this text, Kuang-ti first sought clarification of the essential meaning and deep significance of the Mean by referring to the other classics. To explain the "purpose of the *Chung-yung*" (*Chung-yung chih chih*) in the preface, he appealed to the "The Proclamation of T'ang" (*T'ang—kao*) of the *Classic of Documents*, which stated: "The Lord-on-High has conferred even on the inferior people a moral sense (*chung*), the realization of which is the eternal nature (*hsing*)." Kuang-ti offered this gloss: "The moral sense (*chung*) is centrality [that is, *chung* as in the *Mean* (*Chung-yung*)]. That which is central is also constant, because the mandate conferred by the Lord-on-High is that which the people follow as their nature."

Kuang-ti also summoned the *Classic of Odes* by referring to these lines in the ode of "Humankind" (*Cheng-min*): "Heaven, in giving birth to humankind, also established in it the laws [of nature and humanity]. Since humankind is endowed with this natural disposition (*i*), it cherishes its esteemed virtue (*i-te*)." Kuang-ti contended that the *Mean*'s notion of centrality was the encapsulation of the meaning of these lines, which essentially affirmed Heaven's conferring the good nature on humanity. Thus, the *Odes*, in its own way, also "talked about the principle of nature and mandate [found in the *Mean*]."[41]

While Kuang-ti agreed with Chu Hsi that the first chapter of the *Mean*, preserved by Kuang-ti in the original form, encased the core messages that the rest of the text sought to elaborate, he completely ignored in his commentary the supposed goals of Tzu-ssu, that is, the transmission of Confucius's messages via the "central way." Instead, he elucidated the meaning of *chung* (centrality) and *yung* (ordinariness) in light of the paramountcy of nature (*hsing*):

> The word "*chung*" in the first chapter is specifically spoken of in terms of *t'i* (substance). . . . To speak in terms of nature, it is our constant nature; to speak in terms of the Way, it is the constant Way. . . . The principles of *chung* and *yung* originate in the mandated nature. . . . They are substance's laws as embodied in humanity.[42]

In sum, Kuang-ti, through this particular hermeneutic rendering of the *Mean*, undertaken two years before his death, reaffirmed his own personal understanding of the principal teachings of Confucian philosophy, namely, the centrality of nature and its ethicomoral manifestations. The main ideas in Kuang-ti's *Chung-yung chang-tuan* may be summarized as follows. First, nature was foundational and essential: "The way of nature is the root of moral principles. Nature is embodied in the mind-heart; the way is seen in things."[43] Second, nature was universal: "Human nature is bestowed on me by Heaven-and-Earth, sharing it with all people and things."[44] Third, nature was experiential in that everyone must seek to realize the innate goodness of human nature in the everyday world: "The reception of Heaven's mandate is called human nature. Human nature is the embodiment of the principle of creation and life in the mind. This principle embodied in the mind must be seen working in the daily practicalities. The Way is following the issuance [of principle]. The Way is the path normally followed by people." Fourth, the profundity of nature was naturally manifested in everyday ordinariness: "Nature is the embodiment of the vital principles in the mind-heart. The principles that are embodied in the mind-heart must be manifested in the midst of quotidian activity and utility."[45]

It can thus be readily seen that Kuang-ti's hermeneutic engagement with the classic, the *Mean*, was in prefect concordance with his philosophical premise that human nature was the ontological hinge on which all Confucian arguments turned. It is small wonder that Kuang-ti also read the importance of human nature into the *Great Learning*. As a result, Kuang-ti was prompted to once again take issue with Chu Hsi's emendation and addition to this classic, which he deemed unnecessary if not erroneous. In particular, Kuang-ti pointed to Chu Hsi's creation of a supplementary chapter of commentary (*pu-chuan*) devoted to expounding the ideas of "investigation of things" (*ko-wu*) and "extending knowledge to the utmost" (*chih-chih*). This created text was appended to the original chapter 5 which contained these words: "This is called 'knowing the root' (*chih-pen*). This is called 'the completion of knowledge' (*chih-chih chih*)." The first sentence was regarded by Chu Hsi, following the interpretation of Ch'eng I, as redundant. It should be expunged. The second sentence was most significant, but it was merely the conclusion to some missing text. Hence the need for the supplementary chapter to fill in the textual lacuna.[46]

The *Great Learning*, as is well known, was a text near and dear to Chu Hsi. In his exegetical work on the Classic, the *Ta-hsueh chang-chü* (The Verses and Sentences of the *Great Learning*), Chu cited Ch'eng I, who had explicitly claimed that this one classic was "Confucius's bequeathed text" (*i-shu*), which was "the gateway to initial learning of acquiring virtue." Chu began his discourse by reiterating that this particular text was the foundation of all learning. Programmatically, when "the ancients sequenced learning, [they] in particular relied on preserving [the priority of] this text , followed by the *Analects* and *Mencius*. If scholars follow this in their learning, they will hardly go wrong."[47] In fact, Chu worked incessantly on rearranging the *Great Learning*, so much so that three days before his death, he was still making changes on the chapter, "Making the will sincere" (*Ch'eng-i chang*).[48]

Chu Hsi took the extraordinary step of actually adding words to the transmitted canon because he was committed to expounding the notions of "investigation of things" and "extending knowledge to the utmost" as centerpieces of his architectonic metaphysical system. Chu's reading of the *Great Learning* in effect reinvented it as the locus classicus of the twin ideas. He explained in his supplementary chapter the central idea that "the extending of knowledge to the utmost lies in the investigation of things":

> The intelligence of the human mind-heart is such that it is never without knowledge; all things under Heaven possess principle. It is because principle is not plumbed that knowledge is not extended to the utmost. Therefore, in using the *Great Learning* to initiate learning, scholars will definitely pursue all things under Heaven by

increasingly plumbing them in accordance with a prior principle, so that their ultimate [principle] can be reached. As our endeavor is exerted in a prolonged manner, complete and thorough understanding suddenly arises, so much so that the exterior and interior, and the refinement and coarseness of myriad things are apprehended, and the whole substance and great function of my mind-heart are fully comprehended. This is what is called having investigated things; this is what is called having extended knowledge to the utmost.[49]

Thus, in the *Great Learning*, Chu Hsi found grand and logical unity of his most important precepts, from "investigation of things," through "plumbing principle" (*ch'iung-li*), to "extending knowledge to the utmost." Indeed, in another piece of work on the *Great Learning*, the *Ta-hsueh huo-wen* (Further Questions on the *Great Learning*), Chu argued that "the way of investigating things lies in conceiving principle with regard to every matter, so that things are investigated." This "itemized goal" (*t'iao-mu*) of the *Great Learning* was the programmatic way that the sages had prescribed for learning. "But since the Han and Wei," Chu lamented, "various Confucians have failed to mention it." Even Han Yü, whom Chu praised for once again revealing the importance of the *Great Learning*, failed to examine the idea of "extending knowledge to the utmost and investigation of things," for he erroneously concentrated on the *Great Learning*'s teaching of "rectifying the mind-heart and making the will sincere" (*cheng-hsin ch'eng-i*).[50] Apparently, Chu Hsi placed his exegesis at the service of his philosophy.

Now, Li Kuang-ti, whose philosophy was premised on the ontological primacy of human nature, naturally found that Chu's hermeneutical rendering of the *Great Learning* left something to be desired. Two years before his death, in the same year that he completed his final exegesis on the *Mean*, as we recall, Kuang-ti also finished his "A Discourse on the Ancient Edition of the *Great Learning*" (*Ta-hsueh ku-pen-shuo*), defending the integrity of the classic's "ancient edition." In this piece, Kuang-ti professed that in his fifty odd years of studying Chu's works, he had developed great admiration for the master's understanding of important texts such as the *Changes*, the *Odes*, and Chou Tun-i's "Diagrammatic Discourse on the Supreme Ultimate." These various writings of Chu's never ceased to enlighten and inspire him. But the master's *Ta-hsueh chang-chü* was an entirely different matter. At best, Kuang-ti could only agree with it in the most casual manner. As he put it, there was, between him and Chu, no "tacit agreement through the communication of the minds" in this instance. The reason for such disagreement was that Chu obfuscated the principal points of the *Great Learning*. Kuang-ti maintained that "the two ideas of 'knowing the root' and 'being sincere in self-cultivation' (*ch'eng-shen*) should especially be preserved by those who write about the *Great Learning*. They should not be sullied by the various other themes." What Chu did was the virtual elimination of the idea of "knowing the root." As far as Kuang-ti was concerned, any study of the *Great*

Learning should begin with the "ancient edition" (*ku-pen*) established by the Han exegete Ch'eng Hsuan so as to preserve the idea of "knowing the root."[51]

In another work on the *Great Learning*, Kuang-ti contended that the key to the thorough understanding of the classical text resided in the clause "*ming-ming-te*" (manifesting the clear character), which he glossed in this way: "The clear character points to human nature and not the mind. Manifesting the clear character refers both to 'knowing human nature' (*chih-hsing*) and 'nurturing human nature' (*yang-hsing*)."[52] In sum, the crux of the *Great Learning*'s teachings was "knowing human nature and nurturing human nature." It was not, as Chu Hsi's textual modifications suggested, "investigation of things" and "extending knowledge to the utmost." Hence, Chu's drastic move of adding a supplementary commentarial chapter on "investigation of things" was truly superfluous and infelicitous:

> The two Ch'engs and Master Chu had all emended and edited the text of the *Great Learning*. If their interpretations were accurate, the conclusion of one master would have sufficed and lasted through the ages. Why then had Ming-tao [Ch'eng Hao] edited it, I-ch'uan [Ch'eng I] edited it, and Master Chu edited it? Master Chu's addition of the "Commentary on Investigation of Things" especially elicited posterity's skepticism. If [the idea of] investigation of things required additional commentary, then the ideas of making the will sincere through extending its knowledge to the utmost and rectifying the mind-heart through making its will sincere should also have had their supplementary commentarial chapters.[53]

To Kuang-ti, "knowing human nature" meant "knowing the root." The latter idea, as pointed out earlier, was, for all intents and purposes, disregarded by Chu Hsi as redundant. In Kuang-ti's hermeneutic engagement with the *Great Learning*, he sought to restore the primacy of the notion of the root, whose ontological reality was human nature, and whose experiential expression was "self-cultivation" (*hsiu-shen*). It was not the case that Kuang-ti negated the importance of "investigation of things," but it was only with a firm knowledge of the root that one knew what and how to investigate:

> The mind-heart, body, family, state and all-under-Heaven are things. Self-cultivation, ordering family, ruling the state and pacifying all-under-Heaven are affairs. The root [of them all] is self-cultivation. Therefore, [the classic] says: "Everyone and everything regard self-cultivation as the root." It is not true that when the root is confused, the branch can still be in order.[54]

Kuang-ti then linked the understanding of root and branch to the practice of investigating things:

Things and affairs are things. That which is the root or branch, or the ultimate or beginning, is the principle of things. Investigating it will yield the knowledge of what is prior and what is posterior. . . . In investigating affairs and things, the root and the branch, and the beginning and the ultimate, must all be thoroughly understood. Only then is the entire effort of investigating things fully realized.[55]

With the realization of the entire effort of investigating things came finally the extension of knowledge to the utmost (*chih-chih*). But Kuang-ti made a special point of explaining that the *Great Learning* never intended the word "*chih*" (extension to the utmost) to mean "exhaustive investigation of all things under Heaven." "Extending knowledge to the utmost," Kuang-ti opined, "meant knowing the root."[56] Such knowledge would be manifested experientially in the moral virtues, as Kuang-ti concluded: "Humaneness, uprightness, propriety and wisdom are the investigations of things so as to extend knowledge to the utmost; [they] are the illuminations of goodness in order to know nature."[57]

In yet another earlier work on the *Great Learning*, Kuang-ti attempted again to tie all these themes together to present a synthetic message supposedly delivered by the classic. He began by reiterating his basic interpretation that "what is called the extension of knowledge to the utmost is what is called knowing the root."[58] But what was knowledge of the root? Kuang-ti returned once more to his fundamental philosophical conception, to wit, the goodness of human nature as the encapsulation of a good universe:

Nature is just goodness. The nature of things is like the nature of humanity. The nature of another person is like my own nature. The knowledge that all nature is universally good and that the ultimate root [of such goodness] is in one's self, is the means to knowing nature and illuminating goodness, and the means to knowing the root.[59]

In advancing his philosophical views, Kuang-ti found himself employing the old means of engaging classical books, first and foremost in textual terms. His retelling of the true meanings of the *Doctrine of the Mean* and *Great Learning* within hermeneutic bounds was not simply a rehashing of time-honored and well-worn values, but it was also a way to open dialogue with the ancients and intellectual forebears in a quest for truths as he saw them. Therefore, Kuang-ti, as a staunch follower of Chu Hsi's learning, would nonetheless not balk at criticizing the master's exegetical excess and error.

CONFUCIAN EXEGESIS SEEN IN THE LIGHT OF CONTEMPORARY HERMENEUTICS

A Confucian such as Chu Hsi or Li Kuang-ti, like a Hebrew theologian, a Christian thinker, or a contemporary philosopher of the interpretative enterprise, all play the role of a Hermes (from which the word "hermeneutics" is derived), the messenger of the gods, a prophet of sorts, who, in the words of Martin Buber, "represents the Lord . . . [and] enunciates the message and commands in his Name."[60] The messages of the "gods" and "the Lord" are canonical and scriptural texts, or in other words, the classics that ineluctably impart a sense of the sacral. Just what are the classics? In the broadest terms, they are, in David Tracy's definition, paradigmatic and exemplary texts that "have helped found or form a particular culture."[61] Hence their paradigmatic "public status" and "public meaning."[62] They are the most important element in a community's cultural inheritance, the central testament to its imaginative and mythological universe, comprising the basic assumptions and beliefs; they form "the Great Code," as Northrop Frye describes the Bible, for instance.[63] The Bible, like other classics, so Frye tells us, consists of stories and other narratives that a society must know: "its gods, its history, its laws, or its class structure." These stories are "mythological" in the sense that they are "charged with a special seriousness and importance," and mark off and "outline a specific area of human culture." Hence their historically and culturally acknowledged sacrality.[64]

As such exemplary, public and sacred texts, the classics, to begin with, possess lasting qualities. But more important, their longevity and their refusal to disappear readily from a culture are also a consequence of their "openness to accommodation," in the words of Frank Kermode, welcoming readers and interpreters across time to assume their share of the production of the classics' meanings.[65] This openness is possible because of the general recognition of what David Tracy calls the classics' "excess of meaning," which "demands constant interpretation and bears a certain kind of timelessness—namely the timelessness of a classic expression radically rooted in its own historical time and calling to . . . [the interpreter's] own historicity."[66] To put it another way, the classics have no future other than their invitation to constant historical and finite reinterpretation; or else, their fate is death. The vital classics are capable of staking a strong and irresistible claim to attention both as the encompassing timeless framework and as repositories of universal values. At the same time that they imbue individual passing phenomena with meaning and significance, they demand the hermeneutic intrusion spearheaded by the interpreter's own questions and history.

This inevitable hermeneutic interpolation, as David Tracy, following Gadamer, outlines, has four major characteristics:

> 1. The interpreter initially arrives at the reading of the text with some strong pre-understanding, determined by the interpreter's particular and contingent historical concerns. But these concerns are in turn informed by the memories of the traditions and also animated by the inquirer's fiduciary relationship with the community of other investigators. In brief, there is no fully autonomous interpreter above

history, severed from tradition and exiled from the wider community of other readers.

2. The classics, with their strong claim to attention, draw to them the interpreter. But instead of domesticating the interpreter into their unquestioning eulogist, the classics provoke a confrontation between their identity as immanent transhistorical texts and the interpreter's radical historical alterity.

3. A dialogue then ensues, a dialectical process of engaging the realities and questions disclosed by the texts, marked by the interpreter's negotiations with them. Such negotiations, as in any meaningful dialogue, involve acceptance, rejection, modification and compromise of viewpoints.

4. This dialogue inexorably spills over to the large community of interpreters, insofar as the individual interpreter's preunderstanding is forged by other understandings of the classics. Intersubjectively, the dialogue becomes a broad dialogue with other inquirers, so that a single individual reading acquires the stamp of relevance.[67]

In short, the classics cannot be understood through repeating them; they must be interpreted. Only then, as Kierkegaard insisted, can they be really "repeated."[68]

To state this in Buber's hermeneutic terms, the Word of God in the Bible, and not the rite, was the principal point of "contact between godhead and manhood." Through such Word, God became a person who addresses human beings in a human language. Such address demanded response, so that the "human person not only adopts the word, he also answers, lamenting, complaining to God himself, disputing with Him about justice, humbling himself before him, praying."[69] The person, as the "I," a particular being, in such communication with the Word of God, the "Thou," the universal framework, gained larger insights that transcended limited individual visions. Nonetheless, the Bible, as Buber reminded us, should not be treated as "absolute, sufficing, immutable," although it must be read as "sacred text." The thawing hermeneutic act forestalled such texts from being frozen in time. Through interpretation, their living quality would be invigorated and enlivened.[70]

In light of the foregoing description of the classics and their inescapable hermeneutic corollaries, some palpable commonalities may be discerned between Confucian exegesis and the Western hermeneutic tradition. Both conceive the understanding of particular phenomena in terms of a larger overarching framework. Both strive for understanding of the classics' words through dialogic communication. Both, notwithstanding their acceptance of the classics' cultural function as the preservation of truths, subject these truth-bearing texts to constant interrogation. Both make no assault on the classics' claim to ultimate value, but they dissect the particular ways in which the classics served as the vessels of the ancient sages' pleas and teachings in finite historical moments.

A case in point, as we have shown, is Li Kuang-ti's reading of the classics. Kuang-ti's disagreement with Chu Hsi, across time, via hermeneutic pondering on the Mean and Great Learning, is an example of the tripartite dialogic relation between the sacred texts, Chu Hsi's commentaries and Kuang-ti. As the interpreter, he inevitably brought his vision to bear on the canons themselves and on prior canonical interpretations. As finite historical subject, he approached the classics with his pre-understanding of the Confucian teachings based on the primacy of the goodness of human nature, which was a distinct response to the historical development of Confucian thought addressing the rise and growth of Lu-Wang thinking. Hence, willy-nilly, the timelessness of the classics was qualified by this specific historical insight. Just note the juxtaposition of the following two statements in the preface of his Chung-yung chang-tuan. On the one hand, Kuang-ti claimed, "Because nature is constant, the Way is constant, without the caprice of fads. Is it not true that the sages' teachings, which established the ultimate for human living and which resist changes in the ten thousand generations, are based on this?"[71] On the other, Kuang-ti asserted that although "the myriad principles are replete in the classics bequeathed by Confucius," individuals could only apprehend them after "painstaking thinking and exhaustive quest."[72] In fact, "the sages, while adopting the ways of the ancients [before them], forged their own individual molds."[73] Thus, even if the classics were timeless monuments, they invited constant questioning, thereby staking their claim to attention. Kuang-ti responded to the provocation of the classical text and entered into hermeneutical dialogues with the ancients and their texts, involving in the process the wider community of interpreters.

To the extent that a dialogic relation existed between the hermeneut and the classical text, Confucian exegesis also brings to mind Gadamer's philosophical hermeneutics, which rejects what he calls "Romantic hermeneutics," the sort that sees understanding of classical texts as an "empathic" and "divinatory" process that bypasses history. Such a process renders hermeneutics into psychological interpretions, the intuitive retrieval of the original.[74] Gadamer also faults the sort of mechanistic programmatic hermeneutics that is based on the all-too-sanguine notion of the liberating thrust of critical reason unburdened by tradition. This approach posits that the way to read meanings out of texts is to treat them as objects in themselves, to be approached without preconceptions of the interpreter. Pruned of present prejudices, unencumbered with presuppositions, released from the current time, this mythical interpreter leaps into the past and thus makes his/her presence felt in the objectified text.[75] In so doing, the temporal and chronological gap between the reader and the text can be bridged. While one may well argue that eighteenth-century Ch'ing k'ao-cheng (evidential textual studies) came close to the purport and aim of such programmatic hermeneutics,[76] the sort of Confucian hermeneutics examined here would have found much more common ground in Gadamer's philosophical hermeneutic, which affirms that every interpreter enters into the hermeneutic act bearing the historical effects of tradition. To be sure, Kuang-ti's hermeneutics did bear the rhetorical stamp of what Gadamer would have labeled as "Romantic." It is interesting to note what one of Kuang-ti's junior relations, in a preface he wrote for a collection of Kuang-ti's exegetical writings on the Four Books, had to say about the elder Li's hermeneutic aim:

> The difficulty of glossing the classics lies in the difficulty in gaining access to the minds of the authors. Since the Han and T'ang, there had been many prominent individual schools which had developed their own expertise in strictly adhering to the philological annotations of the original verses and sentences. But often, they could not avoid hairsplitting debates about minutiae. It was only with the emergence of Ch'eng [I] and Chu [Hsi] in the Sung that the hitherto ignored ideas in the classics were apprehended. Using their understanding of moral meanings and principles, they explained the mistakes and lacunae in the terse classical texts, and scholars were relieved to learn that they obtained the real messages which were closely in tune with the minds of the sages. . . . [Kuang-ti] delved into the essence of the classics and plumbed the Six Classics and Four Books not only by broadly studying the exegeses of the Han and T'ang, but also synthesizing their central ideas via Ch'eng and Chu['s learning]. . . . His extensive studies of the various books were always guided by the classics, while his careful investigations of the various ideas were always rooted in moral principles.[77]

From this description, it can be seen that Kuang-ti sought to be in "tune with the minds of the sages." But it is also evident that he invariably complemented formalist philological hermeneutics, or in Dilthey's hermeneutic terms, *Erklären* (explanation), with *Verstehen* (understanding), or the preunderstanding of the classics based on Confucian moral principles.[78] Thus, understanding, after all, in Kuang-ti's hermeneutic scheme, could not be "pure" in the sense that it directly intuited the minds of the sages. It cannot be "Romantic;" it must be guided by critical methods—*k'ao-cheng* went hand in hand with *i-li*. On this score, one is also reminded of Paul Ricoeur's formulation of the hermeneutic process when he suggests that "explanation *develops* understanding" and "understanding precedes, accompanies, closes, and thus *envelops* explanation."[79]

Given Kuang-ti's hermeneutic stance, he would have agreed with Gadamer's assertion that "[h]ermeneutic experience is concerned with *tradition*. . . . But tradition is not simply a process that experience teaches us to know and govern; it is *language*—that is, it expresses itself like a Thou." Without citing Buber, Gadamer goes on to clarify the nature of text-reading via the I-Thou relation: "A Thou is not an object; it relates itself to us. Rather, I maintain that

the understanding of tradition does not take the traditionary text as an expression of another person's life, but as meaning that is detached from the person
who means it, from an I or a Thou. . . . For tradition is a genuine partner in communication, with which we have fellowship as does the 'I' with a 'Thou'."[80]The
clearest expression of the transmitted tradition as language is the classics, in
which are ensconced a culture's "normative sense." Through these texts that
impart a sense of the norms, we gain "a consciousness of something enduring, of
significance that cannot be lost and is independent of all the circumstances of
time—a kind of timeless present that is contemporaneous with every other present." The great canons, albeit once written in the distant past—hence its
ineluctable "temporal quality that articulates it historically"—will always yield
some significant insight into the particular situation of the reader.[81] Thus, to
read the classics is to realize the communicative dialogic relation between the
enduring texts as transmitted tradition and the hermeneut. In this interactive
process, in which the reader and the text are locked in a "hermeneutic circle"
where their questions and answers interpenetrate and unfold,[82] Gadamer affirms
the reader's own biases in the hermeneutic enterprise. Indeed, he sees the fusing
of the interpreter's own historical horizons with that of the texts as the ontological basis of understanding. Our cognizance of the historical role of the texts is
the very condition of our understanding of the texts. For instance, it will be
quite a futile effort to attempt to understand the Bible without prior knowledge
of the paramount influence of the Scripture in the historical life of the West.
The understanding of any texts is the result of the dynamic fusion of one's own
"effective historical consciousness," consisting of one's prejudgments and the
tradition of interpretation that preceded one, and the texts'. This "fusion of
horizons" finally yields "effective history" for the hermeneut.[83] Kuang-ti, the
hermeneut, had his own prejudgments, namely, his philosophy predicated on
the goodness of human nature, and he had Chu Hsi's works on the *Mean* and
Great Learning and also other classical commentaries as the preceding interpretive tradition. In Buber's terms, the reader as the "I," "without forfeiting anything of the felt reality of his activity, at the same time lives through the
common event from the standpoint of the other [i.e., the text as 'Thou']."[84]

This "common event" means that the fullness of the hermeneut's horizons
must be appreciated in the dialogue with the texts. The I and Thou entered into
"a new community," as Gadamer puts it:

> When we try to examine the hermeneutical phenomenon through
> the model of conversation between two persons, the chief thing that
> these apparently so different situations—understanding a text and
> reaching an understanding in a conversation—have in common is
> that both are concerned with a subject matter that is placed before
> them. . . . To reach an understanding in a dialogue is not merely a
> matter of putting oneself forward and successfully asserting one's own

> point of view, but being transformed into a communion in which we
> do not remain what we were.[85]

In light of this notion of a "common event" or "communion," developed through dialogic contact with the classics, we may develop a different perspective in appreciating the meaning of these familiar words uttered by Kuang-ti: "The Way of all-under-Heaven is fully embodied in the Six Classics. The Way of the Six Classics is fully embodied in the Four Books. The Way of the Four Books is entirely within my own self."[86] Customarily, these oft-repeated words are interpreted as an expression of the mystical and holistic Confucian conception of the organismic cosmos. Now, we may explain them more specifically in hermeneutic terms as the fusing of the horizons of the reader and the classical text.

Furthermore, this fusion of horizons not only brings about fundamental change in understanding, but it also in effect creates an occasion for existential transformation. Indeed, Confucian hermeneutics saw understanding as integrally tied to action and commitment. The comprehension and elucidation of texts was an existentialist encounter with the living vital messages of the Confucian classics. As Li Kuang-ti sought understanding of the classics in terms of "knowing the root," that is, awareness of the goodness of our nature, he also prescribed a way of living anchored on individual moral-ethical self-cultivation (*hsiu-shen*), which was the existential result of exegetical understanding of the *Mean* and *Great Learning*: "Knowing that all-under-Heaven and the state both take the self as the root, it is also known that one's self and mind-heart must not be indulgent, slothful and selfish."[87] In point of fact, this Confucian conviction in *praxis* resonates with David Tracy's conception of hermeneutics as *praxis*. Tracy asserts that "[e]very time when we act, deliberate, judge, understand, or even experience, we are interpreting. To understand at all is to interpret. To act well is to interpret a situation demanding some action and to interpret a correct strategy for that action," leading to his conclusion that hermeneutics must be used "as they should be used: as further practical skills for the central task of becoming human."[88] Such praxis would have elicited a hearty endorsement from Kuang-ti.

As with Gadamer, Buber, and Tracy, a Confucian hermeneut like Kuang-ti took the classics or Scripture, the textual embodiment of a vital cultural tradition, as the locus of understanding. Their hermeneutic reflection on the classics was engagement with and participation in a cultural tradition. An avowed Ch'eng-Chu follower like Kuang-ti would readily diverge from Chu Hsi's reading of the classics. With his preconceived notion of the centrality of human nature as the ontological center of gravity of reality, Kuang-ti communicated with the classics. His hermeneutic project achieved the intended agreement with the classics, and vice versa, about a shared reality, a reality defined by the primacy of human nature as the origin of human actions.

If we may generalize from our understanding of the particular case of Li Kuang-ti's hermeneutics, Confucian exegesis was an interactive dialogue with a living past ensconced in the classics. Hermeneutics led not only to a better understanding of the words of the sages but also to their integration in the interpreter's philosophy and life. As Gadamer clearly contends, engaging and understanding the classics do not simply refer to the interpretative relation between the classics as an "object" and the reader as the inquiring subject. The central relation is between the inquirer and whole history of the effects of the classics. To know the classics is to act in accordance with them, or with their spirit. Kuang-ti would have agreed with Gadamer's assertion that "understanding belongs to the being of that which is understood."[89] In sum, to establish and maintain this central relation in pursuit of the classics is to negotiate and renegotiate the boundaries of Confucianism in hermeneutic terms.

NOTES

1. Roger Ames, "Foreword," in Hoyt Cleveland Tillman, *Ch'en Liang on Public Interest and the Law* (Honolulu: University of Hawaii Press, 1994), p. x.

2. John B. Henderson, *Scripture, Canon, and Commentary: A Comparison of Confucian and Western Exegesis* (Princeton: Princeton University Press, 1991), pp. 3–4.

3. Steven Van Zoeren, *Poetry and Personality: Reading, Exegesis and Hermeneutics in Traditional China* (Stanford: Stanford University Press, 1991), p. 2.

4. Wing-tsit Chan, "The *Hsing-li ching-i* and the Cheng-Chu School of the Seventeenth Century," in Wm. Theodore de Bary, ed., *The Unfolding of NeoConfucianism* (New York: Columbia University Press, 1975), pp. 543–48, 553–60, 567–68.

5. Wm. Theodore de Bary, *The Message of the Mind in Neo-Confucianism* (New York: Columbia University Press, 1989), p. 175.

6. I borrow the term from Brice R. Wachterhauser, "Introduction," in Brice R. Wachterhauser, ed., *Hermeneutics and Truth* (Evanston, Ill.: Northwestern University Press, 1994), p.1.

7. On the "contemporary" hermeneutic implications of traditional Chinese exegesis, see Van Zoeren, *Poetry and Personality*, pp. 3-7.

8. See for instance, Jean-François Lyotard, *The Post-Modern Condition: A Report on Knowledge*, trans. G. Bennington and B. Massumi (Minneapolis: University of Minnesota Press, 1984); Michel Foucault, "What Is an Author?" in D. Bouchard, ed., *Language, Counter-Memory, Practice* (Ithaca: Cornell University Press, 1977); Jacques Derrida, *Of Grammatology*, trans. Gayatri Chakravorty Spivak, (Baltimore: John Hopkins University, 1976) and "Structure, Sign and Play in the Discourse of the Human Science," in R. Macksey and E. Donato, eds., *The Languages of Criticism and the Sciences of Man* (Baltimore: Johns Hopkins University, 1970); Roland Barthes, "The Death of

the Author," *Image, Music, Text*, trans. S. Heath (New York: Hill and Wang, 1977).

9. For a discussion on the fundamental differences between the French deconstructionist and the German hermeneutic thinking, see Nathan Scott Jr., "The House of Intellect in an Age of Carnival: Some Hermeneutic Reflections," *Journal of the American Academy of Religion* 55.1 (Spring 1987): 8–13.

10. Ibid., p. 13.

11. David Tracy, *The Analogical Imagination: Christian Theology and the Culture of Pluralism* (New York: Crossroads, 1981), p. 134.

12. Ibid., p. 108.

13. Robert M. Grant, with David Tracy, *A Short History of the Interpretation of the Bible*, 2nd ed. (Philadelphia: Fortress Press, 1984), p. 186.

14. On these central ideas in Tracy's systematic theology, see also his *Blessed Rage for Order: The New Pluralism in Theology* (New York: Seabury Press, 1975) and *Plurality and Ambiguity: Hermeneutics, Religion, Hope* (San Francisco: Harper & Row, 1987). A succinct overview can also be found in Tracy, *Short History*, chapters 16 through 18.

15. Li Kuang-ti, *Jung-ts'un ch'uan-chi* [Complete Writings of Jung-ts'un] (hereafter JTCC) 2.2a, 1b. This collection of writings forms a large portion of the complete collected works of Li Kuang-ti, entitled *Jung-ts'un ch'üan-shu* (Collected Works of Jung-ts'un) (n.p., preface 1829). All of Kuang-ti's writings cited in this essay can be found in this complete anthology. For a detailed and systematic examination of Li's philosophical views on nature, see my "Hsing (Nature) as the Ontological Basis of Practicality in Early Ch'ing Ch'eng-Chu Confucianism: Li Kuang-ti's (1642–1718) Philosophy," *Philosophy East and West* 44.1 (January 1994): 79–109.

16. JTCC 6.2a.

17. Mou Tsung-san, *Hsin-t'i yü hsing-t'i* (The Reality of the Self's Nature and the Reality of the Mind's Nature) (Taipei: Cheng-chu shu-chu, 1968), pp. 21–41. The first quote is from p. 31, the second, p. 37. Mou maintains that this holistic conception of the profound self as the site of transcendence is absent in the West. Hence his coining the term "hsing-t'i," the reality of the self's nature, to denote the Confucian sense of the Absolute located in the individual self. The word "hsing" cannot be adequately translated as "nature," "essence," "substance," "being," or "reality," as they fail to connote the meaning of the self as the "moral creative reality."

18. On the self and its nature as embodiment of the organismic "moral universal," see, for instance, Tu Wei-ming, *Confucian Thought: Selfhood as Creative Transformation* (Albany: State University of New York Press, 1985), pp. 19–28, 35–50. For a succinct examination of the important views on human nature in the history of Chinese thought, see Chang Tai-nien, *Chung-kuo che-hsueh ta-kang*

(An Outline of Chinese Philosophy) (Peking: Chung-kuo k'o-hsueh ch'u-pan-she, 1982), pp. 183–232.

19. See, for example, Ortega's "History as a System," *Toward a Philosophy of History*, trans. William Atkinson (New York: W. W. Norton, 1941), pp. 165–233. My discussion on Ortega's idea of *creencias* is based on Karl Weintraub, *Visions of Culture* (Chicago: University of Chicago Press, 1966), pp. 260–74, and Oliver Holmes, *Human Reality and the Social World: Ortega's Philosophy of History* (Amherst: University of Massachusetts Press, 1975), pp. 122–24.

20. Cf. also Collingwood's doctrine of *Speculum Mentis* that sees philosophy as expatiation upon known experiences. In the words of Louis Mink: "Philosophy is not a specialized form of experience but the self-consciousness of experience in general. . . . The doctrine of *Speculum Mentis* . . . [is] the doctrine that the 'conclusion' of philosophical thinking and the 'experience' on which they are based are names for any two successive stages on a philosophical scale of forms." See Louis Mink, *Mind, History, and Dialectic: The Philosophy of R.G. Collingwood* (Bloomington: Indiana University Press, 1969), pp. 253–54.

21. For illustrative examples of such perspective on learning and thought, see Chang Tai-nien, *Chung-kuo che-hsueh ta-kang*, pp. 497–527.

22. For a detailed examination of the Ch'eng-Chu Tung-lin arguments on the primacy of human nature and their opposition to the Yang-ming position, see my "The Emergence of a New Philosophic Agenda and the Ming-Ch'ing Intellectual Transition," paper delivered in the Neo-Confucian Seminar, Columbia University, March 5, 1993.

23. JTCC 7.24b.

24. JTCC 20.1b.

25. Li Kuang-ti, *Jung-ts'un yü-lu* (Collected Sayings of Jung-ts'un), 26.4b–5a. Hereafter JTYL.

26. JTCC 8.16a. On the meaning of *chung* and *yung*, see Wing-tsit Chan, *A Sourcebook of Chinese Philosophy* (Princeton: Princeton University Press, 1963), pp. 95–99. See also Tu Wei-ming, *Centrality and Commonality* (Albany: State University of New York Press, 1989), p. 16.

27. Huston Smith, "Postmodernism and the World's Religions," in Walter Truett Anderson, ed., *The Truth about the Truth* (New York: Tarcher/Putnam Book, 1995), p. 205.

28. Cf. David Tracey's statement on the hermeneutic history of the Bible: "The problem of interpretation becomes a central issue in cultural periods of crisis. So it was for the Stoics and their reinterpretation of the Greek and Roman myths. So it was for those Jews and Christians who developed the allegorical methods. And so it is for Jews and Christians since the emergence of historical consciousness." See his *Short History*, p. 154.

29. Wing-tsit Chan, *Sourcebook*, p. 97.

30. Note that Tu Wei-ming translates *yung* as commonality. Note also that Wm. Theodore de Bary, in his *The Liberal Tradition in China* (New York: Columbia University Press, 1983), translates the term *hsin-fa* as "the method or system of the mind-and-heart." F. W. Mote has objected to this translation. See his "The Limits of Intellectual History?" *Ming Studies* 19 (Fall 1984): 17–25. On Chu Hsi's compilation, see Ch'ien Mu, *Chu-tzu hsin-hsueh-an* (A New Study on the Learning of Master Chu) (Ch'eng-tu: Pa-shu shu-she, 1987), 2: 1355–88.

31. Quoted in Ch'ien Mu, *Chu-tzu hsin-hsueh-an*, p. 1379.

32. Quoted in ibid.

33. JTYL 7.1a.

34. JTYL 15.7a.

35. Li Kuang-ti, "Chung-yung yü-lun" (Further Thoughts on the Mean) 1a–b.

36. JTYL 7.5a–b.

37. JTYL 8.2b.

38. JTYL 8.2b–3a.

39. JTYL 8.4b–5b.

40. Li Kuang-ti, *Ssu-shu chieh-i* (Explaining the Meanings of the Four Books), "fa-fan" (Explanatory Statement) 2a.

41. *Chung-yung chang-tuan* (Chapters and Sections of the *Mean*), "*hsü*" (preface) 1a–b. Hereafter CYCT.

42. CYCT 3b.

43. Ibid.

44. CYCT 19b.

45. CYCT 1a.

46. On Chu Hsi's modification of the *Great Learning*, see Daniel Gardner, *Chu Hsi and the Ta-hsueh* (Cambridge, Mass.: Harvard University Press, 1986), pp. 36–37. On the general history of the textual revisions of the classic, see Huang Chin-hsing, "Li-hsueh k'ao-chü-hsueh yü cheng-chih: I-Ta-hsueh kai-pen te fa-chan wei li-cheng" (The Learning of Principle, Evidential Studies, and Politics: The Case of Revising the *Great Learning*), in his *Yu-i sheng-i* (Glorious Entry into the Realm of the Sages) (Taipei: Yün-ch'en wen-hua ch'u-pan, 1994), pp. 351–91.

47. Chu Hsi, *Ssu-shu chang-chü chi-chu* (Annotations to the *Ssu-shu chang-chü*) (Taipei: Chung-hua shu-chü, 1983), p. 3.

48. Wang Mou-hung, *Chu-tzu nien-p'u* (A Chronicle of the Life of Master Chu) (Taipei: Shang-wu, 1982), p. 226.

49. Chu Hsi, *Ssu-shu*, pp. 6–7.

50. Chu Hsi, *Ta-hsueh huo-wen* (Queries on the *Great Learning*) (Taipei: Chung-wen ch'u-pan-she), p. 7b.

51. Li Kuang-ti, *Ta-hsueh ku-pen shuo* (A Study on the Old Edition of the *Great Learning*), "chiu hsü" (the original preface) 1a–b.

52. JTYL 1.10b.

53. JTYL 1.17a–b.

54. JTYL 1.13b.

55. JTYL 1.14a, 16b.

56. JTYL 1.16b.

57. JTYL 1.19a.

58. JTCC 6.9a.

59. JTCC 6.11a–b.

60. Martin Buber, *The Prophetic Faith*, trans. C. Witten-Davis (New York: Harper & Row, 1960), p. 58.

61. Tracy, *Plurality and Ambiguity*, p. 12.

62. Tracy, *Analogical Imagination*, pp. 132–34.

63. Northrop Frye, *The Great Code: The Bible and Literature* (New York: Harcourt Brace Jovanovich, 1982), pp. xvi–xix.

64. Ibid., pp. 32–34.

65. Frank Kermode, *The Classic* (New York: Viking Press, 1975), pp. 44–45.

66. Tracy, *Analogical Imagination*, p. 102. This idea of "excess of meaning" may be understood as analogous to Lévi Strauss's theory of a "surplus of signifier" regarding shamanism. The shaman's provides not a direct cure but rather a general language of symbols and rituals that enable the ready expression and release of psychic states that may otherwise be suppressed. See Kermode, *The Classic*, pp. 135–36.

67. Tracy, *Analogical Imagination*, pp. 118–122. See also David Couzens Hoy, *The Critical Circle: Literature and History in Contemporary Hermeneutics* (Berkeley: University of California Press, 1978), pp. 41–78. Hoy's characterization of the hermeneutic procedures is based on his understanding of Gadamer's methods.

68. Tracy, *Analogical Imagination*, p. 103.

69. Buber, *Prophetic Faith*, p. 165.

70. Martin Buber, "Biblical Humanism," in N. Glatzer, ed., *On the Bible* (New York: Schocken, 1982), p. 213. See also *Prophetic Faith*, p. 169.

71. CYCT, preface, 1b.

72. JTYL 1.1b.

73. JTYL 1.3b.

74. Gadamer, *Truth*, pp. 184–97.

75. On Gadamer's objection to such programmatic hermeneutics, see Hans-Georg Gadamer, *Truth and Method*, 2nd revised ed., trans. Joel Weinsheimer and Donald Marshall (New York: Continuum, 1994), pp. 173–218. See also Georgia Warnke, *Gadamer: Hermeneutics, Tradition and Reason* (Cambridge, U.K.: Polity Press, 1987), chap. 1.

76. On the contents, nature and goals of Ch'ing *k'ao-cheng* learning, see Benjamin Elman, *From Philosophy to Philology: Intellectual and Social Aspects of*

Change in Late Imperial China (Cambridge, Mass.: Harvard University Press, 1984), especially, pp. 37–137.

77. "Li hsü" (The Preface by Li), in *Ssu-shu chieh-i* 1a–2b.

78. On Dilthey, see Gadamer, *Truth*, pp. 231–42.

79. Paul Ricoeur, "Explanation and Understanding," in *The Philosophy of Paul Riceour* (New York: Beacon, 1978), p. 165. On this point, see also Steven Kepnes, *The Text as Thou: Martin Buber's Dialogical Hermeneutics and Narrative Theology* (Bloomington: Indiana University Press, 1992), pp. 37–40.

80. Gadamer, *Truth*, p. 358.

81. Ibid., p. 288.

82. Ibid., pp. 265–71, 291–300.

83. Ibid., pp. 300–307.

84. Martin Buber, "Education," in *Between Man and Man*, ed. Maurice Friedman, trans. R. G. Smith, (New York: Macmillan, 1965), p. 97.

85. Gadamer, *Truth*, pp. 378–79.

86. JTYL 1.1a.

87. *Ta-hsueh ku-pen shuo* 4a.

88. Tracy, *Plurality*, p. 9.

89. *Truth*, p. xxxi.

GLOSSARY

Ch'eng Hao	程顥
Ch'eng I	程頤
Ch'eng-Chu	程朱
Ch'eng-i chang	誠意章
ch'eng-shen	誠身
ch'ing	情
ch'iung-li	窮理
chang-chü	章句
cheng-hsin ch'eng-i	正心誠意
chih	致
chih-ch'eng chin-hsing	致誠盡性
chih-chih	致知
chih-chih chih	知之致
chih-hsing	知性
chih-pen	知本
ching-shih	經世
Chu Hsi	朱熹
chung	中
Chung-yung	中庸
Chung-yung chang-chü	中庸章句
Chung-yung chang-tuan	中庸章段

Chung-yung chih chih	中庸之旨
hsin	心
hsin-fa	心怯
hsing	性
hsing-t'i	性體
hsiu-shen	修身
i	意
i-shu	遺書
i-te	懿德
jen-hsing	人性
jen-tao	人道
k'ao-cheng	考證
ko-wu	格物
Ku Hsien-ch'eng	顧憲成
ku-pen	古本
li	理
Li Kuang-ti	李光地
li-i fen shu	理一分殊
ming	名
ming-ming-te	明明德
pen-t'i	本體
pu-chuan	補傳
shan	善
t'ai-chi	太極
T'ang-kao	湯誥
t'iao-mu	條目
t'ien	天
t'ien-tao	天道
t'ien-te	天德
t'ien-ti chih te	天地之德
Ta-hsueh	大學
Ta-hsueh chang-chü	大學章句
Ta-hsueh huo-wen	大學或問
Ta-hsueh ku-pen-shuo	大學古本説
tang-jan chi li	當然之理
tang-jan chih tse	當然之則
tao-t'ung	道統
Tung-lin	東林
Tzu-ssu	子思
wu-shan wu-o	無善無惡
wan-wu i-t'i	萬物一體
yang-hsing	養性

yung (commonality)   庸
yung (utility)   用
Zheng-min   蒸民

9

Treading the Weedy Path

T'ang Chen (1630–1704) and the World of the Confucian Middlebrow

Hsiung Ping-chen

THE BOUNDARIES OF CONFUCIANISM AND THE CASE OF T'ANG CHEN

Considering a notion such as boundary, there are perhaps two lines of argument. Some scholars make sociological or positivist arguments regarding intellectual boundaries. They employ such terms as "legacy," "heritage," or "tradition," suggesting that within a society and among its people, there exist shared sets of notions, values, or ideas that are widely known, commonly held, and openly acknowledged. Thus, discussions, debates, and disputes that may arise are in fact activities that take place among informed members of society. Whether we are dealing with defenders of, or rebels against, tradition, they are all conscious of what they are doing since they operate within an accepted domain of discourse. Therefore, in Chinese intellectual history, we see many figures who are regarded as upholders of the way, but we seldom stop to wonder whether the tradition being upheld (be it a political regime, a cultural heritage, or a philosophical school) is as clearly defined, commonly recognizable, and long accepted as is customarily assumed. By the same token, whenever persons are accused of departing from or transgressing the Way, we again do not sufficiently question the nature of the Way itself in the first place. On the other hand, historians of a more skeptical bent argue that reality is often far more complex and fluid than we assume it to be. Traditions, they argue, be they of a political, cultural, religious, or intellectual nature, are transient. They are living forces that constantly refresh themselves, and in so doing, they continuously clarify and revise principles and ideas, further developing possibilities for and prohibitions against action. Viewed in such a light, a legacy or a tradition, although seemingly inclusive or exclusive in character, is hardly, and ought not to be, of a fixed quality. It cannot mean the same thing at all times, and certainly does not represent the same thing to all people.

Confucianism, with its founding values and leading principles, has been understood both as consisting of fundamental rules that are firm and clear, and as a historical process made up of workings and reworkings by centuries of adherents. In this context, pronouncements from the well-known boundary-setters (or resetters) such as Chu Hsi, Wang Yang-ming, Ku Yen-wu, or for that matter Confucius and Mencius, cannot but be fluid texts that await and experience constant analysis. For however much they may appear to identify themselves with the great tradition, showing total confidence in demarcating right from wrong, they are merely self-proclaimed provincial representatives of their visions of Confucian history and culture. They might have honestly believed that all original Confucian teachings, spirits, and prohibitions could be correctly and precisely grasped, but who, be they mainstream thinkers or marginal self-anointed prophets, could accurately determine what Confucianism actually was? Who or what delegated the legitimate defining agencies of Confucianism? How was Confucianism defined in people's everyday social and intellectual activities?

To consider such abstract notions as legacy, tradition, and boundaries, one should look beyond the texts of the Great Tradition and examine the lives and thoughts of the less well-known followers of Confucianism. We should ask what Confucianism might have meant to its more ordinary adherents. Did their less famous lives contribute to the meanings of Confucianism? Were they concerned with issues different from those tackled by the Confucian thinkers who were considered to be representative of the Confucian tradition? Did they perhaps perceive and wrestle with matters on a different plane? Did common followers care for the same sorts of values and rules as those of the learned Confucian?

With such questions in mind, we turn to an obscure and self-made Confucian intellectual of the seventeenth century, T'ang Chen (1630–1740), who may be deemed as a miserable failure in conventional Confucian terms. The first half of the seventeenth century was a turbulent time in Chinese history. What befell our protagonist represented but a small part of a greater tragedy. T'ang's family was among the thousands of scholar-official landowning families in south China that suffered from both the late-Ming peasant rebellions, and then the Manchu takeover. T'ang's homeland was in Szechwan, which fell victim to Chang Hsien-chung's killing and plundering in 1634. T'ang's grandfather and maternal uncle both fought back in vain, and the grandfather lost his life. In the wake of Chang Hsien-chung's ravages, other elders of the T'ang clan struggled fiercely against the Manchu conquerors. For T'ang Chen and his parents, the immediate results of this Ming-Ch'ing turmoil were the loss of all the family assets in Szechwan and then persecution by Ch'ing authorities because of their "loyalist background." As far as we can tell, during this time the young boy T'ang Chen was away from home, accompanying his father, a district magistrate, in Chekiang. However, T'ang himself did not foster any anti-Manchu or loyalist sentiments. In any event, following the financial setback and under the threat of political persecution, T'ang Chen's formal education suffered. He never received the sound classical education expected of a gentry lad. He and his branch of the uprooted family drifted around Kiangnan and were deprived of their estate and the material comfort that could have come with it.[1]

Thus three aspects of T'ang's life serve as reminders of the price a family like the T'ang's paid during the dynastic change. First, largely because of the Ming-Ch'ing disruption and the harm it inflicted on his family, T'ang Chen was denied the pampered career and the proper education usually expected of his type. Economic pressure forced the young T'ang Chen to labor over the daily needs of the house until his late twenties, when he finally was able to seek long-term employment with the civil service. His impaired education took him no further than the *chü-jen* degree which he obtained at the age of twenty-eight.[2] Lacking the right academic and social credentials for a bureaucratic career, he waited for thirteen years before receiving his first appointment, as a district magistrate of Chang-tzu in Shansi province in the northwest. Even that post did not bring good fortune. After a mere ten-month period, it ended abruptly because of an administrative blunder that could probably have been prevented, had T'ang had better social connections.[3]

Second, financially, T'ang Chen and his family, cut off from the clan estate in Szechwan, had to resettle in the lower Yangtze with few social and economic resources. This condition had a direct and clearly unfavorable impact on T'ang's life. Throughout his entire productive life he scrambled about with small land-holding, in temporary office employment, selling literary services, such as composing memorial essays for the wealthy, running small businesses, for instance opening a *ya-hang*, and borrowing. Sometimes, he starved. All this was perhaps not atypical for the petty intellectuals of T'ang's days. The disasters that forced him to end his civil-service job and his short-lived commercial adventures were but two examples of the sort of handicap suffered by even those of a "Confucian" background.

Third, politically and ideologically speaking, although T'ang Chen himself harbored no anti-Manchu sentiments, the Ming-loyalist background of his close relatives brought inconveniences and barriers in his attempted ascent up the social ladder. He had to change his given name at least once to avoid persecution and discrimination, real or threatened. T'ang, however, continued to hold relatively positive views toward the newly established Ch'ing state, casting it against what he perceived as the corruption, chaos, and incompetence of the late Ming.[4] After being fired from his brief term as magistrate and expelled from the bureaucracy, however, he did begin to reveal a strikingly different outlook toward politics and monarchs. Brooding frustration and concealed skepticism, compounded by the poignant sense of personal failure and humiliation, combined to form a genuine alienation from, and even cynicism toward, dynastic politics and despotic order.[5]

THE BOLD CRITIC

Certain aspects of T'ang Chen's thought are particularly interesting and intriguing. They touch on his views on the nature of Confucianism. Two specifically seem to identify him as a radical and a potential rebel against the Confucian heritage. One is his vehement attack on the cruel nature of Chinese rulership, summed up by his own famous remark that "all kings and emperors are but bandits." Here is T'ang's own description of the circumstances in which the statement was uttered:

> At home one evening, I joined my family in wine. I sat down at the table facing west, while my wife faced east; our daughter An was at the north and my concubine the northwest corner. Wine was poured into the cups while we chatted and joked. I tasted a piece of fish; it was very good. "At the market, this fish, must have been still alive?" I asked. "Not so," the concubine replied. "It died not long before I picked it up. But since it was cold outside, it stayed quite fresh." I then drank my wine and was quite happy. All of a sudden, seized by a thought crossing my mind, I struck the table and sighed. "You were just drinking merrily, why did you all of a sudden hit the table and sigh?" My wife asked. "Those restrained by etiquette have no insight into affairs. I do have opinions, however, that have never been expressed before. People, I fear, would be terrified to hear them. Tonight, the fish reminds me of them again. That's why I sighed." My wife said, "I am only a woman, and may not understand things that concern the gentlemen. But if only you would convey to me just what has occurred in your mind!" I then said, "The way the great Ch'ing dynasty took over the country may be regarded as humane. *But all the emperors from the Ch'in dynasty on were bandits.*" My wife laughed: "Why do you want to call them bandits?" "If some people snatch [from others] bolts of cloths or bushels of grain, do you call them murderous bandits or not?" "They certainly are," she replied. I then continued, "In the case of men killing a single person and robbing him of his cloths and grain, they would be regarded as bandits. *Yet there are those who go about killing all men under heaven and taking away their cloths, food as well as their other possessions. And you don't call them bandits?*" My wife asked me: "When the entire nation falls into chaos, is it really likely that it may be pacified without shedding

a single drop of blood?" "To bring order back to a state in turbulence, bloodshed may indeed be necessary. The kings in the past, however, applied killing only on two occasions: in the case of criminals, and when going to war. If all they did was to ruin every village on their way, to pass and to massacre every city they entered, what in the world was the excuse for their savage activities? While the generals were the ones who were carrying out executions, it was really the Son of Heaven who had committed homicide. While the troops went out slaughtering, it was not they who were decimating lives; it was really the Son of Heaven who had committed homicide. When the bureaucrats drove people to death, it was not really they who were decimating lives; it was really the Son of Heaven who had committed homicide. *The hands that shed human blood may be many, but in fact they were all controlled by the ominous hand of the emperor.*[6]

The indicting thought, seemingly casually expressed in a dinner conversation, was not an accidental one. Apart from the prudently titled "Intimate Conversation" (*shih yü*), which contains such sentiments, there are many other utterances expressing misgivings about the nature of Chinese emperorship that can be found in T'ang's collected essays, *Ch'ien Shu* (The Writings in Obscurity). In addition, the problem, as T'ang saw it, was that the present political system placed all power in one person's hands. The emperor was thus the single person to be held responsible for meeting the needs or causing the calamities of the country. "It is only the emperor who can run the country in an orderly manner, and it is only the emperor who can throw the country into chaos. To govern or to destroy, it is a matter in which no one else can intervene; it is all determined by the emperor."[7] His harsh views, ironically enough, were really his earnest hope that his bitter resentment and scathing accusations would somehow reach the imperial throne, and thus help rectify all the political problems. Such essays as "In Remonstrance of the Ruler" (*ke chün*),[8] "Warning for Future Rulers" (*yüan chien*),[9] "The Rarity of a Good Ruler" (*hsien chün*)[10] and "The Superior Person Rectified" (*i-tsun*),[11] reveal a fervent wish to mend the unmendable. For all his shrewd insight, which pierced through the violent and greedy nature of China's *ancien régime*, it should be pointed out that T'ang Chen never placed blame beyond an individual level. That emperors were bandits notwithstanding, his indignation was never carried one step further to ask whether in fact the entire political order, the authoritarian system, was the evil behind it all. He never asked whether despotism, not despots, was the ultimate machine that legitimized misrule and made murderers out of emperors.

T'ang's rebellious, or in any event, unconventional views were not limited to politics. He also made unusual remarks on social norms and personal ethics. To a group of gathered friends, T'ang revealed rather strong criticism of what he referred to as "the worst crisis of contemporary social life."

Nowadays men often abuse their wives. *While appearing very humble in public, they become ferocious at home.* They do not even mind deferring to lowly servants around the house, but never do they loosen their authority over their women. *Wives are commonly treated as objects for venting the frustration and anger that men encounter elsewhere.* Relationships have become so dreadful: How can one refer to them as "families"?[12]

This social ill became prevalent because, in T'ang's opinion, women were situated in a most unfavorable position. Because of the workaday problems of family life, frictions inevitably arose. On such occasions the husband took advantage of the intimacy of his relations with the wife to inflict violence upon her. T'ang furthermore thought that women, being weaker, were incapable of self-defense; they were isolated and therefore pitiable. T'ang lamented that in his day, the spirit of the *Great Learning* had disappeared because of the deterioration in ethics (*jen-lun*), "of which the husband-wife relationship represented by far the worst instance."[13] The circumstance became even more unforgivable upon realizing that wife-beating husbands were such ingrates. "Has it ever occurred to you men that without a wife your children would not have come about?" "Moreover, how would your house be kept in order? Who would look after your finances? Who would make everything ready for you and keep things in order while you are away?"[14] These duties were unfailingly observed not just by some exceptionally brilliant females. They were the daily routine, T'ang pointed out emphatically, of every single "stupid wife" at home.

T'ang then took another tack in his criticism. He considered the fact that ancient poets were touched when they witnessed the love-making of mandarin ducks. These birds, traditionally depicted in China as the paragon of romantic love, were observed to mate in such a way that the male was beneath the female. Sexual behavior, whether human or animal, told a good deal of what was actually involved in companionship. In their own way, T'ang noted, the mandarin ducks revealed a truth with universal application: "It may be in compliance with the natural endowments of wives that they take a position below their husbands, but only when husbands are willing to accept a position below their wives do they show the magnanimity of a passionate couple."[15] He continued, "When a husband refuses to take the position beneath his wife, it is called male pomposity (*fu-k'ang*); and when there is this male pomposity, there is no peace in the house. The family cannot hold itself together for much longer."[16]

If his message is fascinating to one as being distinctly "modern," we should be cautious about ascribing modern feminist values to T'ang. T'ang himself never had any difficulty with the fact that, at least nominally, women's roles were subordinated to those of men. He said, "it is as natural as the earth's being dominated by heaven, or a minister's subordinating himself to the ruler."[17] Yet for the cosmic order to arrive at a genuine harmony or human affairs to prosper, superior forces in some cases must act submissively to achieve balance with their inferior counterparts: "In truth the virtue of propriety and that of magnanimity are by no means contradictory."[18] Men ought not to feel any discomfort in being leaders who also play supportive roles.

As reflected in his remarks on emperors and political systems, there is both boldness and limitation in T'ang's social critique. He stressed the value, it is true, of men's treating women amicably, fairly and appreciatively, as a logical reorientation of basic Confucian standards of humanity and compassion. And he voiced more than once his outrage toward both disdain for women and domestic violence (*pao-nei*). But it is also important to point out that T'ang's concerns for the status and well-being of women and other gender-related issues lay squarely within the framework of marriage. Women as a category of beings separate from the roles of daughter, sister, wife, or mother did not yet emerge from his discussions. Nor were women themselves perceived as free agents of history. They were shown sincere concern and made objects of serious protest, but never consulted directly or spoken to specifically.

T'ANG'S IDEAS AND THE QUESTION OF CONFUCIAN IDENTITY

In assessing the significance of the seemingly ordinary T'ang Chen and his ideas, which were at times rather extraordinary, we must also consider Confucianism as both a conceptual as well as a socio-cultural construct. In other words, the boundaries of Confucianism were both sociocultural and philosophical in nature. Socially speaking, we should question T'ang's very identity as a Confucian intellectual: Did he fall within or outside the domain of literati? Philosophically, we must define and characterize Confucianism as a body of thought with its main moral-ethical values, discursive contents, conceptual borders, internal diversity, tolerance for potential dissent, and cultural resilience in the face of external attack, so as to gauge the extent to which T'ang's ideas overstepped the Confucian boundary and can be identified as Confucian.

To begin with, the question of T'ang's own identity as a Confucian opens up much for discussion. His status as a middle-ranking provincial official touches upon the question of the sociology of Confucianism. We know fairly little about how ordinary Confucians lived and how they might have perceived the supposedly common heritage. Thus far scholars have interpreted the question of identity mostly in elitist terms. Moreover, T'ang's radical stance on key issues of politics and society makes him quite a good subject for viewing the general intellectual integrity of Confucianism. Was he a conscious rebel or an unintended transgressor? Had Confucianism an intellectual or cultural ground clearly marked out, one that was commonly understood, agreed upon, and upheld by its followers at the level of the rank-and-file? If so, how was the territory defined at any point of time? Through what? And by whom? What means did it possess to define its boundaries, to defend its integrity, and perhaps to punish offenders?

We take as fact that at the personal individual level T'ang Chen was a Confucian. He perceived himself to be one. His life's mission was to become learned by Confucian standards, and he issued all his pronouncements in the position of a self-appointed defender of that great tradition. He was concerned not only with matters of thought. There were times when he actually acted upon what he considered to be his duty as a Confucian disciple, taking note of even the small matters. For example, once, strolling through the outskirts of Su-chou Prefecture, T'ang Chen saw, much to his dismay, a statue of Confucius being worshipped as the God of Earth (t'u-ti shen) in a small shrine. T'ang thought the matter grave enough to warrant a formal report to the local authorities. With the help of a friend, Yu Hui-an, T'ang personally saw to the removal of the profanity.[19] In so doing, T'ang was pleased to be fulfilling the social responsibility expected of a provincial intellectual, proving himself a conscientious defender of the "right" Confucian heritage. T'ang was proud to act as worthy interpreter of the Confucian image, protecting it from the obscene offense perpetrated against the great sage. His authority, nonetheless, perhaps like the little shrine for the God of Earth, could not extend its influence much beyond the rural landscape. What T'ang had done for himself made him only at best a minor figure in the Confucian pantheon.

T'ang was not totally unaware of his limitations in the world of Confucianism. Even in his sixties and seventies, he continued to dedicate as much time and energy as possible to study and reflection. Yet he never quite forgot how poorly equipped he was. Whatever progress he was able to make in his Confucian pilgrimage amounted perhaps to very little in terms of achieved success. Yet he was determined to pursue that to which his deep faith was committed. In his long intellectual struggle to relate his learning to what he saw and experienced, T'ang Chen felt that he had come to grips with something useful and meaningful for others of his ilk. But this something would be radical and critical ideas that he espoused to lambast many aspects of the world in which he lived.

What then do we make of T'ang's more extreme notions, some of which may be considered to be quite "un-Confucian"? His own view was widely at odds with those of others, especially the erudite Confucian highbrow. T'ang himself felt that he spoke as no one but a faithful defender of Confucianism, albeit at times critical. Against the background of contemporary sociocultural and political norms, friends and readers found him a nasty eccentric at best, and a mean foe and dangerous rebel at worst. T'ang was thought of as an awkward man: "He moved slowly in receiving people, talked clumsily, and listened absent-mindedly."[20] Many close to him attributed his unsuccessful life to this "handicap" rather than anything else. They recognized, however, that T'ang was stubborn by nature, especially on matters he deemed important. Regarding learning or social ideals, for instance, he would never let words pass idly by. Whenever such topics were brought up, his sluggishness in speech disappeared: "With those who disagreed, he would argue relentlessly until he was beside himself with anger and agitation." His seriousness toward the issues at stake and his indifference for common courtesy rendered him rough and intimidating at such moments: "He simply would not comply with the norms of the day. If someone incurred his displeasure, not even a thousand men could turn his head around." He was equally adamant and uncowed in openly criticizing the eminent and powerful in society. In return for his "imprudence," he was greeted with aversion and resentment.[21]

More problematic were his rather uncommon and often unwelcome views on society and politics. Friends frowned upon hearing his idea that men should assume a subservient position to that of women, that traditional Confucian ethics of brotherhood (*t'i*) were meant to include considerations for sisters, or that the way of friendship (*p'eng-yu chih tao*) ought to put satisfaction of each other's material needs at the forefront.[22] Of course, his infamous notion that all emperors were bandits, and that rulers were the only ones to be blamed for social unrest and political calamity—he unleashed along the way severe criticism of the Ming's last emperor—brought considerable unpopularity. Friends looked askance at his political radicalism. Among the very few readers who happened to see the first fifty copies of *Ch'ien Shu*, many expressed strong disapproval of his "slandering and false accusation" (*ti wu*) of the Ch'ung-chen emperor and the late-Ming state. Some found his thoughts "saddening, aggravating and hair-raising."[23] Others who saw the reprint a century or so later still considered his proposals "ludicrous and impractical," his opinions "too bitter and extreme," his remarks laughable, and his writings without any solid base and anticlassical.[24] The influential comments of the editors of *Ssu-k'u ch'üan-shu tsung-mu* said the following about T'ang's *Ch'ien shu*: they were "often based on contemporary hearsay, and casual conversations with [the author's] associates." And the *Ssu-ku* editors may not have been far off the mark. Furthermore, to many, their description of T'ang's intellectual standing and Confucian scholarship as "in all not yet accomplished or mature," was an understatement.[25]

Thus, any attempt to establish T'ang's status as a Confucian intellectual, and to appraise his qualifications as a follower of Confucian teaching depends on the particular stance we take on these questions. Subjectively, T'ang believed himself to be a true and faithful Confucian, albeit a poorly equipped and unachieved one. Objectively, a few of his contemporaries and acquaintances were willing to attest to that. Yet this represents but a minority view, even at the time. According to the majority's view, that is, the majority of the self-professed Confucian scholars, he was either a cultural outcast or a dangerous enemy. They would have had a hard time receiving him as an ordinary scholar, or accepting either his acts or his ideas as squarely Confucian. After all, to most typical Confucians, ideas such as a subject's loyalty to his ruler, or a woman's subjugation to her husband, represent unshakable pillars of the Confucian orthodoxy. Yet were they the ultimate judges in history? Who was to determine T'ang's, or anybody else's, qualifications as a Confucian? And by what process?

An ironic twist was added a century or more later, when suddenly, T'ang Chen gravitated in various ways to the center of history and the core of legitimacy. The twist in fate provides rich food for thought for historians considering the forces of inclusion and exclusion in the Confucian world. Early in the nineteenth century, roughly one full century after his devoted son-in-law produced the first fifty copies of *Ch'ien Shu* in T'ang's memory, domestic crises and foreign invasions began to shed new light upon the old scroll. A generation of statecraft thinkers, pressed by political, social, and economic problems, found T'ang's pragmatic wisdom unusually attractive. When Ho Ch'ang-ling (1785–1848) sponsored the compilation of the monumental *Collected Essays on Statecraft* (*Huang-ch'ao ching-shih wen-pien*), no fewer than twenty-one essays out of T'ang's original ninety-seven found their ways into the collection, second in number only to the towering figure of Ku Yen-wu, and first if one were to take as a criterion the proportion of the selected pieces in relation to the original corpus. The choice encompassed a wide range of subjects, although the most radical of the titles were not included, and the editors of the influential anthology customarily offered no comments of their own.[26] But a posthumous honor it definitely was, a far cry from the days when T'ang begged for recognition from men of letters, as evidenced by the incident wherein he was chased away by Wei Hsi's doorman with his first fifteen essays in hand.[27] What had kept T'ang Chen out of the "real" and "established" Confucian circles in the late seventeenth century turned out to be exactly the sorts of proposition that made the early-nineteenth-century statecraft thinkers (still Confucians) group him as one of the insiders. And this does not include the fame bestowed on the same man in the second half of this century by Marxist-socialist thinkers who dubbed him a "progressive spokesman of the petty bourgeoisie."[28] Granted, this latter drama may be seen as a development beyond the Confucian realm, but it surely demonstrates the effect that a shift of cultural boundaries may have upon a single historical character over time.

THE WORLD OF THE CONFUCIAN MIDDLEBROW

The case of T'ang Chen compels us to consider the middle stratum of Confucianism. In the past, our knowledge of Confucianism and Confucian China consisted of two layers. On top was knowledge of Confucianism as a body of thought presented and represented by its elite members. Scholars examined the founding principles of Confucianism, its institutional set-up, as well as the difficulties it encountered in history, but in doing so, they merely focused on high culture and those who were relatively well-informed, well-connected, and well-tuned to the issues of the day. Naturally, the number of "highbrows" was small.

Thus we have also justifiably shifted our attention to the lower level of Confucian world. We not only are looking at "the little tradition" as opposed to the "great tradition," but also at questions of "peasant society" and "popular culture." At the level of the masses, people led lives of a different sort. They uttered voices and upheld values that diverged to greater or smaller degrees from those at the very top. The folks at the bottom were usually kept out of the regular Confucian orbit intellectually and socially, although this is not to say that they were entirely un-Confucian or non-Confucian.

Then there is the logical question as to whether there might have been some people who were adrift in the middle, those who, properly defined, belonged to neither world. The lives and minds of this middle group of the Confucian society should, for a number of reasons, teach us much. First, their personal experiences shed light on the effects that the infinite "layering" process produced in Chinese society and Confucian culture. Second, their intellectual contours should reveal to us the Confucian order from within: How and through what measures were people either "taken in" or "kept out" of the elite culture and social-political circles? What implications did this continuous inclusion and exclusion have for an individual or a group? Third, their daily activities and social interactions should have much to tell us about the functional roles this middle group played within the larger Confucian system. Due to the strategic position they occupied, did it give them particular channels of interaction with those above and below them? Could they thus function somehow as a congealing or integrating element? In times of stress, furthermore, did they tend to be the party that put things together or pulled them apart?

The case of T'ang Chen, and many more like him, informs us on such issues. In my lengthier work on him, I have argued that he and his kind (calling them the provincially educated, or the Confucian rank and file) struggled to keep their minds on par with the elites, but their bodies and hearts had to live out the tough existence of the masses. The implications of acquainting ourselves with this intermediate group are manifold. The ways in which they grasped Confucian teachings may serve to highlight special characteristics of those teachings from the rank-and-file's perspective. Because they were intellectually isolated and materially hard-pressed, subelites tended to approach the orthodox tradition rather individualistically, often resulting in idiosyncratic and eccentric ideas. Yet their inspiration was based on the grim reality of the masses, something elite intellectuals could hardly dismiss. Finally, given the passage of time, the ideas of the middlebrow Confucian can be selectively appreciated and appointed by the elite group, as the case of T'ang Chen and his *Ch'ien Shu* demonstrates.[29]

What about the question of common heritage vis-à-vis individual innovation? In fact, for someone with limited intellectual resources, events personally encountered, voices privately heard, and phenomena accidentally witnessed, cannot but form a more gripping force that philosophical abstractions. To such a mind, although life may at times seem inscrutable, it is more understandable than the pedantic classics.[30] T'ang Chen was speaking from his keenly felt experiences when he proclaimed that moral values did not guarantee administrative competence, that material progress was all that could count for the people, or that men and women were basically the same. Such remarks exhibited neither the uneasiness nor the exhilaration expected of a self-appointed rebel. Instead, he was deeply convinced that even in expressing the least commonly shared views, he was merely brushing the dust off a long-forgotten corner of an ancient inspiration. When the classics somehow failed to yield the right sanction for his positions, he would argue that it was because time had made things different. He believed that Confucius and Mencius would have arrived at exactly the same conclusions, given the appreciation of the passage of time. T'ang pronounced with much delight: "If only the ancient sages would rise up from their graves, they would be bound to change their understanding of the Tao." The spirit and the principles, as he understood them, remained constant, though the vocabularies and the formulae changed. Perhaps the only occasion when T'ang felt alarmed by his own ideas was his uttering of his infamous remark about dynastic founders. But even in expressing this, T'ang felt justified that he was merely stating the obvious. Was it not hallowed Confucian teaching that people ought to propose solutions "to alleviate suffering and to enhance the welfare [of the people]?" Confucius and Mencius would not have objected to this.

In some respects, life could be more "free" under the shelter of ignorance afforded by intellectual and cultural isolation. Under such circumstances, one is forced to make assertions according to one's innate convictions, to elaborate on thoughts that capture one's attention. One can point out the issues that most irritate one. By expressing some unpopular, and mostly unnoticeable, "wild" notions, one does not have to confront the question of whether to raise the banner of revolt. Iconoclasm, in addition to "radical" opinions casually expressed, requires a well-defined tradition consciously fended for and openly denounced. Intellectual rebellion, in this sense, may be as much a product of emotional and psychological alienation as a conscious reaction against a cultural heritage. For this, Li Chih (1527–1602) qualifies much better as a conscious rebel than T'ang Chen. It is little wonder that T'ang, whose confidence in the general merit of Confucianism far exceeded his discontent with it, felt entirely comfortable mounting vigorous attacks while blissfully calling himself a follower. Compared with elite counterparts better versed in classical doctrines and better attuned to the unorthodox, a provincial intellectual might actually be allowed greater space in which to move about, brooding over odd ideas without having to take on the burden of a declared rebel.

T'ang Chen, for one, never quite developed a troubled conscience as a result of his bitter disillusionment with contemporary Confucianism and with what he perceived as China's abhorrent despotism. Indeed, he saw no compelling reason to contemplate the connection between his unhappiness with the reality of Confucian ideals and their ultimate validity. This basic attitude explains why his "rebellious" proclamations lacked the power to shake up the entire system. The numerous irreconcilable contradictions in his opinions on politics and society lay probably as much in this unusual "self-protection" as in his intellectual inability to come to terms with them. He had a genuine interest in being an honest critic, but no motivation whatsoever in stepping out of that framework and declaring war against it.

In certain respects, then, T'ang's life suggests that a sort of "intellectual autonomy" can result from an individual's relatively unimportant social status and isolated cultural environment, even though that freedom was far from totally enviable. A provincial man's marginalization from the mainstream could free him from obligatory preoccupation with the often exhausting but not necessarily fruitful debates over "issues of the day." An independent reading of the classics, moreover, might grant a loser like T'ang Chen more room for innovative thinking, with fewer psychological inhibitions against unorthodox adventures. Devoid of seasoned instructions from formal schooling, or of stimulating meetings with contemporary masters, it perhaps also meant that some of the restraints that went hand in hand with such institutions and conventions were removed as well.

This is not to say that to be a second-rate scholar or a third-rank Confucian was ever admired. Such a person was marked by social inadequacy, cultural deprivation, economic limitations, and political disadvantage. His was very seldom a success story, and the differences between such an existence and that of the more privileged can hardly be overlooked. For example, late in the seventeenth century, when T'ang Chen was scraping through by doing odd menial jobs, the then already celebrated K'un-shang talent (*ts'ai-tzu*), Ku Yen-wu (1613–74), had already completed two major studies, each resulting in a multivolume publication. In addition, Ku seemed financially secure enough to make a series of extensive survey trips around the country "to seek enlightenment and to broaden one's knowledge." As a matter of fact, before the young Ku set out for his first study tour north, he carried with him a letter of recommendation bearing the signature of no fewer than twenty-one prominent scholars of the time, requesting, on his behalf, gracious accommodations and expert cooperation from "all gentlemen everywhere." The letter introduced Ku as a most promising young scholar, alluding to the prestigious achievements of his ancestors. Ku's own remarkable knowledge, according to his recommenders, had grown out of his study of some twelve thousand volumes. The extensive *Strengths and Weaknesses of the Various Regions in China* (*Tien-hsia chün kuo li-ping shu*), which he had recently finished, served, they said, as testimony to the formidable intellectual caliber of their distinguished thirty-two-year-old protégé. Armed with such recommendations, it is small wonder that Ku should have enjoyed the delight of exchanging views with famous men. Specialists showed Ku fresh materials on epigraphy, new techniques of philology, and lent him private copies of rare texts. Numerous academicians even brought him their own works for expert review. Other than the usual scholarly conversations among pedants that often bewildered outsiders, there were heated debates on current issues, discussions on the right interpretations of the Confucian classics, and on the principal guidelines for the proper approach to the tradition, questions that had been in dispute for centuries but were given a fresh new twist. But for people who were not among the group, such as T'ang Chen and others of his breed, they could not partake in anything close to such exchanges. T'ang's life, mostly confined to involuntary solitude, was not an exceptional case. From his own notes and from statements of friends and contemporaries, we realize that T'ang's frustration and loneliness were common to many of the Confucian middlebrow. Frustration in failing to climb upwards and loneliness from lack of recognition beset their mundane lives. Many led miserable lives. Some, like T'ang, would not give up striving to make something of themselves, to become worthy and learned by Confucian standards. But deprived of guidance and assistance from masters, and of encouragement and communication with like minds, they had a hard time escaping intellectual redundancy and cultural alienation.

Yet their experiences, their lives, and their thoughts help us in our foremost query: whether boundaries are real or fluid. Were Confucian boundaries clearly laid out? Or were they vague, blurry, and amorphous? The case of T'ang Chen seems to suggest both. Socially speaking, the line between established Confucian elites and their less privileged counterparts was certainly clearly drawn and judiciously maintained. There was relatively little chance for T'ang's type to become, or to be accepted by, the highbrow. The factor of social class in cultural and intellectual history is just as real and powerful as it is in economics and politics. The boundaries between the highbrow and the middlebrow and the lowbrow were real, especially in terms of people's social place.

Yet intellectually and philosophically, by the seventeenth century, T'ang Chen and his type also demonstrate ways of connecting themselves with the Confucian heritage, often momentarily. There was no institutional setup guaranteeing the transmission of ideas in the orthodox way, and there was no promise that they would get the "right" message on their own. But the fact is that they did consider themselves faithful followers, and their notions of the Confucian teachings correct ones. People did not take them seriously, and they had a difficult time selling the more unconventional of their views. Yet this does not make them any less Confucian. We therefore concede that, in a certain cultural sense and on the plane of ideas, Confucian boundaries were rather fluid and moveable.

Confucianism and the Confucian social order, in comparison with other cultural traditions, belief systems, and social orders, are often exalted for their intellectual tolerance and social inclusiveness. As a secular and civic body of thought, we are told, Confucianism never exhibited the sort of rigid confinement or arbitrary control on individuals or society as did other philosophical schools, religious sects, social organizations or political ideologies, although in practical terms, we are also informed, it served more or less all the same purposes as these other forces. But such and similar claims are half-truths at best, casually stated and wistfully pronounced. The openness of Confucianism and the inclusiveness of the Confucian order is an assumption yet to be tested in history. Until we know better the inner structures of that cultural and social order, through further investigation of its topology, boundaries, and distinctions, our old picture of the Confucian world can only be a partial and blurry one.

NOTES

1. Wang Wen-yüan, *Hsi-shu T'ang Pu-t'ing hsien-sheng hsing-lüeh i-shih-wu tse* (The Record of T'ang Pu-t'ing from Western Szechwan in Fifteen Items), in T'ang Chen, *Ch'ien-shu* (Taipei, Ho-lo Book Co., 1974), pp. 225–29. Consult also Hsiung Ping-chen, "T'ang Chen and the Works in Obscurity: Life and Thought of a Provincial Intellectual in Seventeenth Century China" (Ph.D. dissertation, Brown University, 1983), chapter 1, "A Disinherited Provincial."

2. *T'ang Chen Shih-chi Chung-k'ao*, and "Shih-chi-chien-piao," appendix to T'ang Chen, *Ch'ien Shu*, pp. 253–92. *Ch'ien Shu* is hereafter cited as CS.

3. Wang, in *ibid.*; T'ang, *K'ao Kung* (Evaluating Merits), "Wei cheng" (Government), and "Chüan shih" (Real Power), in CS, pp. 109–13, 115–18.

4. T'ang, *Ts'un yen* (Preserving the Words), CS, pp.113–15.

5. T'ang, "Hsien chün" (The Rarity of Good Rulers), "I tzun" (Superior Person Rectified), "Shou chien" (To Remain in Subjugation), CS, pp. 66–68; 88.

6. "Shih yü" (Intimate Conversations), CS, pp. 196–97. See also Hsiung, "T'ang Chen," chapter 2, "Representative of Practical Wisdom."

7. "Hsien chün" (The Rarity of Good Rulers), CS, pp. 66.

8. CS, pp.119–21.

9. CS, pp. 125–28.

10. CS, pp. 66–67.

11. CS, pp. 67–69.

12. "Nei lun" (Domestic Ethics), CS, pp. 77–78.

13. Ibid.

14. Ibid.

15. Ibid.

16. Ibid.

17. Ibid.

18. Ibid.

19. Wang, "The Record of T'ang P'u-t'ing from Western Szechwan in Fifteen Items," CS, p.228.

20. Ibid., p. 226.

21. "Ch'u chi" (To Be Rid of Weakness), CS, p. 30.

22. "Ming t'i" (Understanding Brotherhood), CS, p. 76; "Chu shih" (Family Life), CS, pp. 78–80; "Wu pi" (The Social Ills of Wu), CS, pp. 170–71. See also Hsiung, "T'ang Chen," chapter 3, "Advocate of Personal Happiness."

23. Wang Yüan, "Shu T'ang Chu-wan Ch'ien Shu ho" (Postscript to T'ang Chen's *Ch'ien Shu*), *Chu-yieh-t'ang wen-chi*, chüan 20, pp. 9–10.

24. Li Tz'u-ming, *Yüeh-man-t'ang jih-chi*, 43:68.

25. *Ssu-k'u ch'üan shu tsung-mu t'i yao*, chüan 125 (rpt., Taipei: Shang-wu, 1993); 24:84, 88.

26. *Huang-chao ching-shih wen-pien* (Taipei: Wen-hai, 1979).

27. Yang Pin, "T'ang Chu-wan chuan" (A Biography of T'ang Chen), "T'ang Chu-wan ch'ien shu hsü" (Preface to T'ang Chen's *Ch'ien Shu*), and "T'ang Chu-wan wen-chi hsü" (Preface to T'ang Chen's *Collection of Writings*), in *Yang Ta-hu hsien-sheng cha-wen ts'an-kao* (Fragments from Yang Pin's Manuscripts).

28. See for instance the preface and postscript to the first reprint of *Ch'ien Shu* in mainland China; also consult, Hsiung, "T'ang Chen," chapter 2 "Conclusion."

29. See also ibid.,"Introduction."

30. Hsiung Ping-chen, "Ts'ung T'ang Chen k'an ko-jen ching-yen tui ching-shih ssu-hsiang yen-sheng chih yin-hsiang" (The Relationship between Personal Experience and the Breedings of Statecraft Thought: The Case of T'ang Chen), *Bulletin of the Institute of Modern History* (Taipei: Institute of Modern History, Academia Sinica, 1985), 14:1–28.

GLOSSARY

Ch'ien Shu	潛書
Ch'ung-chen	崇禎
Chang Hsien-chung	張獻忠
Chang-tzu	長子
Chu Hsi	朱熹
fu-k'ang	夫亢
Ho Ch'ang-ling	賀長齡
hsien chün	鮮君
Huang-ch'ao ching-shih wen pien	皇朝經世文篇
i-tsun	抑尊
jen-lun	人倫
ke chün	格君
Ku Yen-wu	顧炎武
Li Chih	李贄
p'eng-yu chih tao	朋友之道
pao-nei	暴內
shih yü	室語

Ssu-k'u ch'üan-shu tsung-mu	四庫全書總目
T'ang Chen	唐甄
t'i	悌
t'u-ti shen	土地神
ti wu	詆誣
Tien-hsia chün kuo li-ping shu	天下郡國利病書
ts'ai-tzu	才子
Wang Yang-ming	王陽明
Wei hsi	魏禧
ya-hang	牙行
Yu Hui-an	尤晦庵
yüan chien	遠諫

10

Discovering Monotheistic Metaphysics
The Exegetical Reflections of James Legge (1815–1897) and Lo Chung-fan (d. circa 1850)

Lauren Pfister

CROSSING POLITICAL AND METAPHYSICAL BOUNDARIES

Why would an official from eastern Kwangtung seek out foreign Christian missionaries in the newly established colony of Hong Kong in 1843? What motivated Lo Chung-fan (d. ca. 1850), a second degree (*chü-jen*) scholar-official, probably in his mid-fifties, to cross the political boundaries newly established by the treaties that marked the successful British intrusions into Ch'ing China? For it would become a well-known fact that those Chinese officials who came into regular friendly contact with foreigners rarely received imperial approval, and often became the object of imperial disfavor.[1]

Nearly twenty years after that first encounter, when a more mature James Legge had gained a reputation as a missionary-scholar under the name Lee Ya-ko, he briefly recounted some details about this Cantonese scholar in his first volume of the *Chinese Classics*. Calling Lo a "fine scholar" who was "offended by [Legge's] hesitancy" to receive him for Christian baptism, Lo left the red-haired missionary and "enrolled himself among the disciples of another missionary." Still unsatisfied after a short time under missionary tutelage, the Cantonese official retired from his official duties, pursuing "literary studies."[2]

Apparently while at his post in the Hui-lai District of Kwangtung, Lo had read some Christian literature passed on to him by others for his assessment. Although news of the British colony was probably general knowledge, encounters with missionaries or their colporteurs were still relatively rare at this time, even in the busy port of Canton. Had he seen one of the thousands of copies of Liang Ya-fa's *Ch'üan-shih liang-yen* (Good Words for Exhorting the Age), which had come into the hands of many hopeful students, including the young man Hung Hsiu-ch'üan (1813–64), the later prophet-king of the T'ai-p'ing Heavenly Kingdom.[3] Did he search out the sources of these materials to spy on them? Or was his request for baptism an authentic sign of Lo's metaphysical and religious interests? For whatever reasons, Lo risked entering the new colony and located the young and relatively unexperienced missionary educator. Possibly Lo specifically sought out Legge because he had learned that the young Scotsman, at that time only in his mid-twenties, was a scholar already carrying an honorary doctorate.[4]

In fact, Legge had been living with his family and students in Malacca for three years, having initiated his study and teaching of the Ruist canonical literature only two years previously. Most likely, this was the first genuine Chinese scholar Legge had ever met, and so he probably had alongside him his younger Chinese evangelist, Ho Tsun-sheen (1817–71), to help him communicate clearly with the scholarly visitor. Through the awkward dialogue that followed, Legge began to doubt scholar Lo's understanding of Christian claims, and Lo began to doubt scholar Legge's credentials as a competent student of Chinese Ruist literature. At the time there were other foreign missionaries and statesmen in Hong Kong with a far better command of Chinese language, but Lo's initial examination of missionary teachings apparently proved to be a frustrating experience.

Nevertheless, copies of Lo's later "literary studies," located in remnants of Legge's personal library, show that Lo was not totally unresponsive to what he had learned from Christian sources. By crossing over these political boundaries Lo was stimulated to strengthen his metaphysical understanding of Shang-ti in the Ruist canonical literature, and to integrate it into traditional self-cultivation practices and the art of rulership.[5]

On his part, Legge also showed signs of intellectual development after his encounter with Lo. First of all, there was a metaphysical chasm that Legge had to span between the Christian idea of "God" and a variety of concepts in the Chinese correlative cosmological worldview. Only by 1848 had he become convinced that Shang-ti was the equivalent conceptual term for the general idea of God. The transformation of his own ideas came about partly because of the quiet insistence of his Chinese colleague, Ho, and partly due to Legge's growing awareness and sensitivity of the place of Shang-ti in the earliest portions of some Ruist scriptures. Other missionaries simultaneously became convinced that this term was an inappropriate Chinese translation for the Christian "God" because of its associations with a number of Taoist deities in common peoples' minds.[6] In order to resolve this problem, which quickly blossomed into a lengthy and bitter public debate, Legge studied the content and development of the imperial worship ceremonies directed to Shang-ti during the winter solstice.

There was an obvious dilemma for Legge in making these studies. If he discovered a polytheistic or pantheistic cosmology undergirding imperial worship, his search for a cultural bridge in theological concepts would prove to be a failure. In addition, he would have to stand against the fundamental ideas of the authorized Ruist philosophical teachings supporting these ceremonies. But if he could find undeniable proof that the Chinese emperor addressed in his imperial prayers a being equivalent to "God" in monotheistic traditions, this would require a reassessment of missionary approaches to the Chinese scholarly traditions. Any missionary doing so would face a number of cultural and political quandaries that previous debates between Catholic missionaries, papal envoys, and Chinese imperial officials had also not resolved happily.

Space does not allow a lengthy account of Legge's approach to these problems.[7] As an example, we may focus first on what Legge uncovered about the "restorationist" policies that determined the practice of the imperial cult during the Ming dynasty. Because ritual life is such an important dimension of Ruist self-cultivation, the implications of this "reformation" in the imperial worship had implications for both Lo's and Legge's own philosophical ponderings.[8] In addition, Legge's studies of the imperial worship point toward a different range of possible orientations within the Ruist tradition, some with strongly monotheistic beliefs. Lo's own writings are an example of one of these alternative orientations, as will be seen below, something almost completely ignored in contemporary Confucian studies. First, however, a discussion of what Legge discovered about the "restoration" of the imperial worship is in order.

DISCOVERING MONOTHEISM IN THE MING IMPERIAL WORSHIP

In Legge's substantial publication in 1852, he provided documentary evidence for a form of Shang-ti monotheism from the imperial prayers recorded in the *Ta Ming hui-tien* (The Collected Statutes of the Great Ming Dynasty).[9] A careful reader, Legge investigated the relevant original Chinese sources and was able to provide a detailed historical account of the reinvention of the imperial ritual in the Ming, which is now commonly recognized as the Ming "restorationist" policies.[10]

Following the Chinese accounts, Legge suggests that pre-Han royal rituals had been shaped by a cosmology ruled by a single Shang-ti, but the cosmology and the rituals changed fairly early during the Han dynasty, and they remained the standard of imperial practice, defended by Ruist ideologues until the Ming period. But even during the Ming the transformation of the imperial rites was cluttered with controversy. Once the Ch'ing imperial court declared Chu Hsi's (1130–1200) doctrines the interpretive standards for Ruist teachings, a pre-Ming cosmology also complicated the interpretations of the imperial worship, though it did not change the form of ritual. Legge's account can be summarized as follows.

Influenced by a Taoist master the emperor Wen of the Han dynasty replaced worship of the unique *ti* with that of five *ti* in 166 B.C. This precedent broke with previous Ruist traditions, but was maintained in the imperial rituals and supported by a host of Ruist commentators for fifteen centuries. Yet after the overthrow of the Mongol Yüan dynasty by the new Chinese ruler, the Hung-wu emperor of the Ming dynasty (r. 1368–98), other changes were instituted. Desiring to reestablish a firm Han identity through the Ming rule, the first Ming emperor charged ranking Ruist literati with the task of purifying the rites and music according to the ancient classics.

The Ming imperial prayers translated by Legge in 1852 were informed by this restorationist ideology, but they belonged to a later period of the dynasty, the Chia-ching reign (1522–65). Legge partially explains his choice by elucidating the ritual changes advocated by the emperor. These prayers were prepared for special ceremonies in the seventeeth year of the Chia-ching reign (1538), when the terms of reference for Shang-ti were slightly but significantly changed. From that time until the end of the Ch'ing dynasty, imperial prayers at the open altar in the southern suburbs addressed Huang T'ien Shang-ti, "Shang-ti dwelling in the sovereign heavens."[11] Identifying and translating the eleven prayers constituting the full imperial ceremony, Legge underscores the monotheistic elements in these supplications. For example, he points out how Shang-ti is uniquely addressed in self-consciously humble forms of ritualized etiquette by the emperor, while all other spiritual beings are commanded by him, heightening the strict sense of the cosmological hierarchy. At the very same time that the English king, Henry VIII, was "deliberating about the articles" of the new Anglican creed, the Chia-ching emperor in Peking was addressing "the great name of Shang Ti, dwelling in the sovereign heavens." This "spiritual Sovereign" (*shen-huang*) produced Heaven, humans, and Earth, a "creating work" (*tsao-hua*) in which Shang-ti "called into existence" (*chao*) these "three powers" (*san-ts'ai*). In this sense the Chinese Shang-ti is properly addressed as a potter who "made all living things" (*t'ao tz'u ch'ün-sheng*). On a more personal plane, the emperor addressed the apex of the spiritual hierarchy as "our Father" (*ch'in*), but qualifies this in another prayer as the "Lord" (*huang*) who is "the true parent of all things" (*i-chao wu chih tsu-chen*).[12] This Ming precedent obviously provided an instance of a kind of monotheistic worship similar to Solomonic ritual (including sacrifices) and Roman Catholic liturgy (including Legge's anti-Papist rhetoric about the "distorting influences" of mediating saints and other spirits). Although a Victorian missionary might complain about the attendant "spiritual ministers" as Legge did, he was perceptive enough to insist that this in no substantial way detracted from the unequalled status of the imperial Shang-ti. In addition, it also set the precedent for distinguishing a Ruist monotheistic vision from the Taoist polytheism, one of the sources of confusion in early Han ritual as well as among the nine-teenth-century missionaries who opposed Legge's identification of Shang-ti with the general (and Christian) idea of "God."[13]

Though others had written about the imperial rituals, Legge was the first missionary to translate the imperial prayers and unequivocally identify the spiri-tual being addressed in them with the Christian "God."[14] What Legge did not explain, and perhaps did not know, was that the Ming realignment of the imper-ial worship with ancient models (including this monotheistic strain) was itself replete with intense controversy. Inspired by the restorationist spirit, the first Ming emperor not only replaced the worship of the Five Ti with that of a singular Shang-ti, but also decided to worship various levels of spiritual beings in a dis-crete manner.[15] This meant that each spiritual reality was recognized as an inde-pendent entity, and addressed as such in the imperial prayers. Previous to this time, the vast majority of emperors had worshipped these beings as a whole, com-pleting the rituals in a single event during which all of these spiritual beings were acknowledged. By choosing to worship in a discrete manner, the Hung-wu emperor emphasized the hierarchy in which Shang-ti was supreme. Although Shang-ti remained at the top of the hierarchy, other beings now were also addressed in the same worship ceremonies. This new precedent in favor of con-joint worship remained even when the Yung-lo emperor in 1421 officially moved the capital from Nanking to Peking.

Critical Ruist studies during the later-Ming and early-Ch'ing period of the seventeenth century questioned many classical texts in their descriptions of the ancestral ceremonies of ancient rulers, but some identified the ancient *ti* cere-mony as one in which Heaven was addressed in the presence of the ruler's ances-tors.[16] These kinds of questions may well have been live issues in the sixteenth century also. When the Chia-ching emperor required the question of discrete worship to be rediscussed by the Board of Rites, his motivations included insis-tent (what some Ruists considered perverse) filial concerns.[17] In the end, the emperor decided on his own to institute discrete worship in spite of the Hung-wu emperor's precedent, arranging for supporting Ruists to lead the Board of Rites so that his will would be done.

Further innovations were initiated by the Hung-wu and Chia-ching emper-ors, both setting up important changes in the imperial rituals. The former built a large closed temple for the conjoint worship of the heavenly spirits, something that was prescribed only for an open mound. Noting this deviance, the Chia-ching emperor insisted on building not only the open round altar for discrete worship of Heaven in the southern suburbs of Peking, but also designed an open square altar for Earth in the northern suburbs along with special altars with more complex symbolic forms for the Sun and Moon on an east-west axis.[18] These four altars mirrored the yin-yang cosmological principles in the universe and were built along an axis to reflect the correlative positioning of the imperial capital with the heavenly powers.

For some of the Catholic and Protestant missionaries who came to understand these symbols in the light of the Sung Ruist orthodoxy promoted by the Ch'ing dynasty, the cosmological symbols of imperial worship were simply a more colorful way to mirror the organismic wholeness of the material universe. Some sixteenth-century Ruist interpreters who debated these issues with the first Jesuit missionaries apparently held these views, according to Jacques Gernet.[19] Others, such as the nineteenth-century American missionary and Legge's debating opponent William Boone, took the four altars as obvious symbolic references to the polytheism endorsed by the imperial house, supported in Ruist practices of ancestral reverence, and believed by the masses.

These contrary cosmological interpretations of the imperial worship became a source of intense debate among Chinese scholars as well as nineteenth-century missionaries. Imperial records clarified that the liturgical patterns follow ancient precedents in which Shang-ti was addressed as the apex of a hierarchy of spiritual beings. Legge believed this was the "Supreme Being" equivalent to "our God, the true God," one discretely worshipped at the open round altar in the southern suburbs. The metaphysical explanations of Sung Ruists, all of which predated the Ming reformations of the imperial worship, considered these spiritual beings to be subtle material realities organically and dynamically interrelating in a vast and singular universe. Still others saw the discreteness as a multiplicity of deities, requiring a Chinese cosmology (whether Ruist, Taoist, or Buddhist) that was essentially polytheistic. These persons, including Boone among them, felt Legge committed sacrilege later in 1873 when he and others joined hands in a small circle around the center stone of the Altar of Heaven in Peking and prayed Christian prayers to Shang-ti.[20]

PROPOUNDING A SYSTEMATIC MONOTHEISM
IN THE SOUTHEAST OF THE EMPIRE

Few contemporary Chinese scholars were aware of these debates among the Protestant foreign missionaries during the middle of the nineteenth century. Very few at this time, like Lo Chung-fan, had actually sought them out to learn about their metaphysical claims, religious concerns, and institutional expressions.[21] What we find in Lo's commentarial work is an exegetical effort consistent with the mainline tradition of Ruist classical reading, but one also responsive to a certain degree to the new contexts of the foreign missionary presence. In addition, mention should be made of the discussions of the imperial rituals even in the most fundamental texts of the Ruist canon, the Four Books. Although *Shang-ti* is only mentioned once in a very general metaphysical discussion in the *Great*

Learning (Ta-hsüeh), the text Lo would elaborate, explicit references to pre-imperial sacrificial rites of the sage kings were made in the *Chung-yung*, a text Legge named the *Doctrine of the Mean*.[22] Lo was certainly aware of this singular reference, but was concerned in his work to provide a new and systematically integrated Shang-ti-ist foundation for not only imperial rituals, but also for the principles of government and for self-cultivation.

Lo had to be aware that his project would have to be undertaken within certain well-prescribed limits. The specific integration of a monotheistic metaphysics into the Ruist worldview had to recognize that the ritual practice of addressing Shang-ti was the monopoly of the emperor, but reverence expressed toward this being in other ways may not be interpreted as an usurpation of imperial privileges. Furthermore, an integrated monotheistic system orienting a person's moral development and simultaneously qualifying the absolute sway of the emperor was not a regular and integrated feature of any major Ruist thinker's account of self-cultivation or benevolent government. From this perspective Lo Chung-fan's work takes an unusual approach, but it is not without specific relevance to the classical Ruist traditions. With these background assumptions in mind, it is of great interest to explore the ways in which Lo actually worked out his thinking in his commentarial work on the *Great Learning*, a work entitled *Explanations and Discussions of the Old Text of the Great Learning* (Ku-pen Ta-hsüeh chu-pien). It represents a dissenting voice among Ch'ing Ruist scholarship about the basic purpose and meaning of the classic because of its attempt to counter authorized interpretations of the *Great Learning*, appealing to precedents from the Ming dynasty to fortify his own account.

Soon after the establishment of the Ch'ing, the Four Books and Chu's commentaries became the orthodox standards for Ruist scholasticism, but critical dissent from Chu's interpretations gradually grew among Ch'ing Ruists.[23] This has already been noted above in Legge's comments about the work. The *Great Learning* was particularly susceptible to criticism because Chu, following earlier Sung Ruists, had reorganized the passages in the work and in one critical place added his own commentary as part of the "lost" classical work (the famous fifth commentary). Earlier Ch'ing scholars had pointed out these problems, such as Mao Ch'i-ling (1623–1716), who documented four other alternative texts prepared by various scholars after Chu Hsi. Lo not only recognized the controversial nature of Chu's textual changes but also disagreed with his main interpretation of the work.[24] In addition, the treatise reflects the manner in which Lo interacted with foreign missionaries, at times blatantly, other times subtly. Here below we will describe the form and content of the work from four different perspectives in order to show more comprehensively the level of philosophical synthesis it achieves, keeping in mind the uneasy context of mid-nineteenth-century "Sino-barbarian" interactions.

THE STRUCTURE OF LO'S *EXPLANATIONS AND DISCUSSIONS*

Although the two editions of Lo's work are printed in slightly different formats, both follow the traditional mode of distinguishing the classic text by "raising" it to the very top of the page above the subsequent commentarial notes Lo prepared.[25] Unlike some traditional commentaries, the size of the characters used in both the classical and commentarial texts were the same. A smaller sized character, printed in parallel columns underneath the single-character classic passages, was employed only for brief and selective comments on textual redaction problems.[26] (Please see the example in the appendix.)

Following the text standardized in the Han dynasty as the forty-second chapter of the *Book of Rites* (Li-chi), Lo independently divides the book into three sections. The commencement of each division is highlighted by a break in the commentary, initiated by the simple title in the upper right hand corner of the page, "Sheng-ching," the "Sagely Scriptures." Lo's division of the text indicates his emphasis of three major themes: the essential nature of the *Great Learning*, the meaning of making one's intentions sincere (*ch'eng-ch'i-i*), and the means by which the country should be governed (*chih-kuo*).[27] In the first case, Lo takes a strongly theological slant; in the second, he reveals his preference for the basic position taken up by others, including Wang Yang-ming (1472–1529), in contrast to Chu Hsi and the Sung scholars whom Chu followed. The final case provides a further opportunity for Lo to elaborate his counterpoint to the basic interpretive position of the Sung "Renewal School" (*hsin-hsüeh*), preferring the basic value expressed in the introductory passage of the Old Text *Great Learning*, "lovingly caring for the people" (*ch'in-min*).[28]

By the format and structure of the book Lo identifies himself with the Chinese scholastic circles of his day. But his divisions for the book and even this cursory overview of its contents suggest that he intends to assert his authority as a *chü-jen* scholar of Ruist traditions, conserving and protecting the Old Text traditions of the *Great Learning* from their criticisms by certain Sung dynasty scholars. These were not idle concerns in the late Ch'ing period, for Lo's work was an attempt at delegitimating the imperially authorized text and interpretation of this classic. How this situation shaped his use of the knowledge he gained from the Christian scriptures can only be considered after we have more completely described his complaints against Chu Hsi and his followers.

LO'S ARGUMENTS AGAINST THE SUNG "RENEWAL SCHOOL"

The skeptical boldness of the Sung Ruists in challenging the authenticity of the Han dynasty text of the *Great Learning* underscores the flexible nature and liberal rationality possible within Ruist traditions.[29] Lo felt that Chu Hsi in particular had gone too far in inserting his own philosophical assumptions into the text of the *Great Learning*, causing the loss of the obvious meaning of the older text and the misguidance of generations of Chinese students. The crucial trope in Chu's reorganization of the text comes in the first few phrases of the classic, noted in the italicized word below:[30]

> The Way of the *Great Learning* lies in keeping one's luminous virtue bright, in *renewing* the people, and in coming to rest in perfect goodness.

On the basis of a previous suggestion by the Northern Sung scholar, Ch'eng I, Chu replaced one character, so that the former Old Text passage reading "*lovingly care for* the people" (*ch'in-min*) became "*renewing* the people" (*hsin*-min). His reasons for doing so involved a revolutionary reading of the *Great Learning*, breaking away from the traditional understanding that the text was prepared for a sage emperor and promoting instead a kind of populist understanding that all adults could achieve the goals decribed by this classic. In order to reinforce this understanding of the text, Chu very boldly divided the whole text into an initial classical section and ten chapters of highly reorganized commentarial discussions. Believing that he and others had retrieved from the "corrupted" Han dynasty text a more authentic meaning, Chu promoted his "renewal" approach as the best systematic interpretation of the reorganized classic. On this basis Lo justifiably named Chu's interpretive position the "Renewal School" (*hsin*-hsüeh), for in the symbol of this single character's replacement there was involved a very new school of thought about the basic meaning of the text.

The seriousness Lo expresses in his opposition to these textual gymnastics reveals much about the interpretive options within the Ch'ing Ruist traditions as well as the political tensions within the Ruist hierarchy during the late Ch'ing. Taking a stand on the authenticity of the Han text of the *Great Learning*, Lo rejects Chu's division of the work into a "higher" classical section and "subordinate" commentarial sections. Furthermore, in "changing the Sagely Scriptures" (*kai Sheng-ching*) Chu was regularly ripping passages and sentences out of their original context, forcing his meaning (*ch'iang-chieh*) onto the older text. At other times Chu did not even provide interpretive comments on important terms or phrases. For these reasons Lo at one point lampoons Chu Hsi by means of the title of his commentary, *Chapters and Sentences of the Great Learning* (Ta-hsüeh chang-chü): How could Chu even claim to be offering interpretations of "chapters and sentences" when he so willfully refused to accept its original redaction, constructing his own context for his own interpretations, and still at various places not even providing comments on important terms?[31]

A more serious ideological issue arises where Chu and his followers criticize the idea of "loving care" because it suggests a Mohist-styled egalitarian altruism, even approaching a kind of Buddhist compassion. Lo does not reject the connection with Master Mo, but he thoroughly challenges the connection with Buddhist compassion and its meditative techniques. To him, the followers of

Master K'ung (K'ung-men) differ with the followers of the Ch'eng brothers (Ch'eng-men) precisely on this point. The Ch'eng-Chu tradition promoted "renewing the people" by a semi-ascetic form of meditative discipline based on a self-attained moral knowledge. To the contrary, Lo promotes "lovingly caring for the people," seeking to unite all realms within the harmony decreed by Shang-ti. Consequently, Lo believes the Ch'eng-Chu school is Buddhist in the sense that it denies both the cosmology of the Ruist classics and the source of virtuous orientation that leads to ultimate attainment of appropriate virtues.

Chu Hsi's cavalier attitudes toward this authoritative classic alarm Lo also because of the demagogic effect they could produce on others. In a passage where sections of the Book of Poetry (Shih-ching) are discussed, Lo warns about the arbitrariness of the Renewal School's approach through the words of Mencius:[32]

> Those who explain the odes may not insist on one term so as to do violence to a sentence, nor on a sentence so as to do violence to the general scope.

In Lo's mind Chu was "doing violence" to the original text and its basic meanings. The moral consequences of these distortions Lo indicates through a gloss on another Mencian passage (italicized words mirroring Lo's gloss):[33]

> When words are one-sided, I know how the mind of the speaker is clouded over. When words are extravagant, I know how the mind is fallen and sunken. When words are all-depraved, I know how the mind has departed from principle. When words are evasive, I know how the mind is at its wit's end. These evils growing in the mind, do injury to government, and, displayed in the government, are hurtful to the conduct of affairs.

In this context Lo criticizes Chu for "extrapolating the meaning into extremes" (chih-t'ui-chi), and so implies that Chu's renderings are "extravagant." The fact that in his gloss Lo emphasizes the political implications of using extravagant words suggests that he may have considered Chu's teachings to be one source for the political demoralization of the Ch'ing dynasty in the face of foreign powers in his own day.

This implied political critique of the Sung Renewal School's interpretation of the Great Learning becomes explicit in other sections of Lo's commentary. From the viewpoint of self-cultivation, Lo argues that "renewal" is a result of the "loving care" of the people and rulers rather than the precursor to good and wise government. Similarly, it is the "loving care for people" that promotes the virtues of family and social life, causing renewal in a "great harmonious society" (ta-ho-hui). Only a sage-king is able to move further in self-cultivation to the point where he becomes a partner with Heaven and Earth, cooperating in their virtuous creativity (sheng-jen yü t'ien ti ho te). Politically speaking, Lo firmly argues that the *Great Learning*'s sage is "inwardly a sage and outwardly a king" (*nei-sheng wai-wang*).[34] This view consequently condemns Chu's more populist interpretations as inconsistent with the "original" text and a dangerous source of ethical and political misguidance. Lo cleverly stigmatizes Chu's error in very down-to-earth images. Chu is "searching for a mule while riding one" (*ch'i lu mi lu*); in other words, uncritically assuming what he wants in renewal before understanding it. Another image is that while Chu knows that a boat works well on water and a cart on dry land, he tries to use the boat on land and the cart on water. This criticizes Chu's method as an inherently frustrating misuse of categories in self-cultivation.[35]

Making this kind of criticisms of the imperially authorized standards for classical interpretations would have political repercussions, and Lo is self-conscious about these implications. Those supporting the Renewal School's interpretations consider the doctrine of "loving care for the people" (*ch'in-min*) to be a "heterodox" political ideology, *i-tuan*. This was a very serious offense in the Ch'ing period, and yet Lo presents his case for the *ch'in-min* interpretive position with conviction, adducing classical proofs. In fact, Lo places his teaching in the same category as that of the Roman Catholic Christians described in the seventh dictum of K'ang-hsi's *Sacred Edicts*—as a heterodox teaching, an *i-tuan*.[36] Whether or not his Ruist theological framework enhanced this image in his own mind is not mentioned by Lo, since for him the key issues of the *Great Learning* are matters of procedure in self-cultivation and moral goals in governing. How these are extended into a theological setting and justified by Lo is of particular interest in the light of his known contacts with Christian missionaries.

LO'S INTEGRATED RUIST THEOLOGY

From the very first line of Lo's *Explanations and Discussions* the theological element stands out as a prominent feature. The *Great Learning* is that "learning which makes one a fellow of the Lord-on-High and preserves the lofty decree" (*p'ei Shang-ti pao chün ming chih hsüeh*).[37] Several observations can be made even from this short sentence, which typifies Lo's approach. His choice for conveying the meaning of the term "Lord-on-High" is almost always, but not exclusively, *Shang-ti*. Certainly this reflects his classical Ruist background, since it is a prominent word in the *Book of History* (*Shu-ching*) and *Book of Poetry* for what Legge called the "Supreme Being." Also, the phrase *p'ei Shang-ti* itself is a gloss from the *Book of History* quoted once in the *Great Learning*. So Lo displays a concern to construct his own theological interpretation of the *Great Learning* by direct reference to the Ruist classics.[38]

These approaches were remarkably similar to those expressed by the T'ai-p'ing rulers in the 1850s, whose writings regularly referred to *huang Shang-ti*, "the august God." But the T'ai-p'ing writings included a strong antipathy to classical

Ruist traditions in their earlier periods, and regularly pointed to the prophetic status of their ruler, Hung Hsiu-ch'üan, and others.[39] Of these kinds of prophetic ecstasies we hear nothing from Lo. Instead, his direct appeals return to the classical traditions of pre-imperial China and the Old Text of the *Great Learning*. When comparing his use of *Shang-ti* and classical references including the term in his commentary to those found in Chu Hsi's *Chapters and Sentences of the Great Learning* (this work being about one third the size of the nineteenth-century Ruist's commentary), Lo's distinctive theological bent is highlighted. Chu only refers to "Lord-on-High" in this way three times, one being a classical reference, while Lo uses the term fifty-three times in his commentary, twenty-three being quotations from the main classical sources, and another four glosses on those ancient texts.[40]

On the basis of these sources Lo makes some substantial claims about the nature of the "Lord-on-High," the classical Ruist concept of "God." "Heaven gives birth to humans," and *Shang-ti* is identified with this creative activity. *Shang-ti* is for Lo the "sovereign lord of creative transformation" (*tsao-hua chih chu-tzai*), and as with other spiritual beings in the universe, has no physical form.[41] Even though human beings are "the most intelligent of the myriad living things" (*wan-wu chih ling*), their destiny (*ming*) is known and determined ultimately by *Shang-ti*. Being the most sovereign of all beings, "ultimately without form," *Shang-ti* is therefore also the Way (*Tao*). These basic ideas provide a "tao-logical" foundation for explaining the concept of "God."[42]

More significant and interesting is Lo's conceptual integration of this Ruist *Shang-ti* perspective into his claims about "loving care for the people" and his views on self-cultivation. At the core of Lo's critique of the Renewal School is their account of the human heart. With all their emphasis on "investigating things by exhaustively studying their principles" and "making the will sincere," Lo believes that they are acting only on the basis of their "human heart" (*jen-hsin*) and have not yet attained the liberation of the "heart of *Tao*" (*Tao-hsin*). The contrast between the human heart and the heart of *Tao* is anchored in this famous passage of the *Book of History*:[43]

> The mind of man (*jen-hsin*) is restless, prone (to err); its affinity to what is right (*Tao-hsin*) is small. Be discriminating, be uniform [in the pursuit of what is right], that you may sincerely hold fast the Mean.

In Lo's account, the only way a person could gain the "heart of *Tao*," the moral sensitivity that was not at all identical with the "skin bag" (*p'i-nang*, the "insensate" physical heart, *pu-shih hsin*), is through the descent of *Shang-ti* into the human inner being. This can occur only when an attitude of reverence toward Heaven is maintained, and can be lost by petty persons who do not do so (a gloss from the *Analects* 16.8, *hsiao-jen pu wei T'ien*).[44] This "descent of *Shang-ti* into the inner being" (*Shang-ti chiang chung*) is a gloss of another classical passage in the *Book of History*, and appears in many settings in Lo's treatise. Only by this relational fulfillment with the taological God can a human being gain the authentically sincere will that will "keep one's luminous virtue bright," the first step in attaining the Way of the *Great Learning*.[45]

About the claim that this experience of the indwelling presence of *Shang-ti* is the crucial orienting power of human life Lo leaves no question. What one sees, hears, smells, and tastes all takes on new dimensions through this concrete experience of taological synchronization. Only through this living encounter can a person's hearts be made open and pliable, so that the brilliant virtue of a person can mature and be unobscured. Ultimately, one attains to a constant nature (*heng-hsing*) that regularly loves what is best and hates evil.[46] In addition, one truly experiences becoming "one body" (*i-ti*) with myriad things as well as *Shang-ti*, a theme mirroring important ontic descriptions by Wang Yang-ming. On this experiential foundation people can then authentically care for those around them, having received the "lofty mandate of God" as the context in which they must embody the virtues created within their "original heart" (*pen-hsin*).[47]

It is *Shang-ti* who also honors and blesses the virtuous, and so the way of embodying loving care for others, different for the various roles and positions people must take, is enhanced by the destiny the Ruist God sets for these virtuous people. Government is established through the extrapolation of the virtues of familial piety, and so from the core of loving care for others, the nation can be brought into the great harmony envisioned by previous sages.[48] Only the sage will attain the full understanding of these matters, and so ought to be the ruler, but everyone can know the experience of "*Shang-ti* descending into their inner being" and therefore live in harmony with the enlightened mandate. In the end, the virtuous sage does become a "fellow of God" (*p'ei Shang-ti*) and by this means "preserves the lofty mandate."[49] To risk all this by misunderstanding and distorting the teachings of the *Great Learning* is to threaten the world with chaos and to lose the mandate of Heaven. In Lo's view, one can deceive oneself and so deceive Heaven and *Shang-ti*, allowing the "corrupting demon" (*hsieh-mo*) to steal away what good has been planned for human cultivation.[50] Therefore Lo could not have been more intent on opposing Chu Hsi's influences[51] and those who were in agreement with his interpretations: the brothers Ch'eng I[52] and Ch'eng Hao,[53] another Sung scholar named Huang K'an (1152–1221),[54] the Ming scholar Ts'ui Hsien (1478–1541),[55] and the Ch'ing scholar Hu Wei (1633–1714)[56] among others. Believing that he is returning to the fount of sagely wisdom and attacking its enemies, Lo is an informed fundamentalist Ruist with a strong theo-taological philosophical justification for his arguments. His legitimations are drawn completely from the recognized authoritative texts of the Ruist tradition, and so are fully supported by numerous proofs not only in the *Book of History* and the *Book of Poetry*, but also from the *Book of Changes*, the *Mencius*, various editions of the

Book of Rites, the Classic of Filial Piety, the Analects, and others.[57] Nothing could be more formidably Ruist and yet so fundamentally monotheistic.

CHRISTIAN INFLUENCES IN LO'S TREATISE

When we compare Legge's description of the contents of Lo's treatise on the *Great Learning* with the much richer taological system Lo presents, it could be asked at first glance if there is in fact any real or substantial Christian influence in his work at all. Legge had claimed that "[Lo] most vehemently impugns nearly every judgment of Chu Hsi; but in his own exhibitions of the meaning he blends many ideas of the Supreme Being and of the condition of human nature, which he had learned from the Christian Scriptures."[58] If Lo's *Shang-ti* does have sharper defining qualities of creatorship and spiritual form, the conception has nothing to do with a distinctively trinitarian doctrine or any statement related to salvation through substitutionary sacrifice. Legge's emphasis on Lo's ideas about the "Supreme Being" was in fact meant to focus on this more general feature.[59] Again, admitting that Lo does point out how humans may "lose the Way" through a lack of reverential awe expressed toward Heaven, thereby losing also the indwelling presence of *Shang-ti*, Lo nevertheless supports this and other claims with passages from the Ruist classics.[60] Any Ruist scholar would find his explanation compelling, and yet it does not explain the doctrine of sin or sanctification in anything like a Christian anthropology.

What Lo highlights in a manner that is very Protestant-like, almost syncretic, is the indwelling presence of *Shang-ti* as the crux of self-cultivation. While the process of self-cultivation would suggest something more along the lines of a Catholic pattern of meritorious works, the indwelling presence of God moves the religious sensibility away from an altar in a sanctuary to the personal heart. Reminding one of things evangelically Protestant, Lo in one place employs the distinctive metaphor that *Shang-ti* makes the human inner being a temple (*tien*). Here, unquestionably, was a borrowing from the Christian Bible, since the only other classical place where *tien* appears is in the *Book of Poetry*, but within completely different contexts and with dissimilar connotations.[61] Convinced of the power of reverential awe in the presence of an abiding Deity, Lo speaks in Christian metaphors about a Ruist form of spiritual regeneration.

The only place where Lo explicitly refers to "Westerners" (*t'ai-hsi chih jen*) is in a discussion of the seventh-day rest, a very outstanding temporal element of the Christian "Sabbath culture." But once more Lo employs it in a manner unexpected by the Christian reader in the context of a discussion of daily renewal (*jih-hsin*). "Daily renewal" should not only have a personal dimension but also a social one, and in this context Lo mentions the ritual solemnity of the seventh-day rest among "Westerners." His own support for this interpretation comes from one of the commentaries on the twenty-fourth hexagram of the *Book of Changes* (*I-*

ching), the hexagram "Return." There it cryptically states, "In seven days comes his return—such is the movement of the heavenly [revolution]."[62] Interested in attaining and maintaining a great harmony among all beings, Lo believed these heavenly revolutions were models for social rhythms which Westerners had successfully imitated. Whether he felt their model was fully worthy of imitation was not explicitly stated in this work, and nothing more was mentioned about its religious significance among non-Chinese Christians. For Lo it was a matter of cosmic synchronization, part and parcel of the mandate of *Shang-ti* for the human world.

Perhaps the more subtle influence is played out in Lo's regular reference, especially near the end of his work, to the "undefiled" and "completely sacred" character of the "sacred studies" in the *Great Learning*.[63] Here his fundamentalist Ruist trope is mirroring the claims made by missionaries for their own Bible, but Lo utilizes it to castigate the textual distortions of the Sung Renewal School. He is apparently not interested in a comparative religious project between Ruists and Christians, especially in the context of the debate over the reliability of the text of the *Great Learning*. For Lo was fighting a battle to maintain the sanctity and authority of the Ruist traditional world in an age of its impending decay. Even though he was employing new ways to articulate it, sometimes in a manner close to Protestant rhetoric, Lo never left behind his commitment to an original Ruist vision of *Shang-ti* and the ancient sages.

Lo's way was a mediating position, still Ruist in essence but manifesting personal interest in Christianity and cultural influences from its teachings. As far as we can know, he did not adopt a Christian perspective as a Chinese scholar. But there are hints of other transformative changes in his attitudes. One clue comes from the deletion of a phrase in the preface to the 1859 edition of his work, the other from the context of that second edition's publication. In the former case, Lo (or a family member?) dropped the italicized phrase seen below in its original phrasing:

> Master Meng . . . revered the Old Scriptures, seeking to return to the former transmissions, [so that] Chinese and foreigners might hear them. *No matter whether they were [from among] the Nine Barbarians or the eight Man tribes*, [they could] intimately know the Way and use literary means to transmit it.

Did he drop the phrase because of a new respect for "foreign barbarians"? Or was it because there were allied forces holding Canton at the time, and so he feared political repercussions to his allusive and derogatory reference to foreigners?[64] No further hints clarifying his motives are given on this point. The context of his later work will be explained later, when an important European sociological view of Ruist traditions is challenged by use of Lo's later work.

DRAWN IN FROM THE MARGINS OF RUIST LIFE AND THOUGHT: JAMES LEGGE'S CLASSICAL EXEGESIS

Because he taught the *Four Books* to Chinese students for more than a dozen years before writing his own translations and commentaries to them, Legge had time and opportunity to weigh Lo Chung-fan's claims against some of the most influential commentators of Chinese traditions.[65] Indeed, it is because Legge took this scholarly effort and noted Lo's unusual stances that a trace of Lo's works was left for posterity. How Legge himself responded to the major issues of the *Great Learning* and the comments on them within Lo's *Explanations and Discussions* cannot be thoroughly discussed here. Still, a number of details in Legge's commentaries are pertinent in illustrating one of the ways in which he, as a missionary-scholar, could participate in the Ch'ing Ruist traditions on his own terms and be respected by contemporary Chinese literati for doing so.

Although Legge in 1861 chose to present the *Great Learning* in the form of Chu Hsi's reorganized text, the one authorized by the Ch'ing imperial court, he felt compelled to disagree with Chu Hsi's basic interpretation of the work.[66] In this Legge undoubtedly was influenced by Lo's critical arguments against Chu. Both in his decisions about the meaning of the title of the work and in maintaining the Old Text's phrase of "loving the people" in the first phrases of the work, Legge obviously reflected positions promoted in Lo's commentary.[67] Noting at times the difference between "Chu Hsi's arrangement" and the "old arrangement" of the *Great Learning*, Legge in the end criticized Chu Hsi's epistemological claims as "too extravagant" and yet also suggested that Lo's insistence on "harmonizing" diverse elements with the theme of "loving the people" was forced.[68] In spite of his disagreement with some of Lo's judgments, Legge found Lo to be in agreement with his criticism of Chu Hsi's claims about "perfecting knowledge," and explicitly followed Lo's interpretations on the critical phrase, "correcting things" (*ko wu*).[69]

This interaction with Lo's unusual commentary is only one part of Legge's investigation and evaluation of the text. In the end, Legge assumes a position on the value of the *Great Learning* that justifies the adulations of many Ruist scholars and the praises of the French academician and translator of the *Four Books*, Guilliame Pauthier (d. 1873). From another angle, the reductionistic judgment of Charles Gutzlaff (1803–51)—that the *Great Learning* consists only of "a few commonplace rules for the maintenance of a good government"—Legge finds both imprecise and inadequate. While criticizing important aspects of its overall plan for self-cultivation and government, he cites four "seminal principles" that may well be "commonplace," but are also "eternal verities."[70] Based on the criticisms he has gleaned from other Chinese scholars as well as from his own research, Legge assumes a critical appreciation of the work.[71]

This "critical appreciation" includes some reflective judgments on European and British governments and societies from the perspective of the

Great Learning. Legge specifically notes the Ruist emphasis on the exemplary role of those who are in authority, employing it to support Christian ideals of leadership as well as to criticize British bureaucratic institutions and militarism.[72] Here the prophetic role of his own Dissenter Christian convictions are evident, but there is also a suggestion of accommodation of those Ruist principles that hint at a selective harmonization between Ruist and Christian worldviews. Here is a pivotal issue: Could Legge as a Christian missionary be accepted as a scholar of the Ruist canon by Chinese scholars themselves? Did the Chinese Ruist traditions have that kind of flexibility and tolerance?

In a period when European and North American military and mercantile interests were forcing the Ch'ing dynasty to change under heavy-handed policies and treaty provisions, it is easy to imagine that most foreign missionaries would be quickly identified as representatives of these threatening forces. Legge nevertheless was able in 1861 to travel up the East River in Kwangtung Province and prove himself to be an "educated" missionary.[73] When he and members of his group spoke, they sought out audiences in the environment of the local temples, preferring those dedicated to Confucius. By this means these "foreign teachers" responded to the ritual assumptions of Chinese society imbued with Ruist ideals, and so, more often than not, were allowed to speak, and then invited to visit the local teachers or other leaders in the villages and cities they entered. Although at times they were also attacked as unwanted foreigners and deprived of any chance to present themselves publicly, Legge made it a principle to arrange for proper visits to the local civil officials whenever possible. In one case his timely quotation from the *Mencius* so impressed the emissaries of the local mandarin, that initial resistance was immediately overcome, gifts were exchanged, and an audience granted. Even during a time of social upheaval and growing antagonisms against foreigners, a foreign missionary who could demonstrate understanding of the rituals and principles of the Ruist canon was accepted as a honored visitor.

Four years after this event the Ruist scholar Wang T'ao (1828–97), who had begun working with Legge late in 1862 on his translation and commentary to the *Book of History*, wrote a tribute to Legge's Chinese classical scholarship. Wang had worked with other missionaries and had been baptized in Shanghai, but traveled south in 1862 because of the threat to his life due to some questionable contacts he had with the T'ai-p'ing forces. A marginalized Ruist scholar in his own right, Wang would later become a significant figure arguing for reforms, after spending over two years with Legge and others in England, Scotland, and France. But already by 1865 Wang could claim that Legge's position on knotty points on the historical reliability of the *Book of History* was "equitable and impartial, and should be able to put a stop to all disputes." In essence, Wang was claiming that Legge had answered questions that Chinese scholars should take very seriously. He was a participant in their own scholarly traditions, and so Wang referred to him as a *hsi-ju,* "a Western Ruist (scholar)."[74]

But what about Legge's views on the imperial worship? In 1850 Legge published approvingly an English letter of his co-pastor, Ho Tsun-sheen (1817–71), which ended with the following statement:[75]

> I wish that there were many temples or places of worship in China to *Shang Te*, for then it would not be a heathen country, and when His word is spread abroad, they will surely come to be built. Then the Emperor will cease to offer sacrifices to him, and all will know that He is no respector of persons; and, from the Emperor down to the multitutde of the people, all will seek His favour through our Lord Jesus Christ.

Could Ruist traditions accept such a bold-faced hypothetical scenario, a future when the imperial worship would be reduced to prayers like those which Legge and others later offered on top of the open Altar of Heaven in the southern section of the imperial capital? To answer this question, we have to examine the forces that defined the boundaries of the Ruist tradition.

THREE TENSIONS SHAPING THE BOUNDARIES OF LATER RUIST TRADITIONS

1. A Tension between Historical Actuality and Canonical Content

In his work now entitled *The Religion of China*, Max Weber depicted the "Confucian tradition" as one "transmitted only through the study of the old classics, whose absolutely canonical prestige and purified forms of orthodoxy went without question." Although he recognized that there were in fact Ruist literati who opposed the currently accepted norms and employed their classics to support these claims, Weber believed these were unusual cases. Any alternatives of this sort were ultimately ineffective against the indomitable powers of Confucian traditionalism.[76] This position would suggest that Lo and Legge were fated to remain at the very marginal fringes of the Ruist traditions, if they were in fact allowed to participate at all. One would hardly expect them to exist, much less to have some influence, under these conditions.

Yet critics of Weber's judgment point out its weakness. How could it account for the major changes in the scholarly discourse on the Ruist canon in the latter decades of the Ch'ing, leading to the otherwise unexpected ascendency of a reform-minded Ruist school led by the controversial politician and Ruist scholar K'ang Yu-wei (1859–1928)? If traditionalism was a strong force in Chinese traditional society, which no major sinologists or sociologists deny, there were nevertheless certain Ruist ideals that could and did catalyze changes in the Ruist canon and its accompanying ideology during the Ch'ing dynasty. C. K. Yang refers to the tension between "academic ideals" and historical realities; S. N. Eisenstadt speaks of a "transcendental tension." Both recognize that there is an active metaphysical element in "Confucianism," particularly in its Neo-Confucian forms, which Weber simply did not register in his account.[77]

If we assume that the Ruist canonical scriptures did possess an authoritative appeal to those who studied them, in what way could we reconstruct Weber's vision of "Confucianism's indomitable traditionalism" in order to account for this active metaphysical dimension of the texts? C. K. Yang has fairly successfully outlined a response:

> In confrontation with the world, Confucianism . . . kept harking back to the ideal qualities of the *tao* (governing principle of the cosmic and social order) and the 'golden past' when the *tao* was thought to be in perfect operation. This meant that the given world was at ethical variance with the *tao* and the "golden past." . . . What became accepted by the Confucian was [not the world *as given*, but] the world *as interpreted* by the Confucian orthodoxy. . . . Confucian rationalism and asceticism stemmed from this tension or variance between the *tao* and worldly realities, especially during historical crises.

Yang's description of the Ruist value system can actually augment our earlier account of Lo's monotheistic reading of the *Great Learning*. Precisely because *Shang-ti* is the Tao, there is a dynamic power to reconstruct the world under the leadership of a benevolent emperor who "lovingly cares for the people." Though some Ruists would debate the metaphysical equation Lo asserted, others would seriously consider these claims precisely because they were built upon proof texts within the canonical literature

2. A Tension between Radical Traditionalism and Forms of Self-Cultivation

The Ruist traditionalism which Weber deemed to be inconquerable was in fact transformed in subtle as well as radical ways throughout its long history. This was due in part to questions of the *relative authority* of various texts, and the interpretations that arose because of a repositioning of the approach to self-cultivation made possible through the shift of emphasis upon new canonical texts. So, for example, Chu Hsi's reorganization of the *Great Learning* transformed it from being a text dedicated to training future emperors to a text appealing to the sagely possibilities in every adult. Once this text became an authoritative standard of Ruist orthodoxy, the redirection of Ruist political philosophy and its accompanying forms of self-cultivation was complete. But when a minor official like Lo Chung-fan challenged that official tradition as overstated and corrupt because of unjustified textual manipulations, he was acting in the interests of mainline Ruist traditions, and challenging the relative authority of this particular text and its accompanying practices. Legge on his part was doing a similar task on a much broader plane, tackling the whole of the Ruist canon and not just one of its major texts. Precisely because the Ruist tradition is more open, more complex, and more variable than many other religious traditions, it could permit these shifts in emphasis and still retain its anchor in "the Tradition."[78]

Three kinds of shifts in emphasis can be identified within later Ruist traditions. Sometimes these shifts reached the threshold of change because of more radical challenges to the reliability of the texts themselves.[79] Other times the context of crisis, the reassertion of the Tao in a crumbling world order, catalyzed new insights into the ancient texts that prompted new forms of self-cultivation. One of these new forms of self-cultivation, set in opposition to the intellectualist school of Chu Hsi, was the meditative form revealed in the recorded dialogues of Wang Yang-ming.[80] But in the case of Lo Chung-fan, his approach reasserted the importance of certain canonical texts, but also offered a new style of self-cultivation, following lines of Ruist traditions which corrected the extremes of Wang Yang-ming's anti-intellectual leanings.[81]

Still another dimension of self-cultivation, originating from oral teachings handed down from teacher to student, began to take on new importance once the reliability of certain Ruist scriptures was questioned. In the case of the New Text schools of the Ming and Ch'ing dynasties, oral traditions developed from reflections on the Kung-yang commentary to the *Spring and Autumn Annals* (*Ch'un-ch'iu*). This text became the "classical deposit" that had hidden within it special insights into the sagely way. It was claimed that the new teachings could be made available only through the esoteric teachings of a master who had already gained an understanding of these subtle sayings and could apply them to the whole of the tradition. It was precisely this kind of experiential claim that justified the reformist teachings of K'ang Yu-wei, who for a hundred-day period in 1898 effectively governed much of the Ch'ing empire. Compared with K'ang's later utopian vision, Legge's and Ho's Christian projections appear less radical and more reasonable, even though K'ang's approach was based on this fundamental critique of the traditional Ruist canon.[82]

In the light of these kinds of nontraditional self-cultivation methods, Ruist scholars were free to take a more critical approach to the texts and seek harmonization with the wisdom of the sages through personal forms of discipline. In this sense, to quote Eisenstadt, Ruist traditions, both in their classical and Neo-Confucian forms,[83]

> emphasized very strongly a non-traditionalistic, reflexive definition of the nature of the cosmic order and of human existence. This definition contained within itself a continuous principled awareness of the tension between the cosmic ideal and any given reality of the imperfectibility of the mundane order in general and the political one in particular. . . . [There were] great personal tensions involved both in the attempts to maintain such harmony through proper conduct and attitude, . . . necessitat[ing] a very stringent and reflexive

self discipline, as well as . . . the development of a critical attitude to the existing mundane world in general and the political order in particular.

Certainly Ruist scholars who felt this tension, one very evident in the commentary of Lo Chung-fan, might be particularly attracted to a similarly "critical attitude" expressed through Christian missionary teachings and the oral traditions of the Christian "sage" Jesus. The very possibility of this kind of openness within the Ruist traditions, stimulated by a selective use of canonical literature and realized in special forms of self-cultivation, leads to another sort of tension.

3. A Tension between Institutional Mechanisms of Control and Intellectual Autonomy

The burden of Eisenstadt's criticism of Weber is to demonstrate not only that there existed a transcendental tension within the very heart of Ruist traditions, but also that the powers of control were not so much in the vague forces of "traditionalistic" bureaucracies as in a more complex and hierarchical form of imperial dominance. Ruist literati were immediately responsible to the emperor, but were not allowed much access to each other. In this way, collusion was not easily engineered, and the Ruist scholar-official was held personally responsible for the affairs under his jurisdiction.[84]

On the other hand, this form of control also gave the literati much leeway in which to structure their personal and intellectual lives. One of the remarkably autonomous regions of the civil official's life developed in the establishment of schools and academies. Here the Ruist leader was his own master, developing interpretations of and insights into the Ruist tradition. Literati who preferred scholarly pursuits to the mundane chores of bureaucracy could request sinecures that would provide them with the time and support necessary to establish their own academies. Chu Hsi, for example, only worked three full years as a bureaucrat within the Sung empire's system; the rest of the time, he was placed in positions that permitted him to study and teach. This "liberal tradition" within Ruist circles provided opportunities to discover new modes of self-cultivation, which could in turn be promoted by authoritative figures within the broader Ruist-influenced society.

AN EVALUATION OF LO'S AND LEGGE'S METAPHYSICS IN LIGHT OF THE RUIST TENSIONS

Given these tensions, it is intriguing to consider the second edition of Lo's *Explanations and Discussions*. It appears as the third and last section in a morality book (*shan-shu*) entitled *Chüeh-she ch'üan-shan lu*, (Records on Comprehensive Goodness By [The Master Who] Enlightens the Age.) The preface is signed by "the Master from Nanhai who is Willing to Enlighten the Age," and may have been a pseudonym for Lo himself.[85]

The first and largest portion of the work covers themes in meritorious virtuous life and what happens when these works are not performed. Starting from the loving care expressed between parents and sons, the text builds a vision of meritorious goodness which includes humane familial and social relationships, extending to teachers and students, the spiritual world, friendship, speech, sexual relationships, business, the treatment of animals, concubines, and servants.[86] Starting from the principle of "lovingly caring for the people," the Master Willing to Enlighten provides directions for virtuous life in this variety of relationships, often quoting from other literary sources, and occasionally adding his own commentary after various sections.

A host of famous Ruist scholars appear as well as some less known figures, notably Ssu-ma Ch'ien, Han Yü, Chu Hsi, Wang Yang-ming, and Ch'en Pai-sha (Ch'en Hsien-chang, 1428–1500), the last being the only Cantonese Ruist to be officially honored in the temples dedicated to Confucius. As one reads through the moral treatises, there is a growing sense that a community of like-minded Ruists is being formed across the ages to promote the "loving care" of the people, a new *Tao-t'ung* or "transmission of the Way" supporting Lo's own form of a monotheistic moral metaphysics. In the case of Ch'en Pai-sha this is particularly significant, because he also "cherished the thought that human life itself would continue even after death in the company of Heaven and Earth."[87] Not only is there a strong spiritual vision incorporated into this moral philosophy, but it anticipates Lo's later syncretic system. It seems that Lo's religious readings of Ruist traditions are not so eccentric and certainly not without precedents. Significantly, the first section ends in a blessing expressed toward Huang T'ien Shang-ti, "God of the august Heavens," the "Great Name" adopted in the imperial worship in the prayers of the Chia-ching emperor of the Ming dynasty.[88]

The second portion of this morality book is a collection of proverbial statements culled from the writings of a group of notable Ruists. These do not necessarily follow any pattern as in the first section, but they involve personal testimonies of well-lived experiences, covering sayings from as early as the Han dynasty (the scholar Tung Chung-shu) to the Ch'ing (Lo Chung-fan himself).[89] Very notably Ch'en Pai-sha and Wang Yang-ming appear several times followed by commentary. The famous "Western Inscription" of Chang Tsai (1020–77) is also included, supplementing their more flexible and liberal Ruist visions.

From another angle we should ask if the Ruist traditions Lo brought together as his own rendition of the "transmission of the Way" constituted a cultural bridge accessible to "sympathetic" missionary approaches that made use of the classical Ruist concept of *Shang-ti*. It seems more than coincidental that the Nan-hai district of Kwangtung province was also the home of Ho Tsun-sheen (1817–71), the first modern Chinese Protestant theologian.[90] Also the fact that the later reformist, K'ang Yu-wei, another Nanhai man, argued several decades later for a form of Ruist religion that included Sunday services like the Protestants, does not now sound so strange. In fact, the *Chüeh-she ch'üan-shan lu* does actually provide a ritual prayer to be used in community meetings, a suggestion for meeting regularly, and a set of "ten commandments" of its own making to instigate exactly this kind of religious institutionalization of his taological Ruist spirituality.[91]

Under these kinds of institutional adaptations and new teachings, it is not so strange that Wang T'ao, when taken by James Legge to Oxford in 1867, would claim (along lines suggested by Sung Ruists) that, in the "East" as well as the "West," "there are sages whose hearts and principles are the same."[92] The Way was the same for both, but their expressions differed. In the case of Lo, his work was a syncretic product, moved by the "breaking symbols," to use Robert Neville's words, which opened new doors of transcendence in the Ruist classical vocabulary.[93] Not only was there a viable set of religious symbols available for his use in this creative transformation of the meaning of the *Great Learning*, but Lo's further efforts in *Chüeh-she ch'üan-shan lu* also point toward a vaster Ruist tradition stocked full of spiritually connotative symbols.

On the other hand, Lo's form of Ruist spirituality and the traditional Ruist precedents it draws upon suggest that Weber's and others' sociological readings of "Confucianism" are too narrow. But it is not only Weber's sociological analyses that seem restrictive. Tu Wei-ming, Yü Ying-shih, and other contemporary Chinese scholars also present a scenario of Ruist metaphysical possibilities that are too narrow, too tenaciously attached to a twentieth-century readings of certain Ruist traditions that do not fully account for the religious repertoire actually available in their classical and Ming-Ch'ing commentarial traditions.[94] That these religious Ruists may constitute only marginal or minor traditions need not be denied. Yet the fact that some of these traditions did interact positively with Christian teachings, and may have even acted as a culturally sympathetic bridge for Chinese openness toward Christian claims, is an issue regularly denied by too many contemporary Chinese scholars. Even though there are many different Ruist expressions, there is in Lo Chung-fan's taological system a Way very close to, and possibly a preamble to, a Chinese Christian Way.

This kind of institutional openness within Ruist traditions exemplifies the pliability of the Ruist canonical traditions, making Legge's own interests in these traditions as a point of contact between Christians and Ruist scholars all the more sensible. In fact, the institutional flexibility Legge himself experienced after becoming a professor in Oxford provided him the further opportunity to consider his growing respect for "Confucius" in the full light of his missionary and sinological experiences. Like Lo, Legge chose a middling way, and finally clarified his own Ruist-Christian response to Confucius in a sermon of 1886. "Confucius" was his "Master," as was the case with many other Chinese, but Legge added to this attachment his relationship with Christ, whom he called with the apostle Paul "both his Master and his Lord, in the highest sense of that term." Whereas in his early missionary career Legge had taken a far more antagonistic stance against the Chinese sage, he too found a Way that opened a new understanding of Christianity for Ruist scholars and an accommodating approach to Ruist traditions for Chinese Christians.[95]

In summary, in spite of sociological and Chinese interpretations of Ruist traditions as traditionalist and ultimately disinterested in religious concerns, Ming and Ch'ing dynastic expressions of Ruists traditions show a remarkable openness toward metaphysical realms. Not only did the restorationist attitudes of the Ming emperors restore in a fundamentalist turn a strongly monotheistic precedent in imperial worship, but this worship also set the stage for some unexpected developments in a monotheistic moral metaphysics within the Ruist traditions themselves. In addition, it provided the basis for a cross-cultural entrance into the tradition by "outsiders" like Legge who proved themselves and their writings worthy of serious consideration.

NOTES

1. Notable cases of demotion for displaying conciliatory attitudes to foreigners during this period included the sacking of the famous geographer and, at one point, the governor of Fukien Province, Hsu Chi-yü (1795–1873), as well as the imperial Prince Kung (I-hsin, 1833–98), founder of the Ch'ing empire's Foreign Affairs office, the Tsung-li ya-men. See Arthur W. Hummel, ed., *Eminent Chinese of the Ch'ing Period* (Washington, D.C.: Government Printing Office, 1943), pp. 309–10 and 380–84. This work will subsequently be abbreviated as ECCP. Hsü was known to have regular contact with an American missionary named David Adeel (Ya Pei-li, 1804–46), from whom he gleaned geographical and religious information about the Middle East and North America, showing a relatively extensive knowledge of Israel's early history taken from biblical sources. See Hsü's often reprinted *Ying-huan chih-lüeh* (A Brief Record of the Surrounding Seas), first published in 1850, and the sixth *chüan*, which includes numerous references to biblical data. For information on Adeel, see Alexander Wylie's *Memorials of Protestant Missionaries to the Chinese* (Shanghai: American Presbyterian Press, 1867), pp. 72–75.

2. James Legge, *The Chinese Classics with a Translation, Critical and Exegetical Notes, Prolegomena and Copious Indexes* (Oxford: Clarendon Press, 1893), 2nd ed., 1: 25–26. Original edition published in Hong Kong in 1861. Subsequent references to the work will be abbreviated as "CC1," the number standing for the volume in the series.

3. The influence of Liang's writings on Hung has been creatively described in Jonathan Spence's *God's Chinese Son: The Taiping Heavenly Kingdom*

of Hong Xiuquan (Hammersmith, U.K.: HarperCollins, 1996), pp. 51–65. An ear-lier work by Eugene P. Boardman describes the content of Liang's work in outline form. See his *Christian Influence upon the Ideology of the Taiping Rebellion, 1851–1864* (New York: Octagon Books, 1972). See also the more substantial dis-cusssion on this issue in Jen Yu-wen, *The Taiping Revolutionary Movement* (New Haven: Yale University Press, 1973).

4. Legge had received an honorary doctorate of divinity from the University of New York, which no longer exists, in the United States in 1841 for some unspecified efforts as a missionary to Chinese people. Receiving the same honor from the same institution was the older and more established American missionary to China, Elijah Bridgeman (1801–61), the editor for many years of the *Chinese Repository* (1831–50), described in Wylie, *Memorials*, pp. 68-72.

5. An initial study discussing the importance of Lo's writings is Lauren Pfister's article, "Some New Dimensions in the Study of the Works of James Legge (1815–1897): Part II," *Sino-Western Cultural Relations Journal* 13 (1992): 42–44. A more thorough study of Lo's work was also written by Lauren Pfister for the International Conference on the History of Christianity in China, held in Hong Kong in October 1996. The article is entitled "The Way is One, but Its Expressions Are Many: 19th-Century Protestant Influences on Ruist Spirituality in Guangzhou."

6. Legge explained his indebtedness to Ho's convictions, publishing a let-ter by Ho in the final appendix to his *Letters on the Rendering of the Name God in Chinese . . .* (Hong Kong: Hongkong Register Office, 1850). The infamous "Term Question" debates, focusing on how to render properly the idea of "God" in the Christian Bible among other problems, became issues of public interest between 1847 to 1852, but were never decisively resolved even in later public discussions of the problems. Helpful summaries of the problem are found in S. W. Williams's early article, "The Controversy among the Protestant Missionaries on the Proper Translation of the Words God and Spirit into Chinese," *Bibliotheca Sacra* 35 (1878): 732–78, and Douglas G. Spelman's "Christianity in Chinese: The Protestant Term Question," in *Papers on China*, vol. 22A (Cambridge, Mass.: Harvard University Press, 1969), pp. 25-52. Williams covers many of the com-plexities of the problem, but defends the position opposing Legge's commit-ments. Legge offers his own brief summary in the initial portions of *A Letter to Prof. Max Muller Chiefly on the Translation into English of the Chinese Terms Ti and Shang Ti* (London: Trübner & Co. Pub., 1880).

7. See Norman J. Girardot, *The Victorian Translation of China: James Legge, Missionary Tradition, Sinological Orientalism and the Comparative Science of Religion in the Nineteenth Century* (Berkeley: University of California Press, forth-coming). See also my completed book manuscript, tentatively entitled *Dutybound: James Legge and the Scottish Encounter with China: Reassessing the Influences of Chinese Missionary Scholarship, the Development of Victorian Sinology,*

and the Character of Chinese Protestantism, which is in the final stages of assessment by a consortium of presses.

8. Antonio S. Cua, "The Concept of *Li* in Confucian Moral Theory," in Robert E. Allinson, ed., *Understanding the Chinese Mind: The Philosophical Roots* (Hong Kong: Oxford University Press, 1989), pp. 209–35.

9. See the prayers in Legge's *The Notions of the Chinese Concerning God and Spirits* . . . (Hong Kong: Hongkong Register Office, 1852), pp. 24–31, 24–26, 40–42. A number of them were important enough to Legge that he retranslated them for the first university textbook on Chinese religions, *The Religions of China* (Oxford, 1880), pp. 43–51.

10. See Legge, *Notions*, pp. 43–50. Legge actually debated with the American Presbyterian missionary Bishop William Boone (ca. 1815–64), described in Wylie's *Memorials*, pp. 99–102. In the process of discussing the origins of the Five *Ti*, or Five "Lords," Legge demonstrated from other Chinese sources that the account of the Ming religious reforms presented in an influential earlier work by the French priest Claude de Visdelou (1656–1737) was very inaccurate in many details. See a broader account of Visdelou's life and works in Louis Pfister, ed., *Notices biographiques et bibliographiques sur les Jésuites de l'ancienne mission de Chine, 1552–1773* (Shanghai: La Mission Catholique, 1932), pp. 452–57.

11. Legge, *Notions*, p. 25.

12. See Legge's discussion and translation of these prayers of the Ming dynasty Chia-ching emperor and others accompanied with the original Chinese text in *Notions*, pp. 25–31, and retranslated later in his *Religions of China*, pp. 43–53. It is significant to note that the earlier translations in 1852 did receive some careful refinement in the 1880 edition, including the changing of "creating work" to "making work," slightly de-emphasizing the Christian liturgical echo. Still Legge retained the same interpretation of the imperial ritual throughout the rest of his life, greatly influencing his later re-evaluation of the status of Master K'ung, as will be briefly mentioned below.

Two other items of interpretive interest deserve mention here. In his 1852 *Notions* Legge provides an extensive footnote on the theological metaphor, "as a potter," pointing out how prevalent it was in Chinese prayers to *Shang-ti*. Always thinking comparatively, he did not fail to point out certain biblical parallels as well. (See his *Notions*, p. 30.) Anticipating the reactions of some detractors in 1880, Legge also adds a note to explain the character *chao* as the one Chinese word used to describe the power of creating in the Chinese account of Genesis (the Hebrew word, *bara'*). In fact, he was referring to the rendering in the Delegates' version of the 1850s, one of the major Bible translations used during his missionary career. The more popular Union version (*Ho-ho pen*) of 1919 preferred to use the term *tsao* for the same phrase, and so Legge's claim may appear wrong or anachronistic. (See his footnote in *Religions of China*, pp. 48–49.)

13. In his *Notions*, Legge made explicit comparisons between these imperial religious practices and Solomonic and Roman Catholic rituals. In the latter case, there are explicit antipapist criticisms, but they are remarkably muted for their own time in that they affirmed the monotheistic basis of both Ruist and Catholic practices in spite of their other "vitiated" forms of worship. See his *Notions*, pp. 27, 57–59. Other comparisons with classical Jewish forms of religion appear in the same work, pp. 25, 40.

When Legge's position is described as equating *Shang-ti* with "the general (and Christian) idea" of "God," we are reflecting a rhetorical point in Legge's arguments that continued to be a source of misunderstanding. Legge did not mean to identify the Chinese "Supreme Being" with the "Trinitarian God" of Christianity, but rather intended to place it as equivalent to the ideas expressed in the Greek term *theos* and the Hebrew term *ᶜelohim*. Sometimes his own rhetoric was his greatest obstacle for clarifying this point.

14. Legge distinguished the word "God" from the name "Jehovah" in line with doctrines taught in the seventeenth-century Scottish *Westminster Confessions*. These identified the name "Jehovah" with the self-existent eternal being of biblical revelation, while the word "God" was more vaguely associated with natural theological images of a supreme ruler and, perhaps in some cases, a creator or maker. Walter Medhurst (1796–1857), another British missionary colleague from the London Missionary Society, had suggested similar claims at an earlier time, but was never as explicit as Legge.

15. These are described in the Ming dynastic history, the *Ming-shih, chüan* 46, and critically evaluated in Jeffrey Meyer's excellent study, *The Dragons of Tiananmen: Beijing as a Sacred City* (Columbia: University of South Carolina Press, 1991), pp. 80–85. Meyer takes this discrete worship to be directed toward the various spirits of Heaven, Earth, and other realms, but does point out the interpretive ambiguities among the Ruist commentators on these points. In agreement with Legge's basic position he also identifies a distinct hierarchy of spiritual beings in the Ruist cosmology, one that placed Shang-ti at its apex.

16. See a discussion of this particular issue in Kai-wing Chow's thorough work, *The Rise of Confucian Ritualism in Late Imperial China* (Stanford: Stanford University Press, 1994), pp. 137–45.

17. Consult Meyer, *The Dragons of Tiananmen*, pp. 68–73. See also the *Dictionary of Ming Biography, 1368–1644*, ed. L. Carrington Goodrich et al. (New York: Columbia University Press, 1976), the article on "Chu Hou-Ts'ung," pp. 315–22.

18. See Meyer, *The Dragons of Tiananmen*, pp. 91–117, with representations of the structures of each of these altars on pp. 93, 98, 103, 115, and 116.

19. Gernet suggests this metaphysical monism was the basic cosmological interpretation of the Ruist scholars at the end of the sixteenth century. See

Jacques Gernet, *China and the Christian Impact*, trans. Janet Lloyd (Cambridge: Cambridge University Press, 1985).

20. Legge's prayer at the Altar of Heaven became the outstanding incriminating symbol of the "liberal Shang-Te" camp, particularly among his opponents. It came to the surface in publicized debates after a notable speech prepared by Legge in 1877 for the first General Missionary Conference in Shanghai was denied publication in the conference proceedings. "Leggism" consequently referred to any form of accommodating missionary spirit, taking on a discourse life of its own in the *Chinese Recorder*, the most important missionary journal related to Protestant missions in China. This caricature of Legge's actual position has been discussed at length and in various contexts in Girardot, *Victorian Translation of China*, especially part I, chapters 4–5.

21. Only when religious affairs became a responsibility of the *Tsung-li ya-men* when it was established in the early 1860s did Ch'ing officials take a long and closer look into the inter-cultural problems and institutional dilemmas caused by foreign missionaries and their converts. The complexities of these "religious cases" (*chiao-an*) have been explored in Paul Cohen's informative work, *China and Christianity: The Missionary Movement and the Growth of Chinese Antiforeignism, 1860–1870* (Cambridge, Mass.: Harvard University Press, 1963).

An example of the negative responses these religious cases could create in a Ch'ing official's attitudes was evident decades later at the World's Parliament of Religions held in Chicago in 1893. There the "Honorable Pung Kwang Yu," the Ch'ing empire's "Commissioner" assigned by the Tsung-li ya-men, lashed out against a variety of problems caused by missionaries among Chinese Christian communities and their broader contexts. These included unresponsiveness to local Chinese festivals, which provoked resentment and anger among non-Christian neighbors; the unacceptable mixing of the sexes in worship ceremonies; as well as uneducated and immoral "seekers" who used their religious associations with missionaries to gain personal advantages against the Ch'ing civil authorities. Although the commissioner ironically revealed his own elitist assumptions about religious thought and life in his extremely long essay, he clearly had read the Bible (in its translations "far inferior" in quality "to the versions of the Buddhistic scriptures"). Retrospectively it is also certain that he was commissioned in part to leave a lasting impression on his audiences not only about "Confucianism," but also about Ch'ing imperial displeasures with the encumbrances of the "religious cases" caused by the presence of foreign missionaries under the protection of special treaty privileges. The later terrors of the Boxer Rebellion showed how seriously these "dissatisfactions" needed to be taken.

Of special interest to the themes studied here is his insistence that *Ti* is unique and the highest over all spirits (*shen*), the "Spirit who rules this universe of created things, . . . [who] is eternal and unchangeable. . . . Before the creation of the universe he existed, and after the dissolution of the universe he will remain the same." One could wonder about who translated his speech, and whether the translator was fully faithful to the commissioner's original words. See Pung Kwang Yu, "Confucianism," in John Henry Barrows, ed., *The World's Parliament of Religions*, Vol. 1 (Chicago: Parliament Publishing Company, 1893), pp. 374–439, esp. pp. 421–22, 424–26, 434–39.

22. In his translation of the *Chung-yung* for the *Sacred Books of the East* (vol. 28), Legge retranslated the title of the work in a more balanced manner, calling it *The State of Equilibrium and Harmony*. Unfortunately, this more representative translation never replaced his rendition of 1861, partly because he chose only to footnote it in the second edition of 1893 rather than change the title. See Legge, CC1, p. 383.

23. These historical issues are discussed in Daniel K. Gardner's *Chu Hsi and the Ta-hsueh: Neo-Confucian Reflection on the Confucian Canon* (Cambridge, Mass.: Harvard University Press, 1986).

24. One rendition of the text and English translation of Chu's fifth commentary is in CC1, pp. 385–86. Mao Ch'i-ling was a critic of Chu's philosophy, but also studied the development of the *Great Learning* after Chu's skeptical approach to the text stimulated other studies of it. See comments on his text and the names of the four scholars who offered alternative organizations of the *Great Learning* text in CC1, prolegomena, p. 25.

25. The earlier (1850) edition of the *Ku-pen Ta-hsueh chu-pien* (hereafter abbreviated as KPTHCP) by Lo, used larger fonts so that each line had twenty-one spaces. The classical text filled these twenty-one spaces from top to bottom, while the commentarial passages started in the second space from the top of the page. A similar form was assumed in KPTHCP (1859), but it was formated for thirty characters per line. In the earlier edition the commentarial notes were indicated by small circles along side the characters throughout the nine lined columns for each page, while the classical text and its redaction notes were not so marked. In the later edition, both classical and commentarial texts were placed in nine-column pages, but they had no column lines.

26. In some cases there were no redaction notes needed, while in others Lo summarized as many as five different organizations of the text. For example, regarding the placement of a quotation from the *Book of Poetry* on the virtuous attitudes of King Wen, Lo briefly explained the different redactions in the texts prepared by the two Ch'eng brothers, Ch'eng Hao (styled Ming-tao, 1032–85) and Ch'eng I (styled I-ch'üan, 1033–1107), that of Chu Hsi (under the abbreviated form of his commentary's title, *Chang-chü*, lit., *Chapters and Sentences*), the text of the Han scholar Tung Chung-shu (ca. 179 B.C. to 104 B.C.), and the rendition prepared by the Ch'ing scholar Hu Wei (1633–1714).

27. KPTHCP (1859), pp. 1, 10, 26.

28. The denotation of hsin as "renew," according to Chu Hsi, came to him from a passage in the *Book of History* (*Shu-ching*) where the ruler Chung K'ang offered clemency for those who followed wicked rulers, so that "those who have long been stained by their filthy manners will be allowed to renovate themselves." For this passage, see CC3, pp. 168–69 (pt. III, bk. 4, chap. 2, para. 6) and the explanation from Chu Hsi's perspective in Daniel Gardner, *Chu Hsi and the Ta-hsueh*, pp. 89–90, n.54. The character *ch'in* can also be simply rendered as "love," as in CC1, p. 356, and Gardner in the passage above. "Loving care" seems to be a more precise and appropriate rendering in this context.

29. This does not mean, however, that the challenges to long-standing traditions were made without any costs. Chu Hsi died a commoner, stripped of all his earned honors as a Ruist literatus, because of his assertive handling of authorized texts, most notably the *Great Learning*. In his old age he consequently become an object of scholarly scorn from the imperial court during the declining period of the Song dynasty. Only in the year 1313, more than a century after his death, was he reinstated as an exemplary scholar. From then on his commentaries initiated a growing influence to the point of receiving imperial support 400 years later during the Ch'ing dynasty. See biographical details in Wing-tsit Chan, ed., *Chu Hsi and Neo-Confucianism* (Honolulu: University of Hawaii Press, 1986), pp. 596–600, and Wing-tsit Chan, *Chu Hsi: New Studies* (Honolulu: University of Hawaii Press, 1989), especially "Chu Hsi's Poverty" and "The New Tao-T'ung," pp. 61–89, 320–35.

30. This translation reflects a mixture of Legge's and Gardner's renderings, tending more toward Gardner's. See CC1, p. 356 and Daniel Gardner, *Chu His and the Ta-hsueh*, pp. 88–89.

31. See KPTHCP (1859), pp. 16, 27v, 29v, 39.

32. See KPTHCP (1859), p. 29v, citing Legge's version of the *Mencius* 5A:4, CC2, p. 353. Legge called this the "Mencian principle" of hermeneutics, and placed it on the flyleaf of every volume of his *Chinese Classics*. Whether this also reflected the influence of Lo's use of the passage on Legge's understanding of Ruist traditions is never made explicit.

33. KPTHCP, p. 6v. Citing CC2, pp. 191–92.

34. For the phrases quoted above, see KPTHCP (1859), pp. 17–17v, 24v. Lo's arguments described here are most strongly put in pp. 5v–8 and pp. 26v–30.

35. KPTHCP, pp. 21, 31.

36. Lo mentions this in KPTHCP, pp. 2, 31. See James Legge's discussion of the seventh doctrine of K'ang-hsi's *Sacred Edicts* (*Sheng yü*), dealing with a number of other religious groups besides the Roman Catholics, in his second lecture on "Imperial Confucianism" published in the *China Review* 6.4 (October 1877): pp. 223–35, especially the last four pages. There he initially translates *i-tuan* more literally as "strange principles," and he warns that the condemnation of Catholic religion "must be understood simply of Christianity" in general.

37. KPTHCP (1859), p. 1.

38. The phrase *p'ei Shang-ti* appears also in KPTHCP (1859), pp. 7, 32, 36v, 37, 39.

39. An excellent overview of these issues has been published by Wang Ch'eng-ch'ing in his *T'ai-p'ing T'ien-kuo ti wen-hsien ho li-shih—hai-wai hsin-wen-hsien chi-pu ho wen-hsien shih-shih yen-chiu* (The Literature and History of the Taiping Heavenly Kingdom—Studies on New Literature in Overseas Collections and [the Taiping Insurgents] Literary History) (Beijing: Social Sciences Academy Press, 1993), pp. 379–97, 451–74. An older study that still has value in its account and evaluation of the Taiping theology is Eugene P. Boardman's *Christian Influence upon the Ideology of the Taiping Rebellion, 1851–1864* (New York: Octagon Books, 1952). Lo himself used the phrase *huang Shang-ti* following classical precedents in KPTHCP (1859), pp. 6, 7–7v, and 10v.

40. The copy of Chu Hsi's text in my possession is 15 pages in length (9 columns, 17 characters per line); Lo's is 39 pages long (9 columns, 30 characters per line). The numbers of occurences do not include references to the single terms *ti* or *t'ien*, which can also denote "God" in certain classical contexts. Even in reference to these terms Lo's use in comparison to Chu Hsi's is numerically far greater. Of the classical quotations employed by Lo, 6 come from the *Book of Poetry* and 23 are found in the *Book of History*. The passages are located in Legge's rendering of these works in CC4, pp. 443, 436, 448, 452, 529–30, and 620–21; those of the *Book of History* in CC3, pp. 185, 189, 198, 210–11, 286, 295–96, 373, 385, 455, 457, 511–12, 567, 592, and 599. Only a few times are there repetitions in different contexts. A recent and intriguing study of the use of *Shang-ti* and *t'ien* in these two Ruist classics has been completed by Nicolas Standaert in his work on a Chinese Catholic, Yen Mo, called "The Fascinating God: A Discussion on the Name of God by a 17th Century Chinese Student of Theology" (Thesis for licentiate in Sacred Theology, Fujen Catholic University, Taipei, 1994), especially pp. 100–184.

41. This phrase is significant because the term *tsao-hua* also appeared in the Ming and Ch'ing imperial worship as a descriptive term for *Shang-ti*, as Legge pointed out in his translations of the prayers. See the discussions above for details.

42. Find these various statements in discussions of Lo Chung-fan, KPTHCP (1859), pp. 7–7v, 10v–12, 18–18v, 31v, 35v. The importance of this equation between *Shang-ti* and the *Tao* is elaborated in the final section of this paper, as an extension of one criticism of Max Weber's depiction of "Confucian traditionalism." An initial suggestion in contemporary Confucian-Christian dialogue of a "taological" approach to Christian theology was raised in Liang Yen-ch'eng's essay, "Tao-t'i ti Shang-ti yü yüan-chiao" (Taological God and the Perfect Teaching), in Tsai Jen-hou, Chou Lien-hua, and Liang Yen-ch'eng, *Hui-t'ung yü chuan-hua—Chi-tu-chiao yü hsin-ju-chia ti tui-hua* (Concrete

Understanding and Transformation—A Dialogue between Christianity and the New Confucians) (Taipei: Universal Light Press, 1985), pp. 277–308, esp. p. 285ff.

43. James Legge, *The Sacred Books of China: The Texts of Confucianism—Part I, The Shu King* . . . (Oxford: Clarendon Press, 1879), p. 50 (from the "Counsels of the Great Yü"). Compare also CC3, pp. 61–62.

44. See KPTHCP (1859), pp. 20, 38. The original passage in the *Analects* is "hsiao-jen pu chih T'ien-ming, erh pu wei yeh ("The mean man does not know the ordinances of Heaven, and consequently does not stand in awe of them" as in CC1, p. 313).

45. The gloss comes from CC3, p. 185 ("The Announcement of Tang"), which states, "The great God (*huang Shang-ti*) has conferred *even* on the inferior people a moral sense, compliance with which would show their nature invariably right (*heng-hsing*)." This is the *sine qua non* of Lo's taological position on self-cultivation, and so occurs repeatedly in KPTHCP (1859), as in pp. 6, 7, 10v–11, 18–18v, 20, 34, 36. It is associated with another set of phrases from the *Book of Poetry*: "God is with you" (*Shang-ti lin nü*, CC4, p. 436, the ode *Ta-ming*) and "God does not come to us" (*Shang-ti pu lin*, CC4, p. 529, the ode *Yün-han*). It is the latter case by which Lo warns those who are not attentive in expressing their reverential awe toward Heaven.

46. KPTHCP (1859), pp. 6, 7–7v, 36.

47. KPTHCP (1859), pp. 10–10v, 20, 21v, 24–24v, 32.

48. KPTHCP (1859), pp. 3, 5, 7v, 16, 32v–35. So too the benevolent official is one who is "father and mother to the people" (p. 31v), a gloss from the *Book of Poetry*. All true cultivated rulers and humane people are matured in their ability to "lovingly care for the people" (pp. 32, 35, 37v).

49. KPTHCP (1859), p. 39.

50. KPTHCP (1859), p. 10v.

51. Chu Hsi is referred to by his *Chapters and Sentences* as well as his *Collected Sayings* (*Chu-tzu yü-lei*) and his name appears more than seventy times in Lo's treatise.

52. See references to Ch'eng I (I-ch'uan) in KPTHCP (1859), pp. 8, 9, 12, 13v, 17v, 18v, 19v, 22v, 31v, 33v, 35v, 38v–39.

53. See references to Ch'eng Hao (Ming-tao) in KPTHCP (1859), pp. 4, 12, 13v, 18v, 19v, 31v.

54. See references to Huang Kan in KPTHCP (1859), pp. 10v, 21v.

55. See references to Ts'ui Hsien in KPTHCP (1859), pp. 9–9v, 12, 19v.

56. See references to Hu Wei in KPTHCP (1859), pp. 9–9v, 12, 18v, 19v, 39v.

57. In Lo's treatise, the classics on history and poetry are referred to directly 26 times each, the other texts receiving relatively less attention (*Book of Changes*, 13 times; *Mencius*, 10 times; rites-related works, 6 times; the "Doctrine of the

Mean" or *The State of Equilibrium and Harmony* (see CC1, p. 383), four times; and the *Analects* and *Classic of Filial Piety* only twice each.

58. Legge, CC1, prolegomena, p. 26.

59. His awareness that *Shang-ti* was a bridging term, the term best describing the general concept of Deity, was made explicit in his part in the missionaries' "Term Question" controversy, that is, the debate over the proper translation for "God" and other related theological terms. See explanations of this point above.

60. This is notably not like the Figurist search for previously unidentified prophetic anticipations of Christian special revelation in the Ruist classics. Lo's was more direct and less distinctively Christian in his interpretive position. See accounts of Figurist approaches in Claudia von Collani's *P. Joachim Bouvet S.J., Sein Leben und sein Werk* (Nettetal, Germany: Steyler Verlag, 1985), and Knud Lundbaek's article, "Joseph Prémare and the Name of God in China," in David E. Mungello's *The Chinese Rites Controversy: Its History and Meaning* (Nettetal, Germany: Steyler Verlag, 1994), pp. 129–48.

61. Lo's phrase is found in KPTHCP (1859), p. 21, where *Shang-ti* is described as "dwelling in the inner being" (*chü chung*) so that within the chest there is a temple (*i tien*). Taoist imagery should not be discounted in this case, but the parallel with the Christian image in 1 Corinthians 6:19 ("your body is the temple of the Holy Spirit") is striking. The term *tien* appears twice in the *Book of Poetry*, meaning "guardians" and "to sigh," and does not appear in any other major Ruist classic. See CC4, pp. 403, 502.

62. Quoted from James Legge, *The Sacred Books of China: The Texts of Confucianism—Part II, The Yi King* (Oxford: Clarendon Press, 1882), p. 233 (in the first appendix to the *Book of Changes*). See the passage in KPTHCP (1859), p. 15v. Discussion of the full-orbed cultural model expressed in Protestant "Sabbath culture" is developed in my forthcoming book, *Dutybound: James Legge and the Scottish Encounter*, chaps. 1, 3 and 8.

63. See for example KPTHCP (1859), pp. 32, 36, 39.

64. British and French armies had taken over military rule of the capital city of Guangdong Province in early 1858 and remained there until October 1861, one of the military actions involved in the second Opium War campaigns.

65. This Legge did in both Malacca (1840–43) and in Hong Kong (1843–56) as the principal of the Anglo-Chinese College (*Ying-hua shu-yüan*), including a three-year furlough of Legge and his family in Britain accompanied by three of the male students and one female student (1845–48). One account of his activities in Malacca is presented in Brian Harrison's *Waiting for China: The Anglo-Chinese College at Malacca, 1818–43, and Early Nineteenth-Century Missions* (Hong Kong: Hong Kong University Press, 1979), esp. 103–15, and another covering his activities in both Malacca and Hong Kong in my forthcoming book, *Dutybound: James Legge and the Scottish Encounter*, chapters 3 and 6. Revealing biographical details of some of the students can be found in Carl T.

Smith, *Chinese Christians: Élites, Middlemen, and the Church in Hong Kong* (Hong Kong: Oxford University Press, 1985), pp. 143–54.

66. It should be mentioned that although Legge published Chu Hsi's rendition in CC1, he translated the Old Text of the *Great Learning* as the 39th chapter in his translation of the *Book of Rites* in the *Sacred Books of the East*, Vol. 28.

67. See Legge's discussions in CC1, prolegomena, pp. 28–29 and in the commentary, pp. 355–56.

68. See Legge, CC1, prolegomena, pp. 31–33, and in commentary pp. 371, 376, 378. Gardner feels Legge is too hard on Chu Hsi, insensitive to qualifications Chu adds to his commentary in other places. See Daniel K. Gardner, *Chu Hsi and the Ta-hsueh: Neo-Confucian Reflection on the Confucian Canon* (Cambridge, Mass.: Harvard University Press, 1986), pp. 107–08.

69. See Legge's references to Lo's criticism of Chu Hsi's supporting a more democratic vision of sagehood and its epistemological implications in CC1, prolegomena, p. 33, and his agreement on *ko-wu* in the commentary, p. 358. Disagreements with Lo's interpretations occur in the commentary on pp. 367–69, 376, 379.

70. Initiating his critical comments on the value of the *Great Learning* by quoting from both Pauthier and Gutzlaff, Legge later identified these four "seminal principles": that government should purpose to "make its subjects happy and good"; that all authorities at various levels of social organization must strive toward "personal excellence"; that personal excellence itself is "rooted in the state of the heart" and is the "natural outgrowth of internal sincerity"; and that the golden rule is promoted, although it is stated in a negative form. See CC1, prolegomena pp. 27–28, 33–34.

71. So Legge indicates that his discussions over the range of application of the *Great Learning*'s teachings have included talks with "intelligent Chinese whose minds were somewhat quickened by Christianity" (CC1, prolegomena, p. 29). Whether Lo Chung-fan was among these is not certain, but Legge may well have been thinking of Hung Jen-kan (1822-1864), an assistant evangelist in Hong Kong under Legge and Ho Tsun-sheen for four years (1854-1858), and then later a high official in the ill-fated Taiping Heavenly Kingdom.

72. This remarkably bold use of a Ruist principle against "society in the West" and the standards of British imperialism is stated in CC1, prolegomena, p. 105.

73. The trip occurred during the month of May in 1861. Legge was joined by one junior missionary colleague, John Chalmers (arrived in Hong Kong in 1852), and a small group of Chinese Christians from Hong Kong and Canton. See the accounts published in the *China Mail*, supplement to no. 853 (June 20, 1861) and the edited version in *The Missionary Magazine and Chronicle* (London) no. 304, n.s. no. 21 (September 2, 1861): 249–60. These have been elaborated in greater detail in Girardot and Pfister, *The Whole Duty of Man*, part I, chapter 6.

74. See the copy of the hand scroll written by Wang T'ao and translated with commentary by Lindsey Ride in copies of CC1 published after 1960 in Ride's "Biographical Note," pp. 15–18.

75. See this letter in the last "Note" of James Legge's *Letters on the Rendering Of The Name God in the Chinese Language* (Hong Kong: Hong Kong Register Office, 1850), p. 73.

76. See Max Weber, *The Religion of China*, trans. H. Garth (New York: Free Press, 1964), xxxviii and pp. 163. For further accounts of Weber's description of "Confucian bureaucracy" and its effect on the ideology based on the Ruist canon, see Lauren Pfister, "Reassessing Max Weber's Evaluation of the Confucian Classics," in Jon Davies and Isabel Wollaston, eds., *Sociology of Sacred Texts* (Sheffield, U.K.: Sheffield Academic Press, 1993), pp. 99–110.

77. See Weber's *The Religion of China*, p. xxxviii, and S. N. Eisenstadt, "This Worldly Transcendentalism and the Structuring of the World: Weber's *Religion of China* and the Format of Chinese History and Civilization," in *Max Weber in Asian Studies*, ed. Andreas E. Buss (Leiden: E. J. Brill, 1985), pp. 46–64, here esp. 48.

78. This is precisely the kind of claim made by John B. Henderson in his broad-minded study entitled *Scripture, Canon, and Commentary: A Comparison of Confucian and Western Exegesis* (Princeton: Princeton University Press, 1991), esp. pp. 38–50, 100, 121–22.

79. The textual problems that surfaced because of variant textual readings are still problematic for contemporary scholars in Ruist studies, though most have admittedly put these textual matters aside in order to address the more penetrating problem of the survival of the Ruist traditions in the modern world. The importance of the conflict between "Confucianism" and modernity, especially outside of the People's Republic of China, was underscored by the May 1958 Ruist declaration of four major Chinese scholars in Hong Kong. The significance of this text within the general crisis of "modern Confucianism" has been clarified by Hao Chang and developed in its relation to the religious tendencies of contemporary Ruist traditions by Lauren Pfister. See Hao Chang, "New Confucianism and the Intellectual Crisis of Contemporary China," in Charlotte Furth, ed., *The Limits of Change: Essays on Conservative Alternatives in Republican China* (Cambridge, Mass.: Harvard University Press, 1976), pp. 276-302, and Lauren Pfister, "The Different Faces of Contemporary Religious Confucianism: An Account of the Diverse Approaches of Some Major Twentieth-Century Chinese Confucian Scholars," *Journal of Chinese Philosophy* 22 (1995): 5–80.

80. Wang Shou-jen, later styled Yang-ming (1472–1529), was a Ming Ruist who had an intense intellectual and spiritual battle in seeking to attain sagehood by means of Chu Hsi's methodology. His alternatives were legitimized by focusing on Chu Hsi's distortion of the meaning of the text of the *Great Learning*, and so set a precedent that Lo Chung-fan explicitly followed. See discussions of his

life and works in Julia Ching, *To Acquire Wisdom: The Way of Wang Yang-ming* (New York: Columbia University Press, 1976). Other special studies worth reading are Tu Wei-ming's *NeoConfucian Thought in Action: Wang Yang-ming's Youth (1472–1509)* (Berkeley: University of California Press, 1976), and Antonio S. Cua, *The Unity of Knowledge and Action: A Study in Wang Yang-ming's Moral Psychology* (Honolulu: University of Hawaii Press, 1982).

81. Of particular importance to Lo in this regard are the works of other Ming scholars, Ch'en Hsien-chang (styled Pai-sha, 1428–1500) and his disciple Chan Jo-shui (styled Kan-ch'üan, 1466–1560). These are made evident in the larger context of the morality book mentioned above, *Chüeh-she ch'üan-shan lu.*

82. A major work on K'ang Yu-wei is Hsiao Kung-ch'üan's *A Modern China and a New World: K'ang Yu-Wei, Reformer and Utopian, 1858-1927* (Seattle: University of Washington Press, 1975). K'ang's utopian vision has been described and evaluated in Lauren Pfister's "A Study in Comparative Utopias—K'ang Yu-Wei and Plato," *Journal of Chinese Philosophy* 16 (1989), pp. 59–117.

K'ang was so convinced of the need to shift the emphasis of the canon, that he attempted in 1902 to raise to canonical status *another* chapter of the *Book of Rites*, the *Li-yün* or "Evolution of the Rites." This kind of oral tradition built upon "New Text" scriptures and their interpretations can still be found among some sectors of Chinese scholarship, although it is far less available now than it was at the turn of the century, and never represented anything more than a minority perspective within the "Great Tradition" of Ruist orthodoxy. Nevertheless, David Pankenier of Lehigh University, editor of *Early China*, told the author that he spent three years under the tutelage of one of the relatives of the last emperor of China, receiving training through the esoteric teaching method of the New Text approach.

83. S. N. Eisenstadt, "This Worldly Transcendentalism and the Structuring of the World: Weber's *Religion of China* and the Format of Chinese History and Civilization," in Andreas E. Buss, ed., *Max Weber in Asian Studies* (Leiden: E. J. Brill, 1985), pp. 46–64, here p. 49 in passim.

84. Eisenstadt, "This Worldly Transcendentalism," pp. 54–58.

85. *Chüeh-she ch'üan-shan lu* (Hsün-i District, P'ing-pu village: Liang Ch'ung-te Hall, 8th year of Hsien-feng (1859)), preface. No direct evidence on the identification of the "Master who enlightens the age" (or as in the text, the "Master Willing to Enlighten") is presented in the work, but quotes from Lo's own work suggest that possibly he, a relative, or a student may have been the editor working under this pseudonym.

86. This is not a comprehensive list, but these topics do appear in this order. This first *chüan* is 163 pages in length.

87. Quoted in Huang P'ei and Julia Ching, "Ch'en Hsien-chang," in L. Carrington Goodrich and Chaoying Fang, eds., *Dictionary of Ming Biography,*

1368–1644, Vol. 1 (New York: Columbia University Press, 1976), pp. 153–56, here p. 155.

88. *Chüeh-she ch'üan-shan lu*, p. 163 (entitled *shih T'ien hsin chu*). See above for descriptions of this Ming emperor's prayers and their translations by James Legge.

89. Lo's contribution is a set of four proverbs related to the cultivated way to see, hear, speak, and move in life, a commentary on a famous saying of Master K'ung to his student Yen Yüan (*Analects* 12.1; CC1, p. 250). See *Chüeh-she ch'ün-shan lu, chüan* 2, pp. 34–34v. This section is completed in forty-one pages.

90. See my paper presented in Jerusalem at the international worship on "The Bible and Chinese Culture" (June 1996) entitled "A Transmitter but Not a Creator: The Creative Transmission of Protestant Biblical Traditions by Ho Tsun-Sheen (1817–1871), the First Modern Chinese Theologian."

91. *Chüeh-she ch'üan-shan lu, chüan* 1, pp. 117v–18v.

92. Wang T'ao, *Man yü sui lu*, in Chung Shu-ho, ed., *Tsou hsiang shih-chieh ts'ung-shu* (Changsha, China: Yueh-lu, 1985), pp. 97–98.

93. This idea of symbols which lead us to the brink of transcendence, "breaking symbols" in that they both breakdown in their normal meanings but also breakthrough to new meanings, is fruitfully investigated in Robert C. Neville's book, *The Truth of Broken Symbols* (Albany: State University of New York Press, 1995).

94. See comments about the lack of symbolic resources for a theistic God in the Confucian tradition in Tu Wei-ming's *Centrality and Commonality: An Essay in Confucian Religiousness* (Honolulu: University of Hawaii Press, 1976), pp. 69, 116. A more recent and more open position, but one still arguing against a Ruist form of monotheistic moral metaphysics, is Yü Ying-shih's *Ts'ung chia-chih hsi-t'ung k'an Chung-kuo wen-hua ti hsien-tai i-i* (Looking at the Contemporary Significance of Chinese Culture from [the Perspective of] Value Systems) (Taipei: Shih-pao wen-hua, 1992).

95. See Legge's sermon of November 25, 1886, "The Bearing of Our Knowledge of Comparative Religion on Christian Missions," p. 10, held in the School of Oriental and African Studies Library, University of London CWM/ South China/Personal/Legge/Box 4. Legge's intellectual pilgrimage as it related to his change of attitudes toward "Confucius" has been described in greater detail in my article, "Some Deeper Dimensions. . . . Part II," pp. 45–48.

是遵古經。追復先傳。庶中外得聞。無論九夷八蠻。悉知道以文傳。文以字順。字以義顯。原本瑞光煥然。億兆中有志士興焉。斯道卜大光矣。書以識之。价之羅仲藩

羅仲藩嘉慶十五年舉人南海縣志選舉表後改名仲衡南海續志藝文畧官惠來教諭又選舉表附錄

聖經

南海羅仲藩註辨

大學之道在明明德在親民在止於至善 此節之下董氏改本核古之欲明明德於天下者蔡虛齋改接物有本末一節而章首補所謂致知在格物者一句

大學。配上帝。保峻命之學。明。昭明也。德是道之得於身者。在天曰顯道。在人曰明德。若著之恭從明聰睿。見爲仁敬孝慈信者是也。親者。親之也。明德親民。即修己安百姓也。止。住也。居也。如北辰之居其所焉。至善。盡善而無間然之謂。至善無止境。無止之止。不息

GLOSSARY

I. Names and Terms

Chan Jo-shui (Kan-ch'uan)	湛若水 (甘泉)
Chang Tsai	張載
chao	肇
Ch'en Hsien-chang (Pai-sha)	陳獻章
ch'eng-ch'i-i	誠其意
Ch'eng-Chu	程朱
Ch'eng I (I-ch'uan)	程頤 (伊川)
Ch'eng Hao (Ming-tao)	程顥 (明道)
Ch'eng-men	程門
ch'i lu mi lu	騎驢覓驢
Chia-ching	嘉靖
ch'iang-chieh	強解
chiao-an	教案
chih-kuo	治國
chih-t'ui-chi	致推極
ch'in	親
ch'in-min	親民
Chou Lien-hua	周聯華
chü chung	居衷
Chu Hou-ts'ung	朱厚熜
Chu Hsi (Hui-yen)	朱熹
Chung K'ang	仲康
Chung Shu-ho	鍾淑和
Han Wen-ti	漢文帝
Han Yü	韓愈
heng-hsing	恆性
Ho Tsun-sheen (Fuk-tong)	何進善 (福堂)
hsi-ju	西儒
hsiao-jen pu chih Tien-ming, ho pu wei yeh	小人不知天命, 可不畏也
hsiao-jen pu wei T'ien	小人不畏天
Hsiao Kung-ch'üan	蕭公權
hsieh-mo	邪魔
Hsien-feng	咸豐
hsin	新
hsin-hsueh	新學
hsin-min	新民
Hsü Chi-yü	徐繼畬
Hsün-i	貴邑
Hu Wei	胡渭

Huang K'an	黃幹
huang	皇
huang Shang-ti	皇上帝
Huang T'ien Shang-ti	皇天上帝
Hui-lai	惠來
Hung Hsiu-ch'üan	洪秀全
Hung Jen-kan	洪仁玕
Hung-wu	洪武
I-hsin	奕訢
i-t'i	一體
i-tien	一殿
i-tuan	異端
i-chao wu chih tsu-chen	億兆物之祖真
jen-hsin	人心
Jen Yu-wen	簡又文
jih-hsin	日新
kai Sheng-ching	改聖經
K'ang-hsi	康熙
K'ang Yu-wei	康有為
K'ing Wen	文王
ko-wu	格物
K'ung-men	孔門
Lee Ya-ko	理雅各
Liang A-fa	梁阿發
Liang Ch'ung-te	梁崇德
Liang Yen-ch'eng	梁燕城
Lo Chung-fan	羅仲藩
Mao Ch'i-ling	毛奇齡
ming	命
Nan-hai	南海
nei-sheng wai-wang	內聖外王
p'ei Shang-ti	配上帝
p'ei Shang-ti pao chün ming chih hsueh	配上帝保峻命之學
pen-hsin	本心
p'i-nang pu-shih hsin	皮囊不是心
P'ing-pu	平步
Prince Kung	恭親王
Ruism/Ruist	儒教 / 儒家
san-ts'ai	三才
shan-shu	善書
Shang-ti	上帝
Shang-ti chiang chung	上帝隆衷

Shang-ti lin nü	上帝臨女
Shang-ti pu lin	上帝不臨
shen	神
shen-huang	神皇
sheng-jen yü t'ien ti ho te	聖人與天地合德
Ssu-ma Ch'ien	司馬遷
ta-ho-hui	大和會
T'ai-hsi chih jen	泰西之人
T'ai-p'ing Heavenly Kingdom	太平天國
T'ai-tzu	太祖
Tao	道
Tao-hsin	道心
Tao-t'ung	道統
t'ao-tz'u ch'ün-sheng	陶此群生
Ti	帝
ti	禘
tien	殿
t'ien	天
Tsai Jen-hou	蔡仁厚
tsao	造
tsao-hua	造化
tsao-hua chih chu-tsai	造化之主宰
Ts'ui Hsien	崔銑
Tu Wei-ming	杜維明
Tung Chung-shu	董仲舒
wan-wu chih ling	萬物之靈
Wang Ch'eng-ch'ing	王成慶
Wang Shou-jen (Yang-ming)	王守仁 (陽明)
Wang T'ao	王韜
Ya Pei-li	雅裨理
Yen Mo	嚴謨
Yen Yüan	顏淵
Ying-hua shu-yuan	英華書院
Yü Ying-shih	余英時
Yung-lo	永樂

II. Books and Articles

Analects	論語
Chang-chü	章句
Chu-tzu chang-chü	朱子章句
Chu-tzu yü-lei	朱子語類

Ch'üan-shih liang-yen	勸世良言
Ch'un-ch'iu	春秋
Chung-yung	中庸
Chueh-shih ch'üan-shu lu	覺世全書錄
Ho-ho pen	和合本
Hui-t'ung yü chuan-hua—Chi-tu-chiao yü hsin-ju-chia ti tui-hua	會通與轉化 — 基督教與新儒家的對話
I-ching	易經
Ku-pen Ta-hsueh chu-pien	古本大學註辯
Kung-yang chuan	公羊傳
Li-chi	禮記
Li Yün	禮運
Man yu sui lu	漫遊隨錄
Meng-tzu	孟子
Ming-shih	明史
Sheng-ching	聖經
Shih-ching	詩經
Shih T'ien hsin chu	事天心祝
Shu-ching	書經
Sheng yü	聖諭
Ta-hsueh	大學
Ta hsueh chang-chü	大學章句
Ta Ming hui-tien	大明會典
tai-p'ing T'ien-kuo ti wen-hsien ho li-shih—hai-wai hsin-wen-hsien k'an-pu ho wen-hsien shih-shih yen chiu	太平天國的文獻和歷史 — 海外新文獻刊部和文獻事史研究
Tao-t'i ti Shang-ti yü yuan-chiao	道體的上帝與圓教
T'sung chia-chih hsi-t'ung k'an Chung-kuo wen-hua ti hsien-tai i-i	從價值系統看中國文化的現代意義
Tsou hsiang shih-chieh ts'ung-shu	走向世界叢書
Ying-huan chih-lueh	瀛環志略
Yün-han	雲漢

Contributors

Kai-wing Chow is Associate Professor of History and East Asian Languages and Cultures at the University of Illinois, Champaign-Urbana. He is the author of *The Rise of Confucian Ritualism in Late Imperial China: Ethics, Classics, and Lineage Discourse* (Stanford University Press, 1994).

Kandice Hauf teaches at Babson College. She did her doctoral work at Yale University and is completing a monograph on Wang Yang-ming.

John B. Henderson is currently Professor of History and Religious Studies at Louisiana State University. His major publications include *The Development and Decline of Chinese Cosmology* (Columbia University Press, 1984), *Scripture, Canon, and Commentary: A Comparison of Confucian and Western Exegesis* (Princeton University Press, 1991), and *The Construction of Orthodoxy and Heresy: Neo-Confucian, Islamic, Jewish and Early Christian Patterns* (State University of New York Press, 1998).

Tze-ki Hon is Assistant Professor of History at State University of New York, Geneseo. He has published several articles on historiography and the *I-ching* including "Teaching the Book of Changes," which appeared recently in *Teaching about Asia*. He is completing two book projects: one on modern Chinese historiography, and the other one on eleventh-century Chinese thought.

Hsiung Ping-chen is research fellow and division head at the Institute of Modern History, Academia Sinica, Taipei. As a specialist in the cultural and intellectual history of late imperial China, she has published monographs and articles on provincial intellectual life, history of infants and children, as well as Chinese pediatrics.

Yuet Keung Lo teaches in the Chinese Department of Grinnell College. He is currently working on a book on the writing of Chinese Buddhist laywomen's biographies in late imperial China, and another on the parable tradition in early

China. His most recent article, "From Analogy to Proof: An Inquiry into the Chinese Mode of Knowledge," appeared in *Monumenta Serica*.

On-cho Ng is Associate Professor in the Department of History at the Pennsylvania State University. He has published many articles on the intellectual history of late imperial China, that have appeared in journals such as the *Journal of the History of Ideas*, *Philosophy East and West*, *Journal of Chinese Religions*, and *Journal of Chinese Philosophy*. He is completing a book on early Ch'ing Ch'eng-Chu Confucianism.

Michael Nylan is Professor of East Asian Studies and History at Bryn Mawr College. She is the author of two books, The *Shifting Center* (Monumenta Serica, 1992) and *The Canon of Supreme Mystery* (State University of New York, 1993). A third book, on the history and interpretation of the Five Confucian Classics, is in final revision. Work is proceeding on the fourth, a study of domestic life in early China.

Lauren Pfister is Associate Professor in the Religion and Philosophy Department of Hong Kong Baptist University, and Assistant Editor of the *Journal of Chinese Philosophy*. His research has focused mostly on nineteenth-century Ruist/Confucian and Chinese Christian issues, and he has published extensively on the eminent Scottish Sinologist James Legge. He is currently engaged in two team projects, one on James Legge and another on Feng Yu-lan.

Index